The Struggle for Water in Peru

The Struggle for Water in Peru

COMEDY AND TRAGEDY
IN THE ANDEAN COMMONS

Paul B. Trawick

STANFORD UNIVERSITY PRESS

STANFORD, CALIFORNIA

Stanford University Press
Stanford, California

© 2003 by the Board of Trustees of the
Leland Stanford Junior University

Printed in the United States of America
on acid-free, archival-quality paper

Library of Congress Cataloging-in-Publication Data

Trawick, Paul B.
  The struggle for water in Peru : comedy and tragedy in the Andean commons /
Paul B. Trawick.
    p. cm.
  Includes bibliographical references and index.
  ISBN 0-8047-3110-1 (cloth : alk. paper) —
  ISBN 0-8047-3138-1 (pbk. : alk. paper)
    1. Water-supply—Peru—Cotahuasi River Watershed. 2. Irrigation—Peru—
Cotahuasi River Watershed. 3. Social structure—Peru—Cotahuasi River
Watershed. 4. Social conflict—Peru—Cotahuasi River Watershed. 5. Water-
supply—Government policy—Peru. I. Title.
  HD1696.P54 C683 2003
  333.91'00985'32—dc21   2002009779

Original Printing 2003
Last figure below indicates year of this printing:
12 11 10 09 08 07 06 05 04 03

Typeset at Stanford University Press in 10/13 Minion

Contents

Preface: A Note on Theory ix

A Note on Orthography xv

Introduction: Reading Social History in a Cultural Landscape 1

1. The Setting: A Valley on the Edge of "The Abyss" 17

2. Early History: Story of a Hole on the Map 39

3. Huaynacotas: Irrigation and Ethnicity in an Indigenous Community 71

4. Pampamarca: Hierarchy and Inequity in a Colonized Community 110

5. Cotahuasi: Domination and Social Decline in a Hacienda District 150

6. A Failure of Good Intentions: The Military's Attempt at Land Reform 199

7. Failure Again: Water Reform, Drought, and the Legacy of Class Conflict 228

8. Water into Blood: Irrigation Improvement, Corruption, and the Coming of the Shining Path 273

Conclusion: The Story of Irrigation in the Andes—"Comedy" and Tragedy in the Commons 291

Glossary of Quechua Terms 307

Notes 309

Bibliography 327

Index 341

Tables and Illustrations

TABLES

1. Cotahuasi Valley Population, 1572–1981   51
2. Basic Principles of Irrigation in Huaynacotas   86
3. Spring and Tank Capacities in Cotahuasi District, 1988   157
4. Landownership in Cotahuasi District by Hectares, 1981   214
5. Landownership in Cotahuasi by Number of Owners, 1981   214
6. Land Acquisition in Household Sample   214
7. Decline in Springwater Flow During Drought, 1987 vs. 1988   239

MAPS

1. Peru and Location of Study Area   2
2. Provinces and Major Roads, Department of Arequipa   4
3. Altitude Zones and Watersheds, Department of Arequipa   18
4. Ecological or Land-Use Zones in the Cotahuasi Watershed   32
5. Prehispanic Settlement Patterns in Cotahuasi and Pampamarca   50
6. The Planting and Watering Sequence in Huaynacotas   77
7. The Ayllu Territories and Major Canals of Pampamarca   114
8. The Planting and Watering Sequence in Pampamarca   116
9. The Irrigation System of Cotahuasi   154

FIGURES

1. Average Monthly Precipitation, Cotahuasi and Puica, 1964–1988   23
2. Annual Precipitation, Cotahuasi and Puica, 1964–1988   25
3. Population Collapse and Recovery, 1572–1981   52
4. A Typical Irrigation Unit   89
5. Terrace Destruction and Corral Building   175
6. A Typical Hacienda Unit   180

PHOTOGRAPHS

1. Huaynacotas and Its Surrounds   72
2. A Terrace System   73
3. River Gorge Dividing the Fields of Pampamarca   112
4. View of Cotahuasi   152

Preface

A Note on Theory

Having written this book in the early 1990's, and finding myself revising it for publication now several years later, I feel obliged to comment briefly at the outset on the turn that much of cultural anthropology took while I was in the field, and to situate my work within the discourse that characterizes the discipline today, which reflects a state of crisis. I refer, of course, to the rise of hermeneutic or interpretive anthropology, as a challenge to "scientific," "positivist," or "realist" anthropology, and the prevalence today of the postmodern point of view.

Many contemporary theorists have a deep suspicion of any coherent narrative, such as I will present here. According to them, the only correct approach to the study of culture today is aesthetic and subjective, rather than objective, historical, or even practical. This attitude seems to me to rest on a misguided rejection of the effort toward objectivity, a state that can be approached or approximated but never actually achieved, and what I see as an obsessive concern with the Self and the problem of ethnographic authority.

Much hand-wringing occurs over the fact that anthropologists have the power, or the privilege, to go somewhere far away to live and study, often under harsh and even dangerous conditions involving great personal sacrifice, and write a book about another people and another cultural reality. The book will then be read by a small circle of people—other anthropologists—and ultimately have little or no impact on the world whatsoever, especially if it is an interpretive account. Sadly enough, history shows this to have been the fate of most that we have done in the discipline; yet many people today would somehow accuse us of going too far, of the sin of excess.

The assumption seems to be that, in doing ethnography, we necessarily have to speak "for" Others, to represent them to the rest of the world, meaning that the goal is to translate their values, concepts, and most deeply held beliefs into terms meaningful to people in the West. This approach is rightly criticized for both epistemological and moral reasons; yet many people are opposed to any other kind of analysis and any other set of aims, seeing careful observation of people's behavior within its material context, and even logical thought itself, as just another form of ethnocentrism and arrogance. If these people are right, then we should pack up our collective tent and go home, because anthropology, as well as most other scholarly disciplines, has become useless.

The perspective has left interpretive and postmodernist anthropologists with no grounds for doing anything constructive about the plight of the people that they study, having no valid argument to justify the effort. After all, if representing Others is so problematic, requiring so much self-reflection, then figuring out, not only what they want but also what they might truly need, can only be worse, to say nothing of acting on their behalf. We are thus forced, despite all the talk about power and hegemony, to sit back and let history, the working-out of that power throughout the globe, take its course and watch as the number of victims mounts. In the meantime, hand-wringing will provide plenty of grist for the academic mill, so that some of us, at least, will be able to watch it all from a safe and comfortable distance, unlike those Others that we study.

The account presented here is not primarily hermeneutic, being concerned with "meaning" mainly in a practical or material sense. Nor do I intend to put myself at the center of the analysis; rather, I plan, in a quite old-fashioned way, to take myself out of it as much as possible, to disappear sometimes from the scene. The account is descriptive and highly analytical, but it is also interpretive in some places, and its methods of analysis and persuasion are sometimes little different from what I understand interpretivists to be advocating and often doing extremely well. For the most part, however, I will read the landscape, its ecology, and the concrete and productive things that people do there in order to make a living, interpreting local practices as they are distributed and patterned in space.

Those practices, it should be noted, are "social facts" that have specific functions and, in a sense, speak for themselves. Contrary to what some critics of social science might claim, what people in the valley I studied do to make a living—how they cultivate and irrigate, how they share water—has nothing to do with me, my theoretical perspective, or my "lofty" position in society. And this book is not about me, but about them. Indeed, as I revise this book now, many years after the initial fieldwork, I find that they have examined my work, through several publications written in Spanish and published in Peru, mainly for their benefit; they have discussed it at length in public meetings and given it their vote of approval. Thus I have no need to wear my professional ethics on my sleeve, something that has lately become a cottage industry in the discipline.

As far as I am concerned, the politics of ethnography and representation are between them and me, and not anyone else.

What follows, then, is a certain kind of analysis of the ethnographic "present" (in this case mostly the late 1980's but also the 1990's, when I made several return visits), as well as an approximation of what must have happened in the past, both distant and more recent. It is a probabilistic account, based on what I think is for the most part sound evidence, but one that no doubt will be improved upon and corrected by other people in the future. It is an effort to analyze and interpret the present so as to be able to imagine, in a realistic and highly plausible way, the past. In that sense, however, it tries to be as objective as possible and is "scientific," for which I make no apology. From the beginning, I felt that the wedge that was being driven between humanism and science in anthropology was to a great extent a false one, based on a serious misrepresentation of science and even a certain amount of bad faith. And, unfortunately, it is now clear that this was indeed the case, as recent work by several authors (Roscoe 1995; Bowlin & Stromberg 1997; Lewis 1998) and other writers of the late 1990's has shown.

The focus here will not primarily be on texts, or anything that can be considered a text, but on practices and techniques, sets of material relations as well as the logic behind them. After all, some kinds of "meaningful" behavior are largely functional; they are not so much expressive as practical, even though they may be accompanied by ritual acts that are expressive indeed (see Lansing 1991). Their ramifications, however, can extend far above that limited material domain into the cognitive realm.

When I spoke with people about these matters in the field, especially in reference to the past, I did not collect long statements or testimonials but questioned them and commented in a dialogue, trying to get at the reasons behind what they said, sometimes reasons I alone perceived as relevant. When they spoke of conflict, of people stealing and fighting over irrigation water, or defying rules and customs, I asked them who was doing this, and also why they thought it had happened, but most of all I tried to clarify the circumstances as much as possible through further questioning. Gradually, by working systematically in several communities, I began to develop a general perspective, an understanding of what had happened in irrigation, a knowledge of some of the factors that lay behind that dynamic and could create such change and conflict. But that perspective was ultimately my own, not wholly shared by anyone else in the valley.

Before I go further, I should point out that my account will, much of the time, be gender-specific. Irrigation and most of the activities associated with it are primarily men's work, although women can and do participate in almost any aspect of it when the absence of a man makes this necessary. Moreover, society in most Peruvian communities—though not all of them, a subject that I will not broach here—is very male-dominated. Therefore, when I use the masculine pronoun it will be quite deliberate, indicating that, although my statement may encompass all local households, I am talking specifically about men and thus only roughly one-half of the local population. Otherwise, I will use the designation his or her, or vice versa.

Given all that I have said here, my main goal can hardly be to speak "for" Others, to define their identity for them, represent them to the rest of the world, or fully capture their native point of view. I have always felt that attempts to do so were highly subjective and often far removed from the real problems that people face, especially peasants, who everywhere encounter tangible threats to their existence. That, I think, is a good reason for doing research that is ecological and economic, work that is concrete and sometimes rather limited in scope. Where I speak of more abstract and symbolic things, such as the moral basis of village life or the culture and ideology of corruption, I try to interpret and deconstruct those phenomena in much the same way that other kinds of anthropologists would. This means that I necessarily speak in two distinctly different voices in the account: one as objective as possible and perhaps a step removed from the people of whom I speak, the other much more subjective, up close and personal. I have tried to separate these voices out as clearly as possible from each other. However, my main interests here are in practice and in history—ecological, technological, and social history—in telling the story of irrigation in the Andes.

My study did allow me to arrive at important conclusions and recommendations for policy, for taking action in the present. This is the one sense in which I do speak "for" the local people, on their behalf and with their common welfare in mind. I feel no need to justify that effort, especially in a situation where other agents and agencies, vastly more powerful than I or any other anthropologist, are making recommendations based on far less evidence and virtually no knowledge about the people whose lives will be severely affected. My recommendations, like the description, the analysis, and the account itself, will no doubt be criticized, corrected, and perhaps even rejected in part by my friends and colleagues both here and in Peru. But that is as it should be.

Many people contributed to the completion of this book, and to the research on which it is based. The fieldwork was made possible by generous grants from the Fulbright Foundation for Educational Research and the National Science Foundation in Washington. The project itself was conceived under the tutelage of three mentors at two universities: Harold Conklin at Yale, my dissertation adviser, and Richard Adams and Richard Schaedel at the University of Texas at Austin, where I had previously done graduate work. Other Yale professors were inspirational teachers and role models during its inception: Richard Burger, William Kelly, Harold Scheffler, and Timothy Weiskel. My anthropological collaborators in Peru, whose help and support were also crucial, were Rodrigo Montoya Rojas—whose work in an adjacent region inspired and shaped my own—Luís Montoya Rojas, Max Neira Avendaño, and Pablo de la Vera Cruz. Special thanks go to the people who read my doctoral thesis, on which this book is based—to Harold Conklin and Richard Burger and, perhaps most of all, to Enrique Mayer, now also at Yale. Although Mayer was not one of my collaborators in the field, I was strongly influenced by his work in conceiving the project and carrying it out, a debt that is acknowledged at many points in the text. His advice was also crucial in revising the manuscript and improving it in a number of ways for publication. In that regard, Laure Pengelly, my editor and friend, contributed perhaps more than anyone to making the book what it had the potential to be.

Numerous people in the Cotahuasi valley, far too many to list here, provided patient and insightful collaboration. Special thanks go to my hosts, Victor and Elena Honderman, who made me part of a hard-working and knowledgeable family for nearly three years. In Huaynacotas, two brothers, Jesús and Rey Chirinos Roncalla, opened doors in the community and taught me a great deal about the local way of life. In Pampamarca, three people, Leoncio Quispe Casani, Pascual Quispe Flores, and Gustavo Hinojosa Loayza, were indispensable sources of knowledge, contacts, and assistance. A special debt is also owed to Hernan and Aurora Andía, of Cotahuasi, and to Silvio Rubio Benavides of Tomepampa, true friends who looked after my welfare during a period of political turmoil. My thanks go also to Herbert Wilkes, who provided the kind of friendship and sympathy that only a fellow foreigner could have offered.

Most crucial were the companionship and moral support given by several people. My former wife, Laura Hillier Nightingale, saw me through the first few months of fieldwork and, unfortunately, shared in the chaos that it unleashed in my personal life. Throughout the long period of isolation that followed, my mother, Anne Hoell, my grandparents, James and Lillian Deason, and my sisters, Helen Hausmann and Camille Trawick, sent encouragement from a distance and kept me from losing faith in my ability to achieve my goal. Letters from my adviser, Harold Conklin, were also critical in this regard, as was his un-forgettable trip to visit me in the field. Faced with a person with such a great love for knowledge, and for fieldwork, I could hardly have done anything but persevere. But the greatest debt of all is owed to my dear friend and wife, Susan Mitchell, without whose help and companionship I would never have been able to see the research, or the writing of the book, through to the end.

P.B.T.

A Note on Orthography

The tabulation below is a pronunciation guide for Quechua terms used in the text. Although the Cusco-Collao dialect has only three vowels—a, i, and u—the last two are pronounced differently, lowered somewhat, when they are preceded or followed by a glottalized consonant. These lowered allophones—o and e—are included here, as is common in scholarly publications in Peru; they are shown in brackets. The consonants in parentheses are borrowed from Spanish.

Consonants	Labial	Alveolar	Palatal	Velar	Postvelar	Glottal
Voiceless stop	p	t	ch	k	q	
Aspirated stop	ph	th	chh	kh	qh	
Glottalized stop	p'	t'	ch'	k'	q'	
Voiced stop	(b)	(d)		(g)		
Fricative	(f)	s				h
Nasal	m	n	ñ			
Lateral		l	ll			
Simple trill		r				
Multiple retro-flexive trill		rr				

Semi-vowels	Labial		Palatal			
	w		y			

Vowels	Front	Central	Back
High	i		u
Mid	[e]		[o]
Low		a	

Reading Social History in a
Cultural Landscape

This book is about water: how the most vital natural resource is distributed, utilized, and above all shared in a unique and troubled part of the world. It is an anthropological study of irrigation and water management among peasant communities in the Andes mountains of Peru. Based primarily on research carried out from 1986 through 1990 in a remote valley on the western slope of the sierra,[1] during the most violent and turbulent period of that country's modern history, the analysis focuses on villages whose terraces and canal systems date back hundreds of years to the time of the Incas and beyond. My main purpose in living there and studying the communities was to examine the changes that these ancient landscapes, and the whole tradition of water use associated with them, had undergone in recent times—a "dry" enough subject, at first glance, but an important one that had received little attention in previous work.

In this valley, as in many others throughout the Andean highlands today, settlements that probably once shared the same local tradition now tend to differ markedly in even the most basic aspects of water use. By doing a comparative ethnographic study, one focusing on different villages at the same time, I tried to find out how far they had actually diverged from one another in their development, and to learn why this diversification, much of it evidently fairly recent, had taken place. More important, by tracing the process carefully in different kinds of places, I hoped to find out how it was related to ongoing changes in the other domains—socioeconomic, political, and cultural—of Andean community life. I wanted to learn the history of irrigation in the highlands, to be able to tell that familiar New World story of Conquest, Colonialism, and expanding global Capitalism from a hydrological, as well as an ethnic, point of view, as I will try to do here. And I will do it simply by talking about all of these places, about local people, how they do things, and the very different kinds of communities in which they now live. The value of this effort seems obvious enough in a region where irrigation is essential for agriculture—indeed central to every

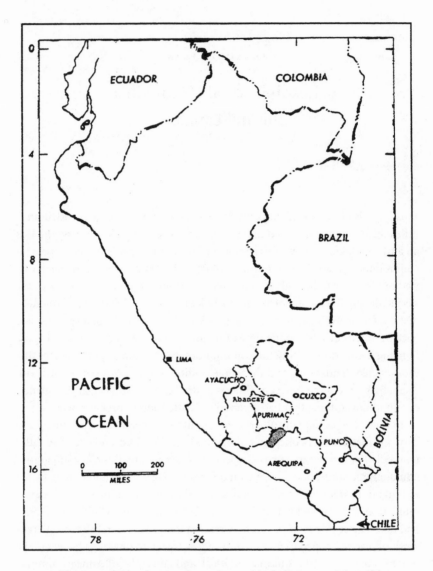

MAP 1. The state of Peru showing the study area (shaded). Source: Adapted from a map by the Instituto Geográfico Nacional, Lima

aspect of rural life—and where water is chronically scarce today, a source of real strife and conflict.

To undertake the study was daunting, since it required me to learn local agricultural practices, to evaluate their functional significance, and somehow also trace them back to their historical roots. The notion that local villages had once had much more in common technologically than they do today seemed beyond doubt and was useful as a point of departure, but it was an open question just how much alike they had formerly been. The fact that their canal systems were built by the Incas and their predecessors did not necessarily mean that water had originally been distributed and used in the same way in each case. Instead, it was likely that a certain amount of variety had always existed in the valley because not all places have the same terrain or the same problems of water supply. Allowances also had to be made for idiosyncratic differences, since, in irrigation as in many other pursuits, the same ends can often be accomplished by alternative means.

The challenge, of course, was to identify these "authentic" differences and distinguish them from those of more recent, and exogenous, origin. In theory, new practices could have arisen autonomously through innovation, or they could have emerged in response to changes whose main inspiration lay outside the communities themselves, in the political economy of the colonial and modern periods. For example, I knew going in that, during the late-nineteenth and early-twentieth centuries, regional trade had intensified throughout the sierra, leading to a dramatic increase in the number of private agricultural estates devoted to commerce and long-distance transport. This expansion of the haciendas, although known to have occurred at the expense of adjacent peasant communities, depriving them of land while ruthlessly exploiting their labor, was bound to have led to some significant changes in agricultural practice at the local level. Yet these had never been closely studied, nor had their impact on water use—and ownership—ever been examined.

It was also likely that rural administrators acting on behalf of the national government, or other external agents of change, had imposed some new practices. In a few of the villages, the state had administered irrigation for a long time, making it crucial to consider the changes that official policies for water management had set in motion at the local level. Despite the government's long and widespread involvement, its impact on this, the most basic aspect of village life, had not been thoroughly examined in any previous study.

Unfortunately, few historical documents contain information on these subjects, which might be used to supplement the memories of people still alive. Nevertheless, I felt certain that I could learn a great deal using standard ethno-

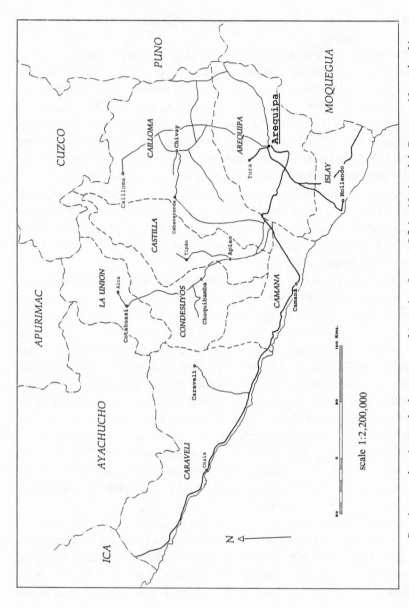

MAP 2. Provinces and major roads, department of Arequipa. Source: Oficina Nacional de Recursos Naturales, Lima

graphic methods—such as participant observation, focused interviews, and the collection of oral histories—in a study of the practices, and especially the knowledge, of people in this one small region. By looking closely at a few villages that were of common ancestry and that had always exploited the same type of environment, yet that were markedly different from one another today, I thought it might be possible to discover some of the factors that had caused communities throughout the sierra to diverge in recent times. This comparative approach has a long history of use in social anthropology, but it had seen surprisingly little use in ethnography, in research done by a single observer in a given area, and it had never been tried in work on irrigation.

After four months of combing the southern highlands, I was convinced I had found the best spot to study: the Cotahuasi valley of the department of Arequipa, a remote and little-known place lying high on the western slope in the southern part of the country. Like all of Peru's watersheds that drain into the Pacific, this one is quite arid, and irrigation has always been even more vital to agriculture in this province than in the more humid inter-Andean valleys farther to the east. When I first visited the area in 1984, it seemed particularly suitable for my research, much more than other provinces in the same desert region (see Maps 1 and 2).

For one thing, although the local canal systems were clearly prehispanic, some of them seemed to be virtually intact while others had obviously been modified in significant ways. This was immediately evident in the landscape itself. In many villages, agricultural terraces still covered the mountainsides, vast sculpted gardens that seemed as ancient as the Andes themselves. Yet in other places much of this original landscape had either been abandoned or deliberately destroyed. Based on a previously published study of another valley (Mayer & Fonseca 1979), as well as my own earlier experiences in Peru, I felt sure that the latter development, the destruction of terracing, somehow lay at the core of the processes of change that I wanted to understand.

The location was also particularly attractive because of the diversity of the local population, in terms of both ethnicity and class. It included, at the extremes, peasants, or *campesinos*—people who are culturally largely indigenous or Andean and whose primary language is Quechua—and a large group of elite families, landlords who consider themselves to be both culturally and linguistically distinct, being the direct descendants of Spanish settlers and other people who came to the valley from elsewhere. In between is a group of peasants who, although bilingual, speak Spanish primarily and identify themselves as mestizo (*gente mestiza*), people of mixed cultural heritage. Interestingly, the three groups live in close proximity, sometimes even within the same village (see Onuki 1981:13–14).

These differences in culture, in identity, and above all in practice, as I experienced them and ultimately came to understand them, will be explained in the chapters that follow. Because of them, the valley seemed to offer a glimpse back to a time when indigenous people and people of Spanish heritage lived together side by side in small highland communities. In most parts of the sierra this era had ended several decades earlier, when hacienda owners had withdrawn from the countryside to the major towns and cities, putting their estates into the hands of local mestizo managers. Since what I hoped to understand was the interaction of Andean and Spanish traditions, not just in irrigation but in other domains of life as well, it seemed important to work in an area where the emigration of the landlords had only recently begun, which was the case here.

Beyond all this, the valley was extremely remote and, compared with adjacent ones, still in a rather marginal position within the commercial economy. The local people had never really practiced commercial agriculture, except for pasture and livestock-raising, and no major development projects had ever been carried out. This relative marginality, it seemed to me, would have limited the scope and pace of change, and reduce the number of variables that had to be taken into account in the study. The area was in fact changing rapidly, as it turned out, like all highland provinces, and had its own peculiar history of involvement in the market economy. But the lack of any enterprises involving the investment of external capital seemed to provide a setting in which both continuity and change might be studied more effectively than was possible in other, less remote parts of Peru. Unbeknownst to me, that situation would end abruptly soon after I began fieldwork, giving me the chance to observe, in their early stages, processes of change that had begun in most areas long before, but had never been closely examined.

Finally, the valley was one of the most obscure parts of the entire sierra, being virtually unknown in the anthropological and historical literatures. Aside from a few brief ethnographic surveys (Bowman 1916; also Bingham 1922; Onuki 1981), only one scholar had worked in the area (Inamura 1981, 1986), and the high-altitude community he studied engaged primarily in camelid herding. Apart from that, nothing had apparently ever been written about the place, other than numerous references in the Spanish chronicles and the sketchy accounts in the colonial *visitas*. Curiously, these sources indicated that, despite its small size, the valley had once been a very important place, the political center of one of the four quarters of the Inca empire and the home of one of its most powerful ethnic groups. Yet almost nothing else was known about it, and the valley remained a hole on the historical map. Since I intended to do an archival search, and to do some preliminary archaeological surveys in an effort to date

the local canal systems, Cotahuasi seemed to offer an opportunity to make contributions in several areas of study.

In contemplating all of this, I felt certain that two assumptions could safely
be made. First, the components of the original Andean technology had to share
some kind of underlying logic, whether explicit or not, and should therefore fit
together into a coherent pattern. Although this would also be true of any Spanish innovations, their rationale would not necessarily be the same, which might
make it possible to identify practices introduced so long ago that local people
had come to consider them traditional. And second, the patterns of change
could only be recognized through a more comprehensive analysis of hydraulic
and agricultural practices than most previous authors had provided.[2] There was
a puzzling variation in techniques both within and among the different villages.
Whereas earlier ethnographers had tended to accept such diversity as endoge-
nous, or at least treat it as a given, for me it was something to be explained. And
I would have to become familiar with the conditions of water use in several
communities if I was to have any chance of success.

The Research Hypothesis: A Local Tradition Once Shared

At the time I began my fieldwork, in 1986, there had been some major advances in ethnographic research, but these had created a degree of controversy
over the nature and significance of Andean irrigation. Recent work had cast
into question the notion, once widely held, that a distinctive technology had
evolved autonomously and spread throughout the region during Inca times, an
ancient heritage whose basic elements were thought to have survived in many
communities despite centuries of Spanish domination. The first detailed studies of highland watering systems—all following on the innovative work of
William P. Mitchell (1973, 1976)—had revealed a striking variation in nearly
every aspect but size; nearly all the systems are small-scale, serving less than a
thousand hectares of land (see Hunt 1988, 1989). A variation that included
everything from basic organization to watering techniques made it appear
doubtful that any widespread native tradition had ever existed, much less an
egalitarian one, as many scholars had previously thought.

Some authors had reported on communities where irrigation was highly
centralized, or "unified," operating according to strict rules and procedures
(Mayer & Fonseca 1979; Fonseca 1983; Gelles 1984, 1986; Valderamma & Escalante 1986; see also Hunt 1988, 1989), whereas others had described ones that
were "acephalous," or lacking any effective central authority (Bunker & Seligmann 1986; Guillet 1987). Still others had found systems that alternated between

the unified and acephalous modes, depending on the water supply (Mitchell 1973, 1976, 1981). The first type sometimes operated relatively smoothly, according to those rules and procedures, whereas the second tended to be rife with competition and conflict over water rights, in most but not all cases (Paerregaard 1994). The third, not surprisingly, lay somewhere in between.

The diversity was just as striking when it came to distribution and watering methods. In some villages, sectors of land and their individual fields were irrigated in a fixed sequence; in others, irrigation took place in a flexible, irregular, or even haphazard order, so that some people got water more often than others. Some communities were characterized by terraces that were relatively flat and watered from the bottom upward, others by sloped fields watered from the top downward, and still others showed a mixture of landscaping and watering techniques.

Because it was difficult to see any clear pattern in all this diversity, a tacit consensus had emerged by then—somewhat less prevalent today (Treacy 1994a, b; Guillet 1994)—that a significant amount of regional and local variation must have existed in the distant past, just as in the present, at least in terms of the principles governing organization and use. Finding this view questionable for several reasons, I set out to test an idea that was more consistent with my own knowledge and understanding of Andean reality. I felt that the community types documented in the literature had all emerged out of the same general sequence of historical development, under the influence of a similar, but variable, set of factors. And I thought that some of them, if not all, did indeed derive from an indigenous prototype, an original hydraulic tradition that may have been quite widespread and uniform in its general characteristics.

This hypothesis was based on my assumption that, throughout the highlands, the current state of hydraulic and landscaping practices in each community is the outcome of three lengthy phases of development, three sets of changing historical conditions. These provided a context in which changes in irrigation were likely, indeed virtually certain, to take place. They were (1) the establishment, during prehispanic times, of deliberate methods for managing scarce water among populations approximating those found in the region today (Cook 1981); (2) a massive reduction in the intensity of land and water use throughout the colonial period as the indigenous population collapsed, a sustained phenomenon that must have created an extraordinary situation of resource abundance; and (3) a gradual re-intensification as the indigenous population recovered, combined with the simultaneous growth of regional export economies in many areas, growth that was based on the expansion and proliferation of haciendas, or private agricultural estates.

It was clear that, in all cases, the population recovery had taken place under ecological, socioeconomic, and political circumstances never experienced by Andean people before. But in this valley, and apparently many others, a crucial variable, and an obvious one to any person familiar with the region, lay in the fact that, in some villages, the process had been dominated by a resident ethnic minority, who were the owners of those commercial estates, while in others it had not.

During my first visit to the valley in 1984, I had noticed two important things: that the *hacendados* largely controlled irrigation wherever they lived, and that their methods of water use were somewhat different from those of people in the peasant villages. I had not learned how they maintained this dominance, but upon starting the study, I quickly saw that it depended to some degree on another critical factor: the extent to which the state, with its legal and administrative institutions, had become involved in community affairs. It was striking that these two outside influences had manifested themselves differently from place to place, and that in a few villages they seemed hardly to figure in at all.

I therefore selected three places where I thought it might be possible, through a comparative analysis, to document the transforming effects that the landlords, and the presence of the state, had had on the local hydraulic tradition and the local way of life. My hypothesis was that, over large portions of the sierra, these alien and dominating influences had acted in broadly similar but diverse ways on a single local tradition, producing much of the variation found within the region today. They thereby undermined that tradition, contributing to a process of ecological, technological, and social decline, to a "tragedy of the commons" (Hardin 1968) whose symptoms had been widely noted, but which, in my opinion, had never been adequately explained.

The idea that the tradition in this valley, at least, had once been rather homogeneous came from two sources. The ethnohistorical accounts of Garcilaso de la Vega (1966 [1617], 2: 56–57) and Cieza de León (1959 [1553]: 199–200) strongly suggested that, at the time of the Incas' conquest of the area, a single ethnic group had inhabited the upper watershed. The amount of variation originally present was likely to have been relatively small where this was the case, and where environmental conditions were fairly uniform, as in a relatively small valley. The second source was, again, Garcilaso (1966 [1609], 1: 248), who claimed that, under Inca rule, irrigation in arid parts of the sierra had been carried out everywhere in the same manner, at least during times of water scarcity:

> In districts where the quantity of water for irrigation was small, they divided it proportionately (as they did with everything they shared out), so that there should be no

dispute among the Indians about obtaining it. This was only done in years of scanty rainfall when the need was greatest. The water was measured, and, as it was known from experience how long it took to irrigate a *fanega* of land, each Indian was accordingly granted the number of hours he needed for the amount of land he had, with plenty to spare. Water was taken by turns, according to the order of the plots of land, one after another. No preference was given to the rich or nobles, or to favorites or relatives of the *kuraca*, or to the *kuraca* himself, or to royal officials or governors. Anyone who neglected to irrigate his land at the proper time received an ignominious punishment.

The climatic and hydrological conditions described in this account, scarce water and scanty rainfall, prevail throughout much of the Andes today, and there were good reasons to think that they must have been just as common in the distant past. It therefore seemed possible that a single tradition had once predominated, not only in this valley, but over a vast area of the highlands. Yet it seemed unlikely, given all the chaos of the colonial period, that the tradition might have survived in some places.

Three Communities Along a Continuum

The three villages chosen for study were selected for two basic reasons. They have in common the distinctive kind of hydraulic system found almost everywhere throughout the sierra—small-scale, vertically oriented canal networks fed by mountain springs—yet they cover a wide range of the diversity found in the highlands today. All three are stratified into groups of large and small landowners and grow basically the same array of crops, including cultivated pasture for animals, but they vary in their ethnic composition and their degree of autonomy. They also vary in altitude, proximity to roads and adjacent provinces, and other factors, forming a kind of rural-urban continuum (Mintz 1953), though all within a very rural context.

The first, Huaynacotas, is a remote community of peasants who, although largely bilingual today, communicate with each other primarily in Quechua. Rather closed and located at high altitude, the pueblo has remained relatively independent of hacienda influence, never having allowed any landlords to actually settle there and acquire land, and unaffected by the national government's many interventions into local water affairs. The second, Pampamarca, is another remote village, also predominantly Quechua-speaking, which has long been controlled by a small minority of resident "Spanish" landlords, but where the impact of state institutions has likewise not been strongly felt in irrigation. The third, Cotahuasi itself, is a district composed of several communities, where Spanish is the primary language. The center of local commerce and state provincial administration, it remained thoroughly dominated, up until the advent of Peru's agrarian reform in 1969, by a group of elite families of Spanish descent, merchants who were the owners of major agricultural and herding estates. Here, outlying peasant villages, annexes where Quechua was formerly the main language, have long shared their irrigation system with a dominant town, and provided the local haciendas with both water and labor. These villages are the only ones in the province that are accessible by road.

Methodology: How to Be in Three Places at One Time

The communities lie a considerable distance away from one another and, by the time I arrived, personal security had become a serious problem for a foreigner, so that my options in studying them were limited. There were rumors that the violent revolutionary group known as Sendero Luminoso, the Shining Path,[3] was moving into the region and occasionally making its presence known in the more remote villages. Given the difficulties of travel and communication, I could not tell how real the threat was, but it meant that the police and the provincial authorities could not guarantee my safety in these areas and were unwilling to accept any responsibility for my protection. They advised me to spend most of my time in the lower part of the valley, which was safe at the time, and told me that, although I could go to the villages higher up, my visits should be few and limited to brief periods, and that I should not travel alone.

Given these restrictions, which I had no choice but to accept, I set up my home base in Cotahuasi, the provincial capital and one of the three places I wanted to study. Since this was the hub of commerce in the valley and the point of departure, a central place to which people from every village traveled fairly often, I adopted the only strategy available to me: one that combined short visits to the other pueblos with intensive interviews conducted in the town.

During an initial two-week stay in each of the other sites, Huaynacotas and Pampamarca, I prepared a detailed diagram of the irrigation and land-use system, with the help of local water distributors and other informants, by using an enlarged aerial photograph purchased from the National Aerial-Photographic Service in Lima (1:22,500 approximate scale).[4] At that time, I explained my interests publicly to the village authorities and the local people, and got the names of individuals who would be willing to talk with me about irrigation, in exchange for a small payment, whenever they visited Cotahuasi. Since the villagers proved to be generally cooperative in both cases, my list of informants began to grow after my initial visits.

These diagrams facilitated the subsequent interviews, which were conducted over a period of more than three years, from January 1986 through March 1990, both in Cotahuasi and in the city of Arequipa, where there is a large migrant community that includes people from every village in the valley. I found that, once I became familiar with the irrigation and land-use systems, the socio-economic composition, and the political structure of each community, I was able to do research on all three places at more or less the same time. I focused my routine work on Cotahuasi and its satellite hamlets, but I would interrupt this to work with anyone from the other two pueblos who came to town.

The method was less than ideal, of course, and it caused me to spend much more time in the valley than I had planned, amid worsening and increasingly worrisome conditions. Because the Sendero Luminoso guerrillas were then (1986) threatening to expand their operations from their base in Ayacucho, immediately to the west and north, into the southern part of the sierra, the newly elected government in Lima began to pour large amounts of money and personnel into the province, designating it an Emergency Development Microregion. Unfortunately, the influx of cash and equipment—much of it intended for irrigation improvement—created opportunities for corruption and thus posed further hazards for my research, as well as my safety.

Over the next two years, many cases of the misuse and theft of public funds came to light, on the part of outsiders as well as provincial officials who were members of the ruling party, the American Popular Revolutionary Alliance, or APRA. This discovery led to a series of confrontations between the local people and the party leadership, which escalated, nearly erupting into violence and ultimately resulting in several arrests. Being a witness to these incidents, as well as to the pervasive corruption, I found the local authorities becoming less and less cooperative toward me and more skeptical of my motives for being there as time went on.

From the beginning I had been aware of suspicions that I might be an agent of the Central Intelligence Agency or a member of Shining Path, suspicions that were hard to dispel completely, since I was dealing with people who had a lot to hide. Later these feelings began to be expressed in various forms of obstruction and harassment, and ultimately in outright threats against me by certain members of the ruling party.[5] It soon became clear that, in traveling alone out of necessity to the other villages, I was putting myself in jeopardy on more than one front.

Probably because the government's newfound interest in the valley caused a great deal of outside publicity to be focused on the place, Sendero Luminoso took a greater interest than it might have otherwise. Rumors of the guerrillas' presence in the villages circulated increasingly until late 1988, when they let it be known, through a series of acts culminating in terrible violence, that they were indeed a force to be reckoned with. These incidents ultimately forced me to withdraw in early 1989 to the city of Arequipa, where I continued my research for another year.

The tragic sequence of events—a story to be told in the penultimate chapter—made it impossible for me to spend as much time in the other two communities as I had planned.[6] The security conditions forced me to rely more heavily on the out-of-situ interviews than I would have under other circumstances, but I found that I was able to compensate for this in two ways. I was mainly interested in a limited set of hydraulic and agricultural practices that could be discussed, or even physically demonstrated, wherever canals, terraces, and irrigation water were found, as in Cotahuasi. And since I knew from the beginning that my trips to the other villages would be few, I spread them out over the two-and-a half years of fieldwork, during which I conducted many hours of preparatory interviews with residents of each community. I found that, by gathering most of my information in these conversations, I was able to devote my actual visits almost exclusively to confirming or correcting what I had learned.

The interviews were conducted in both Spanish, the national language of Peru, and Quechua, the Inca language, still spoken by millions of people in the highlands today. Although most people in the valley were fully fluent in Spanish, it was crucial, if I was to understand Andean concepts of irrigation, to be able to converse to some extent in Quechua as well, especially when I was working in the peasant communities. Although my training in the latter, at Yale initially and later in Cusco, never made me a fluent speaker by any means, it did allow me to use the language effectively in fieldwork.

The Materialist Focus of Research: Differences in Practice

My goal was to do a study of each community that was both ethnographic, in that it documented the current state of irrigation in all its aspects, and historical, in that it showed how local practices had changed through time. Since I had to begin with the present, my initial interviews and observations were mainly concerned with answering a number of standard questions about practices and conditions in each village, ones designed to provide a basic knowledge of the current state of irrigation in each community. Accordingly, each ethnographic section of the book will, in roughly the same order, describe the landscape, the ethnic and socioeconomic composition of the population, the irrigation and land-use systems, local techniques of water distribution and use, landscaping practices, canal maintenance, and labor exchange in agriculture, providing also a brief social history of each place. In discussing each of these matters with people, I was careful to check their knowledge of any changes in practice that had occurred, not only during their own lifetimes but also those of their parents and grandparents. Although this knowledge was very unevenly distributed within each village population, the questioning eventually provided a substantial amount of historical information.

Ultimately, though, it was the comparative method itself, the analysis of similarities and differences in practice between the communities, that proved most critical in revealing how Andean irrigation had changed through time. However, in order to account for the changes that had taken place and comprehend their impacts on village life, it was necessary to understand as fully as possible the context—the demographic, socioeconomic, and political conditions—in which they had occurred. Three sources provided this kind of information.

The first were the genealogies, and the personal and family histories, of my best informants, who always included several of the larger landowners in each community. Throughout the valley, the wealthier "Spanish" families were tightly linked by ties of kinship, the result of a strong tendency to marry only among themselves, so that my work with the landlords in one village invariably provided information on those in other communities as well. Since these families had always controlled local commerce, the interviews eventually yielded a great deal of information about the valley's economic and social history. Along with my conversations with smaller landowners and former peasant tenants, they provided crucial data on the conditions of work on the haciendas, and, more generally, on the culture and life-style of both peasants and the provincial elite.

Documents, the second source, were found in the following archives: the office of the Provincial Council in Cotahuasi, the National Archive in Lima, the Historical Archives of the Departments of Cusco and Arequipa, and the Library of Congress in Washington, D.C. These documents included items covering the entire history of water legislation, as well as other laws affecting relations between rural communities and the state. Demographic data were assembled from the published censuses of 1876, 1940, and later years, as well as from late-eighteenth- and early-nineteenth-century records found in the departmental archive in Cusco. The archive also yielded legal records providing extremely valuable information on socioeconomic and political conditions during the late colonial period.

Finally, I gathered archaeological data—surface artifacts, descriptions of architectural features, and dwelling counts—during surveys of the ancient sites found within each community's territory. These brief studies were done in order to accomplish three things: (1) to trace the early development of irrigation technology; (2) to estimate very roughly the pre-Conquest population of each area; and (3) to determine how changes in settlement patterns imposed by the Spanish during the sixteenth century had affected water distribution. All of these were crucial parts of the puzzle that I wanted to solve.

My research followed in the tradition of Julian Steward (1955b), Karl Witt-fogel (1955), Edmund Leach (1961), Harold Conklin (1980), William Kelly (1982, 1983), and many others, all of whom had tried, in one way or another, to deter-mine how irrigation has shaped social and political life in relatively arid parts of the world. Since my main concern was with people's use of material and hu-man resources—land, water, and labor—in transforming the physical environ-ment and deriving a livelihood, the theoretical orientation and the methodol-ogy were mainly those of ecological anthropology, following Steward (1955a), Roy Rappaport (1968, 1984), Robert Netting (1986), and many others. But since I was especially interested in agency, or the perspective of the individual, in an-alyzing knowledge, practice, and motivation at that level, the study was also economic, informed by current theory in that area of anthropology too. My contribution was to do an ecological and economic study, contextualized as thoroughly as possible, that was both comparative and historical.

Although the method stressed the observation of processes at the local level, I was of course aware, like any ethnographer today, that rural communities are and always have been caught up in the dynamics of larger systems: regional, state, and global. Yet I was convinced that, if these external influences had af-fected village life in truly significant ways, they must have done so in part by changing the use of the most important resource: water. Consequently, I felt that tracing the history of irrigation, even within this one small province, would almost certainly shed new light on the many processes of change that are reshaping the region today. These include, most importantly, the widening stratification within rural communities, the commercialization of peasant agri-culture, the demise of traditional authority and customary forms of coopera-tive work, and, above all, *mestizaje*, the "creolization" of highland culture. These trends, all indicative of basic changes in values and in social identity, had been documented and discussed in nearly every recently published work, but their relationship to ecological and technological change had never been closely studied. The reader, of course, will judge the degree to which I was successful in doing all this, and casting both the present and the past in a new light.

ONE

The Setting

A Valley on the Edge of 'the Abyss'

The Cotahuasi River emerges from headwaters high along the continental divide in the central Andes, then descends southward through a vast canyon that narrows and deepens as it approaches the Pacific Ocean. About halfway along its course, the river flows over a precipice into a chasm so deep that, from that point onward, almost until it reaches the sea, it can neither be seen nor heard from the mountain slopes high above. There, in what is perhaps the deepest gorge on earth, the river takes on its real name: Ukhuña, or, in the hispanicized version, Ocoña, meaning "now in the depths" or "now in the abyss."[1] When local people speak of the river or the watershed as a whole, that is the name they use. Cotahuasi is the largest village along the banks, but, apparently in recent times, that name came to embrace the river's upper reaches, an area also known as "the valley," where the slopes are less steep and where most of the population resides.

The area has always been exceptionally remote, and even today it remains little known outside the immediately surrounding region. Unlike most of its counterparts along the western Andean slope, this valley cannot really be considered coastal, since the most heavily populated portion lies in the heart of the sierra, cut off from the sea. Snow-capped peaks and high tundra enclose it on three sides, yet these provide the only major access because the canyon below is nearly impassable and blocks entry by way of the river channel.

Although extremely remote, the location for a long time had considerable advantages as the only fertile and sheltered place for more than a hundred miles in any direction (see Maps 1–2). Up till the time that roads and motor vehicles penetrated the surrounding plateau, during the 1950's, the province lay at a strategic intermediate point along ancient transport routes linking coastal valleys to the south and west with highlands to the north and east. Local merchants carried out a brisk trade in products from the two regions, moving them overland on caravans of mules. The distances involved were so great that these people enjoyed a monopoly, which is why few outsiders ever visited the place.

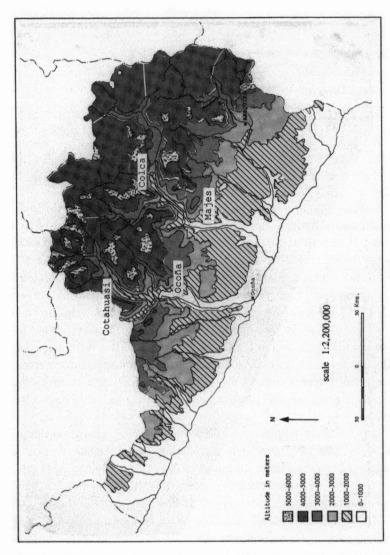

MAP 3. Altitude zones and watersheds, department of Arequipa.
Source: Adapted from Oficina Nacional de Recursos Naturales map.

The first foreigners to reach the valley in modern times were Hiram Bingham and Isaiah Bowman, leaders of a 1912 Yale expedition, who stopped in Cotahuasi en route to completing the first scientific transect of the Andean cordillera. In published reports, they spoke of an oasis hidden among arid mountains where "Indians" lived under the thumb of landlords of Spanish descent, and where a violent, drunken uprising had recently been suppressed by the local authorities. These images attracted me and led me to travel there for the first time in 1984. Although I did not realize it until events unfolded much later, they were still strangely appropriate despite seventy years of change and were a harbinger of tragic events to come. Mainly, though, it was Bingham's (1922: 54–55) striking description of the landscape that had aroused my interest: of vast terraced mountainsides made lush and green by irrigation, which seemed to him to have remained the same for centuries—just as they did, at first glance, to me.

Geography, Topography, and Remoteness

The valley lies along the northern edge of a unique geological formation known as the volcanic plateau of Arequipa. This barren undulating tableland, called the *meseta* or *puna*, is part of a zone of ancient eruption and tectonic uplift that extends far to the south, through the Atacama desert of Chile, varying in elevation from 2,000 to over 4,700 meters, or 7,000–15,000 feet (Bowman 1916: 199–203). Some of the highest landforms are found in the north, in the area surrounding the Cotahuasi-Ocoña and Majes valleys, where altitudes average around 4,300 meters, or about 14,000 feet (see Map 3). Two of the world's biggest volcanoes, Coropuna and Ampato, rise above the plain there to heights of 6,200 meters (21,000 feet), dominating the landscape along with other major peaks (see Bingham 1922: 23–49).

The plateau forms the western flank of the famous *altiplano*, or high plain, of the central Andes and southern Peru, the wool-producing region surrounding Lake Titicaca. This vast plateau, like its counterpart in Tibet, represents the upper limit at which humans can subsist and live on a long-term basis. Within this context, however, the meseta is unique, not only because of its volcanism, but also because rivers have cut down into it through a process of orogenic faulting and fluvial erosion and created the deepest canyons in South America, and perhaps in the world (Bowman 1916: 233–73). Among these, the canyon of Ukhuña is foremost, reaching a depth of more than 3,000 meters, or roughly two miles from the rim to the bottom, not including the adjacent mountains.[2]

The vertical scale of both the valley and the canyon is enormous, with great extremes of altitude lying within very close range of each other. From the river at its lowest point, 1,200 meters (4,000 feet), the canyon walls and the slopes of the volcano Solimana rise almost straight up for about three miles to a height of 6,000 meters (19,000 feet), all within a horizontal distance of only seven miles. Here, a day's climb on horseback can take a person all the way from the driest subtropical desert to the equivalent of arctic tundra and even to glacial habitats. Andean valleys have long been recognized for this distinctive vertical ecology, and this is one of the places where the feature was noted scientifically for the first time (Bowman 1916). Although the upper watershed is not quite so deep, extending from 2,300 meters to about 5,300, the environmental parameters are similar in both areas, and they form a single geographic and hydrological unit.

The vastness and height of the surrounding plateau make the valley quite remote from adjacent regions of southern Peru. To the south, Arequipa, the second-largest city in the country and the capital of the department of the same name, is 200 kilometers away in a straight line, 455 kilometers by road, and twelve to fourteen hours by bus. Before the dirt road was completed in 1960—one of the highest in the world and doubtless one of the worst, but the only one connecting the valley with the outside world—this trip took eight days and followed the path of a major roadway built by the Incas. To the north, it is four days' walk or horse ride to Puquio in the department of Ayacucho, the only important town between Cotahuasi and the department's capital, Ayacucho city. To the east, Cusco, the capital of the Inca empire and of the present department of Cusco, is roughly 250 kilometers away as the crow flies, or about six days away on horseback. Going westward, one can follow the remains of the Inca road to Kuntisuyu—passing down into the canyon, then up and across the plateau—to arrive at the coastal village of Chala in three or four days. This stone-paved highway, which once linked the ancient capital of Cusco with the valley as well as the sea, was the most important transport route in the region before the Conquest.

Throughout much of its history, the valley was tightly integrated into networks of trade and transport that extended in all directions. Within these archaic systems, the location was clearly not the great disadvantage that it has become today. Paradoxically enough, the development of motorized transport and the expansion of roads during the 1950's and 1960's had the effect of shifting Cotahuasi and its people into a more marginal geographic and economic position than they had ever been in before, and of bringing a kind of "golden era" to an end, at least for a certain segment of the population. When overland transport ceased to be carried out on the backs of mules, llamas, and other beasts of burden, what had long been a central place and a hub of economic activity became a remote area, whose role in regional trade had been eclipsed.

Even though the area can now be reached by road, the costs of transport have elevated the prices of goods brought to and from the valley far above those that prevail elsewhere in the southern highlands. As a result, the population suffers today from a new kind of isolation, one created by a market and transport system based on fossil fuel, which has reduced the scope if not the frequency of its exchange with the outside world. As we will see later, this is true even though much of the population now travels outside the valley on a regular basis and, like people throughout the sierra today, is in close contact with family members who have migrated to urban areas. Two cities, Arequipa, with a population of about 1,000,000, and Lima, with more than 8,000,000, are now the focus of nearly all external trade—mainly cattle for sale in urban markets—and communication.

The Hydrology of the Watershed

Among the valleys of the western Andean slope, this one is unusual for the large number of high peaks that enclose it and supply it with water. Among Peru's fifty-four coastal rivers, the Cotahuasi is second in size of watershed, second in area of snow-covered peaks and lakes, first in humid area, fifth in annual flow, and first in dry-season flow (Chavez 1982: 31). All of this reveals a cruel joke of nature, since the valley's topography allows most of the water to escape from the local irrigation systems. The river is so deeply entrenched that most of it has remained unavailable for agriculture up to the present day. Of all the local communities, only four—Alca, Tomepampa, Taurisma, and Mungui—are able to make use of the river or one of its tributaries, each on a rather small scale. The vast majority draw upon the only other water sources that are available: alpine springs.

Thus the valley has an enormous hydraulic potential, mostly unexploited. It is by no means unique in this respect, however; throughout the upper reaches of the western slope, and even in most inter-Andean valleys, river gradients are steep and water channels are always deeply incised. The only peculiar thing about this watershed, aside from its size, is that, owing to the extraordinary steepness and depth of the canyon, the water cannot be diverted and used until it actually reaches the very narrow coastal plain to the south, so that most of it ultimately pours into the sea. All of the other western rivers are tapped heavily along their lower reaches, as they approach the coast, but this is rarely the case higher up. In fact, throughout the sierra proper, it is unusual for the water of major rivers to be used extensively or on a massive scale for irrigation.[3] In this sense, Cotahuasi is a typical highland valley.

The top of the watershed is Nevado Coropuna, one of the biggest volcanoes in the world (6,377 meters, or about 22,000 feet), which looms over the valley but is not actually visible from there. The third-highest peak in Peru, Coropuna is still widely revered and worshipped in the region and regarded as the second-most-important Apu, or mountain deity, in Andean cosmology (Valderamma & Escalante 1980; Gose 1994). Site of one of the most sacred oracles in the Inca empire—one of only two where the Apus routinely "spoke"—it was adorned with a major temple (Cieza de León 1959 [1553]: 152), whose remnants still lie undiscovered somewhere on its slopes. There, priests and nuns once devoted themselves to interpreting the mountain's behavior and to receiving the souls of the dead, who, during ancient mortuary rites, were "sent" there from communities throughout the altiplano to reside in their afterlife. Many peasants and herders still follow this ancient practice today, giving one indication of the singular importance that the valley and the surrounding region, formerly known as Kuntisuyu, once had in the Andean world. The volcano's original name was probably Qoripuna, or "Puna of Gold."[4]

Rainfall, Drought, and Irrigation

Like other western valleys, this one cannot be cultivated on the basis of rainfall alone, and it is subject to frequent droughts that tend to strike the entire southern sierra. Although they vary greatly in intensity, these can have a devastating effect on agriculture and on the economy and on social life in general. All of this means that such crises occur on an irregular basis but are a constant in the sense that they are a feature of the physical environment.

Rainfall throughout the Andes is proportional to altitude. The yearly rains, which here fall almost exclusively in January, February, and March, come from the east, rising over the mountains from the Amazon basin. As these clouds of tropical origin pass over the range, they discharge most of their moisture, creating a rainshadow over the valleys below (Bowman 1916; Brush 1977a). The shadow is more pronounced in the west and creates more aridity than in the east, in part because the valleys are so deep, but mainly because the clouds have traveled over the entire width of the range by the time they arrive.

Data recorded at a weather station installed in the town of Cotahuasi in 1964 by SENAMI, the Peruvian weather monitoring agency, showed an average of only 259 millimeters of rainfall per year, at an altitude of 2,673 meters. In con-

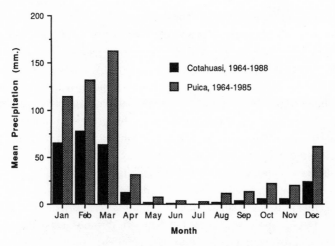

FIG. 1. Average monthly precipitation, Cotahuasi and Puica, 1964–1988. Source: Servicio National Meteorológico, Arequipa.

trast, the station at Puica, located in the upper part of the valley at 3,600 meters, reported an average of roughly twice that amount (see Fig. 1). Consequently, the lowest part of the study area can be classified as arid, and the highest zone as semi-arid at best. Rainfall in the canyon, where there are also scattered villages, is a lot more scarce, though no data in that case are available.

The average precipitation in Cotahuasi is roughly only half the minimum needed for the cultivation of maize, the primary staple crop.[5] And Puica, though it receives much more, is seriously deficient as well. Thus the vast majority of the lands now in production have always been intensively irrigated, and much of the valley would not be cultivable at all without watering. A tradition does exist, however, of dry-farming certain high-altitude lands, located between 3,700 and 4,100 meters elevation. As in most parts of the sierra, these areas are devoted mainly to tuber production through the well-known system of sectoral fallowing (see Guillet 1981; Orlove & Godoy 1986). But even here, many of the lands are irrigated for planting at the beginning of the rainy season and then watered periodically if the need arises, since any decrease in normal precipitation, such as commonly occurs, will devastate the harvest. There are also extensive fallowing lands that lack this advantage, not being accessible to springwater, but these now lie abandoned because of recurrent droughts in the last half of the twentieth century. Irrigation is therefore crucial for the long-term cultivation of the area.

The early inhabitants of the valley went to great lengths to mitigate the ef-

fects of climate, to overcome the rainshadow, by constructing canals and terraces that redistribute water over a tremendous vertical range. These systems
tap major springs and groundwater flows created by glacial runoff and by seep-
age from alpine lakes among the surrounding peaks. In addition, each network
contains smaller springs that emerge farther downslope, within the cultivated
areas. Wherever possible, natural stream channels were simply modified in order to create the main paths of distribution, so that great vertical swaths of land
could be covered without building extremely long canals. From an engineering
standpoint, the biggest challenge obviously lay in creating flat surfaces that
would allow the water to be absorbed, through terracing.

The landscape is rugged and convoluted, including everything from sheer
cliffs to gentle hillsides to small flatlands, and it is generally steep: unmodified
gradients average about 30 percent (27 degrees). Without terracing, irrigation
of the steeper areas would be futile and destructive of water and soil, since the
water would simply run off. However, the technology has other important
functions as well, which apply to all kinds of terrain, as we will eventually see.
Evidently, the arable parts of the valley were originally leveled in their entirety
for this reason. In recent times, however—meaning the period since the Spanish families arrived and colonized the place—much of the landscape has deliberately been returned to its previous state. The logic of this transformation, the
destruction of terracing, will be explained later; it emphasizes the production
of food for animals over the growth of food for people, and is of Spanish origin. Its impact on local irrigation has been profound, changing the very nature
of the technology in many communities.

The canal systems cover only a few hundred hectares and would be considered small scale by most standards (see Hunt 1988, 1989). Nevertheless, they are
quite imposing, especially to an outsider, an impression that Bingham (1922:
54–55) captured in his account, where he described the panorama from high
above Cotahuasi, overlooking terraces that extended, apparently unbroken, for
a vertical mile.

Figure 2 shows the average annual precipitation in the rainy season for Cotahuasi and Puica over the twenty-four-year period 1964–88. The data, adjusted
from the weather station reports, are intended to highlight the only agricultur-
ally significant precipitation, that which falls from January through March.
Rainfall outside of this period is minimal and sporadic and has little effect on
cultivation. The Cotahuasi data represent conditions in the pueblos of the
lower part of the valley, and the Puica data those in higher villages like Huaynacotas and Pampamarca, all three of which are found at roughly the same altitude.

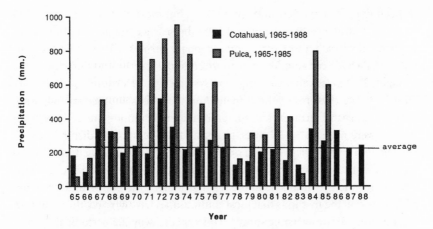

FIG. 2. Annual precipitation, Cotahuasi and Puica, 1964–1988. The minimum rainfall needed for cultivation without irrigation is 650 mm. Source: Same as Fig. 1.

The figure reveals that, in spite of the rainshadow effect, climatic fluctuations tend to affect the two zones at the same time and to a similar degree. In Cotahuasi, the standard deviation in total rainfall during this period was 93 millimeters, indicating that the typical variation between years was on the order of 36 percent. Puica, even though it usually got about twice as much rainfall, showed a similar deviation of 185 millimeters, or 31 percent of the mean annual total. This, of course, is a highly unstable pattern.

What is noteworthy is the dramatic increase in years with below-average rainfall beginning in 1978. More than half the years in the succeeding decade were ones of drought, a frequency that, according to the local people, was unprecedented. This trend has since shown some signs of abating when I was there, but it may in fact still constitute a major climatic shift. Only the future will tell whether the persistent droughts, apparently related to the oceanic phenomenon known as El Niño, are indeed part of a long-term weather change, because the stations' reports are the earliest available.

The important point, for the moment, is that recent decades have shown considerable variation. There were consecutive droughts in the first two years of record, none in the decade that followed (1967–77), and six in the years 1978 –88. The last cycle generated a recurrent water crisis in nearly every local village. Without exception, dry-farmed lands that lacked access to water were abandoned, and in most cases the water supplies of irrigated lands were seriously deficient. A major reason for the crisis, aside from the dearth of rainfall itself, is that the springs became quite unstable. Much of their volume is constant, coming as it does from glaciers and alpine lakes, but most of them are also highly dependent on the recharging provided by the yearly precipitation. In the vast majority of cases, both primary and secondary springs will dwindle substantially after a bad year, roughly in proportion to the severity and duration of the drought. This means that the irrigation systems fluctuate, quite inevitably, according to the rhythms of the climate. And that raises another crucial point.

The canals and terraces, and the other material components of local technology, were not created in order to negate these temporary disturbances in rainfall. Rather, they were built in order to alter the rainshadow effect, which is a permanent condition. The impact of drought can only be mitigated to a limited extent, and the means lie in the realm of water distribution and irrigation technique—in the methods that local communities have devised, through time, for adjusting to the available supply. This explains why the periodic droughts, although widespread, are much more serious in some villages than in others. The capacity of many communities to adapt has been diminished by numerous changes in practice that have occurred since the Spanish Conquest. The full significance of these changes will become clear when we examine the various plans that the communities have attempted, or proposed, for resolving the water problem.

The conditions just described—vertically dispersed springs, unstable groundwater flows, and steep terrain—are almost universal in the highlands and form a distinctly Andean pattern. The local systems that were developed in order to cope with them—the physical structures, as well as their techniques and principles of operation—are therefore unusual and highly sophisticated. In many important respects, these Andean systems, which are properly called communal traditions, contrast sharply with the riverine ones of the coast, which are large scale, tap a single water source, have a more horizontal orientation, and typically operate on different principles. As we will see, the people who depend on them for survival identify strongly with their customary way of doing things and play a vital role in its continuation. The canal systems are maintained through elaborate unifying ritual, and the most important factor by far in sustaining the traditions, specifically the rules and principles for water use, is the constant vigilance, leadership, and participation of the people themselves.

However, roughly half the local villages can no longer be described as indigenous, either technologically or culturally, mainly those that lie near the valley bottom. At first glance their irrigation systems seem much like the ones higher up, but closer inspection reveals differences so basic that they can only have originated in a separate sequence of development. The chapters that follow will show that most of this variation emerged as a result of conditions and events that transpired long after the structures were built, many of them quite recent and most of them exogenous in origin. This applies to differences in landscaping, in watering technique, and, perhaps most importantly, in hydraulic organization.

Technological changes turn out to be crucial in explaining many of the ecological, sociocultural, and even political differences among the communities, including their relative ability to adapt to drought. In reality, the recurring water crises can be attributed as much to the decline of prehispanic traditions as they can to a disturbance in rainfall patterns, which have apparently always been rather unstable. Far more than climate, it is irrigation that has changed, and most other aspects of Andean life have changed along with it.

Irrigation's Many Functions

In arid and mountainous settings like this, irrigation actually fulfills several important functions. To say that it supplements scanty rainfall, or that it counteracts the rainshadow effect, is to generalize in a way that obscures some of its complexity and significance. First of all, irrigation is used to overcome the seasonality of precipitation, thereby making it possible to sow plants and allow them to begin to mature before the onset of the rains. The most important staple crop, maize, requires nine months to mature, but the rainy season lasts three to four months at best. Irrigation is used to lengthen this natural growing season and thereby widen the array of crops that can be grown (Mitchell 1976). Without it, even the production of fast-maturing plants (potatoes, wheat, and barley), which take roughly five months to grow, would be precarious, and agriculture would be restricted to the higher altitudes where rainfall is greatest.

Irrigation is also used in a complex and ultimately unsatisfactory way to supplement the rainfall in times of drought. During normal years, supervised distribution ends in each village once it becomes obvious that the rains have begun in earnest and remains suspended until the planting season of the following year. If the rains fail to achieve a consistent daily pattern, however, irrigation must continue, under special emergency conditions, throughout the wet season until shortly before the harvest. And if the rains begin and then stop prematurely after the cycle has been terminated, watering will be resumed once it becomes clear that a serious situation has developed. Every local community faces this problem and must take appropriate action, which in each case is decided upon by an assembly of water users. Generally, the emergency measures are customary ones that go into effect automatically once a decision has been reached. They cannot eliminate the effects of drought, however, but only mitigate them to a certain extent, because irrigation and rainfall play different, though complementary, roles in agricultural production.

The irrigation of food crops begins in late August, during the middle of the dry season (April–December). It is used first for seed germination and thereafter for slow but steady plant development until the rains come. Because this is when the water supply is quite low, most villages will irrigate the plants no more than eight times from September through December, or only about twice a month, even under the best of conditions. The goal is to see that the plants achieve a critical minimum of growth in this period, so that they can later take advantage of the rainfall, which normally induces a four-month growth spurt that is the main phase of crop development. When the rains fail, however, the best that irrigation can do is to allow a minimal harvest to be salvaged. During a drought, even if the supply is carefully rationed, as in the higher-altitude villages, the frequency of irrigation will at best remain about the same as it was during the dry season. Compare this with what people consider to be a "normal" season, when the soil is thoroughly moistened by rainfall almost daily. The function of irrigation with respect to drought, therefore, is only to mitigate or minimize the resulting damage, not really to replace the rain that fails to come.

Finally, irrigation is used to water perennial plants that have no special growing season. These include fruit trees in household gardens (apples, oranges, and avocados), but the most important one by far is alfalfa, a crop that the Spanish introduced locally during the seventeenth century for pasture. Highly resistant to both frost and drought, alfalfa can survive for months without water, yet it has an extraordinary capacity to respond to frequent watering by growing faster and producing multiple crops or cuttings. It is irrigated year-round and is cultivated in every local community, but the extent of its production, as well as the methods by which it is watered, differ markedly from one village to the next. In this case, irrigation makes it possible to produce a crop on a continual basis, often independently of the rainfall, and to do so at a wide range of elevations. Because alfalfa is used to feed animals rather than people, however, its cultivation, which is expanding in most places, involves a fundamental shift in the whole ecology of land and water use.

Temperatures, Seasonality, and the Rhythm of Cultivation

Highland irrigation has another peculiarity. Its schedule is determined not merely by the annual variation in springwater and rainfall, as one might expect, but also by the yearly fluctuation in temperatures. In both the upper and the lower part of the valley, the climate is fairly mild: average annual temperatures are 15–17 degrees C in Cotahuasi (at 2,700 meters) and 8–15 degrees in Puica (at 3,600 meters). The effects of high altitude mitigate those of tropical latitude (15 degrees south) and vice-versa, but a pronounced diurnal variation in temperatures widens with increasing altitude. During the winter dry season (June–August), daytime temperatures show surprisingly little change, but at night they begin to drop so severely that frosts become common at all elevations. The threat of frost imposes a severe constraint on the timing of cultivation, and, consequently, that of irrigation, not only on the western slope (Treacy 1994b; Gelles 1986, 1994; Guillet 1992), but in the inter-Andean valleys to the east as well (Mitchell 1976; Bunker & Seligmann 1986; Bolin 1990).

Since crops must be harvested before the first frost and cannot be sown again until the frost period ends, a dead or slack season truncates the production cycle. In each community, planting and watering begin with maize in late August or early September, in order to allow the necessary nine months, then proceed to other crops as the planting cycle continues. The last of the planting is done just as the rainy season gets under way—the only arrangement possible under these conditions—and it is at this point that organized watering normally ends. Then, with one major exception, all cultivation and all irrigation cease after the harvest in early June.

The result is that irrigation ends at the time when the water supply is at its highest, just after the rains, and it does not begin again until the supply has declined dramatically. Even more important, in most cases the flows will continue to dwindle as they are being used during the early part of the agricultural year. During the three-month cold period, when the springs are at their peak, water is free for the taking and can be used by anyone on a first-come, first-served basis. Nonetheless, alfalfa is virtually the only crop irrigated, since it alone is nearly immune to the effects of frost. Even though pasture production is substantial in some villages, this means that, in all of the communities, water is, and probably always will be, used least at the very time when it is most available

The Changing Landscape

It is important to note that alfalfa has come to dominate the crop-rotation cycle in many villages, along with a wild grass called the *kikuyo* or *grama*, another import that competes with it. Nearly everywhere in the lower part of the valley, a household will have at least one tiny plot of alfalfa to feed the family cow; and many people grow much more because they are involved in the cattle trade. If a pasture field is well cared for it can produce alfalfa for twenty years or

more, but the battle against the grama is constant and the invading weed usually takes over a field completely long before that.

A field may lie out of use in this condition for many years, apparently abandoned, until the soil is turned over through a labor-intensive process called a
rompeo, or breaking-up. At that point, potatoes will be planted for one or two
years to take advantage of the soil fertility that alfalfa has created through nitrogen fixation. This stage will then be followed by up to five years of maize.
When maize productivity declines, wheat or barley will be planted for a year or
two, and if the soil improves enough because of this crop change, maize will be
planted again. Ultimately, however, the only thing to do with an exhausted plot
is to plant it in pasture and start the rotation cycle over again.[6]

In the lower part of the valley, the demand for alfalfa, together with the need
for soil regeneration and for the periodic breaking-up, drives this whole rotation process. Furthermore, in some communities much of the landscape has
been modified, through terrace destruction, to accommodate the production
and harvesting of the plant. Alfalfa is the only cash crop, and in these villages
more than half the plots are really pasture fields, in one phase or another of the
rotation cycle. Even the terraces that remain intact in the steeper areas are
planted in it periodically and rotated in the same manner. Thus, especially at
the lower altitudes, the whole landscape changes according to a rhythm dictated, not by one plant, but by two plants that compete with each other. Both
were introduced to the region and are not native to it, and both have a tremendous thirst for water.

Ecology, Land Use, and Hydraulic Organization

In extreme topography like this, all climatic conditions vary according to the
elevation—not just rainfall and temperatures, but solar radiation, relative hu-
midity, even wind patterns. Throughout the Andes, these conditions have
shaped the edaphic and biotic components of the environment to create several
distinct kinds of habitat. Map 4 shows the distribution of these habitats based
on J. A. Tosi's (1960) method of classification. Although the Tosi criteria are
simplistic (Rengifo Vasquez 1984: 57–58), they remain useful in illustrating the
general pattern of natural life in this kind of setting: a series of ecological tiers,
or "floors," arranged along a vertical axis (Bowman 1916; Weberbauer 1945;
Dollfus 1982). Local people recognize these environments as discrete zones, and
they have traditionally considered them suitable for particular forms of exploitation. The western slope features four of these culturally defined habitats,[7]
out of the eight identified for Peru as a whole by Javier Pulgar Vidal (1946).

They are, as shown in Map 4:

1. The *yunka* or *canyón* (1,200 to 2,300 meters), a hot, lowland zone of small, spring-fed irrigation systems, producing mainly fruits, grapes, and wine

2. The *qheshwa, valle,* or *quebrada* (2,300 to 3,600 meters), the temperate zone, and the main area of irrigation, maize production, and agriculture in general, as well as the most heavily populated area

3. The *suni* or *echadero* (3,600 to 4,000 meters), a cool upland zone devoted to tuber cultivation in systems of sectoral fallowing, both irrigated and rain-fed, and to the grazing of cattle, sheep, and goats

4. The *puna, altiplano,* or *meseta* (4,000 to 5,000 meters), a frigid zone where llamas, alpacas, sheep, and some cattle are grazed in areas with enough natural pasture

Two points must be understood about this pattern of diversity. First, the lowest and warmest zone, the yunka, lies in the canyon, a sparsely inhabited area whose tropical climate differs from the more temperate alpine zone above. These lands are well separated geographically and do not form part of the production systems in the valley itself, the area of my study. The second point is that the amount of terrain actually exploited at each elevation is extremely limited. None of the four zones forms an unbroken belt or "floor" and to speak of them as ecological or natural life zones is to obscure the crucial role that groundwater, and its redistribution through irrigation, has always played in making the valley habitable. As Enrique Mayer (1985) has pointed out, the inhabited area consists of "zones of production," circumscribed lands whose fertility is as much a creation of human technology and culture as of nature.

The lands under permanent cultivation lie in the qheshwa, and these are confined to areas that can be watered by the major springs or, in a few places, by the river (also true of the yunka). The suni lands, immediately above, rely mainly on rainfall and are much more extensive, since they are worked through the method of sectoral fallowing. But they too are irrigated for planting wherever possible, and as noted earlier, the areas without access to this water now lie abandoned. Most extensive of all are the herding grounds in the upper suni and puna, but even these areas are circumscribed, since good pasture is abundant only around places where snow-melt collects and alpine springs emerge.[8] All of these inhabited areas are surrounded by slopes and mountainsides that are so dry as to be unsuitable for agriculture and, in many cases, even herding.

The result of this zonal configuration is a scarcity of arable land that is extraordinary even by Andean standards. The province covers 4,715 square kilometers—roughly the size of a large American county—but of these only about 3,120 hectares, or 0.06 percent of the total, are now under cultivation.[9] The ex-

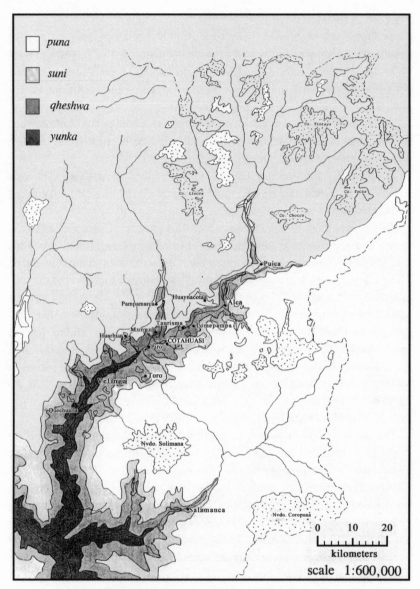

MAP 4. Ecological or land-use zones in the Cotahuasi watershed. Source: Adapted from Oficina Nacional de Recursos Naturales map.

act amount has varied markedly, mainly because of depopulation during the colonial period and the abandonment of dry-farmed land during droughts. It is clear, though, that on a provincial level, the proportion of the landscape under intensive irrigation has never been very much greater than it is today. In general terms, the small size of the irrigation systems, like that of the villages themselves, reflects the low rainfall and the small capacity of the alpine springs. No community has more than 400 hectares of irrigated land or more than 1,400 people.

In any populated area, the exploited lands lie superimposed one above the other, usually in a contiguous manner, and they are linked together by canals that direct the water from up above down below. The higher-altitude peasant communities tend to control land in all three zones and to have their own irrigation systems, a type of land use that is widely found throughout the Andes and is known to be a very old form of adaptation (see, e.g., Murra 1972; Webster 1971; Mitchell 1976; Mayer 1974b; and Golte 1980), but whose hydraulic dimension is often overlooked.

The vertical arrangement makes the best use of available resources by confining animal herding to the upper zones, where pasture grows naturally on the precipitation and groundwater, and reserving irrigation water for the fertile land below, where only crops for human consumption are grown. This is plainly the most productive and efficient arrangement, one in which two very scarce resources, land and water, are used to achieve a high degree of food self-sufficiency and to support the greatest possible number of people in a given area.

This combination of agriculture and pastoralism still prevails in the higher-altitude communities,[10] even though they lost many of their puna lands long ago to the landlords who live in the lower valley. The arrangement is dependent, of course, on their control of alpine springs. Since arable land is of little use without irrigation, the control of water is essential for a diversified exploitation of the land, and the amount that a village has determines how much territory it can cultivate on a permanent basis. Water is thus the primary limiting factor in this kind of setting, but its availability depends as much on cultural factors as on environmental ones. Nature limits the quantity flowing through a given area at any point in time, but it is the political system, the system of legal rights, that determines the amount that each community can actually use. In these circumstances, water is not merely a resource but, along with land, a basic kind of property.

This underlines John Murra's (1972, 1975, 1985) point that "verticality," the

exploitation of multiple ecological zones, is not a feature of the Andean environment but a general type of political structure, one that can be based on any
one of several forms of control over land. The contiguous, three-zone pattern,
which has been called the "compressed" type (Brush 1977a), is one of these, but
few people have recognized that, in many cases, flows of irrigation water form
the central axis around which it is constructed. This is true not only along the
western slope, but in the inter-Andean valleys to the east as well, where the
maize-growing zone is semi-arid and requires irrigation. In these settings, a
change in landownership in the higher zones, where the primary water sources
are located, can therefore result in major changes in the use of land down below, changes in the very base of community life.

Where local communities control land in only one or two zones, one invariably finds that two or more of them use the same canal network and share at
least some water sources. For example, in the district of Cotahuasi, two villages
and three hamlets, all at different elevations, overlap in their use of major
springs and are interconnected by long canals. Another local village, Visve, receives its water from a pueblo located a considerable distance upslope. From a
purely hydrological standpoint, this kind of variation is curious, since the valley's larger settlements are separated from each other by large expanses of barren uncultivated terrain. For the sake of resource conservation alone, the logical arrangement would seem to be that each community would be fully
independent.

That is in fact the traditional Andean pattern. Without exception, the villages that remain indigenous today, such as Huaynacotas and Pampamarca,
have always been largely autonomous in this respect. In other places, such as
Cotahuasi district, that integrity was breached early in the colonial period,
when the Spanish altered the territories of the original prehispanic communities by imposing major changes in settlement patterns. New villages were set up
on low-altitude lands that had belonged to communities higher upslope, so
that separate settlements and discrete social groups were now forced to share
water. This is how the transformation of the local technology, of the customary
ways of distributing and using the resource, began. It created a legacy of conflict
that persists to this day.

Reading the Pattern of Abandoned Land

The percentage of land under irrigation in the province today seems remarkably similar to that of Inca times, but numerous areas fell out of use after

the Conquest and have remained so ever since. Although putting them back into production would probably not raise the total figure for the valley by more than 25–30 percent, that could make a significant difference to people in the communities where they are found. Their distribution is very uneven locally, a pattern that helps to reveal how irrigation, and the whole ecology of land and water use, have changed in recent times.

The pattern is different in some other parts of the department of Arequipa, such as the Colca valley, where roughly 40 percent of the irrigable land still lies abandoned. This is partly because the population there never recovered fully from the collapse that followed the Conquest (Cook 1982; Denevan 1986; Denevan et al. 1987). In the Cotahuasi valley, populations in the high-altitude villages returned to their prehispanic levels some time ago, and the majority of them now seem to be close to the capacity that the water supplies, the land, and the technology can sustain. Consequently, in peasant communities like Huay-nacotas and Pampamarca, little or no abandoned land exists within the confines of the canal systems.

Among the exceptions to this pattern, the most notable is Cotahuasi, a district composed of communities that share the largest irrigation system in the province. It is striking that in a district that has been the center of the commercial economy ever since early colonial times, much of the land originally irrigated has not been put back into production, even though the total population is close to its pre-Conquest level. One has to be cautious in interpreting this fact, since it is possible that both the climate and the water supplies have changed. Nevertheless, the situation in the other two communities would seem to suggest that any contractions in the supply have been counteracted by adjustments in land and water use. This clearly has not happened in Cotahuasi.

The villages in this district have many significant commonalities, but perhaps the most revealing one is that they produce more alfalfa than any others in the province. Much of the territory surrounding each pueblo has been converted to producing pasture for animals, primarily cattle for sale in urban markets, and the amount in the area around the town itself exceeds 50 percent.[11] Many of the properties on which this is done are former haciendas, estates that were broken up in part by the agrarian reform of 1969. The biggest estates, those that were located around the capital, were once the prime maize-growing lands of the villages higher upslope, whose water Cotahuasi has long shared. And it is in the vicinity of those villages that large expanses of abandoned terrain are found. Once alfalfa's impact on water use is examined, this pattern will be understood.

Two Zones of Culture and Their Overlap

The valley, the canyon, and the surrounding highlands form a single political unit, the province of La Unión, which is part of the department of Arequipa. The seat of local government is in Cotahuasi, which oversees eleven administrative districts (*distritos*), each of which has a subordinate capital. Most of these are villages that, like Cotahuasi, lie on relatively flat land along the valley bottom.[12] Their jurisdictions extend upward all the way to the provincial boundary on the plateau, incorporating peasant villages and hamlets, called *anexos*, and small herding stations on the puna, called *estancias*.

Note that, from a political, economic, and even cultural perspective, the valley population is distributed in two distinct levels or zones. The lower one is predominantly Spanish in culture, with a Spanish-speaking population, many of whom refer to themselves as *españoles* (see Onuki 1981: 12–15) and trace their ancestry back to the Spanish landlords who came to dominate local politics and commerce in early colonial times. This zone is where the biggest haciendas were located, and, despite several attempts at agrarian reform, most of the valley's larger properties and bigger landowners are still found there today. People in this zone are generally involved in business ventures of various kinds, primarily cattle production and retail trade. They hold all of the major political offices, and they are generally in closer contact with the national or urban society than those who live higher up.

The vast majority of people in the upper zone are indigenous peasants. By this I mean that they are Quechua-speakers who, although fully bilingual today, address each other primarily in that language. They refer to themselves in everyday discourse as *runakuna* (and explain that this means *gente indigena*), thereby distinguishing themselves from the people of the district capitals and the lower valley in general. Those people, who are at least partly of Spanish descent, they refer to as *mistis* or, alternatively in the case of the dominant landowning families, *españoles* (see Onuki 1981: 14), distinctions that also apply to the landlords who dominate several of the upper, otherwise indigenous villages. In addition to language, a distinguishing feature of the runakuna is their practice of certain rituals that were formerly widespread in the Andes, such as offerings made each year to the springs and the mountain deities.

The runakuna are subsistence farmers who have only sporadic involvement in commerce. Traditionally, their role in the provincial and national economies has been that of wage laborers and, to a certain extent, consumers, rather than that of producers or distributors. They acquire money through periodic wage work, either in the lower valley or in neighboring provinces, and through occasional sales of cattle. They typically buy a small range of items in the stores of the lower zone, but they do not produce crops for the market, and most of them grow most of the staple crops they consume.

The peasants who live in the lower zone and in the few places where the two zones overlap, that is, in the annexes or satellite villages of Cotahuasi district, constitute a third group. They consider themselves to be mestizo, or *gente mestiza*, and are quick to distinguish themselves in this way from the runakuna.[13] The runakuna do likewise with them, either lumping them in with the mistis or accepting their own characterization, mestizos. Many of these people have very little land of their own; most formerly worked on the valley's major haciendas, which were found within the territories of the annex communities themselves, and supported themselves by sharecropping. Today they rely heavily on wage work and various kinds of petty commerce.

As for the meaning or significance of the mestizo distinction, for the moment it indicates only that Spanish has become these people's main mode of communication, and that they have come to identify, to some extent, with the values, attitudes, and practices of the dominant society. I make no claims here about the extent of their alienation from indigenous culture, although the linguistic change is certainly significant in this respect. That question will, among other things, be a central theme of the analysis presented in the chapters that follow.

It is striking that the mestizo pueblos, the annexes of Cotahuasi district, have long shared their irrigation water with the haciendas and the provincial capital down below.[14] However, a final, crucial feature distinguishes them from the other high-altitude villages and links them with the district capitals along the valley bottom. The national government is involved in the administration of their water, a relationship that began in 1940, shortly after Peru's Ministry of Agriculture was founded. Until very recently, an employee of the ministry with the formal title "technician" oversaw usage as decreed by Peru's Water Code of 1902 and the General Water Law of 1969, the second of which made the state the legal owner of all the country's water.

In theory, the state's jurisdiction extends to every local community, but the government is actually far too weak and poor to be able to exercise its authority over the daily affairs of most of them. Except for those in Cotahuasi district, villages continue to have de facto control over their water and to use it in a customary manner. As is the case in many parts of the sierra, the high-altitude villages maintain their autonomy because they are too remote to allow close supervision.

In the chapters that follow, we will see that this kind of independence has been essential to their survival as indigenous communities: full control, not just over alpine springs, but over the procedures through which their water is shared and utilized. We will also see how some of the processes mentioned here—the establishment of haciendas, water sharing by different communities, the cultivation of pasture for livestock, terrace destruction, and resource management by the state—all of which are exogenous in origin, have contributed to the alteration and decline of the Andean way of life.

TWO

Early History

Story of a Hole on the Map

The Cotahuasi valley's early history can be traced in its general outlines by using a variety of sources, many of them rather obscure. It is a story of domination by successive empires or states, always meeting with strong resistance by the local people, a struggle that climaxes periodically in violent rebellions. The province is not only remote and extreme in terms of geography, but rich in valuable resources, and each distant government has found it difficult to control the place, particularly the local landlords and political bosses who have run the valley, exploiting both these resources and the indigenous population, ever since colonial times. As we will eventually see, this relationship with the state continues today, and it was played out dramatically during my fieldwork.

First Occupations and the Huari Intrusion

Little is known about the valley's earliest inhabitants. Only two archaeological studies have been done, both of them surface surveys that did not involve excavation and are unlikely to have yielded remains from the first occupations. A reconnaissance of the entire watershed (Chavez 1982) identified twenty-seven prehistoric village sites, and my own brief survey located nine more, all in the upper part of the valley. Both investigations yielded ceramic remains (potsherds) that showed the area was heavily populated by the time of the Huari era, also known as the Middle Horizon, from A.D. 700 to 900, but no artifacts from earlier periods were found. Other information, however, confirms that people were present long before this.

The valley is rich in high-quality obsidian, an especially valuable material for making stone tools. Comparison of the trace element content of samples that I collected from the local source with the chemical signatures of obsidian tools from prehistoric sites throughout much of Peru shows that this material was being widely traded in the Andes during the period known as the Early Horizon, from 900 B.C. to 200 B.C., and during later periods as well (Burger & Asaro 1977: 43–36; Burger et al. 1996).[1] The people who mined and exchanged it almost certainly lived there in permanent residence so as to maintain control over the sources, which continued to be of primary importance in the Andes until the period known as the Inca Horizon.

Throughout much of Peru, the period A.D. 700–900 was marked by the expansion of Huari, a state whose center lay in the present department of Ayacucho. Its dominance is known to have extended well into the southern highlands at that time, but the full extent and nature of its influence have yet to be determined (W. Isbell & McEwan 1991). In the Cotahuasi valley, far to the south, the prevalence of Huari ceramic remains in all the early sites is striking and suggests an invasion or colonization of the area. But other than domination and the extraction of tribute and valuable minerals, the state's relationship with the local people remains unclear, particularly its role in developing irrigation.

The oldest ceramic pieces encountered in both Chavez's survey and my own are typical examples of early Huari (or Middle Horizon) pottery styles known from neighboring regions: Robles Moqo 1B and Viñaque. They have been found in every early village site located thus far, which in Chavez's view (1982: 166) suggests that the valley came under Huari influence early in the state's expansion. Especially abundant in the upper watershed is Qosqopa, a post-Huari but pre-Inca style that also predominates in sites in the neighboring Majes and Colca valleys (Pablo de la Vera Cruz,personal communication). Apparently the populations in these three areas were in close contact at the time, as they clearly were during later periods, when they seem to have formed some kind of ethnic group that may have specialized in mining, as we will shortly see.

Some evidence suggests that the valley was under the control of Huari administrators. Two major sites seem at first glance to exhibit the distinctive architecture (referred to as orthogonal cellular; W. Isbell 1991) that typifies Huari administrative centers in other regions: the compounds of Collota and the neighboring site of Netahaha near Cotahuasi (see Chavez 1982). In each case, the ground plan consists of large rectangular units with narrow dwellings surrounding central patios. These features and others, such as plastered walls and subterranean drainage canals, distinguish the sites from other local settlements of the same period. However, Justin Jennings and Willy Yepez (n.d.) have shown that the basic elements of the local architectural style were simply reworked or reassembled in the two sites, and that the construction technique itself is different. This suggests that local elites were simply copying the Huari and argues against colonization and direct state control over the valley.

The prehistoric village sites share some of the following characteristics: double-faced walls of stone and masonry, rectangular houses, plazas, and distinctive ceremonial structures. There is no way to tell on the basis of surface surveys alone how many existed before the valley came under Huari influence. There may be a local pottery style predating Huari that still lies undiscovered—possibilities that can only be explored by excavating.

All of the Middle Horizon remains in the vicinity of the modern pueblos of Cotahuasi and Pampamarca are located on steeply sided ridgetops, directly overlooking slopes covered with terracing, presumably for the same purpose they now serve: to provide the irrigation water that is that necessary for farming in this environment.[2] In every case, the nearest water source is rather distant, so that even if existing stream channels were simply modified, even small-scale irrigation required the building of a substantial canal, typically 4–8 kilometers long. Most of these canals are heavily reinforced, with retention walls on the downslope side made of large stones and earth, some reaching a height of 3 or more meters. All were simply dug out of the ground and then lined with a layer of gravel, creating a surface that allowed considerable filtration of water along the entire length. All of them are still in use, as are most of the terraces, and they form the core of today's irrigation systems.

Again, it is unclear which of these sites date to the Huari period or which were built earlier by the local people about whom so little is known. The Middle Horizon literature until recently provided little information on the subject, focusing largely on the Huari state's accomplishments in urban development and bureaucratic administration (e.g., W. Isbell 1988; W. Isbell & McEwan 1991), while neglecting the accompanying agricultural expansion that must have been necessary. The findings of the Colca Valley Project (Denevan 1986) and the more recent Cotahuasi Archaeological Project (Jennings & Yepez n.d.) suggest that this may have been a serious oversight. They show that the majority of the terraces in the two valleys were built during the Huari period, and that although numerous village sites existed there previously, the state did either oversee or somehow inspire a major expansion and intensification of agriculture in the region. One thing, in any case, is clear: most of the valley's irrigation systems were built before the end of the Huari period, and although they may have been expanded somewhat later on, they have been in continuous use for at least a thousand years.

The most common elements in the Middle Horizon village sites are small, highly uniform structures, obviously domestic ones. A rough count of the numbers in the four sites associated with Cotahuasi suggests a population of at least 2,250 people,[3] without taking into account another group that may have existed in Cotahuasi itself, of which only traces remain (Huari ceramic fragments from looted tombs). It therefore seems possible that the population living in the area a thousand years ago approached that of today, roughly 3,000 people. In Pampamarca, the numbers are much smaller but, again, appear to have been fairly close to current levels: perhaps some 700 people.

The First Revolt: Political Relations Between the Kuntis and the Incas

In the years following the breakup of Huari, the local people are thought to have been a part of some kind of regional ethnic confederation, whose nature is poorly understood. At the time I began my fieldwork, only three things were known about the groups in this alliance: that they resided in the adjacent Cotahuasi, Majes, and Colca valleys (Galdos 1985, 1988); that they were in contact and probably engaged in regular trade; and that they were the most powerful people in the Arequipa region. They are also thought to have spoken Aymara rather the Quechua dialect used in the valley today (Manrique 1985; Mannheim 1985; Galdos 1985). The Spanish chroniclers referred to them as the Kuntis or Kuntisuyus, meaning simply "the people of the West."

The information Chavez and I collected shows that the inhabitants of these valleys remained in close contact after the end of Huari, a relationship that has since been further documented by the Cotahuasi Valley Project (Justin Jennings, personal communication). In both ceramic collections, most of the later sherds are of a pottery type known as Chuquibamba (Chavez 1982: 172), the same pre-Inca style that predominates in the parts of the Majes and Colca valleys known to have been Kunti territories (Pablo de la Vera Cruz, personal communication).[4] Chavez (1982: 166–67) feels that the style shows a strong altiplano influence (post-Tiahuanaco), but the main point is the more local sphere of interaction revealed by its distribution. Apparently this is Kunti pottery.

It is important to note that in all three valleys the style appears quite late in the intermediate period and continues to be present, with some modifications, throughout the Inca Horizon. Thus the only published data on the Kuntis present a problem for interpretation: before their conquest by the Incas, and after being dismembered from the Huari state, were these people engaged in some kind of enduring alliance, or were they linked by trade alone? It may be that they only united to fight the Incas, a political association that persisted thereafter simply because they were incorporated into the same administrative province within the empire: Kuntisuyu.

One thing is clear. The Incas, who were a despotic people, very serious about their role as conquerors and "civilizers" of the people of the Andes (Patterson

1991), met with extraordinarily fierce resistance in their efforts to subdue the Cotahuasi valley. Garcilaso (1966 [1617], 2: 56–57) documents the first in a long series of conflicts, an account that differs little from the oral history everyone in the valley seems to know. After two months of struggle in the rugged mountains above Alca, at the eastern end of the watershed, the army of the Inca Mayta Capac defeated a local force that had been assembled by the residents of the area around Alca, who seem to have achieved a certain level of political and ritual dominance in the area (Justin Jennings, personal communication), though not the region. They then surrendered. The rest of the valley submitted shortly thereafter.

According to Cieza (1959 [1553]: 199–200), the truce lasted only a short time. The Kuntis revolted during the reign of Capac Yupanqui, Mayta Capac's son, and assembled a massive military force—one probably coming from all three valleys—which marched on Cusco, the Inca capital, with intentions of destroying it. Not until this army had been routed twice, supposedly at a cost of over 6,000 lives, and been pursued back to the valley for a final decisive battle did the Kuntis submit in earnest and begin to pay tribute through the *mita*, or labor tax. Local people claim that the names of several local settlements reflect this history and date back to the Conquest, names derived from Quechua, the Inca language, rather than Aymara: Alca itself, supposedly derived from *sallqha*, "savage"; Willaq, "guardian" or "sentry"; Qhawana (Cahuana), "observatory" or "lookout"; and Ayawasi, House of the Dead.

The Incas put an end to all this resistance by establishing their administrative capital at Mawka Llaqta, above Puica, and another, smaller one at Cahuana, immediately above Alca. Although not recognized as such by the present inhabitants, Cahuana was apparently the local center of imperial government. Both the prehispanic settlement and its irrigation system were clearly built under Inca direction.[5] The ancient site, today called Qhaqha, is a typical example of Inca provincial architecture, featuring dwellings with high gabled roofs and walls with trapezoidal niches and doors. Located on a steep, fortified ridgetop, the complex centers around two plazas, each faced by large rectangular buildings that are distinct from all the other structures. These clearly had a non-domestic function and suggest that the site was a military garrison or administrative center of some kind. It no doubt was also a *tampu*, a resting-place for traveling soldiers and messengers: a stone-paved stairway and road passes directly through the site, climbing some 1,000 meters to the puna above and continuing on to the Majes and Colca valleys.

Cahuana's irrigation system differs from that of most other settlements in the valley. The main canal is roughly 6 kilometers long and as much as 5 meters high in places, with retaining walls made of large rocks and earth (some stone faces cover a square meter). Its most unusual feature is the lining of fitted stones, locally called *pilcha*, on the bottom and sides of the canal to prevent water loss. The secondary canals are also stone lined, and are opened and closed with carved-stone plugs called *takapu*, which fit precisely into the canal mouth or gate. The main reservoir, which stores water for the system, is one of the largest ancient ones in the province, 35 meters wide by 4 meters deep, with walls reaching a height of 7 meters at the lower end. Circular in shape and now lined with cement, it is said to be built of large closely fitted carved-stone blocks plastered over with earth. A second, smaller tank, for overflow, lies immediately below it and reportedly has the same construction.

These Inca hydraulic features are absent in most of the pueblos in the upper valley, between Cotahuasi and Alca.[6] They are reported to be present in some irrigation systems in the canyon, but that area was outside the scope of my study. This evidence indicates that the Inca occupation began a second major phase in local irrigation development. Chavez's (1982) report contains no information on water systems, but it does document a proliferation of sites in all the local ecological zones during the period of Inca rule, particularly in the canyon. This expansion and colonization achieved a degree of vertical control far beyond what the Huari had been able to accomplish. When the results of my brief study are added, it becomes clear that many other settlements came under the dominance of both groups, most of which have yet to be investigated. But more important, my findings indicate that irrigation development played a crucial role in the establishment of Inca hegemony. Hydraulic expansion was necessary, not just in order to establish administrative centers like Cahuana and colonies in the canyon, but also in order to open up new lands for cultivation and the extraction of tribute.

According to local lore, the Incas made improvements in the irrigation systems of certain villages after they finally conquered the valley, as a reward for the people's submission and loyalty. People currently living in Taurisma, a community in the valley bottom, claim that the Incas did this for their ancestors, and that they brought water for the first time to the village of Huillac, above Alca. Taurisma seems to be the only pueblo where this bit of oral history has survived. Several elderly people now living in Arequipa told me this story, independently in Spanish, claiming to have heard it from their parents. According to them, after the Incas defeated the local army, the leaders of the original communities, the *ayllus* (corporate kinship groups) of Taurisma, gave the Inca ruler a royal welcome and pledged their obedience.[7] In so doing, the leaders—known as Tawa Rimaq, or "the Four Speakers" (from whom the pueblo's name is supposedly derived)—gained the Inca's favor. He rewarded them by putting the soldiers and engineers of his army to work improving and expanding the irrigation system. He had previously done this for the people of Huillac.

Two major projects were supposedly completed in only two months. One was the rebuilding of a canal called Puka Puka, which serviced the old Huari site of Tulla, high above Taurisma. Apparently the terrain around Tulla was the ayllus' original territory. Today, this canal lies in disrepair, virtually abandoned, but segments of Inca stone paving like that of Cahuana can still be found along it, and a lengthy section is cut into the face of a cliff in typical Inca fashion. It is surrounded by one of the largest areas of abandoned terracing in the province, covering over 100 hectares. Thus it seems likely that this part of the story is true, that the Incas improved the canal and expanded the irrigated area belonging to these ayllus, lands that are located high in the qheshwa zone.

The other project is said to have been the construction, along the valley bottom, of the 10-kilometer-long canal and aqueduct that passes through Taurisma and on to another area. This is one of only four canals in the province that draw water from the river, and it is by far the largest. Most of the canal is still in use, and it is the principal source of water for Taurisma, whose irrigated land now lies exclusively along the valley bottom. The lower portion of the canal, which once watered a vast area of flatlands called Collota, was abandoned long ago and stayed in that condition until recently.

In 1989, a group of Taurisma residents decided to rebuild the abandoned portion, a long above-ground aqueduct, in order to reclaim the lower part of Collota for cultivation. In the course of their work, they found large numbers of pottery sherds in the fill of the canal wall, which I took to a colleague in Arequipa for analysis All of them proved to be Inca utilitarian ware (de la Vera Cruz, personal communication). Since the lower part of the canal was never used by the Spanish, the sherds tend to date the canal and confirm the story.[8]

Much of this information is anecdotal and second-hand, but it is significant for two reasons. First of all, since the *pampas* of Taurisma and Collota have no other source of water,[9] it suggests that the Incas were the first to irrigate this area, the most extensive flatlands in the valley, and that they did it by drawing water from the river. This finding is consistent with numerous comments by early Spanish observers, with the observations of Murra (1960) and many archaeologists (D'Altroy 1987; Levine 1987), and with recent archeological work in the Colca valley (Denevan 1986), all of which indicate that the Incas were the first to irrigate low-altitude lands along the valley bottoms.

Second, the location of the canal suggests that the main reason the Incas built it was to open up new lands for tribute production. The pampa of Collota begins 2 kilometers below Taurisma and is well separated from its present territory. It is immense by local standards, covering an area of more than 200 hectares, only about a quarter of which has been farmed in historic times (the upper end). The canal traverses this entire expanse, within which the only remains of habitation, either prehistoric or colonial, are the site of Collota itself. Although the compound was built in Huari times, abundant evidence exists of a Late Horizon occupation: Inca utilitarian pottery and fancier Inca provincial ceramics (Chavez 1982: 6, 173).

These must surely have been the lands of the Inca and the Sun, imperial property devoted to the support of the state and the church, respectively, from the proceeds of the mita labor tax. The lands are found in the only cultivable area that was previously unexploited, one clearly separated from the production systems of the local ayllus. By developing such areas with their own source of water, the Incas could have provided for tribute payment without interfering with the subsistence needs of those communities, as seems to have been their policy. Moreover, these very warm lands along the valley bottom could be cultivated and irrigated on a completely separate schedule from the community lands, again without interfering with subsistence. It can be no coincidence that this pampa is the most extensive part of the valley that was abandoned after the Spanish Conquest, which destroyed the very political structure whose main local function was to administer such lands.

We have seen evidence that the Incas invested heavily in the valley and its people: two military conquests, the colonizing of the canyon, and large-scale hydraulic and agricultural development. All attest to the great importance that the region called Kuntisuyu had within Tawantinsuyu, the Inca empire (Garcilaso 1966 [1617], 2: 56). Two questions, then, arise: why was this part of the empire the object of so much attention, and what did this have to do with the prominence of the Kunti people?

The standard explanation would be that the valley was subjugated in order to consolidate the empire and increase the extraction of tribute, just like any other region. But beyond this, the valley provided unique resources, and access to resources, that may have given it singular status within the Inca political economy. The most important of these by far was gold. Although it is not widely known, the canyon of Ocoña is the richest gold-bearing zone in all of Peru, with some 200 mine claims pending even today (Fidel Vera, personal communication), despite heavy exploitation by the Spanish during the seventeenth and eighteenth centuries. According to Victor Oehm (1984: 13), it is one of only two regions with actual veins of gold rather than alluvial deposits, and it is by far the richest (see also Raimondi 1944: 49). Many abandoned colonial mines lie close to Inca sites in the canyon (Chavez 1982: 60); they are surrounded by shallow shafts that do not have the characteristic stone arch used by the Spanish. According to the descriptions of George Petersen (1970: 68), the mines must be prehispanic. Their presence throughout the valley indicates that this area was a major source of gold for the Incas, one that has remained unknown in the archaeological literature.

Another valuable resource was the aforementioned obsidian, which is abundant in the area around Alca and of very high quality. Again, trace element analysis (Burger & Asaro 1977: 35–36; Burger et al. 1998) has shown a match between the local stone and Inca tools from Cusco, the imperial capital, confirming that the valley was a major source of lithic material for the empire, as it had been for the earlier Huari (Burger & Asaro 1977: 45–46).

Also of great importance was rock salt, which came from a huge mine in the village of Huarhua, directly across the valley from Cotahuasi. This enormous network of tunnels is still in production, in a pueblo where there is clear evidence of Inca presence. One of only two sources of rock salt found in Peru (Llano Zapata [1761] 1904), the mineral is said to have unusual chemical properties that lengthen the preservation of cooked food, making it an important item in the diet of herders in the region today. It continues to be the most highly valued product in barter networks that extend throughout the northern altiplano (Concha 1975: 75; Inamura 1981: 72). The mineral itself is called *warwa* in the Cusco dialect of Quechua (Lira 1970: 418), the official language, and it is unclear whether the village was named after the salt or vice-versa.

Finally, the valley gave the Incas their most direct route to the coast, with its marine resources. Garcilaso (1966 [1609], 1: 184) notes that the Inca regularly enjoyed fresh fish brought to Cusco by runners who passed along the road to Kuntisuyu, a major artery of the imperial road system. Other transported products were probably *cochayuyo*, a dried algae, and *chalona*, dried fish, both of which remain important foods in the southern Andes today (Masuda 1981a). Despite the great importance of this road, which passed through the Cotahuasi valley, up onto the puna at Charcana and onward to the coast at Chala (see Cieza de León 1959 [1553]; and Bingham 1922), it was not included in John Hyslop's (1984) massive study of the Inca highway network, probably because of its remoteness and difficulty of access. This, of course, was the route along which the gold, obsidian, salt, and fish were also transported—no doubt by llama caravan—to the imperial capital.

The Cotahuasi valley thus seems to have been the heart of Kuntisuyu, one of the four quarters of the empire, which is known to have been inhabited by an ethnic group whom the Spanish called the Condes. Presumably following customary usage, the Spaniards referred to the valley as the Condesuyos of Cusco, also ascribing the Conde name to the people of Chuquibamba, Pampacolca, and Viraco in the Majes valley, to those of the Cabanaconde area of the Colca valley, and to still others in the area around Santo Tomas in the neighboring province of Chumbivilcas, immediately to the east (Poole 1987). These Conde populations are known to have lived dispersed among other ethnic groups in the region (Galdos 1985, 1987), but no one has ever explained why they were especially powerful or prominent.

Deborah Poole (1987: 260) has made the intriguing observation that, after their final conquest by the Incas, the Condes of Chumbivilcas seem to have been given more autonomy than other groups in that area. The evidence from Cotahuasi suggests that the Kuntis may have been given certain privileges because they specialized in the exploitation, and possibly also the transport, of resources vital to the empire, whose main sources lay within their territory.

It is also possible that, prior to the Inca conquest, the Cotahuasi valley was in some sense the center of a unified Kunti mining region. The gold is much more abundant in Cotahuasi and of higher quality than in the Majes and Colca valleys, however, and the salt is exclusively found there. But valuable minerals, including important sources of obsidian, are present in all three, and there is no reason to assume that the local Kuntis were in any kind of preeminent position before the Incas arrived. The available evidence, mainly the diversity of agricultural and mineral resources in all three valleys, seems more suggestive of autonomy for the three groups than of heavy interdependence among them. The simplest interpretation at present is that the threat of growing Inca hegemony brought these groups into a much closer alliance than they had ever achieved before.

This discussion has shown that the valley was anything but marginal and isolated in the prehispanic world. The Incas may have considered the region remote, as contemporary Peruvians do, but it was important enough to them that they made heavy investments in its people and resources. In fact, their contributions far exceeded anything that the Spanish Crown or the Peruvian republic would provide during the next few hundred years. Some of these, such as the imperial road system, would eventually become outdated and largely obsolete,[10] but the irrigation works continue to be important today, when the scarcity of water and of cultivable land is a major concern of almost everyone.

Conquest and Collapse During the Colonial Period

The conquest of the Andes by people as ruthless and bloodthirsty as the Spanish was of course cataclysmic in itself, but it was accompanied by a catastrophe unprecedented in human history. According to Noble Cook (1981), Peru's population of about 9,000,000 people in 1530 was reduced to roughly

600,000 by 1620, a decline of 90 percent, or nearly nine people out of every ten, in only ninety years. This population collapse was the combined result of recurrent epidemics of European diseases, forced labor in colonial mines (the Spanish *mita*), and the war of conquest itself, along with later rebellions. Although the effects were disastrous on all aspects of Andean life, the impact of these factors, particularly the diseases (smallpox, measles, influenza), varied significantly among regions. Remoteness, high altitude, and a scarcity of resources attractive to the conquerors provided some areas with a degree of protection and slowed the pace of change. For a brief while, the Cotahuasi valley was one of these favored areas.

Soon after the Conquest, the people of the upper watershed were divided into five *repartimientos*, or populations of tribute payers: Achambi (including Tomepampa); Cotahuasi; Pomatambo (incorporating Huarhua, Mungui, and Pampamarca); Huaynacotas; and Alca. Of these, Achambi was a royal grant paying tribute directly to the Spanish Crown, and the others were given as *encomiendas*, or labor grants, to individual conquistadores or their widows (Cook 1975:123–30; Levillier 1925: 159–62). At a higher level, the ayllus, or peasant communities, were put, quite illogically, under three different regional administrative units. Huarhua, Pampamarca, and Huaynacotas were assigned to the province of Parinacochas in Ayacucho, to the west, and most of the other communities to the Condesuyos of Cusco, to the east. The remaining groups in the canyon, such as the ayllus of Salamanca, became part of the Condesuyos of Arequipa, to the south. For administrative purposes, then, the valley was divided.

Before local populations had declined substantially, they were forced to resettle, by the Viceroy Francisco Toledo, in the famous *reducciones* of 1572. This uprooting founded the Spanish-style villages that are the pueblos of today; the goal was to make the people easier to control, extract tribute from, and convert to Christianity. The inhabitants of these dispersed ayllus were forced to move and unite into a single village centered around a church and plaza. Map 5 shows the original settlements for Cotahuasi and Pampamarca.

In Cotahuasi, the villages that were left behind were later destroyed during the "extirpation of idolatries" (Arriaga 1968 [1621]). This was a massive assault on native religion, intended in part to keep the Indians from returning to their ancestral homes.[11] Eventually, the populations in most districts were allowed to disperse again into smaller units located within the cultivated lands belonging to each ayllu. But these too were new settlements, established at a lower altitude than the original ones, and they formed the annexes of today. This further move does not appear to have happened until the early eighteenth century (see Villanueva 1982 [1689]: 319–20).

The first document containing population counts for the valley is Toledo's

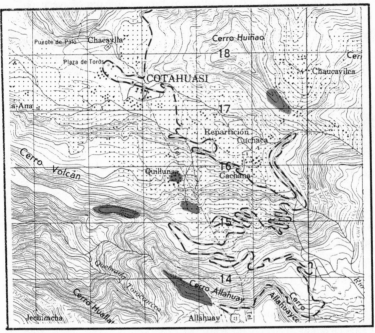

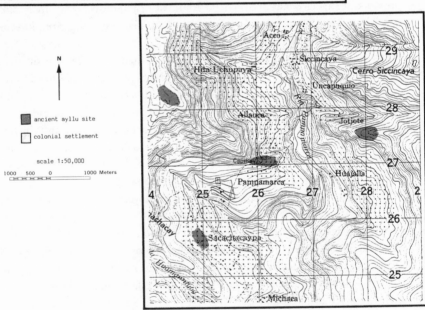

MAP 5. Prehispanic settlement patterns in Cotahuasi (top) and Pampamarca (bottom). Adapted from a map by the Instituto Nacional Geográfico, Lima.

TABLE 1

Cotahuasi Valley Population, 1572–1981

	1572	1621	1689	1724	1785	1831	1876	1940	1981
				Cotahuasi (district)					
Total	3,000	1,266	1,000	1,214	1,151	958	2,958	3,353	3,126
Men	506	302	—	251	179	149	1,436	—	—
				Alca (district)					
Total	4,490	2,731	580?	1,030	624	1,882	6,863	5,440[a]	5,374
Men	938	630	—	213	129	365	3,040	—	—
				Tomepampa (district)					
Total	3,070	2,666	416	372	299	527	934	1,311	1,022
Men	730	283	—	77	62	85	461	—	—
				Huaynacotas (pueblo)					
Total							672	1,114	1,073
Men							318	—	—
				Pampamarca (pueblo)					
Total							616	806	942
Men							310	—	

SOURCES: *1572*, Cook 1975: 129–30; *1621*, Vasquez de Espinoza 1943: 577; *1689*, Villanueva 1982: 319–20; *1724, 1785*, Poole 1987: 271 (except Cotahuasi 1785 total, from ADC 1785a); *1831*, ADC 1831; *1876*, DNE 1876: 434–37; *1940*, DNE 1940: 120–23; *1981*, Peru, Oficina del Consejo Provincial.

NOTE: No figures are available for Huaynacotas and Pampamarca until 1876 because they belonged to a different administrative province in the earlier years. I have included the districts of Alca and Tomepampa for illustrative purposes.

[a]Includes Puica.

visita, or royal population inventory, which took place in 1572 (Cook 1975: 129–30). As shown in Table 1, it stated that Cotahuasi district had 3,000 people, including 506 males. Totals for two other districts are listed in the table for illustrative purposes because Huaynacotas and Pampamarca were not included with Cotahuasi in the visita.

The 1572 figures suggest that the populations were just beginning to decline and were still in a fairly balanced state. The relative low percentage for men is probably mainly due to the effects of the Spanish mita (forced labor in the mines for all men eighteen to fifty), which had already begun, though at least some men absconded to avoid being counted. In any case, once these possibilities are taken into account, the numbers in most areas appear quite close to those of today. This again suggests that Inca-period populations were probably roughly equal to or greater than present-day ones.

It is likely that, until Toledo ordered that tribute be paid largely in money, rather than merely in crops, animals, or cloth as before, which could only be

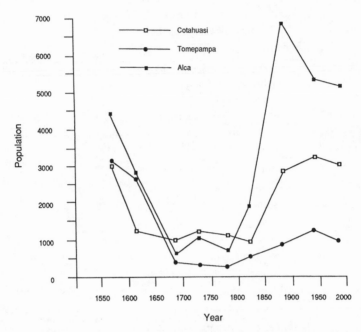

FIG. 3. Population collapse and recovery, 1572–1981. Sources: See Table 1.

obtained by selling those goods to outside intermediaries (Glave 1987), there was relatively little movement of outsiders through the valley. The visita, or inventory, of Francisco de Acuña (1965 [1586]: 312), taken only fourteen years later, reveals that no mines had yet been established in the upper part of the watershed, a situation that would have helped to isolate the area and probably limit the spread of new diseases. This seclusion apparently prevailed until the turn of the seventeenth century, when the discovery of gold in the valley proper brought an influx of Spaniards to the entire area.

Few people outside the province seem to know that the valley was one of the first places that the Spanish came to in search of the sources of Inca gold, probably because published information on early colonial mining is scarce. In 1550, the second gold-mining settlement in all of Peru was founded deep in the canyon at the Inca village of Chaucalla (see Boggio 1983: 13; and Chavez 1982: 172). However, it appears that the early prospectors limited themselves to the major mines in that area and did not discover the sources in the upper valley, most of which are much smaller, for some time. In the visita of the Viceroy Martín Enriquez, from 1581 to 1583, ten years after Toledo's (Levillier 1925: 159–62), for example, the figures for the valley are nearly identical to the previous ones, again very close to present levels, suggesting that the population may still have been fairly intact. In contrast, the early-seventeenth-century visita of Antonio Vasquez de Espinoza (1943 [1621]: 55) shows marked changes and notes the existence of "rich mines of silver and gold in the whole province . . . in the midst of which are [the pueblos of] Alca, Taurisma, Cotahuasi, Pomatambo, and others." Clearly, there had been a huge surge of mining activity in a period of thirty-five years.

The 1621 document reveals the devastating impact of the diseases that accompanied the first Spanish settlers, as well as the effects of the mita. It showed a sharp reduction in the population of each village since the previous count and far fewer men than women (see Fig. 3 and Table 1). A major contributor here must have been the mita to the mines at Huancavelica, far to the north, which had begun in 1566 (Boggio 1983: 14–17). Although the accuracy of this visita has been rightly questioned (Cook 1975: xx–xxi), the data are probably close enough to confirm that the valley settlements were by then in rapid decline.

This downward trend continued throughout the seventeenth century as epidemics continued to take their toll and men were forced to work the local mines, as well as to serve in the mitas to Huancavelica and now (since 1624) Caylloma (Boggio 1983: 19). Curiously, there is no record of a local mita in colonial documents dealing with the labor tax (see Purser 1971; and Fisher 1975). It is clear, however, that both large- and small-scale mining were going on within the valley during this time, and that Indians from the immediate area were the only labor force available.

By 1689, all this activity had reportedly reduced Cotahuasi's population to about 1,000 people, including twenty Spaniards, a drop of 66 percent in less than a century (Villanueva 1982 [1689]: 319–20). All of the valley pueblos had apparently been decimated, and the vast majority of the population were women. Alca had reportedly dwindled to only 580 people, and Achambi had almost ceased to exist, having only eleven (see Table 1).[12]

The shortage of tribute payers was so acute that local priests complained of the poverty of their *doctrinas* and urged that the labor tax be reduced (Villanueva 1982 [1689]: 319–20). Most of the Indians who survived the work in Huancavelica or Caylloma never returned, opting either to stay on as wage laborers, who were somewhat better treated than mita workers, or to seek refuge in distant villages. As outsiders in other communities, *forasteros*, they could be hidden from the mita and avoid serving, and probably dying, in the mines.

The mita, which we know had originally been a short period of service to the Inca, carried out at state expense, had been converted by the Spanish into a life-threatening burden that drained the valley of able-bodied men. The result, as shown in Figure 3, was a collapse from which the village populations did not begin to recover until 150 years later. It set the stage for a long period of hardship and turmoil for the local people, since the tribute payments and other demands on their time continued, and most of the impact fell on the women who stayed behind. The effects on all aspects of life must have been devastating, but perhaps the most basic one, from the standpoint of the political economy, was in most places a loss of land, much of which now lay abandoned because of the population collapse. In the larger districts like Cotahuasi, Tomepampa, and Alca, Spanish settlers gradually moved in, appropriated prime farmland and set themselves up as feudal landlords, forming the first haciendas, or agricultural estates. Thus began a slow process of commercial expansion that would ultimately transform local society and leave no aspect of the economy—the use of land, labor, and especially water—untouched.

Gold Mining, Muleteering, and the Origin of the Haciendas

By the end of the seventeenth century, four estates had been established on the best lands within Cotahuasi's territory: Piro, Pitahuasi, Cachana, and Cancha (Villanueva 1982 [1689]: 319–20). During the next century, which was the height of the mining era both in the valley and in the canyon below, two more estates appeared, again on choice lands belonging to the ayllus: Chaucavilca and Aquerana (ADC 1785a). These haciendas were used for three purposes: growing food crops for the owners and their families; growing a crop surplus for sale to mita laborers and other workers in the gold mines in the canyon (ADC 1794: 18); and, above all, producing alfalfa as fodder for the mules the landlords used to transport foodstuffs, mining supplies, and manufactured goods throughout the Arequipa region. Presumably, local Indians were sometimes forced to work on the estates, but other people must have been readily available, since we know that thousands of forasteros (mita refugees) were roaming the southern sierra at the time, searching for protection from the labor tax (Sánchez-Albornoz 1978). And this, of course, the haciendas could provide.

As for irrigation water, that was simply expropriated, in huge amounts, along with the land. In Cotahuasi, the entire flow of one of the three major springs, called Armanca, ultimately became private estate property; and the other two, Wakajara and Cutirpo, were divided up among the haciendas and the four local ayllus. The estate water was later subdivided and sold, along with part of the land, but together with some later additions, it continued to be private property until the agrarian reform some 200 years later. The amounts were enormous because of the peculiar characteristics of alfalfa, a very "thirsty" plant, and because of the peculiar rhythms of long distance trade, as we will eventually see.

The mines that these haciendas supplied were some of the largest and most important in all of Peru.[13] The biggest operation by far was the royal mine of Montesclaros, founded in the canyon in 1612 and put under the administration of the viceroy who gave it his name. The most famous mine in Peru in its time, it is said to have been worked by a force of 600 mita laborers and to have yielded more than two metric tons of gold a year until it was abandoned after a landslide in 1797 (Palma 1951; Raimondi 1887: 73; Boggio 1983: 14). The Indians who worked it over a period of 170 years must have been conscripted from local villages, since no other nearby area could have provided the necessary labor. An even richer site was Huayllura, an old prehispanic mine discovered in 1830, which produced more than 6,000,000 pesos' worth during its three years of existence (Raimondi 1887: 69; Babinski 1883: 5; Palma 1951). The name refers to a specific nineteenth-century claim in the canyon, as well as the surrounding district, which contains many other sites worked during the seventeenth and eighteenth centuries.[14]

The upper watershed also contains many significant deposits, especially in the mountains near Huaynacotas, Pampamarca, and Puica (Raimondi 1887: 76–80), where one can find the remains of colonial mills, or *quimbaletes*. Men from throughout the valley were obviously working several claims, the most important of which was Pararapa, on the puna above Huaynacotas. There, over 100 shafts tapped into a massive horizontal vein (ADC 1794: 18; Raimondi 1887: 77–78).

The valley's mining history is part of the story of local irrigation because it stimulated a regional trade in which the agricultural estates, and the whole business of muleteering, or *arrieraje*, had their origin. Most of the local pueblos were integrated into a production system spanning three ecological zones, in which the use of all essential resources—land, water, and labor—was subordinated to the demands of mineral exploitation, on the one hand, and long-distance transport, on the other. A few of the peasant communities—Huaynacotas, Cahuana, Ayahuasi, and Huillac—felt the demographic impact of this system but were never colonized by miners and suffered little loss of land. Others, such as Pampamarca and Puica, were colonized but lost only a small amount of territory, simply because the local mines and estates were rather small. But for the ayllus of Cotahuasi, Tomepampa, and Alca, the land and water expropriated by the estate owners would ultimately prove to be enormous losses.

The members were probably not all that concerned at the time. Land and water became abundant, after all, as the Indian population dwindled. Since labor was now the scarce resource, the impact of those losses, as well as others that followed soon after, must not have been felt nearly so acutely as it would be later on. Not until the nineteenth century, when mining and the mita ended, and the native population began to grow, would the consequences begin to become evident.

Today, people in Cotahuasi recall that the principal Spanish families, such as the Perezes, Gastelús, Vera-Portocarreros, and Moriberóns, established themselves and became rich in the mining and muleteering business. All were involved in long-distance trade extending from the valley all the way to Arequipa, and several were the owners or part-owners of local mines. Unfortunately, there are no surviving records of their mining and mercantile activities. But we know from other sources that the unusual integration of mining and agriculture fostered a concentration of power in the hands of these local elites. Because of the area's remoteness, the colonial government found it especially difficult to control this process, a situation that seems to have led to the acquisition of still more estate land.

During the late eighteenth century, it was quite common for the government to take legal action against local *kuracas*, the traditional leaders of indigenous communities (also referred to as *caciques)* who were responsible for collecting tribute money and overseeing the use of community lands. These actions were often initiated by the local Indians themselves (O'Phelan 1983, 1987; Bonilla 1987a) for crimes such as confiscating tribute, expropriating the lands of mita workers who never returned home, even using forced labor on those lands—essentially for becoming landlords at the communities' expense. This kind of legal confrontation happened in Cotahuasi in 1785, when the most prominent kuraca in the valley, a woman who represented all the ayllus of Cotahuasi, Tomepampa, and Toro, was accused of tribute theft (ADC 1785a). The sole heir of a family that had led the local communities for some 200 years (Acuña 1965 [1586]: 313), she had accumulated a considerable amount of land and other property. It appears that she, and previously her father, had in fact been embezzling tribute over a period of more than twenty years. Although at some point colonial officials seized all her property and fined her 1,000 pesos, the document does not reveal the final outcome of the trial. It does show, however, that the local Indians, and the leaders of each individual ayllu, spoke out against her in the investigation.

A similar event happened nine years later (ADC 1794), when the priest of Alca district—a Spaniard who, oddly enough, also happened to be the primary cacique and tribute collector for the local ayllus—became the central figure in a controversy over mita labor. The colonial government had ordered local Indians to begin doing their mita service at the mine of Orcopampa, in the neighboring province of Castilla, instead of making the long trip to Huancavelica or Caylloma, a change that would seem to have been very much to their advantage. However, with the priest as their advocate and spokesman, the men steadfastly refused to go, arguing that the mine was unsafe and its owner corrupt and abusive.

This protest led to a confrontation in which the mine owner alleged that the priest was concealing over 100 tribute payers in order to employ them at Pararapa, the largest gold mine in the Cotahuasi valley, which was partly under his control. He had supposedly been offering them protection from the mitas to Huancavelica and Caylloma in exchange for labor service, not only in the mine, but also on a local hacienda that he owned. The price of concealment supposedly included the workers' tribute payments, which had allegedly been going into the priest's pocket.

No record seems to exist of any action taken against the man after the accusations were made, which suggests that the incident may have been covered up. Nevertheless, I think it reveals how the local mines were worked and provides insights into the dynamics of power in this unusual situation. Why would Indians from throughout the valley rally behind a Spaniard who was guilty of most of the abuses committed by the cacica they had denounced earlier in Cotahuasi? The answer would seem to be that he provided protection from the mita and the opportunity to work the local mines instead of going on the long death march to Huancavelica, something that the cacica could not offer.

It seems likely that a conspiracy did exist, that it involved other local communities as well, and that it had been going on for some time. Pararapa was a mine nearly on the scale of Montesclaros, employing a rotating work force of more than 100 men at a time, which could not have been provided by Alca alone (Raimondi 1887: 77–78; Fidel Vera [former owner of the mine], personal communication). Although other explanations are possible, such a conspiracy would help to explain the fact that every pueblo in the valley, not just Alca, joined in the boycott of the new mita. The justification given—an unsafe mine with a corrupt and abusive administrator—is suspicious, since those conditions were the rule in Peru at the time, not the exception (Boggio 1983). The Indians seem to have been objecting to the mita itself, which they may have been avoiding entirely (ADC 1794: 26).

Several villages, such as Pampamarca and Puica, had smaller mines and haciendas in their territories that may have been worked under the same arrangement. And if, as it appears, the colonial government never knew of the existence of these, not even Pararapa (Fisher 1975), the owners were not only evading mineral taxes but operating a major labor refuge in which the conditions of work were completely free of outside control. In addition to enriching them, this free hand in labor, which may have been going on for decades, would have given these men an extraordinary amount of control over the indigenous population, as the priest of Alca clearly had, power that could easily have been used to acquire more land.

Other documents reveal that, by the end of the eighteenth century, landlords involved in the mining economy had gained control over the local cacique positions, and with it, the control of community lands. This is consistent with the trend Scarlett O'Phelan (1987, 1983) found throughout much of the sierra: the growth of the power of local landlords toward the end of the eighteenth century at the expense of the native elites. The final blow for the kurakas came after the Tupac Amaru rebellion of 1780, which spread all over the southern Andes, even to places as remote as Cotahuasi (Cristina Herencia, personal communication), until the colonial authorities ruthlessly crushed it. Thereafter, most kurakas throughout the region were replaced, whether or not they had participated in the uprising. The landlords of Cotahuasi seem to have benefited from this action, since it enabled them to displace their indigenous competitors and, in many cases, probably acquire some of their property as well (see Poole 1987: 269). Thus here, where landlords and ayllu members lived in close proximity, it was almost exclusively the former who ultimately profited from the population collapse. Very few people of indigenous heritage were able to accrue and hold on to ayllu land.

That still holds true today in villages like Pampamarca and Puica, where "Spanish" families, always composing a small ethnic minority, have lived ever since the mining era. They are the only large landowners in those communities; there are no "rich" peasants. Evidently, it was only in the few places that the landlords never colonized—Huaynacotas, Cahuana, Ayahuasi, and Huillac—that the kuracas managed to accumulate a substantial amount of property, so that the indigenous population became stratified. In this respect, the relationship between native and Spanish elites seems to have been one of competitive exclusion. This is not to say that all of the kuracas in Cotahuasi were usurped, but rather that the few who survived probably did so through close alliances with the Spanish, under terms largely dictated by them (Spalding 1974).

It was also during the late eighteenth century, the height of the mining era, that some of the communities began to take steps to protect their territory from expropriation. The people of Ayahuasi, for example, sought formal legal recognition of their lands at this time, presumably because they were under threat.

Unfortunately, the colonial authorities obliged them by placing the lands in the hands of the kuraca on the community's behalf, in accordance with Spanish concepts of property (see Pease 1986).[15] In Huaynacotas and Huillac, which evidently took the same action, some of the communal lands eventually became the private property of the indigenous elites, particularly the herding grounds on the puna, and were passed down to later generations. A few of the grazing lands were eventually recovered by the communities during the twentieth century, however, when they succeeded in getting them recognized as communal property.[16]

As for the herding grounds of Cotahuasi and Alca, the elite families ultimately acquired most of that land during the nineteenth century. Depopulation had left large expanses of the puna uninhabited and largely unexploited, and, despite the fact that they belonged to the communities or their leaders, the landlords began to take over these areas as soon as it became profitable to do so. This was the fate of most of the herding grounds belonging to Pampamarca, Puica, and the other villages where Spanish families lived.[17]

Hacienda Expansion After Independence

The valley became a single province again shortly after Peruvian independence in 1821, through a brief armed struggle typical of the *caudillo* era of factional politics. Until that time, the watershed had belonged to three different administrative units, the *intendencias* of Ayacucho, Cusco, and Arequipa, a fragmented arrangement that the first republican government in Lima sought to maintain. Because it was arbitrary and did not take geographic and economic realities into account, leaders of the local elite families protested and demanded that the valley be unified as a single province. When vested interests within the government stoutly resisted the change, the local elites took up arms in 1835 and formed a provincial militia. The Cotahuasinos, led by men who had fought with distinction in the war against Spain, won in a brief conflict against a counter-insurrectionary force, and thereby succeeded in founding a province that they appropriately called La Unión.

The haciendas expanded and proliferated in the decades that followed, as the landed families became heavily involved in the wool export trade, which came to be based in Arequipa (Flores Galindo 1977). This was a role for which they were well prepared, since success depended on their ability to make long journeys at high altitude, transporting large amounts of goods through areas scarce in natural pasture for cargo animals. The landlords of Cotahuasi had long since solved this logistical problem in supplying both themselves and the mines with food and merchandise. For them to become successful wool merchants, it was only necessary to expand the scope of their activity and to increase their holdings of agricultural and pastoral land. The valley's location destined it to become a major center in the trade, and the estate owners were quick to exploit this advantage by acquiring new property, expanding their mule herds, and increasing their production of alfalfa. As the export economy flourished, so did the number of routes over which goods moved, joining lowland and highland populations in a complex network of exchange that extended throughout the southern Andes and ultimately reached the United States and Europe, the sources of wool demand.

A flurry of studies in the 1970's and 1980's have done much to correct the notion that haciendas were static and uniform enterprises, built on a model imported wholesale from Spain. The term is now used to refer to a number of types of institutions, some of which underwent complex historical changes (Keith 1976; Montoya et al. 1979; Montoya 1980; Bertran 1975; Skar 1981). However, even though most scholars would now agree that the hacienda was not necessarily a bastion of feudal relations and a hindrance to market development wherever it appeared, few have shown highland landlords playing a progressive role in regional economic affairs (Montoya et al. 1979 and Montoya 1980 are the notable exceptions).

In Cotahuasi, it is clear that the landlords were at the forefront as rural entrepreneurs during the late nineteenth and early twentieth centuries, and that their activities had a profound effect on the communities upon which their success depended. Here, the haciendas were in many respects a force for change, despite the landlords' efforts to exclude their workers and sharecroppers from the benefits of commercial growth. By absorbing neighboring ayllus as a labor force and encroaching on their resources in a process of capital accumulation, the hacendados unleashed a dynamic that left no aspects of local life untouched, and that is still ongoing in many parts of the valley today. Without considering this impact, contemporary variation in the use of land, water, and labor cannot be understood, nor can current processes of socioeconomic and cultural change.

As elsewhere in Latin America, the estates were rather closed units, based on relations of patronage that were paternalistic, exploitative of the work force, and sometimes abusive. Various definitions of the hacienda have been offered through the years, but that of Eric Wolf and Sidney Mintz (1957: 360) is still the most useful: "an agricultural estate operated by a dominant landowner and a dependent labor force, organized to supply a small-scale market by means of scarce capital, in which the factors of production are employed not only for capital accumulation, but also to support the status aspirations of the owner."

For Cotahuasinos, the term simply means a relatively large property under one owner, often consisting of several tracts dispersed in different areas of an irrigation system, or even in different villages. But the other features of the definition clearly apply.

Dedicated to a mixture of subsistence, barter, and commercial activities, the thirty or so haciendas in the province averaged only about 20 hectares in size, with the largest one reaching only 60. These were relatively small properties producing a modest agricultural surplus for barter in the acquisition of wool, but at least half their land had to be planted in alfalfa, for fattening cargo animals before and after long journeys onto the puna. The Cotahuasi hacienda was a family-run enterprise devoted largely to livestock-raising and transport, which gave it unusual ecological and social characteristics. Such estates may have been common in the sierra, where muleteering was the basis of commercial success (Manrique 1983; Urrutia 1983), but they had little resemblance to the big plantations of the coast and the valleys along the eastern slope.

The estates were part of a two-tiered system of production, in which their counterparts on the puna, small herding haciendas owned by the landlords, provided a steady supply of wool.[18] The merchants usually added to their own stocks of fiber by bartering with independent herders throughout the surrounding region for manufactured goods purchased in Arequipa, alcohol bought in the neighboring Majes valley, and food crops produced on their valley estates. This exchange was the heart of the wool business; it made it possible to accumulate substantial amounts of fiber from a vast region by providing herders with essential foods and goods that they could not easily acquire.

It has long been recognized that Andean herders rely heavily on lowland food products for their subsistence (Flores Ochoa 1968; Thomas 1972; Webster 1973; Orlove 1977b). But few authors have noted that this dependence was the basis of the wool trade. Cotahuasi merchants were successful because they took these food products and other essential goods directly to the altiplano, thus relieving herders of some of the burden of long-distance travel, which they had traditionally borne out of necessity.

The business was made possible, of course, by mules. Soon after their introduction by the Spanish, these animals had come to replace the llama as the main beast of burden in the southern Andes (Manrique 1983; Urrutia 1983; Valderamma & Escalante 1983), because they easily adapted to the hardships of the harsh environment and could carry about twice as much weight. The use of mules made it possible to reorient the production systems of the valley toward increased provisioning of the surrounding puna during the late nineteenth and early twentieth centuries. This new arrangement complemented the traditional pattern of vertical integration based on llama transport, in which herders acquired food crops through yearly exchange with neighboring agriculturalists (Concha Contreras 1975; Inamura 1981). The shift evidently allowed the pastoralists to concentrate more on herding and less on exchange and transport; they reportedly increased the percentage of alpacas in their herds and reduced their frequency of migration. In this way, they were able to expand wool production within a finite amount of terrain as the demand for alpaca fiber grew.

In most cases, the hacienda owners were also involved to some degree in the overland transport of cattle for sale in urban markets. Although this was done by a few on a significant scale, here *ganadería* was generally of secondary importance, a characteristic that distinguishes the Cotahuasi estates from those of southern Ayacucho (see Montoya et al. 1979; and Montoya 1980). In any case, the cattle business rested on the same ecological base as the wool trade, the cultivation of pasture for animals involved in long-distance travel at high altitude, and it reinforced the same set of traits: distinct forms of land and water use, and a complex division of labor that allowed unusual mobility, both geographic and socioeconomic, to certain workers involved in transport.

Some estate owners were the descendants of conquistadores who had received lands in encomienda, such as the Perez and Loayza families of Cotahuasi (Cook 1975: 129–30; Villanueva [1689] 1982: 319–20). Others were the heirs of royal officials sent from Spain to oversee the Crown's encomiendas, such as the Benavides of Tomepampa. Still others were merchants drawn to the valley from neighboring provinces by the opportunities for enrichment and higher status, such as the Vera-Portocarreros from Castilla and the Aspilcuetas from Parinacochas. These were the *castas*, the principal landed families, who formed the elite core of provincial Spanish society.

The Cruz family of Cotahuasi were landowners of another sort. They were not hacendados but worked as arrieros, professional muleteers in the transport business. They are descendants of the only kuraca family that managed to accrue and hold onto ayllu land; their name appears in colonial documents going back more than two centuries (e.g., ADC 1785a). But with the exception of the Cruzes and a second family that was apparently not of elite ancestry, all of the independent muleteers in the district were members of the castas. Peasants typically had too little land and too few animals to be able to engage in the business on their own, though some made a good income from renting their animals (usually burros) and their services to the landlords.

The "status aspiration" of the castas was a provincial Spanish life-style in which all manual labor was done for them by indigenous people. Other accouterments of this status were large homes, manufactured clothing, a few imported luxury items, horses, and the pursuit of education and leisure. Two of the means by which they maintained their status, to the exclusion of people not of Spanish descent, were strict class endogamy and a school system that for a long time was closed to everyone else.[19]

Expansion, Privatization, and the Decline of Indigenous Life

It is clear that the ayllus of Cotahuasi lost much of their land to the haciendas, that they became a dependent work force, and that estate encroachment had much to do with their transformation into communities of a more mixed, or mestizo, cultural heritage. The expansion was a lengthy process that extended well into the twentieth century and occurred in two distinct phases. The native population increased throughout that time despite the loss of territory, and no widespread abandonment of "Indianness" occurred. It was not until other factors came into play, ones related to hacienda growth but not in themselves due to the loss of territory, that the decisive cultural shift, often termed mestizaje, took place. Here, again, the population figures tell the story.

According to an 1830 fiscal census, the district of Cotahuasi contained only about 960 people at the time the province was founded, consisting of roughly 710 *indios*, now largely dispersed in four hamlets, and a group of criollo families who were concentrated in the pueblo of Cotahuasi itself (ADC 1830, 1831).[20] The numbers indicate that, unlike native populations in many other parts of the Andes (Gootenberg 1991), the local ayllus had not yet begun to recover from collapse. This was also true of the district of Tomepampa, whose total constituted no more than 40 percent of the level recorded in the earliest colonial visita. Alca had made some headway, but its total too was still short of the 1572 level (Table 1).Yet the Cotahuasi estates had already grown to thirteen, an increase of six since 1785. There were still four ayllus,[21] but three of them had lost some of their territory, and only one of them, Quillunsa, was still a relatively independent community.

The census shows that the haciendas were located on the best lands in the district, the pampas, but it does not reveal how extensive the properties were. Judging by the numbers of people listed as working them at the time, however, both ayllu members and forasteros, they must have been rather small, and they cannot have taken up all of the flatlands where they were found (ADC 1830: 114–16). It is obvious that the estates had partially displaced the ayllus in these areas, absorbing some of their territory and population, but that there was still plenty of room left for expansion.

During the next five decades (1831–76), every district in the valley grew dramatically as the native population began a strong recovery. By 1876, the few independent communities for which earlier figures are available, the dispersed ayllus of Alca district, had grown an average of roughly 260 percent (DNE 1876: 434–39). This vigorous rebound, which was probably under way in Huaynacotas and Pampamarca as well, must have been due largely to the earlier termination of the official mita there, with all of its demographic consequences. Elsewhere in the valley, forced labor probably continued on the estates much as before, as in other places (Davies 1970: 19–43), despite numerous efforts by the Lima government to abolish it legally.

A still greater expansion occurred in the Spanish villages. The district capitals of Cotahuasi, Tomepampa, and Alca more than quadrupled in size, with an average increase of 460 percent. Since little had changed to affect fertility and mortality among the inhabitants, this increase can only indicate a sizable influx of people from outside the province, which the family histories of several of my informants confirm took place. Yet it is curious that, with one major exception, the 1876 census does not show the addition of even one new hacienda in these fifty years, at least in Cotahuasi. Significantly, the only new property was a herding estate that had incorporated all of the pasture lands in the entire district.

Apparently, the existing estates simply expanded farther onto the flatlands, taking them over entirely. The neighboring ayllus, left with only the surrounding slopes, were absorbed as a dependent work force. Two of the ayllus in the 1830 census, Collana and Andamarca, were no longer listed in 1876, but the population figures suggest that Collana had become part of the hacienda of Cachana, and Andamarca had been absorbed by the estates adjacent to Cotahuasi itself. These two pampas had become hacienda communities, probably composed of several properties under different owners, including small holdings belonging to the ayllu members. Only two ayllus were unaffected by the expansion: Reyparte, which had lost much of its territory long before, and Quillunsa, the one ayllu that was still fairly intact.[22]

Although the populations of all these hamlets had increased by 1876, it is important to note that only Quillunsa had grown at a rate comparable to that of independent communities in the valley: roughly 142 percent. The district as a whole had more than doubled in size, mainly because of the growth of the elite population, and had reached the level recorded in 1572.[23] But the hacienda communities of Cachana and Chaucavilca had lagged far behind, averaging only 40 percent growth. Although other factors may have contributed to this slow rate, it must have been largely due to the loss of land and the conditions of work on the estates.

It was the legalizing of the buying and selling of indigenous community land, part of the liberal program enacted by Simón Bolívar and other leaders of the Peruvian revolution that had made this expansion of the haciendas possible

(Davies 1970: 19–31; Delran 1981: 100). Those decrees enabled the landlords to do legally what they had already been doing for some time, but it appears that they also made new forms of land acquisition possible. We have seen that the estates had increased in number over the course of the colonial era, a process that occurred in violation of laws protecting Indian territory. Obviously, the landlords did not need legal permission to make these acquisitions, especially in a remote valley such as this. Nonetheless, the reforms must have facilitated the land transfers and given them a permanence they had not had before. For the first time, peasants became the legal owners of their parcels and could sell their land to outsiders. More important, the transactions ceased to involve the communities at all and became strictly a matter of negotiation between individuals. It thus became possible to acquire indisputable titles to ayllu lands.

Although Bolívar and other early heads of state had also repeatedly decreed that forced labor was to end, it does not appear that the conditions of work on the estates had changed significantly by 1876, given the slow growth of the hacienda communities. If traditional servitude had ended by then, one would expect a rate of increase more comparable to that of the independent ayllus. It seems clear that these small hamlets were in no position to resist either the land grabs or the labor demands of the landlords. And the state could obviously offer little protection, since for all practical purposes governance of the countryside had "evaporated" earlier in the century (Gootenberg 1991: 144). A significant change in work relations did eventually occur, but apparently not until the turn of the century, when a rise in wool prices and a boom in exports (Flores-Galindo 1977: 94–133) stimulated further estate expansion.

Unfortunately, another census was not taken until 1940, by which time the local wool trade had reached its peak and important changes in the valley economy had long since taken place. Although no data are available for the intervening years, the 1940 figures reveal the impact of earlier developments (DNE 1940: 120–22). For one thing, they show that the growth pattern of the previous century had reversed itself. The population of the pueblo of Cotahuasi had declined 26 percent, whereas that of the annexes and the rural sector had almost doubled and now accounted for 60 percent of the district total.

One of the most spectacular cases was Quillunsa. That independent ayllu, which had grown substantially during the previous period, had continued the trend, to double in size between 1876 and 1940 (114 percent growth). Chaucavilca, the one ayllu with some territory for expansion, had also increased at roughly its previous rate, growing 51 percent. The other communities of Cachana and Reyparte, most of whose land the hacendados had taken long before, had declined slightly like Cotahuasi, by 19 percent.

Even more significant, though, were the fifteen new estates listed in the 1940 census (DNE 1940: 120). Although the change in numbers since 1876 could reflect some difference in the way these properties were counted, it is clear that new haciendas had been established by this time on ayllu lands throughout the district, including several in Quillunsa. Many are still intact today, some even under the same ownership, and all of them survived until the agrarian reform of 1969. Several were reportedly purchased during the first two decades of the twentieth century, when wool prices in Arequipa began to rise steeply in response to growth in demand stimulated by the First World War (Flores-Galindo 1977: 69–72, 150–52).

A final change was a direct result of this expansion: the number of people who resided in the countryside, outside of the annexes and the capital, had exploded, increasing 324 percent by 1940. At a total of 994, these people now constituted 29 percent of the district population. Many of them were clearly forasteros, poor peasants who came from other districts and regions to work on the estates, and who were not incorporated into the annex communities. The parents of several of my informants came to Cotahuasi at this time, from nearby provinces in Ayacucho and Apurimac. Perhaps more significantly, others came from the ayllus of the districts of Alca and Puica. These villages, which had shown the most rapid growth during the previous period, had all declined to some degree by 1940. In three of the four cases, the change was substantial, an average of 33 percent, and it seems to have been caused by pressure on resources, since estates were not a factor.

It is important to note that few of the immigrants, if any, came from Huaynacotas or Pampamarca. Those villages, which have much more land than the annexes of Alca, had grown 65 percent and 24 percent, respectively, continuing a trend that obviously began much earlier. For some reason, they seem to have recovered from collapse more slowly than the others, a process that continued at a moderate pace throughout the twentieth century. It is unclear why they had not grown as large as the Alca ayllus by 1876.

The forasteros were a vital part of the labor force of the Cotahuasi estates, one with a very specific role, but they were not the only workers, indeed not even a majority of them. Traditionally, roughly half of the fields on each estate property were subsistence plots, many of them worked by members of the annex communities under sharecropping arrangements. These parcels provided the surplus crops that the landlords used in barter for wool. The other half consisted of alfalfa fields, tended by resident outsiders and their families, the *mayordomos*. Many of the sharecroppers also lived on the estates, and though some of these workers too were outsiders, most were members of the ayllus with little or no land of their own. In fact, these estate workers reportedly made up the majority of the dispersed rural population.

At some point during the period of estate expansion, the landlords turned away from traditional labor servitude, or *colonaje* (see Caballero 1981: 263–77), in favor of these sharecropping arrangements and various forms of wage labor. Colonaje was the full-time labor tenancy of the colonial period, in which people worked for five days a week on the landlords' special fields as rent on plots they had been loaned for their own subsistence, which they tended to on weekends. Most of my elderly informants, both landlords and peasants, insist that there was no true servitude on the Cotahuasi estates in their own time, that of their fathers, or even of their grandfathers. If they are correct that full-time servitude was an "ancient" tradition that ended long ago, then the shift must have occurred at about the time of the census of 1876, after forced labor was officially abolished.

However, regardless of when it happened, I do not think that the move to sharecropping was impelled by these liberal reforms, for two reasons. For one thing, it primarily reflected the hacienda owners' need for more surplus crops for barter. Throughout most of the nineteenth century, sheep wool was the main focus of the export trade, wool produced on the landlords' own puna estates. It was only toward the end of the century that the prices for alpaca fiber climbed high enough for it to dislodge sheep wool as the product of choice (Flores-Galindo 1977: 71–72). At that point, the landlords began to barter with independent herders on the surrounding puna, and the regional trade fairs of Lampa, Incahuasi, and Nana Alta developed, where the merchants did their best business (ibid., pp. 69–79; Urrutia 1983: 59–61). Soon they were able to use food crops to double their money, and they must have turned to sharecropping at about this time. The new arrangement was preferable because it gave peasants an incentive to work harder and increase their production, and because it required less supervision by the landlords.

Moreover, the shift to sharecropping was not complete, and it did not bring labor servitude to an end. The landlords did rent out many of their fields, but they retained certain forms of obligatory work as part of the arrangement, a practice that persisted right up until the agrarian reform of 1969. Such forced labor—gathering a year's supply of firewood for the men, work as domestic servants in the landlord's house for the women—simply became periodic, rather than constant as it had been before. If the adoption of sharecropping had been a response to the liberal reforms, perhaps pressed on the hacendados by community members now aware of their rights, this would not have happened. Instead, these forms of servitude, which the landlords framed as forms of reciprocity traditional in the ayllus, went on much as before. This manipulation and distortion of custom was a continuity with the colonial past, reflecting the landlords' continued power to ignore or evade the decrees of the Lima government.

We have seen that the Cotahuasi estates expanded throughout the nine-teenth century, and that this loss of territory prevented the full recovery of most of the ayllu populations. Those that lost most of their land early on eventually began to decline, and those that were affected less severely experienced retarded growth. The one ayllu whose territory remained intact grew at a rate compara-ble to the independent native communities, but it too was finally penetrated and absorbed into the dependent work force. At the same time, substantial numbers of workers came into the district from the outside, though these peo-ple remained a separate and dispersed population. We have also seen that servi-tude was an integral part of hacienda labor relations, that it persisted despite its official abolition, and that this reflected the landlords' continued power to cir-cumvent the authority of the state.

These were clearly unusual conditions, not only within this valley but within the highlands as a whole. In a recent study of the demographic and social his-tory of the region, Paul Gootenberg (1991) has shown that indigenous commu-nities in many areas experienced a long period of stability during the nine-teenth century. This was marked by sustained population growth, freedom from interference by landlords and the state, and a strengthening of their "In-dianness." Gootenberg argues that the liberal reforms of Bolívar did not imme-diately result in aggressive moves by landlords against the land and labor of na-tive villages, that persisting low man-land ratios allowed most communities to withdraw into self-sufficiency, and that the first significant moves toward mes-tizaje, which he refers to as the abandonment of "Indianness," were delayed un-til the early twentieth century.

This is precisely what occurred in the ayllus of Alca district, in Huaynacotas, and, to a certain extent, in Pampamarca. And Gootenberg has shown that the trend prevailed throughout much of the sierra. It is important to point out, however, that these communities, like many of the ones Gootenberg discusses, are still indigenous today. The people, although now largely bilingual, mainly speak Quechua among themselves, they live in neighborhoods called ayllus and wear a traditional peasant style of dress, and they engage in a number of rituals devoted to the Andean mountain spirits, including burnt offerings and coca-leaf divination—rituals that have declined in most of the other annex commu-nities.

Gootenberg argues that the expansion of regional trade after the War of the Pacific (1879–95) stimulated the first major assaults on indigenous community resources. Massive land grabs, renewed oppression, and widespread peasant re-volts shook the sierra as a result. Because this onslaught occurred in a context of land scarcity, produced by the sustained population growth of the previous century, a threshold had been crossed, and the effects on native life were so severe as to induce a subsequent turn toward mestizaje. Although these events did occur in Cotahuasi in this period, I have shown that the encroachment actually began much earlier, inducing a growing scarcity of land and creating harsh conditions of work that restrained early demographic growth. But that is not my main point.

The villages where all of this happened, even very early on, did not soon cease to be indigenous. The hacienda communities of Cachana and Chaucavilca, which lost land in the seventeenth, eighteenth, and early nineteenth centuries, were still predominantly native villages in 1940. Like Reyparte and Quillunsa, they were still called ayllus, though they had long since ceased to be listed that way officially, and the meaning of the term had probably changed. In the 1940 census, which claims to be based on people's own categorizations of themselves, some two-thirds of the rural population of Cotahuasi district still identified themselves as indios (DNE 1940: 25, 120). Although official statistics are not the best measure of such things, my informants agree that most local peasants had held onto their language and indigenous identity, despite their incorporation into the haciendas. Land had long since become very scarce, people had been dependent on the landlords for decades, and some ayllu populations had even declined. But "Indianness" still prevailed.

Of course, many other people had come to identify themselves somewhat differently by this time, a trend that would grow rapidly during the next two decades.[24] The 1940's were in fact a watershed in this respect, even though most of the estates had been established much earlier and the total population had long since grown as large as it is today.[25] These economic and demographic factors, which have been the main focus of all the relevant studies done to date, simply cannot account for the pivotal change, at least not in this particular case. It cannot be fully explained without examining what had recently happened, and what was about to happen, to indigenous people's rights to water and to the whole system of local irrigation.

The Missing Element: Water

With respect to land, encroachment and privatization had not contradicted indigenous peoples' concepts of property as strongly as one might think. Within the ayllus, household plots had been held permanently under usufruct and inherited within the family, which is little different in essence from private ownership (Benavides 1988). The liberal reforms had simply made these people full legal owners, so that they could sell their land to outsiders—a significant

step, in concepts of tenure and property, but not a sea change. Far more important was the fact that hacienda expansion had involved the privatization of water, a resource that had heretofore been communally owned and cooperatively
managed. This conversion had begun with the founding of the earliest estates,
but it was legally sanctioned and encouraged with the passage, in 1902, of a new
water law (Pasapera 1902). The Water Code of 1902 was a profound change that
introduced a degree of inequality and privilege previously unknown in the annex communities.

Strangely enough, water privatization has hardly been discussed in the literature, though it has been documented briefly in one important ethnographic
study (Montoya et al.1979: 78–79). By 1940, this process, which obviously took
place in many hacienda-dominated parts of the highlands (e.g., Mitchell 1994),
had deprived the local ayllus of much of their water, undermined their customary way of sharing the resource, and unleashed a struggle within each community as the remaining supply tightened. This "tragedy of the commons" (to
use Hardin's familiar term), the prevailing of selfishness and conflict over cooperation and concern for the common good, has been widely documented in
Andean irrigation systems. In Cotahuasi, it accelerated dramatically after the
state agricultural bureaucracy got involved, beginning in 1941, a turning point
from which a whole series of other changes followed.

In order to appreciate the impact of these events, however, and to comprehend the effects of developments occurring long before this, we must first have
some knowledge of indigenous irrigation.[26] Fortunately, there are a few local
villages that we can turn to where most of these changes never took place,
whose traditions and way of life seem more intact. There, we might expect to
find a different, more hopeful situation arising out of a distinct history, one
that, even though it too has been born of extreme hardship and catastrophic
change, might be characterized as "comic" rather than tragic. According to the
classical definition offered by Smith (as cited in McCay & Acheson 1987a:
15–16), comedy is "the drama of humans as social rather than private beings, a
drama of social actions having a frankly corrective [and mutually beneficial]
purpose." Let us see now whether the traditional means of managing water
among people who still call themselves runakuna can be characterized in this
way.

THREE

Huaynacotas

Irrigation and Ethnicity in an Indigenous Community

One village in the valley is notorious for having managed to resist the coloniza-tion of the province in a way that no others did. Its people are said to be purely "Indian," exceptionally proud and fierce, and to live a distinctive kind of life. Among residents of the lower part of the valley, the Huaynacoteños are said never to have allowed the Spanish to gain a foothold by acquiring any of their land and actually settling there, as happened in most other places, and to have maintained many of their "Inca" traditions up to the present day. The story turns out to be more complicated than this, but the reputation is well deserved. Huaynacotas is extraordinary in many ways and is an authentic Andean com-munity. Neither a pristine isolate nor a backwater relic of the distant past, it is a place where people have struggled to hold on to their ethnic identity and maintain some control over the direction and pace of change. And history, it turns out, has equipped them to do that in an unusual way, through a tradition built around irrigation and water-sharing.

The village sits in the upper part of a huge bowl or amphitheater formed by the surrounding mountains that tilts southward onto high cliffs overlooking the Cotahuasi River. Terraced and sculpted from top to bottom, the basin forms a vast garden that descends toward the river in step-like fashion, facing out over a breathtaking view of the valley below. As one climbs through this landscape toward the pueblo for the first time, up stairways and footpaths cut into stone, seemingly as old as the Incas, a sense of anticipation builds. One becomes aware that this must indeed be a remarkable place.

Located at an elevation of 3,400 meters, or about 11,500 feet, in the upper qheshwa zone, Huaynacotas is one of the bigger settlements in the valley, with only slightly fewer people than the provincial capital, officially 1,073 in 1980.[1] It is one of the few legally recognized peasant (*campesino*) communities, whose land and water are officially protected from purchase by outsiders, a legal status finally achieved by community leaders in 1965.[2] It is the only one that has ever dared to expel provincial officials—leaders of the elite society of the valley bot-

PHOTO 1. Huaynacotas and its surrounds

tom—from its borders, as happened almost forty years ago. No other village has been able to establish its own *colegio*, or high school, a luxury otherwise reserved for the district capitals. These features reflect a long struggle for social and political autonomy, and attest to the Huaynacoteños' strong sense of ethnic identity. They have apparently always been fiercely independent; a visitor in the eighteenth century noted that they were operating their own gold mine (no doubt near Pararapa, high above the village), which they worked cooperatively so that each household could pay its monetary tribute in gold without having to depend on outside intermediaries (Llano Zapata [1761] 1904).

The village is composed of three ayllus called Kupe, Ch'eqa, and Wayki—groups of related families that date back to the reducciones of 1572 and beyond. As in all Andean communities, these are residential and social units that are organized on the basis of bilateral inheritance and descent but do not control discrete territories of agricultural land, as they did in their original settlements. People in the ayllus generally follow the common Andean pattern of having several scattered plots of land dispersed throughout the village territory, with only a few small sectors still belonging to a specific ayllu. This pattern evidently results from a long history of intermarriage among the three groups. The ayllus ceased to be endogamous long ago, probably during the era of depopulation,[3] a time when they may have been too small for this ancient practice to be viable.

Evidently, intermarriage and criss-crossing patterns of inheritance have since led to the mixed pattern that exists today.

The three populations are fairly equal, but they are differentiated internally into two strata that are explicitly recognized and often talked about: the large landholders, known in Spanish as *mayoristas*, and the smallholders, or *minoristas*. The former, most often referred to as *chakrasapa*, "people with many fields," are distinguished in this way because they have six *topos* or more (1 topo = 0.35 hectare) of irrigated land.[4] These families number fewer than fifty and account for less than 20 percent of the village population (264 households). Their typical landholding, including dry-farmed land, is said to be only about three hectares (ten topos), and no household has more than five. Irrigated land does not exceed three hectares today, although some families did formerly have as many as five.[5]

The smallholders are usually referred to as *chika chakrayuq*, "people with just a few fields." Within this stratum, one subgroup is relatively well endowed with land and the other is not. The first consists of families with 3–6 topos (1–2 hectares), just enough land to be largely self-reliant in the production of staple crops. These households make up no more than 40 percent of the total population, or half of all smallholders. The remaining families have 1 hectare or

PHOTO 2. A terrace system

slightly less and make up 35 percent or more of the village total, perhaps 40 to 50 percent of all minoristas. Families with less than 1 topo are called *wakcha*, "the poor," and reportedly constitute less than 10 percent of the population. These people have to rely mainly on the exchange and sale of their labor, both within the community and outside it, to meet their food needs. Only four families are without any property at all, and these are referred to rather unflatteringly as *mana chakrayuq qella*, "lazy people with no land." They have lost their land on account of alcoholism.

The people are all native Quechua speakers who address one another primarily in that language, but the vast majority have long also been fluent in Spanish. They acknowledge their indigenous ancestry (describing themselves as "runakuna" or "gente indígena") but give greatest emphasis to their shared identity as village members, *llaqta masis*,[6] or *comuneros*, people who have an attachment to the community, its territory, and its customs. As in most Andean pueblos, this connection to place of origin is fundamental, a bond with the village and the landscape that confers a sense of uniqueness and overshadows broader notions of ethnic affiliation (Montoya 1980).

Although the differences in wealth are significant, they are minimal compared with the hacienda communities of the lower valley and other places where landlords have long resided. The largeholders own approximately 40 percent of the total land, but their holdings average only about 2 hectares under irrigation. Even the wealthiest households, twelve in all, today have only about 3.[7] What truly differentiates them, however, especially the "richer" families, is their ownership of livestock and pasture. The eight wealthiest families have small estancias on the puna, herding estates of a few hundred hectares where they keep sixty to eighty llamas and alpacas, perhaps ten or fifteen mixed-breed cattle, and a number of sheep. Most of them also have a few fine dairy cows—up to four or five in the bigger households—which they keep in the village and feed primarily on alfalfa. The other mayoristas have up to eight or ten *wakas chuskas*, or mixed-breed cattle, that graze on the community's fallow lands and uncultivated slopes.

The rest of the population typically has a couple of mixed-breed cattle and some sheep and goats, which again are kept on the fallow lands and the upper slopes. Because most of the surrounding puna came under private control a long time ago, some of it by the local elite families, the majority of the populace now has limited access to natural pasture. Landlords of the lower valley own the big estates on the puna above, but a few smaller properties have remained in the hands of these local families, who are said to have been the leaders of the community since time immemorial.

These private pasture lands apparently date back to the time of the kurakas (caciques). Everyone seems to agree that the wealthiest families have always led the community, and it is clear that they have dominated important posts such as *teniente gobernador*, or mayor, during recent times. The lands probably came under the control of their ancestors during the late eighteenth or early nineteenth century, when, as we saw in the last chapter, the neighboring communities of Ayahuasi and Huillac, immediately across the valley, acted to protect their pasture lands from expropriation by registering them in Arequipa and legally placing them in the kurakas' hands. If Huaynocotas ever took such a step, there is no record of it because it was not under the jurisdiction of Arequipa at the time, but instead answered to Ayacucho, where no such records seem to be available. The lands were evidently divided up among other prominent families sometime after that.

Huaynacotas never seems to have experienced any major influx of outsiders, such as happened in Cotahuasi during the mid-nineteenth century. No early demographic data are available, but it is clear that growth during the first half of that century was significantly slower here than in other native communities, such as the annexes of Alca. As late as 1876, the first year for which there are census data, the population was only 672, a little more than half the current level. Growth occurred at a moderate pace after that, with the population increasing only 66 percent in sixty-four years, reaching 1,114 by 1940 (DNE 1876: 435, 1941: 121). Immigration does not appear to have made any contribution to this expansion. Here there was no influx of landless campesinos, because the community was never penetrated by the landlords and no agricultural estates were ever established. As a result, the process of differentiation was truncated, and the local mayoristas remain little more than campesinos-writ-large, or first among equals.

The population today is slightly less than it was in 1940 (1,073 in 1980), but it probably reached its height in the early 1960's and then declined significantly. Although no figures are available for the peak years, it is clear that, like most places in the valley, Huaynacotas has seen a substantial permanent outflow of families to the city. This serves to illustrate a point that I will emphasize later. People migrate for different reasons and in response to a number of factors, only one of which is the quality of village social life. Furthermore, the community, even though it is extraordinary in many ways, is not some kind of utopia, free of toil and conflict. People will have problems wherever there are significant differences in wealth between them. And a peasant's life is hard.

Hydraulic Structure and Land Use

Huayacotas's irrigation system is one of the biggest in the province, second in size only to Cotahuasi's, and it is widely said to be the best organized and most efficient. That it has earned this reputation is curious because people elsewhere in the valley seem to know almost nothing about how the system actually operates. Spanning elevations from 3,100 to 4,100 meters, the canal network covers roughly 400 hectares of land (see Map 6), terrain that is cultivated more intensively than in Cotahuasi and other villages in the lower valley. [8] The population density here is greater, with much less cultivation of food for animals. All three of the villages use the same basic technology, but in this case local practices have not been altered or displaced by the methods usually associated with pasture production. Alfalfa is grown on a very minor scale, and it is irrigated in the same customary way as any other crop. This difference turns out to be crucial and, along with many other unusual ways of doing things, it distinguishes Huaynacotas from all but a handful of local communities.

The system is fed by a pair of springs in the mountains above, whose water is diverted through two main canals into two independent hydraulic units down below, each of which has its own storage tank. Because the springs are small and quite vulnerable to drought, this dual canal system is organized and operated so as to conserve a scarce resource whose availability fluctuates markedly from one year to the next. The larger of the springs, called Orqon, is highly dependent on rainfall and far more unstable than the other, Warmunta.

Because of the general vulnerability of the supply, one of the first conservation measures taken here was to build the two major reservoirs, Waskaqocha and K'uchuqocha, that store the waters of Orqon and Warmunta, respectively. These tanks help to minimize waste and facilitate distribution over the intensively irrigated lands down below. In addition to making it possible to limit watering to the daylight hours, an obvious benefit of storage is that, by multiplying the volume passing through the main canals during the daytime, with a minimal increase in surface area, the evaporation and filtration of water are reduced. Unlike Cotahuasi's bigger reservoirs, which were built only during the last fifty years, these tanks are apparently prehispanic, indicating that conservation has been a major concern here for a very long time. [9]

The village territory encompasses two kinds of cultivated land in different ecological zones, one of which is irrigated intensively, the other only once or twice if at all (see Map 6). The lower of these, referred to as *sara chakra*, or "maize fields," are indeed used mainly to grow maize but are also planted in other staple crops,

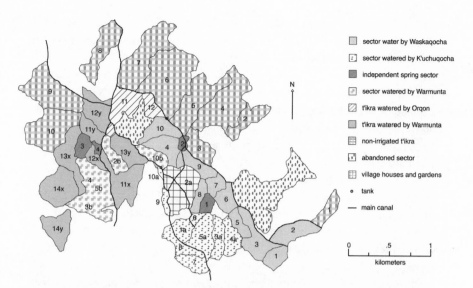

MAP 6. The planting and watering sequence in Huaynacotas. Units are watered in the sequence numbered. The paired numbers indicate that the two units are watered simultaneously. The x-y pairs are t'ikras, and they, like all the other t'ikras, alternate in three-year fallow.

K'uchuqocha tank (Warmunta spring)	[K'uchuqocha tank cont.]	Waskaqocha tank (Orgon spring)	Unwatered t'ikras
1a Oqo	10a Qochasiki	1 Lluqlla	1 Suntu Suntu
1b Lluqlla	10b Qochapata	1x Huaynapata	2 Cruzpata
2a Huertas (gardens)	11x Latawichu	1y Qaraqara	3 Chunkayumi
2b Ch'akiqucha	11y Uchuqu	2 Killalli	4 Qaraqara
3a Motanqa	12x Hueco	3 Campanario	5 Munyapata
3b Sirque	12y Pawsarima	4 Trapiche	6 Ch'ichi
4a Qurma	13x Ch'akiqucha	5 Ch'ilkapuqyu	7 Chuchulla
4b Qushmi	13y Qallwani	6 Waynapata	8 Qiruni
5a Akcha	14x Kabanya	7 IstuGrande	9 Waqanya
5b Qirone	14y Qusmi	8 Tamana	10 Cabracancha
6 Waykicha		9 Ch'iqya	11 UchuUkhu
7 Uchuwaru	Independent spring sectors	10 Yumari	12 Wayqo
8 Pisqanturka	1 Uklli	11 Quntanya	
9 Sinya	2 Q'irune	12 Istu Chico	
	3 Qushmi Chico		

such as broad beans, quinoa, and some alfalfa. These fields are found within the qheshwa zone at elevations of 3,000 to 3,600 meters. The majority lie below the reservoirs within the two main watering units, called *waskaqocha qarpana* and *k'uchuqocha qarpana*, respectively ("waskaqocha," "k'uchuqocha irrigation"). Each of these areas has a network of primary and secondary canals leading from the tank off-take. It is important to note, however, that numerous maize fields lie above, and out of reach of, the two reservoirs. The only way that those fields can be watered is with the daytime flow from the springs as it passes through the upper main canals. Much of the time, the same flows that are stored at night in the tank are used during the day in this manner.

The other type of terrain consists of rotated fallow lands, which are used to grow potatoes and other Andean tubers, broad beans, and barley. These are located in the upper qheshwa and suni zones at 3,500 to 4,000 meters. Called *t'ikras*, they were formerly used for sectoral fallowing and are sometimes referred to by the most common name for such fields in the literature, *laymi*, (Orlove & Godoy 1986; Guillet 1981; Fuji &Tomoeda 1981; Mayer & Fonseca 1979). Here, however, some of them are irrigated for planting and then watered once more if the need arises, for example during a mild drought. Thus the word t'ikra is particularly appropriate, coming from the verb *t'ikray*, "to turn over," "rotate," "transfer," or "empty something from one container into another" (Beyersdorf 1984: 114; Cusihuamán 1976: 150). The rotation cycle on these lands was formerly five years long: a year's production of potatoes and other tubers and another year of broad beans, followed by three years of rest. That is why the units occur in multiples of five: two were traditionally cultivated while three lay fallow. Only eight of the units are accessible to water and were irrigated, however; the majority were dry-farmed. All of the t'ikras, including the irrigated ones, were abandoned during the 1970's when the drought set in.

Both of these "production zones" (Mayer 1985) are divided into named sectors (see Map 6). The irrigated sectors are defined spatially by the canals that service them, and the fallowing ones topographically. Because animals are allowed to graze freely on the fallowing fields when they are taken out of production, those sectors are surrounded by boundary walls to protect them when they are under cultivation. All together, there are twenty-nine maize sectors, covering roughly 300 hectares, or 74 percent of the area under irrigation. The irrigated t'ikras span about 110 hectares and constitute approximately 26 percent of the total area, though only a few were cultivated at any one time because of fallowing. The dry-farmed ones lie in several major units covering perhaps 250 hectares, but the same was true of them.[10]

Just as in most villages, there are also several independent sectors watered by secondary springs, each of which has its own tank and small canal network (see

Map 6). Sometimes distinguished as *pukyu chakra*, or "spring fields," all of them lie within the maize zone and produce the typical array of *sara chakra* crops, but they are independent of the main hydraulic network, being given additional water only if a spring dries up during a severe drought. Here, just as in other indigenous communities, the principle is that *pukyu yaku*, or "secondary spring water," is always used in place of main irrigation water, so that there is no duplication and no one is favored within the system.

Oversight of the system is divided between two *campos*, or water distributors, each assigned to one of the main canals. This position can only be held by a mature male who is thoroughly familiar with the system, but most men are qualified and are expected to serve at some point in their lives. The position is one of the most important *cargos*, or posts, in the civil-religious hierarchy around which village life is centered, involving a year of nearly constant work for the benefit of the community. As in most Andean villages, a candidate normally volunteers, sometimes under considerable pressure, but he must be approved by the members in a public assembly. The campo is responsible for filling the tank at night and releasing the water at dawn, for dividing the water flow into shares, for ensuring that sectors and fields are irrigated in the proper order, for enforcing customary rules for water use, and for overseeing the maintenance of the canal system. His jurisdiction extends over the entire area served by his spring and tank, but it does not include the sectors of the secondary springs, which are independent and have their own campos.

Achieving Equity in Water Distribution

The distribution systems that these men oversee are some of the most complex and dynamic in the entire province. Each is managed in such a way as to produce uniform conditions of water use and to even out the effects of fluctuations in the supply. The rules that govern this process are of two types: those that determine the distribution of water between sectors and those that control its motion within sectors. A campo must rigorously apply all rules of both types in his half of the system, or conflict will break out and water will be wasted. Were this to happen repeatedly, it would lead to his removal from office and a great loss in his prestige, in damage to his reputation.

DISTRIBUTION BETWEEN SECTORS

The order in which sectors are irrigated is established by custom and never varies. This traditional sequence, called a *mita* or *turno*, determines which *yarqha*, or secondary canal, must be opened so that water can be diverted into it from the main canal, the *hatun yarqha*, or "big canal." In each half of the system, the campo must carefully coordinate the use of the canal and tank water, adjusting to the amount available at different times of the year. More important, because all the maize-growing sectors in each area are to be irrigated during every cycle of the system, they must be on the same schedule and receive water with exactly the same frequency.

The sectors are irrigated in the order in which they are planted, and that in turn depends on the crop; maize typically comes first in the planting cycle. Thus watering may begin anywhere from early September to late October. Once all of the maize-growing sectors have been sown and irrigated, the same order is then repeated for the next watering. At that point, the t'ikras used to be added to the end of the cycle, upon planting in December. The schedules for the two hydraulic divisions are indicated by the numbering and grouping of sectors in Map 6.

The basic unit of distribution, the *raki* (meaning a single share or allotment), is a standard portion of the volume of the main canal flow that is considered adequate for one user to employ on a single parcel.[11] The quantity is not physically measured but simply dispensed *ñawiwan*, "by sight," and it is determined by the amount of water available at a given time. The full volume of each system is roughly 2 rakis, 1 from the springwater above the tank and 1 from the tank itself. The two rakis can either be used separately in different sectors of land or be combined in the same one, thanks to a large canal that allows the springwater to flow into tank at night but to bypass it during the daytime. As indicated, the actual amount available to be doled out varies with the velocity of the water, which waxes and wanes with seasonal and yearly fluctuations in the spring flow.

When the two rakis are combined, they are usually used within one sector. A secondary canal that borders a parcel will hold both but no more. Under normal conditions, a combined raki will irrigate two adjacent plots of 1 topo each in the customary amount of time, roughly two hours.

The conditions under which the rakis are used separately differ slightly in the two halves of the system. In the Orqon-Waskaqocha section, the two flows are combined most of the time because only two sectors lie above the tank, both of them abandoned t'ikras. During the maize-planting cycle in September and October, the flow of the upper main canal is added to the tank outflow through the bypass, so that both rakis can be used to finish the planting down below as quickly as possible. This system proceeds until the first irrigation of maize, called *allapay*, is completed, which normally takes about two months.[12]

The sequence is then repeated for the second irrigation, called *allway*, which takes roughly the same amount of time. When, at that point, the t'ikras above had been added to the end of the order, the daytime spring flow would be detained there, and the tank water would be used to start the cycle over again in the lower sectors. For a brief period, this created two mini-cycles that were simultaneous but that advanced more slowly, both of which had to be overseen by the campo. Once the upper sectors were finished, the two flows were combined for the rest of the cycle, at which time the cycle was repeated if necessary. Normally this is not required, since the rains usually begin in early January, near the end of the second irrigation. The watering will end once the campo and the community become confident that a typical wet season is under way.

The arrangement is much more complicated in the Warmunta-K'uchuqocha section, where six maize sectors lie above the tank and six irrigated t'ikras as well. At the start of the planting cycle, the daytime springwater flow is used to irrigate the upper maize lands, and the tank outflow is used in the other sectors below, with 1 raki going to each area (the order and timing are shown in Map 6). Then, once all the sectors above have been planted but one (unit 10b), the two flows are combined to water the remaining lower units, including the household gardens in the village itself. When the only maize lands left are the two sectors lying immediately above and below the tank, they are then watered separately with the two flows. This two-month sequence is then repeated for the second irrigation, which again takes approximately sixty days. The procedure for watering the t'ikras was the same here as in the other half of the system, so that their abandonment has simplified the whole process in both.

As the dry season and the first half of the agricultural year progress, the spring flows diminish, and the tanks do not fill completely at night. The flows of each spring and tank gradually decrease, so that the two rakis become smaller in the sense that they arrive at the fields more slowly. The campo must allow the amount of time that each sector is irrigated to lengthen somewhat in order to compensate. Following a season of normal or heavy rains, the overall cycles in both halves of the system stretch out to about two months during planting, as we have seen. But when the rains do not come on schedule, the cycle quickly extends to roughly three months, approaching the outside limit for a complete crop failure. Under these conditions, the campo must either shorten the sectors' irrigation time or take some land out of production. In rare cases, it is even necessary for the campo of Waskaqocha to request additional water from the K'uchuqocha section, whose spring is less severely affected. Such supplements are given only with the consent of the other campo and an assembly of his water users.

The t'ikras were traditionally irrigated only for field preparation and planting, after which the rain alone was usually sufficient for plant development. Once the rains began in earnest, they were also adequate for the maize fields down below. Consequently, during the period from January through March, the canal systems were closed off so that the springwater and runoff could bypass the pueblo through a ravine, the same procedure that is followed today.

Once this happens, the campos' work is finished, and the water is free for the taking on a first-come, first-served basis. People who want to irrigate their alfalfa or maize must climb up to the ravine bypass and divert water into a main canal and on down to their fields below. If they do this, they are responsible for preventing blockage and overflow along the entire watercourse, something that can easily cause serious damage to nearby terraces and crops. Then, after the rains have ended, the campos may take up the cycles again, for one more watering before the harvest. Since the rains increase the spring flows, the cycles run much faster than they do during the dry season.

All of this, again, assumes a "normal" year. If the rains are seriously deficient and fail to reach a normal frequency of falling daily, supervised distribution will continue throughout the wet season until a month before the harvest. And if the rains start out heavy but then cease prematurely, the cycle must be resumed after being interrupted, at a time decided by the community.

A final feature should be noted. The water is distributed only five days a week in Waskaqocha territory, and six days a week in K'uchuqocha. On the other days, the water of the tanks and the main springs is sent down to two communities in the valley bottom, in customary arrangements that date back very far in time. These neighboring hamlets, Visve and Luicho, were apparently established on low-altitude lands that once belonged to Huaynacotas, and they remain closely affiliated with the village today.[13] Although dominated by haciendas, they are mostly indigenous, and many Huaynacoteños have property there, especially the mayoristas. It is likely that these lands once belonged to a fourth ayllu that no longer exists, and that the four together formed part of a system of dual or moiety organization, the well-known *saya* system, known to have been widely imposed by the Incas (Murra 1980; Zuidema 1986; Gelles 1995). In any case, both communities send their own people to store, release, and guard the water, so that the campos of Huaynacotas are not involved. Thus the village, though it is highly independent, does share some of its water. As we will see, a very different situation prevails in other places where communities share water, such as Cotahuasi district.

DISTRIBUTION WITHIN SECTORS

Clear rules determine the order in which a sector's fields are irrigated and for how long, and thus how long each sector will take. Because the sequence is customary and known to all users, who are responsible for the actual watering, applying these rules requires only communication and supervision and does not involve any physical labor on the campo's part. In most other communities, watering schedules are somewhat irregular and are typically discussed at formal weekly meetings, but here the campo is able to alert users on a casual, house-to-house basis. Since every landowner knows the fixed order in which the water is to be used, he merely has to be informed of when it will arrive at his parcel.

Within each sector, irrigation always begins at the far end of the lowest canal and works its way up gradually, terrace by terrace, then on to the next canal higher up, and so on through the entire area. All of the plots are watered contiguously in this bottom-to-top sequence, regardless of whether they are planted in food crops or alfalfa. Thus the time at which they are serviced depends on their location. The order is fixed, and there is rarely any variation; no special or auxiliary share is ever given to certain crops, nor is preference ever given to certain people. In effect, water is granted to fields rather than households, and just as in the case of the sectors, the landscape itself determines the distribution order. This is a central principle of indigenous irrigation, reportedly practiced in the other relatively independent communities of Cahuana, Ayahuasi, and Willaq.

The amount of time that each landowner irrigates is the time that it takes to flood the terraces in his parcel with the one raki that he is given. Because everyone uses standard water-pooling features (*atus*), this period varies only according to the size of the plot, the soil type, and the velocity of the water. The pooling technique itself, along with the even division of rakis, ensures that, regardless of size, for a given soil type the ratio of surface area to water consumed will be uniform, or directly proportional. This proportionality among water shares is another crucial feature of the local tradition.

Note that with the pooling method (to be described in detail below), it is difficult for someone to irrigate a parcel for longer than necessary or to use more water than other people with the same size plot and soil type. The only way this can happen is if someone irrigates twice by returning to refill or top off his terraces after finishing, once they have had time to drain slightly, a practice called *kutipay*. Such duplication is normally prohibited, except in the few places that have poor soil; because it is difficult to detect once it is done, the campo must not let it happen. He is always aided in this task, however, by other users in the immediate vicinity, who are invariably preparing their fields and waiting to irrigate. The contiguous watering order ensures that an irrigator's neighbors are always waiting and watching to see when he finishes, so that this kind of abuse is normally prevented. This is perhaps the most important function of the sequential distribution pattern: it creates transparency by making irrigation a public affair.

A landowner who does not show up or is unable to irrigate at the proper time will be skipped and put last in the canal order. The campo will usually assist someone who is short-handed, however, in order to avoid the loss of water that results from changing the sequence, provided that this has not become a habit. But once the water has passed from one canal to the next, it is not allowed to return until the following cycle.

The requirements for receiving water are that people have their fields prepared for irrigation; that they abide by the rules against hoarding (i.e., duplication) and water theft; that they have contributed to all communal work projects (*phaynas* or *faenas*) for maintaining the canal system during the previous year or paid a penalty; and that they respect the authority of the campo. Infractions are punished by the loss of a turn, a fine, or a loss of water rights for the entire year, depending on their severity. The campo decides on these sanctions by consulting with the other village authorities.

ADAPTING TO DROUGHT

As we have seen, field and sector watering times gradually elongate as the dry season progresses, stretching out the time between cycles to three months. When the rains are seriously deficient, wet-season irrigation becomes necessary, and the campo must truncate this process and conserve water. The cycle cannot exceed 100 days without causing serious damage to crops.

The campo conserves water by taking some of the upper sectors of land out of production.[14] The decision is made rather naturally, as it were, and the process is a familiar one to all concerned. What happens is that the first irrigation proceeds very slowly and so does not finish before the second irrigation, whose date is more or less fixed, is to begin. So when time runs out, the sector then being watered is finished, and any remaining ones are simply dropped from the cycle. This is only done with the approval of the users, but for two reasons they rarely protest. All of them understand, first, that the action is necessary for everyone's welfare, and second, that the impact falls rather evenly on people because their plots are scattered throughout the village territory. Since no one has all or even most of his or her land concentrated in the upper sectors that are dropped from the order, the emergency measures affect no one person more than another. These measures, I should add, have not had to be taken for some number of years because the sectors that used to be dropped were the irrigated t'ikras, all of which were abandoned by the 1980's.

The Logic of an Egalitarian Tradition

The functions of the hydraulic system as a whole are to achieve efficient water use, while dispensing the resource equitably on a uniform schedule, and to distribute evenly the impact of droughts. The practice of starting irrigation at one end of a sector and moving systematically, always servicing contiguous parcels in consecutive order, promotes these goals in at least three ways. The first was explained to me by a campo, who pointed out that water loss through filtration decreases dramatically once the soil of a canal surface become saturated or waterlogged. Thus it is best to concentrate irrigation in one area, saturating a secondary canal and using it until all the terrain around it has been watered, rather than jumping around erratically, as happens in Cotahuasi and other communities. This approach minimizes the total surface area of canals in use at any one time, and thus the water loss.

Beyond that, the contiguous order facilitates the campo's task, since he does not have to run up and down over a large area in order to supervise the usage. He has the water users' assistance in doing this, as we have already seen. Perhaps most important, the arrangement makes it difficult for the campo himself to commit an infraction; he cannot favor certain people over others by changing the order or allowing someone to irrigate twice, simply because the neighbors will notice. The system is, from the standpoint of the users, highly transparent.

At the sector level, watering times and resource consumption are regulated by the custom of using standard pooling features on each terrace, so that all parcels are irrigated in the same way. This procedure limits variation in the efficiency of individual technique, ensures soil saturation while avoiding the waste of water, and, most important of all, guarantees that people's allotments are strictly proportional to the extent of their property. The arrangement is thus one of proportionality, or "equity" (Hunt 1992), in the sense that no one is allowed to deprive others of water by using more than the amount to which he is entitled, nor can he legally get it more often than everyone else. The other basic principles of local irrigation are shown in Table 2.

It is easy to see that all fields and all users within each subsystem absorb equally both the seasonal decline in the supply and the impact of drought. The cycle extends gradually and uniformly with the decrease in flow up to a certain point, after which the campo curtails this process through a standard conservation procedure that affects all households in roughly the same way. In the rare cases when it becomes necessary for the less-affected half of the system, K'uchuqocha, to give water to Waskaqocha, which is more drought-prone, the effect is still felt quite evenly because, again, nearly all Huaynacoteños have land

TABLE 2

Basic Principles of Irrigation in Huaynacotas

Principle	Description
Autonomy	The community owns and controls its own sources of water
Contiguity	Water is distributed to fields in a fixed contiguous order based on their location along successive canals
Uniformity	Everyone receives water with the same frequency, and everyone irrigates in the same conservative way
Proportionality (equity)	In rights: No one can use more water than the size of his land entitles him to or legally get it more often than anyone else
	In duties: A person's contribution to maintenance must be proportional to the amount of land he has
Transparency	Everyone knows the rules and has the ability to confirm, with his own eyes, whether or not those rules are generally being obeyed—that is, can detect and denounce violations because of the contiguous order of watering
Regularity	Things are always done in the same way under conditions of scarcity; no exceptions are allowed, and any sudden expansion of irrigation is prohibited

in both areas. Hence the users of K'uchuqocha can usually achieve consensus to mitigate the crisis in this manner. A major canal exists specifically for this purpose, connecting Waskaqocha with the other main canal. It has reportedly "always" been there and is obviously prehispanic, evidence that droughts have occurred frequently over a very long time.

As for the independent springs, these may or may not dry up during a given drought, but if they do, they are added to the cycle of a neighboring sector and given main water in the usual manner. Since most springs are affected by declines in rainfall, having land in these sectors is not necessarily an advantage. Although during normal years the cycles of some of them could feasibly be shortened, in all cases but one the campo simply adds their flows to the main water after their cycles have been completed, making the time between waterings in those sectors conform to the rest of the system. Rather than being restrained within a small area to yield an advantageously short cycle, as happens in Cotahuasi and many other places, secondary water is distributed here communally and equitably just like any other. This strict observance of equity may explain why land in the independent sectors is not concentrated in the hands of mayoristas or other prominent families. No privileged users exist within this irrigation system. Exceptions are permitted only in cases of emergency—trips, accidents, or illnesses—and the campo must explain the reasons why someone got water out of turn to the affected parties. Although it is possible for a campo to offer these explanations as a pretext to benefit a kinsman or friend, the truth will eventually come out. In such cases, people will not hesitate to confront him physically, even violently, and denounce him to the other authorities. If he is then judged to be guilty, the penalty is severe, but graded according to the offense: from removal from office to a loss of water privileges for the remainder of the year on one parcel. Matters hardly ever reach this extreme, since a campo is always given several warnings in the form of complaints and threats.

Note that all community members have the same rights as users of the system (de facto claimant rights, in the terminology of Schlager & Ostrum 1992, otherwise known as "communal" rights), and no exceptions are permitted.[15] This is the only sort of "egalitarianism" that exists in the indigenous communities, one where people's water rights are both qualitatively equal and quantitatively proportional. This relative equality arises directly from the technology and the organization that local tradition has provided, but it bears repeating that the vigilance of the water users is essential in maintaining it.

Monitoring, an essential function in any irrigation system, is pervasive and routine, spread out among users throughout the system, rather than a special task put entirely in the hands of the water distributor. Such assistance is crucial because, in the steep and convoluted terrain, it is ultimately beyond the capacity of any person, no matter how physically fit, to divert the water from the main canal, guard against theft, and monitor water use, all at the same time. Under this kind of regimen, other people can see what is going on; and since they always know roughly where the water should be and how fast the cycle should be advancing in a given area, they tend to know an infraction of the rules or other problem when they see one. They are quite confident of their ability to protect their own rights, and this has everything to do with their strong tendency to obey the rules and respect tradition.

Infractions and other causes of conflict are said to be very rare in Huaynacotas, but because of the extreme scarcity of the resource, they do occur. This will happen to some extent in any irrigation system, no matter what the rule, and of course there is always the possibility that the rules will not be enforced, especially when the penalties are harsh, as is the case here. However, in such a transparent system, this kind of corruption cannot happen repeatedly without being discovered by the other water users.

By way of illustration, there is one local landowner who was notorious for breaking the rules and taking water out of turn. The man would confront the campo if he objected, threatening him in an effort to force him to accept someone else getting bumped down in the watering order. The head of a relatively wealthy family with a fair amount of power in the community, this man and his sons often used strong-arm tactics to get their way and prevent any penalties from being imposed. The abuses reportedly continued for several years, but ultimately led to various forms of social ostracism and informal sanctions by the other comuneros, who were quite aware of what was going on. The main one was a dose of the same medicine: persistent water theft. Partly as a result, the family was eventually forced to leave, selling their land and moving to the city. Such defiance, or "free-riding," is always possible, and no system of rules and sanctions can ever fully prevent it. The important point in this case is that it led to ostracism rather than the spread of the same cheating behavior within the community. Again, theft is extremely rare—this is the only case the campos could cite of it becoming a problem—because people are able to protect their own rights. Another important issue, that of the corresponding duties of households to the community, is more ambiguous, as we will see shortly, and has been resolved through a process of dialogue and confrontation between the mayoristas and the smallholder majority.

Uniformity and Proportionality in Water Use

The terraces of Huaynacotas are all virtually level, and they are irrigated exclusively through what I call the bottom-up or pooling technique. Alfalfa fields are terraced like any other plot. A contiguous group of terraces belonging to a single farmer, called a *pata-pata* or *andenaría*, is watered through this traditional procedure, referred to in Quechua as *qarpay*, "to irrigate." Figure 4 depicts a typical irrigation and landholding unit, which is usually referred to simply as a *chakra*, the generic word for field or parcel.

Once a landowner has been told by the campo that water will be sent to his part of the sector, he must prepare for its arrival by ensuring that the catch basins, or atus, are in order and have no breaches in their walls. He must also clear the canals of obstructions and close the earthen barriers that direct the flow, so that the water will pass all the way to the far end of his lowest terrace. This usually means that the only atu remaining open will be the last, or lowermost, one in his plot. Upon arrival, the water is diverted from the adjacent secondary canal, the *yarqha* or huch'uy yarqha, by means of a temporary dam of large rocks and sod, called a *yut'a*. The yut'a must be placed diagonally across the canal and built high enough so that all the liquid will flow cleanly to one side without spilling over the edge. The water then passes over and along each terrace through temporary earthen canals, the *yarqha*, dropping cleanly between levels by passing over small platforms that extend out from each terrace

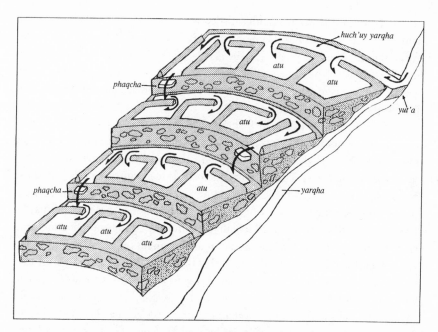

FIG. 4. A typical irrigation unit. As the arrows indicate, the gate (yut'a) at the canal (yarqha) opens onto a small canal (huch'uy yarqha), whose water flows down the phaqchas (falls) into succeeding levels.

edge. These platforms, called *phaqchas* ("falls"), are permanent features made from large flat stones; their purpose is to keep the water from damaging the walls. The water quickly reaches the bottom terrace, called the *siki pata,* or "base terrace," where it passes through the canal all the way to the far end.

The atus, which are built each year out of moistened and compacted soil from the terrace, cover virtually the entire plot. They vary in size according to the width and length of the terraces (4 by 5 meters is typical) and are built to a height of 35–40 centimeters, with walls thick enough to withstand the weight of water of that depth.[16] After the water flows into and fills the first atu, the irrigator seals its opening with a piece of sod taken from the wall of the one below. The sod is placed directly across the canal to form a barrier, the yut'a, which blocks the flow and so fills the second atu. If the flow of water is large, two atus may be filled at the same time, but they are always watered in sequence until the whole terrace has been flooded to a depth of 30–35 centimeters.

The small area formed by the phaqcha (fall) and the portion of canal of which it is a part usually do not have to be watered, since this edge of the terrace has normally been well moistened while water was passing over it to the terrace below. If the person is not satisfied with the result, he will block the fall and flood this section in the same manner as before, and so on for all the atus. Although no crops are planted in the canals, it is essential to flood as much of the plot surface as possible so that the entire terrace will be deeply saturated. This procedure is repeated until the whole series of terraces has been inundated from top to bottom to a uniform depth.

The terraces of a parcel may be oriented in slightly cantilevered fashion, so that the direction of water flow alternates within the plot, as in Figure 4, or they may descend like slightly tilted stairs, with the canals and water running the same way at each level. The stair arrangement is sometimes necessary because of a slight cross-slope of the terrain, but the design of the unit often simply expresses the aesthetic preference of the individual farmer. Either method may be used on wide terraces that are virtually flat, and the configuration sometimes changes through the years. The cantilever arrangement redirects the flow of the water at each level, slowing it down, so that the higher terraces absorb moisture from the canals while the lower ones are being watered. This is advantageous on wide parcels located near the main canal and high along a secondary one, where the quantity and velocity of the water are sometimes greater than down below. A third arrangement is frequently used on ridges, where the center of each terrace is sometimes elevated, so that the two halves are inclined slightly away from each other as the terrace bends around the ridge. There the path of the water through the parcel will be down the middle, and the water will be directed alternately to either side.

Terrace irrigation is normally a job for three family members, typically the males, though in some cases it can be risked by only one or two. Women, of course, are perfectly capable of doing the work, and they might take over the task if their husbands are absent, although this is rare. Widows typically rely on kinsmen or hired workers to irrigate fields for them.

One person fills the atus and is responsible for repairing any breaches that might open in their walls. The second must maintain an unobstructed flow over the whole group of terraces and halfway up the route to the main canal above. If blockage from rocks or debris should occur and go unnoticed, water will be lost and flood adjacent terraces and walls, producing a danger of collapse. The third person must constantly inspect the rest of the feeder canal for the same reason, all the way up to the point where the campo has diverted water into it from the main canal. This task of monitoring, called *qhaway*, "to watch over," is necessary because the landowner is responsible for any damage caused by obstruction and flooding up above while he is irrigating. Of course, watchfulness also prevents theft. The campo inspects the water route higher up in order to discourage theft and detect any violations that might occur, especially above the tank, where it is most likely to happen. But this task becomes the irrigator's responsibility once the water leaves the main canal.

The atu technique ensures that the proper amount of water sits on virtually the entire terrace surface long enough to soak in, including the part taken up by the canals. In the deep, loamy soil that predominates locally, called *yana hallp'a,* or "black soil," water retention is good and filtration is slow, so that when the water supply is fairly high, it takes about two hours for the atus covering a topo of land to fill. As it slowly soaks in, this water will thoroughly moisten the terraces to a depth of about 1.5 meters. With other types of soil, the process takes longer. In rocky or gravelly soil, called *ranra hallp'a,* retention is poor and the water drains more quickly, so that some of it is lost. It therefore takes more than two hours a topo for the atus to fill and fully saturate the soil. This is the one situation where double-irrigation (kutipay, i.e., returning to top off one's atus after they have had time to drain a little) is allowed.

Soil variation is ordinarily the only factor that causes one farmer to irrigate for longer, and to consume more water per unit of land, than another. The gravelly soil occurs only in a few scattered areas.[17] *Aqo hallp'a,* or sandy soil, is even less common than the gravelly type, retains water even more poorly, and takes longer to irrigate. In any case, the same principle is observed in these areas as for any field: when one's atus are finally full, irrigation is complete. The regulation of watering time is thus an inherent feature of the technique itself. As we shall see, this technique, practiced in this village exclusively, is used alongside other methods elsewhere. In Cotahuasi, in particular, a different technique leads to a widely varying consumption of water per unit area.

The pooling technique makes it possible for as much as three months to pass between waterings without seriously jeopardizing the harvest, which usually happens toward the end of the dry season and always occurs then during droughts. Maize plants are watered a maximum of four times after a wet year and only three after a dry one. This arrangement is viable because of the great amount of water stored in the terraces through saturation to such a great depth; plants continue to draw on moisture deep in the subsoil long after the surface has dried out. Agronomists working in the valley, who have little knowledge of agriculture in remote villages like this, find it hard to believe, but the technology does in fact achieve this result (see Treacy 1994a, b; Gelles 1994; and Guillet 1992 for similar observations in the Colca valley). Even so, the Huaynacoteños recognize that theirs is hardly an ideal state of affairs.

Everyone is of course aware that a shorter cycle would increase agricultural production. People speak with envy of the two-week cycle that the hacendados of Cotahuasi formerly enjoyed, and they would love to irrigate once a month, as the Cotahuasinos sometimes do now. The problem is that the pueblo has had to reapportion and stretch out its water supply steadily over the last century in response to demographic growth. As we saw, the population almost doubled between 1876 and 1940 and grew still more in the 1960's. The amount of land under irrigation was presumably expanded during this process by putting terrain that was abandoned in the colonial period back into production. If current customs were followed, the expansion must have been carried out in such a way that it did not favor any landowners or any particular parts of the territory; the cycle was probably just extended, gradually and uniformly, to its present minimum time of two months.

Some forty years ago, the Huaynacoteños worked hard to increase the supply by beginning to construct a long canal up to an alpine lake that lies about 20 kilometers from the village. The hope was that this canal, built through *faena*, or communal labor, would make it possible to increase the watering frequency in the maize lands, to put the t'ikras under continuous irrigation, and, above all, to eliminate the effects of the periodic droughts that seem to cause greater hardship every time they occur. Unfortunately, the project, which was financed by the state and other outside agencies, ran into serious technical problems and was abandoned. Thus the people are left to their own resources, having stretched their technology to its limits.

How to Build a Terrace

The last several decades have seen a surge of scholarly interest in terracing and other landscaping technologies in the Andes (e.g., Earls & Silverblatt 1978; Donkin 1979; Denevan 1986; Guillet 1987, 1992; Mitchell & Guillet 1994). A lot of discussion has focused on the agronomic functions of terracing, and a number of significant benefits have been demonstrated. However, my own interest as an ethnographer studying the technology was not in any indirect or unintended benefits that it might have, but rather in the conscious purposes that it serves in the minds of people who use it. Without exception, Huaynacoteños offered one simple rationale: terracing is necessary for the efficient irrigation of steep terrain.

New terraces are rarely built here, and then only on a very small scale. People do it today for the same reason they suppose that their ancestors did, so that water can be completely absorbed. As I was told many times, "Chakra patakuna sumaq pampay pampan kayta atinku, hallp'a qarpaqtinku llapan yakuta ch'on-qanampaq" (Field surfaces have to be flat, so that the soil will absorb all of the water when irrigated). This explanation shows that the primary function of terracing is water conservation, and that terracing and irrigation are thus components of a single technology. Erosion control and soil conservation are benefits that people recognize, but they do not usually mention these results on their own. This finding agrees with that of Guillet (1987, 1992) and Treacy (1994a, b) in the Colca valley, and it probably holds true throughout the western Andean slope.

The importance of water conservation is reflected in the Huaynacoteños' method of terrace construction, which is called *chakra mirachiy* ("to enlarge one's terrain"). As the term suggests, new terraces are rarely built, though existing ones are sometimes expanded, because the vast majority of the lands within reach of the canal system are already terraced and in production. Apparently known to everyone, the technique can only be practiced during the rainy season, when the soil is wet and easy to excavate and compact, since a lot of water is required, and the campo cannot give this out of turn in the dry season. But once new terracing is built, the campo is obliged by custom to include it in the watering cycle, regardless of the state of the supply. In principle, any land that one can irrigate without having to extend a secondary canal, or build a new canal, is free for the taking and must be given water once it has been landscaped. But in fact the owners of adjacent plots have first rights to that land, and they almost always exercise them—to such an extent that building terraces has become synonymous with enlarging a parcel. This practice probably reveals how land and water use were expanded as the community recovered demographically during the last century, by putting previously abandoned terrain back into production.

A farmer always begins construction at the bottom of his parcel, regardless of its topography.[18] There he excavates a flat trench about half a meter deep along the entire length, following the natural contour and making a right-angle turn into the slope at each end. It is not considered necessary to excavate the trench down to bedrock, and terrace foundations are often simply laid in deep subsoil. The ditch is then filled with large angular stones (at least 40 centimeters long on one side), which are fitted together as closely as possible and placed with their longest side pointing into the hill; a shorter side extends vertically upward to form part of the wall face. The stones are usually gathered or excavated from the parcel itself, but if necessary they are brought from the surrounding hillside. The stones are placed as close together as possible and shimmed with rocks and moistened dirt called *ripyu*, so that the stones will bind firmly to each other and stand up to the terrace's repeated drying and saturation. This effect is referred to as *rumi hap'ichiy*, "to make the stones grab."

In this way, the wall base is built up until it extends about 20 centimeters above the trench, when it is covered with a layer of soil excavated from the slope behind. At the same time, more dirt is dug from the slope and filled in behind the wall, until a level surface has been formed at the top of the row of stones, extending into the hill. The damp soil is then compacted as thoroughly as possible by vigorous stamping with the feet, an action known as *tushnuy* or *saruy*. This entire first phase of construction is called *simyentay* (Hispanicized—"to put down the cement or base").

The same procedure is then repeated to form another layer of wall on top of the base. This is again done with stones from the hillside; these must be angular and oblong, with a *rumiq chupan* or "tail" (tapered long side), which is pointed toward the inside of the wall and into the terrace. As before, a shorter flattish side extends vertically above to form part of the outside wall face. This process of placing stones is called *rumi tiyachiy*, "to make stones sit"; the objective is to contain the soil filling the terrace and direct its weight inward along the upper surface of the stones.

The same process is followed for the corners at each end, which are excavated and built into the hillside, usually all the way to bedrock, a phase of the work called *kantun pirkay*, "to wall the corners." The terrace ends have to be made especially strong if the structure is to withstand repeated irrigation. Finally, a layer of soil is excavated from the slope behind the wall and filled in on top of the previous level, to a height slightly exceeding that of the new layer of stones. The entire surface is then compacted, again by stamping it with the feet or with a *combo*, a wooden pole.

If the natural soil is deep *yana hallp'a*, the black earth that predominates in the valley, it is simply excavated from the slope behind and filled in as the wall is built. Rocks encountered in the subsoil are removed and used in wall construction. If the subsoil is rocky or gravelly, it will be removed if possible, and good soil will be brought in from elsewhere for fill. Where this cannot be done, the topsoil is removed with a shovel and put aside, and the rockier subsoil used to fill the bottom of the terrace, after which the topsoil is put back to form a good soil cap.

Huaynacoteños try to avoid leaving rocks or gravel in the fill because it allows water to seep through the soil before it is thoroughly saturated. It can also prevent plant roots from penetrating deeply and interfere with plowing. Terraces with gravelly soil exist only where there is no other option.

The excavation of prehispanic terraces in other parts of the Andes has turned up some cases of gravelly and rocky fill that appears to have been deliberately graded in particle size as one digs deeper. At least two authors (Bingham

1922; Bonavía 1967) have suggested that this was an Inca technique designed to promote filtration and the redistribution of excess water between terraces. Although the gradation might be a useful adaptation to other Andean environments with ample rainfall, it is clearly inappropriate for an area where the majority of communities suffer from water scarcity even in normal years. I have examined many terrace profiles, both in Cotahuasi and in the indigenous communities, and never found any evidence of such fill, although I often did find that stones or gravel had been placed in the bottom layers. I find it difficult to believe that the Incas employed the technique in such an arid region, even if rainfall was somewhat greater than today. Here, terraces are built to retain both rainfall and irrigation water, which are rarely so abundant that people need to be concerned about dealing with an excess.

Huaynacoteños do not employ any sort of rudimentary tool to level terraces, but simply do the job by eye (*ñawiwan* or *al tanteo*). When there are not enough stones readily available to make a wall high enough for a level terrace of the desired width, they will finish the wall with large adobe bricks called *taphya*. Normally, these bricks are used to build the double-faced boundary walls, or *taphial*, that restrict the movement of grazing animals. When necessary, they may be made on the spot to finish up the job. Another method of coping with the leveling problem is to leave a slope along the surface of each terrace, but break it up into miniature level terraces called *waqllapata*. These can be created quickly during the final phase of construction by building low walls of rock on top of the main soil cap and backfilling them. The main disadvantage is that these mini-terraces are weak and need constant repair.

The aversion of people in Huaynacotas to irrigating slopes can hardly be exaggerated. Again, the point was made to me several times: "chakra pata sumaq pampay pampan" (the field surface has to be very level). People claim that a sloped terrace will eventually slump and collapse if it is irrigated on a regular basis, especially if the subsoil is rocky or clayey. Since most farmers have plenty of experience working as wage laborers in Cotahuasi and other communities of the lower valley, they have seen many fields in this condition and assisted more than once in the necessary repairs. On the other hand, they have also seen that it does not happen very often, and that the problem is not all that severe. They do, though, have another, more important reason for objecting to slopes.

The consolidation and enlargement of terraces is sometimes practiced locally in order to build alfalfa fields, just as in Cotahuasi and elsewhere. Here, however, the work is done only in certain contexts and carried out in a different manner. Construction is considered feasible only where it is possible to create a large flat surface that will absorb water well. To achieve that, the builder must limit the number of terraces to no more than two or three and thoroughly excavate and redistribute the topsoil and subsoil, procedures rarely followed in Cotahuasi. The objectives are the same here as elsewhere: to facilitate the use of an ox-drawn plow, instead of the native *chakitaqlla*, or foot-plow,[19] and, more important, to create a bigger animal pasture. But sloped fields as such are simply out of the question. There is no formal rule against them, only a custom that they ought not to be built. People offered different justifications for this bias. For example, when I asked farmers what would happen if someone built one, most of them, especially those who had served as campos, replied that it would not be given water because it could not be irrigated properly without wasting the resource. Some also pointed out that this would lead to conflict within the community. Others insisted that no one would do such a thing because the field would not absorb water well enough for maize plants to survive the long period between waterings.

Such statements reveal a clear perception that sloped fields, which now prevail in the communities of the lower valley, necessarily encourage waste, inequity, and conflict. They also indicate that the practices typically associated with pasture production in other villages are seen to be incompatible with the welfare, both physical and social, of the community. Huaynacoteños are thoroughly familiar with these practices from their work in the lower valley, but they see them as inappropriate and also as essentially foreign. Several men pointed out to me, quite emphatically, that slope irrigation is the way that *mistis* do things, not runakuna. The techniques and principles of irrigation are significant because they seem to form a central part of Huaynacoteño ethnic identity. Local farmers' concept of themselves, both as community members and indigenous people, is closely related to the customary way that they share water, landscape, and irrigate. They perceive their traditions as contrasting and opposing the way that things are done in the lower valley, and they see their technology as the only authentic and appropriate one. To them, the way that *mistis* do things—mestizos and non-indigenous people in general—is alien, wasteful, and basically irrational.

Working Together on the Canal System

The upkeep of the canal and tank system is not very demanding of time and labor, requiring only two principal *phayna*, or communal work projects, every year. Just as in most Quechua communities, this labor is carried out during the fiesta of Yarqa Aspiy, also known as the Water Festival. The event is held on two consecutive days in July, the 18th and 19th, that come shortly before the village's saint's day celebration of San Juan (July 29). The ritual and symbolic dimensions of the work are much the same here as in other Andean communities described in the literature.[20]

The most significant difference between the maintenance work in Huaynacotas and that in most other local communities is that all households, both mayoristas and minoristas, must participate directly in the labor. Each family is required to provide at least one adult male for the task or else pay a *multa*, or penalty. The two campos, who are both the sponsors of the fiesta and the directors of the work, take roll call and check compliance within their halves of the irrigation system, aided by assistants called *comisarios*.

Ordinarily, participation in the event must be personal. Hiring substitutes is permitted only under unusual circumstances, and never for mayoristas. In addition, largeholders are expected to contribute extra labor and large amounts of *trago*, or cane alcohol, to the event. This is seen as compensation for having more land and using more water than the average person. The rule is not a formal one of the sort enforced by the campo, but rather an obligation that the majority have traditionally imposed on the wealthier minority. A tacit agreement of long standing holds that this arrangement, again one of proportionality, is fair. And though the custom carries considerable moral force, it is up to the minoristas to enforce it. For example, should a largeholder fail to bring along a few bottles of alcohol, he would be criticized and ridiculed as a "misti" and "patrón," and the complaints would continue until he corrected his breach of custom. (I use "would" here because this is only hypothetically the case: no one I talked to could recall an instance of this actually occurring.)

No count is taken of the exact number of workers provided by each family; a list, or *relación*, of users (the Padron de Regantes) is checked only to ensure that any absent households later make compensation. Yarqa Aspiy is one of the most important village celebrations, and all male members of each household usually attend and work enthusiastically, without concern for the precise sharing of responsibility among families. Although women and girls do not participate in the work itself, they cook and serve all the food for the work parties. This solidarity makes it possible to clean both the tank and the main canal of each half of the system all the way up to its source at the spring in a single day. All the men working together clean the tanks, whereas separate work teams service the canals in topographically defined sections, called *suyus*.

Smaller projects for the maintenance and repair of the secondary canals, called *huch'uy phayna*, are arranged by the campo on separate days with the members of each sector. The same is true for the independent sectors, which are the responsibility of their respective campos. Major maintenance work on the water system adds up to approximately ten days a year, depending on the extent of any necessary canal repairs, which amounts to only about four or five days of work for each family.[21]

It is important to emphasize that the duty of each household to contribute one laborer or else pay a penalty is a minimal or symbolic one, which merely ensures that each family at least makes this small gesture to the community in return for its use of communal water. In the case of the mayoristas, this contribution is considered necessary but not sufficient. For the smallholder majority, the wealthy are obliged not only to participate but also to provide significant amounts of alcohol as a simple matter of fairness. The largeholders cannot simply buy their way out of this obligation by providing more than one worker. The smallholders insist, moreover, that this extra contribution must be proportional to the amount of irrigated land those farmers have. Thus, though custom dictates that all households must perform certain minimal duties for the community and pretends to a fundamental equality, it is overruled by the majority's insistence that households should be differentiated according to relative wealth.[22] The smallholder majority enforces that argument through a process of dialogue and confrontation, an arrangement that is probably not unique to this community, but that has not been reported previously and may have been misunderstood.

Reciprocity in Agricultural Work

Minoristas in Huaynacotas carry out the work of irrigation and cultivation in the same way as their counterparts in the lower valley do, through forms of mutual aid that have been widely discussed in the literature. They do not employ wage labor very often, and, with the exception of widows, who may have no other option, they almost never use it in subsistence work. Households are usually large enough to be self-sufficient in routine agricultural tasks, but when work requirements exceed the capacity of the nuclear family, as in sowing and harvesting, assistance is first sought through the institution of *yanapakuy*, or generalized reciprocity (see Mayer & Zamalloa 1974; Lambert 1977). The extra hands they enlist are typically adult children who live nearby in their own homes, along with their spouses, and sometimes siblings of the household head.

This family work force is periodically supplemented under a variety of circumstances through *ayni*, the exchange of labor with kin and neighbors of the same socioeconomic status. In an important review of the literature on this practice, Bernd Lambert (1977: 18) has concluded that in Andean villages "non-kinsmen seldom exchange labor on an *ayni* basis." But Huaynacotas has long been largely endogamous, so that nearly everyone was until recently related in some way, whether reckonable or not, to everyone else.[23] Therefore, to observe that ayni partners are usually kin is to say very little.

For Huaynacoteños, ayni in its most common form is a reciprocal exchange or loan of labor between neighbors who have a roughly equivalent amount of land and therefore the same amount of work to do. Its purpose is to allow the major tasks to be completed as quickly as possible on each parcel, usually in a single day, so that the cultivation cycle is closely tuned to the development of crops, and so that all of a person's fields are on the same production schedule. It does not reduce the total amount of labor that each household has to invest in subsistence work.

For reasons of mutual convenience, ayni is very often practiced between people whose fields lie quite close to each other or who reside near each other in the same barrio or ayllu (Mayer & Zamalloa 1974). But though partners are usually chosen with this in mind, they must also be workers as reliable and efficient as oneself if the exchange is to be equal. In general, partners may be first cousins or close affines as well as neighbors, but they are usually some sort of kin simply because they live in the same village or are members of the same ayllu.

Partners who are first cousins, called *wawqey*, or *primos hermanos*, will often cite the closeness of their kin ties as the reason for practicing mutual aid. However, persistent questioning—for example, "why these particular cousins?" or "do you do *ayni* with all your first cousins?"—will reveal that the same factors are at work in these relationships as in those between more distant kin or nonkin: the size and proximity of the partners' plots and their mutual compatibility as workers. In my interviews, kin were always mentioned along with *compadres* (the godparents of one's children) and friends in defining the social circle within which ayni partners were sought. But often no strong preference for relatives was either stated or implied. I questioned people specifically and was told that, though close kin should help each other, many things could interfere with the arrangement, and that in any case ayni could equally well be, indeed often had to be, practiced with distant relatives or even unrelated neighbors.

In most of the ayni work parties I participated in, and on which I gathered data, I found that one or more partners fell into the category of *karu ayllu*, the circle of nonkin and distant relatives who begin with second cousins and extend out from there, people who were usually introduced simply as compadres.

Though some students of reciprocity have noted this pattern before (e.g., Mayer & Zamalloa 1974: 77–80), most authors continue to stress the primary importance of kinship in these relationships.

Some significant and fairly recent changes might help to explain this situation—for example, alcoholism, which makes certain close kin unreliable, and the high rate of out-migration, which makes others unavailable. Nevertheless, the congruity of work to be done and the mutual compatibility of partners are the critical factors in the establishment of these work partnerships. My point is not that kinship is unimportant, or that it does not influence the formation of these bonds, but that the institution of ayni does not rely on kinship to hold it together or make it work. Its inherent benefits accomplish that, so long as it is practiced between people who have the same level of commitment to work and roughly the same amount of work to do.

In their own descriptions of the practice, Huaynacoteños emphasize other considerations that can and do stand on their own over a long period of time. That is why the relationships are usually long term and are often so highly valued that reciprocity takes on a generalized aspect, something that has not been noted in the literature. Here I am not referring to the prevalence of *compadrazgo*, spiritual co-parenthood, which speaks for itself. In addition, ayni partners commonly look after each other's fields in minor ways, without request, when the other person is absent, such as by protecting crops from theft or from damage by pests or livestock. Such care occurs situationally as the need arises, without keeping a count of the favors, and it does not seem to depend on the two parties being closely related or related at all.

Such services may be small in comparison to those that siblings provide each other, but their importance is reflected in the strong preference for neighbors as partners. The pattern indicates that it is here, in the equal exchange of subsistence work (much more so, I think, than in ceremonial sponsorship), that social bonds readily extend beyond the bounds of the close kindred into the *karu ayllu*, the distant kindred and beyond. This explains why the use of ayni has not diminished in Huaynacotas in recent decades, even though the rate of emigration has steadily increased.

COMMONALITIES IN ASYMMETRICAL EXCHANGE

Work relations between the large and small landowners of Huaynacotas reveal social dynamics of equal if not greater importance than ayni. If capital accumulation is taking place rapidly in a community, then norms of reciprocity are likely being manipulated and distorted, and this is where the cutting edge of change will probably be found. Despite a slowly widening stratification within the population, one finds an unusual continuity in work relations. In this respect, the behavior of mayoristas in Huaynacotas has been, and continues to be, distinct in fundamental ways from that of their counterparts in the lower valley.

I cannot discuss the economic position of these families in detail. It has changed significantly in recent decades but remains limited by their relatively small land holdings (by provincial standards) and their dependence on Cotahuasi middlemen for the purchase and transport of their commercial products. The bulk of their cash income has long come from livestock sold to cattlemen from the lower valley, which in most cases are their own rather than ones purchased from a neighbor for resale.[24] The few families that own estancias on the puna were once able to supplement their incomes by selling small amounts of wool to valley merchants, but this money source diminished in the early 1960's with a steep decline in international prices and remained relatively insignificant thereafter. Fortunately for them, the local cattle trade began to flourish at about the same time, so that the two or three head they sold every year fetched enough of a price to compensate for the drop in wool profits and stabilize their incomes. All that ended with the economic disruptions of the late 1980's, when a severe recession sent the cattle trade into decline along with everything else.

Despite this loss of income, they are still clearly better off than the minorista majority. They live in slightly better homes, and they are more fully equipped to carry out agricultural and domestic work, having a broader array of tools and utensils, including oxen and plows. The primary goods that distinguish them from minoristas are their herds of livestock, kept either in the fallow lands or on the puna, and their dairy cattle, which allow them to consume milk and cheese more often because their cows are more productive than most criole breeds. Only one family in the late 1980's had purebreds (*overo negro*); the others had at least a few cross-breeds that had been bred selectively for milk production. The key importance of the livestock is directly reflected in the mayoristas' use of irrigated land; roughly one-third to one-half is always planted in alfalfa, for feeding the dairy cows and oxen and for fattening up beef cattle for sale. This land use contrasts with that of the typical minorista, who rarely has more than one tiny plot of perhaps a quarter of a topo (1 *cuartillo*) of pasture, if any at all.

The largeholders' remaining fields are planted in subsistence crops no different from those of any other village member. A few of the wealthier families are able to purchase some chemical fertilizers, though they use these only sporadically, and they generally cannot afford pesticides. Otherwise, the largeholders use these fields for their own subsistence, just as the smallholders do. They do not sell any of their produce, and the only significant barter they practice is with herders on the puna, for llama and alpaca meat. As in the rest of the valley and in most Andean communities, barter is now of little importance within the village (see Figueroa 1982, 1984); it is mainly a way to acquire new varieties of crop seed.

A final aspect worth noting is that, like many of the minoristas, most of the wealthier families now have modest homes in the *pueblos jovenes*, or shanty-towns, of Arequipa. Many have sent at least some of their children to schools there; and the more established families are able to afford to send one or more children (generally male) to the colegio in Cotahuasi. On the whole, then, their children are better educated than the minoristas' (although few of them have gone on to achieve professional status).

The homes themselves are typically quite humble and in many ways indistinguishable from the urban homes of minoristas, which reveals a crucial point. These landowners are not "*indios gamonales*," or Indian bosses, or truly wealthy people by provincial standards. They are not former *arrieros* and *laneros* (wool merchants); they do not own trucks or major stores, although some own small shops.[25] They are not *ganaderos*, or professional cattle-buyers; and none is a career politician. Throughout the years, these people, who are peasants too, have spent their income from cattle and wool sales primarily on education.

As I see it, the crucial issue in the history of work relations here is the extent to which the smallholder majority has been able to influence the terms under which this wealthier minority operates. Hindsight has shown that this is where the most significant and meaningful differences between local communities lie, in how people of different economic strata work together. In this village, the wealthy seem to be bound by norms that are essentially egalitarian, in the sense that no one is exempt from the physical work of cultivation. Wealthy families do not engage in exchanges that define certain tasks as beneath their status, unlike the landlords of the lower valley, nor do they use reciprocity to replace the labor of family members who live in the community but are simply unwilling to work. Traditional labor exchanges are not employed in activities devoted to capital accumulation; they are used according to standards of equity or fairness, in such a way that the labor supplements rather than replaces the work force of the household.

These conditions prevail, not because the mayoristas have unusual virtues, but mainly because the minorista majority has imposed certain constraints on their behavior, through a process of communication, negotiation, and confrontation. The operative norms, to be examined below, are customary ones of long standing, which clearly have their own origin and rationale. They consist, at one and the same time, of positive affirmations of the common values of fairness and shared work, and negative constraints that require the local elite to behave in ways different from hacendados.

The following is a compilation of the conditions and principles governing the labor relations of mayoristas in the pueblo as I understand them. It is based on conversations with both large and small landowners, as well as participant-observation in several work parties.

Most routine irrigation and cultivation work is carried out by the nuclear family, supplemented as necessary through the arrangement of yanapakuy with adult siblings and children. This includes the planting and watering of alfalfa and the tending of livestock. Mayoristas do not engage in ayni exchanges with smallholders (or anyone else) because their plots are generally larger, so that the days of work exchanged would be unequal, and the relationship therefore exploitative. For them, ayni is limited to loans of goods, such as plow and oxen, tools, or cane alcohol, things that can be reciprocated precisely in kind and amount, and to food preparation and other work involved in ceremonial sponsorship.

For the major periodic tasks on subsistence fields, the mayorista families rely exclusively on *mink'a*, the exchange of work for special foods, *chicha* (corn beer), alcohol, a portion of the eventual crop, and a drunken fiesta afterward. Just as in ayni, a mink'a work party performs some major task such as planting or harvesting, but here it is composed of two distinct groups—a detail that has not been noted in previous discussions of reciprocity. The core of the labor force consists of members of the host household, including any married sons and their wives, as well as some adult siblings of the landowner, a few friends, compadres and *ahijados* (godchildren), and one or more special mink'a partners, depending on the size of the field. These special partners are the first people to be invited to a mink'a. If they accept, they are expected to work the whole day from about nine o'clock until sundown. All of them are nominally free to refuse the invitation, but their participation is largely governed by other reciprocal relationships with the landowner, such as yanapakuy or compadrazgo.

The special partners, called *mink'aq*, are in fact poor people with little or no land who, in exchange for special compensation, have agreed to assist in all the mink'as throughout the year on the parcel being worked. In return, they are allotted one or two terraces in that same plot for their own use, which are sown in conjunction with all the others but whose crop they will keep for themselves.[26] This customary arrangement, called *wakllay*, is similar to practices that have been reported in other highland regions (Fonseca Martel 1974: 95–96). The partners sometimes work on other parcels as well, again in exchange for land for their own use.

In most cases, the partners also provide the host with occasional wage labor for smaller tasks, but for this they receive, in addition to the money, favors such as the use of a plow and oxen, foods such as cheese and meat, or loans of tools or small amounts of cash. Since there is considerable competition for mink'a partners, the landowners have to maintain these work arrangements from year to year through a series of small reciprocations. Poor people tend to work for families with whom they have such a special relationship, but the labor is only periodic, and they are free to change partners each year once they have fulfilled their mink'a obligations.

The other members of the work party—more distant kin, compadres and ahijados, and friends—are not obligated to participate, and, unlike the members of the core group, they do not have to commit themselves when they are invited. If they decide to come, they will do so, along with their families, but they are not necessarily expected to be there on time. This means that the work force in a mink'a grows throughout the morning, which is why the core group has to start early and provide the bulk of the labor. These are the only people obligated to work steadily the whole day, thereby maintaining the pace for the others, and they are specially compensated for this commitment. Though all attending people must be generously fed and given drink, it is only the members of the core group (except for the special partners) who receive large shares of the eventual harvest, a shawlful of at least 1 *arroba*, or 11 kilos. Other people usually receive a smaller portion, and only if they participate in the harvest itself. Nowadays, each person who works most of the day is also given a token wage, equivalent to about ten or fifteen cents, an arrangement that reportedly emerged, at the insistence of the smaller landowners, during the 1970's, the years of agrarian reform.

The work is differentiated into various tasks, but the division of labor within the core group must be uniform. If the field owner, for example, distances himself too much from the actual physical labor by resting excessively or drinking and talking with his family, he will be joked about and ridiculed by the others as a misti, a mestizo, or a *qella patrón*, a "lazy host." This sort of banter goes on constantly, but it is usually done purely in jest. For example, on one of the occasions I witnessed, there was an especially long pause in the host's work because he spent a long time serving liquor and talking to some helpers, then went on to take even longer in serving his wife and himself, conversing with her all the while. I heard a member of another task group say in a loud, mocking voice: "Ay, Taytay Patrón, ñachu misti runaña kapunki? Manañachu llank'anki?" (Well, Señor Patrón, have you finally become a *misti*? Do you no longer work?). The man's reply also played up the stereotype and drew a lot of laughter: "Aswanmi uqyayasaq. Qan ruwapuwachaqsikiqa, imasqataq llankayman" (Better that I just drink. Why should I work when I have you to do all my work for me?). Such exchanges are intended as parodies of hacendado-sharecropper relationships in the lower valley, but they have a more serious side, an indication that too much distance from the work is considered unacceptable.

Huaynacoteños will not continue to help someone who assumes the posture of being "worked for," and who differentiates himself or herself too much from the rest of the party. The owners are masters of ceremonies who must see that their helpers are given plenty of drink, but the husband and wife cannot simply take on the roles of host and manager. This is what I was told; I do not know if any actual boycotts have ever taken place. People simply said that they do things this way "*por costumbre*," and that any other arrangement would be unfair. The underlying principle, however, seems to be that mink'a must take the form of a supplement to the household work force, of assistance rather than labor service. The basic asymmetry in socioeconomic status that arises because the host is a mayorista and patrón is mitigated through an acknowledgment that all are equal with respect to the work itself. As several people explained to me: "Kay llaqhtapi, aylluyuq minkakunapi kuska igualmanta llank'an" (Ayllu members in this community work together in *mink'a* as equals).

The role of compadres and ahijados in mink'a is somewhat different here than in the pueblos of the lower valley, and in this case there has recently been a change in practice. Smallholders typically seek out mayoristas to be the baptismal or marriage godparents of some of their children, a lifelong spiritual bond. In return, the parents and child were formerly obligated by custom to work for the godparent whenever he requested it, a duty that endured for an indefinite number of years. Depending on the level of support the *padrino* provided for the child as his part of the bargain, this arrangement could sometimes lead to lifelong service for little in return. This kind of situation has long been common in Andean communities (Benavides 1988), and it is by no means unheard of even today in Huaynacotas.

Nevertheless, most mayorist here have only four or five primary godchildren. To have many more, say twenty or thirty, as hacendados typically did, is now considered improper and is explicitly recognized as a form of vice, a means of gaining a cheap labor force. Although I cannot say to what extent the mayoristas' treatment of their godchildren conforms with this view, it is at least the case that the numbers involved are relatively small.

Obviously, the issue of fairness in these relationships is a sensitive one. It reportedly became a matter of contention and negotiation between members of the two strata during the agrarian reform of the early 1970's, when social mobilization efforts by the national government led to a widespread rejection of traditional labor relations in the valley. The duties of compadres and ahijados were redefined at that time, and they are now considered to be a matter of personal choice. At least in theory, these "clients" now work for their patron only as much as they think is appropriate. They are invited to mink'a events just like everyone else, and they are free to participate or not according to the importance they attach to the relationship. There is clearly still some room for manipulation, but at least a new norm exists to govern the interaction.

Note that mayoristas often reciprocate by working in other people's mink'as. For example, they will assist their sibling helpers in the core group, who are generally also largeholders and whom they are obligated to help at least occasionally, though no count is kept. A mink'a exchange, however, is a one-day affair that is considered complete once it has ended. The tendency to reciprocate with work in the future lies in the ongoing relationships involved, not in the exchange itself.

Another kind of work arrangement common in the Andes, sharecropping, is not practiced by the wealthy families, apparently because they and everyone else consider it exploitative. However, migrants who spend most of their time elsewhere but who want to retain some land in the community do often make sharecropping arrangements with a brother or close relative, usually for half the inputs and half the crop. Since people will rarely agree to do this work for a nonrelative, wealthy families who leave the community usually cannot find enough kin to work all of their land and are forced to sell part of it. These families do practice sharecropping, but they are no longer mayoristas, and they visit the community at most only once or twice a year.

For any work other than mink'a that is done on mayorista lands, smallholders demand a wage, or *jornal*. This includes all labor done in alfalfa fields. Poor people do seek regular wage work, both within and outside the community, but they typically work for several different landowners because virtually all local families do the majority of their own routine subsistence work themselves. The mayoristas never hire others to irrigate in their place, and only rarely hire someone to look after their cattle, primarily because of the risks involved: water damage to adjacent parcels, animal damage to neighbors' crops, or the death of cattle through *aventacón*, or overeating. Landowners of their means are understandably reluctant to entrust these tasks fully to others when it is they who would have to pay the penalty for any damages or absorb any loss that might occur. Such hiring is periodically necessary because of the absence of household members and close kin, but the labor takes the form of assistance and does not involve any overt differentiation in the division of labor.

The majority of wage work is devoted to occasional tasks such as repairing collapsed terraces and building field walls or houses (except roofing). The wage is a substantial one and is always supplemented with food and drink, but it is still significantly less than the going rate in the lower valley. Plowing is another common form of wage work, but this is mainly practiced by smallholders, a large group of people with plows and oxen who sell their services. The wage for this specialized work is much higher, and the landowner provides alfalfa for the animals. Mayoristas, it should be noted, do not usually hire these workers because most of them have their own plows and animals.

Poor people, for their part, now derive their incomes, both in cash and in kind, from periodic work, not just for local mayoristas, but also for large landowners in the lower valley. They do not depend on continual or obligatory work for one or two families. Again, no one in the community (with the exception, under special circumstances, of certain widows) employs other people in order to rid themselves of the burden of subsistence, in the manner of a valley hacendado, whether through mink'a or through jornal. This constraint is maintained, not only by limits on the frequency of these labor exchanges, but, as we have seen, by constraints that the minoristas have imposed on the conditions under which the two kinds of work can take place.

In effect, subsistence labor and commercial activity have long been segregated into agricultural and pastoral domains, respectively. But it is social conventions, or rather social pressures, that have kept these realms discrete, by confining traditional reciprocity to food production. Smallholders have consistently demanded a wage for pastoral work and other kinds of chores; this has ensured that no one can make money directly off of labor acquired through reciprocal exchange, and that work in the commercial domain is always rewarded with some of the income to which that labor contributes.[27] At the same time, within the subsistence domain the minoristas have insisted that work always be shared and take the form of assistance, rather than labor service. Thus no one can provision himself exclusively, or even primarily, through the work of others. Again, the only exception to this pattern are certain elderly widows who have few kin and who are forced to rely on the help, whether paid or not, of others.

In both kinds of labor exchange, the operative principle is that remuneration must be made with some of the labor's ultimate product. In the case of mink'a partnerships, the reciprocation must be a substantial one that tradition has defined as equitable or fair: the usual food, drink, and the like, but also the harvest from a sizable portion of the land being worked, and, since the 1970's, a token wage for each day of work. Though some observers might feel this is not a fair return for several days of labor, it is enormous in comparison to the typical mink'a arrangement in the lower valley, as we will see.

Irrigation as the Moral Foundation of Village Life

What, some may ask, does all this have to do with irrigation? I could respond, for a start, by pointing out that conditions in the hydraulic realm are consistent with those in the domain of labor relations; that is, there are no glaring contradictions. But I would go beyond this to argue that the central idea governing reciprocity, that of people's responsibility for most of their own subsistence work, is sustained by, if not derived from, the hydraulic tradition itself. Irrigation is the cornerstone of cultivation, the only task repeated several times a year on each plot, and despite the simplicity of the mechanisms that govern it, it is a matter of considerable risk and great concern. Any households that turned the task entirely over to someone else would do so at their own peril. Some of the risks involved have already been mentioned, but there is another more fundamental one that must be considered.

The equity among water rights is central to this village's social life. Adherence to a customary arrangement based on what are said to be ancient procedures—the fixed irrigation sequence and the uniform watering technique—is by no means automatic. Huaynacotas, again, is not some kind of social utopia. People do occasionally fight over the water because it is sometimes stolen, given illegally, or otherwise taken out of turn. It is only the constant and very public vigilance of the users that guarantees continuity in practice and protects people's rights. This pervasive monitoring provides the primary deterrent against theft and inequity, and is the only check on the campos' potential for favoritism, both of which would lead to breakdown of the system if they went unrestrained.

The implications of this situation are profound: obviously a person cannot entrust the protection of his most fundamental right to his neighbor, particularly when he is "rich" and the neighbor is poor. People who have more land and use more water than others must, more so than anyone else, protect their rights personally and publicly, with a shovel in the act of irrigating. If a mayorista turned this most basic task over to wage laborers, it would be resented as behavior befitting a landlord, a transgression of sorts, and people would readily take advantage of the situation. The family would certainly become a target of theft and would probably have problems with the campo over premature termination of their watering.[28] This means that all villagers must do a substantial part of their own subsistence work if they are to maintain their rights to water. Indeed, the very legitimacy of those rights seems to depend on a personal attachment to the work and to the peasant way of life itself.

It may seem paradoxical that such a contentious reality should help to sustain a fundamental equality, one that makes cooperation between members of different strata possible, but that is evidently the case. Here it bears repeating that neither is a mayorista permitted to send a replacement to carry out the maintenance duties upon which his rights depend. The notion that certain kinds of work must be done personally, like the concepts of proportionality and equity, has become a basic moral principle in communal life.

We have seen that, despite its unusual solidarity, Huaynacotas has long been a stratified and to some extent a divided community, like most Andean villages. Its customs are therefore not merely survivals of a communal Inca past, but evolved mechanisms for allocating scarce resources and mitigating internal conflicts in a manner reasonably acceptable to everyone. After all, the largest landowners here would have to be seen, from a purely socioeconomic point of view, as nearly equivalent to any hacendado in terms of class, at least those who have estates on the puna. Yet their behavior is distinct in fundamental ways; they are accountable, as comuneros and *llaqta masis*, to the interests of the other village members.

The basic inequalities in the ownership of agricultural and pastoral land seem to have been established more than a century ago. Rather than try to eradicate them, the comuneros of Huaynacotas have instead sought to prevent them from widening, so that their own subsistence was assured and the community was preserved. They have accomplished this through a process of negotiation and confrontation governed by the notions that they all work their own land to feed themselves, that no one is above certain tasks, and that people do not subsist or enrich themselves primarily off of the labor of others. This ideology, and the specific norms and principles that express it, lie at the heart of local ethnic identity, which, according to my understanding, is manifested in a strong sense of attachment to the landscape itself and to tradition. Those norms and principles did not merely evolve as a form of resistance to, or protection from, the exploitative relations prevailing historically in the lower valley (Scott 1985, 1990), though they are significant enough as a critique of what goes on there. Rather, they are based on long-standing continuities in the hydraulic tradition, and they are sustained, quite literally, by the irrigation system itself.

FOUR

Pampamarca

Hierarchy and Inequity in a Colonized Community

The integrity of local tradition in Huaynacotas reflects the fact that no Spanish people have ever lived there, a situation that the villagers have struggled to preserve because it gives them a significant degree of autonomy in managing their own affairs. But it is not unique among the communities in the province, as many people in the lower valley seem to think. A few others have maintained this kind of independence, namely, Cahuana, Ayahuasi, and Huillac, and it is striking that the same irrigation practices seem to be found in all of them (e.g., terracing, water pooling, contiguous distribution). The pattern suggests that a single hydraulic tradition may have once prevailed throughout the entire valley, at least at the higher elevations, which was my original hunch.

It is not necessary to study all of the "autonomous" villages to test this hypothesis, which in any event cannot be confirmed on the basis of these examples alone. They are the exception today, and it is necessary to look also at the villages that have lost this kind of independence, which are the rule. The typical "indigenous" community in the valley is one where people of Spanish descent have resided as a small but dominant ethnic minority for a very long time. One such place is Pampamarca, where, for more than a century, a group of elite families has lived alongside a Quechua-speaking peasant population.[1]

The Spanish first came to Pampamarca in search of gold, establishing mines at Catatoria and Ayapata, on the puna above the pueblo, sometime during the seventeenth or early eighteenth century. Once there, they expropriated farmland and irrigation water and founded two small estates, which served as bases of operations for the mines. These oldest haciendas, called Molino and Aqo, still show traces of mining activity,[2] and there is evidence that their owners lived in the village at least part of the time. They obviously contributed to the local church, an abandoned eighteenth-century building that is large and extravagant, compared with the small chapels found in places like Huaynacotas. During this early period, there were probably only a few people, perhaps two families, and although their presence certainly must have had a great impact, it is not likely to have disrupted customary practices such as irrigation.[3] The major changes in that domain clearly came later, after the mines were exhausted in the late eighteenth century, when a new influx of outsiders began.

Two new families, the Aspilcuetas and Zanabrias—both of them relatively poor branches of the lower valley castas—acquired some of the estate property and moved into the village around the time of Peru's independence. Five others joined them by the end of the century: the Sotos from Cotahuasi, the Cornejos from Taurisma, the Cervantes from Chuquibamba, and the Bordas and Hinojosas, both from neighboring provinces in Ayacucho. The Soto family, which did not actually live in the pueblo, somehow managed to take control of most of the pasture lands on the puna and became heavily involved in the wool trade. The others seem to have been attracted by prospects created by the accompanying growth of the provincial economy. They went on to do a modest local trade in a few manufactured goods, especially alcohol from the Majes valley, and to raise cattle on a small scale. Some also bartered for wool on the puna, but since they had no herding estates and only a modest amount of farmland, the business was of minor importance.

Some of these landlords also had property in other villages, but most of them lived in Pampamarca with their wives and children for most of the year.[4] As the elite families did wherever they settled, they assumed the leadership—political, economic, even religious—of the community, largely displacing the kurakas who had governed it before. They redefined the prerogatives that went with high status, making themselves owners of a lot of land and irrigation water and becoming privileged people to be served by tenants and other dependents. They introduced alfalfa, which was essential to their livelihood, and thereby promoted the same changes in land and water use that occurred in Cotahuasi, though on a more limited scale.

The local people and the newcomers managed to coexist for a long time in an uneasy alliance. The village was able to absorb the impact of the landlords without seriously disrupting local custom mainly because of abundant water, enough of the resource to support what were in effect two ecologies of land use and two hydraulic traditions. From a social point of view, the village community is in some respects like that of Huaynacotas. But the physical space itself, and the things that people do in the process of making a living, are distinctly patterned and inscribed with a history that reveals itself to the attentive eye. One can look back into the nineteenth century and even beyond, to trace the outline of a familiar story: a tale of privatization, domination, and the coopting of local tradition, leading ultimately to resistance against the legacy of the colonial past.

*

PHOTO 3. View of the river gorge that divides the fields of Pampamarca

Located at an altitude of 3,400 meters (about 12,000 feet)—five hours' climb above Cotahuasi and the road—Pampamarca is every bit as visually striking as Huaynacotas, a vast garden that appears to hang from the huge rock face looming over it, a great amphitheater of cliffs that is apparently part of a collapsed crater. The village, although notably smaller than Huaynacotas, looks much like any other annex: a cluster of adobe houses with high patio walls, about a third of them now with roofs of corrugated tin instead of the traditional thatch. From the central plaza, which doubles as a football field, one looks eastward over terraces that descend, gradually and seemingly without a break, toward a nearby river, a major tributary of the Cotahuasi. There the land falls off abruptly, giving way to a narrow canyon about 600 meters deep. On the other side, a great green-and-yellow checkerboard of fields stretches off in the distance. Getting across this gorge is not easy, even though only a stone's throw separates the two sides. The pathway zigzags steeply down, crosses a rickety footbridge, and then climbs right back up, costing a person on foot more than half an hour.

In the late 1980's, the village comprised five elite families, numbering about forty people, and four ayllus with roughly 900 members, for a total of 157 households in all.[5] However, at least 20 percent of these people, and probably more, no longer resided there full time, having migrated to Arequipa and Lima and to lowland zones such as Camaná and the Majes valley. One of the ayllus, Qhayawa, was much larger than the others, with seventy-five families, compared with forty-two in Qocheqa, and about twenty each in Kupe and Ch'eqa.[6] Since every household now had at least one member living elsewhere, the total resident population was probably no more than 700 people, or 12 percent smaller than in 1940 (see Table 1).

Again, the ayllus are residential and kinship units that divide the population, and the "urban" space of the settlement itself, into four neighborhoods, or barrios. They are also sociopolitical groups, each of which has its own civil and religious hierarchy, or *cargo* system.[7] But these ayllus, unlike those of Huaynacotas, are above all independent hydraulic and landowning units (corporate groups), each with its own canal system and its own water sources. The names refer, not just to kin groups and neighborhoods, but to discrete sections of the village territory that straddle the canyon, with two lying on each side, as shown in Map 7. The members of the Qhayawa, Kupe, and Ch'eqa ayllus maintain secondary homes in small hamlets in these outlying areas, simply because the lands lie quite far away from the pueblo itself. Thus the population is more dispersed than Huaynacotas's. There are no traces of Andean moiety organization here, no grouping of the four ayllus into upper and lower halves, but again it is likely that these did once exist.

Although each ayllu has its own territory, members of other ayllus can and do possess land within each one. In fact, most people have property in more than one irrigation system. Because the four groups are too small to be endogamous, intermarriage between them has obviously led to a mixture of landholdings similar to the pattern in Huaynacotas, though not so extreme. The sale of land between members of different ayllus has also contributed to this process.

The village is stratified both ethnically and socioeconomically, but the pattern has changed significantly since the 1960's, when the wool trade declined and the hacienda era came to an end. During the height of that era, in the 1950's, the only large landowners were the seven elite families from the nineteenth century, the mistis, also referred to as *principales*. All of them had 6–15 hectares of land, usually in more than one property, or *fundo*. Two other Spanish families, poor by local standards and not considered landlords, had only about a hectare each. The heads of both were teachers at the village school, which was established by 1930.

Today, the minoristas or comuneros have an average of slightly less than 1 hectare (2–3 topos) of land, but most have at least the 1 topo considered neces-

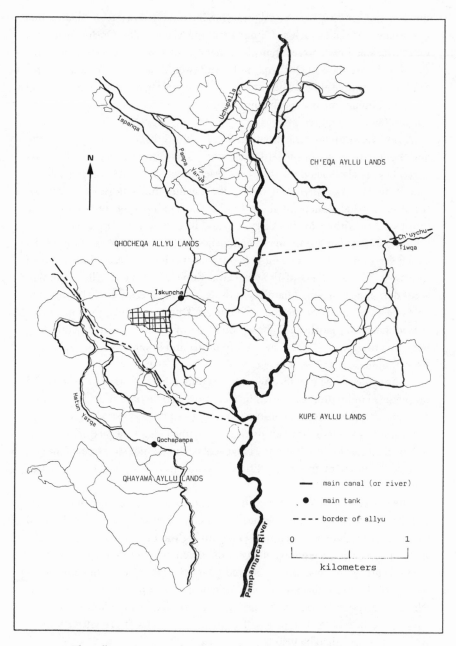

Within the map:

Uchupalla

Ispanqa

Pampa Yarqa

CH'EQA AYLLU LANDS

N

Ch'uychu
Tiwqa

QHOCHEQA ALLYU LANDS

Iskuncha

KUPE AYLLU LANDS

Hatun Yarqa

Qochapampa

QHAYAWA AYLLU LANDS

—————— main canal (or river)

● main tank

- - - - border of allyu

0   1

kilometers

Pampamarca River

MAP 7. The ayllu territories and major canals of Pampamarca

sary for survival. Very few people are without any fields at all, although the size of family holdings has declined somewhat as the population has grown. Between 1940 and 1987 the total population, both resident and nonresident, increased steadily, but only by 17 percent, a rate that for some reason was significantly slower than that exhibited by most other villages in the Andes (see Mitchell 1991a,b). The most likely explanation is heavy out-migration, both seasonal and permanent, a trend brought about in part by population growth.

Toward the end of the hacienda era, several comunero families were able to acquire additional land and in effect become mayoristas, with 2–3 hectares, although none has reached the level of the mistis. Referred to as *medianos propietarios* by other comuneros,[8] they are slowly occupying the commercial and political niche being given up by the landlords, who began leaving the pueblo after the wool economy bottomed out and agrarian reform broke up the haciendas in the lower valley. There are now only five hacendado families, which are clearly in decline. The landholdings of three have been subdivided through inheritance and sales, and the younger members of a fourth now live most of the year in Arequipa, leaving only one whose property and stature in the community are still fairly intact. Thus Pampamarca today is a community in economic, social, and even political transition.

The Irrigation System

The four canal systems service approximately 340 hectares of land, ranging in altitude from 2,700 to 3,700 meters. Most of this terrain is covered with terraces, the bulk of which are irrigated through the same water-pooling technique used in Huaynacotas. Certain areas, however, are now watered by a more recent method that requires less labor but uses a lot more water. This method, used on slopes, is associated with the destruction of terracing, a process that began when the Spanish established the first estates. These differences provide clues about the ways the indigenous hydraulic tradition has changed under their influence, not only in Pampamarca but in other local villages as well.

The largest ayllu territories, those of Qhayawa and Qocheqa, lie on the west side of the canyon. They are watered by two big springs, Ch'ewqa and Ispanqa, which emerge from the cliff that looms over the village (see Maps 7 and 8). In each case, the water is diverted into a pair of relatively short canals, the uppermost of which leads to a major tank. The flows of both springs are large and remain steady even in times of drought, a happy circumstance that Pampamarca alone enjoys in the whole of the region. They surge with the seasonal rains, then return to and maintain a normal flow no matter how little rain has fallen.[9] As a

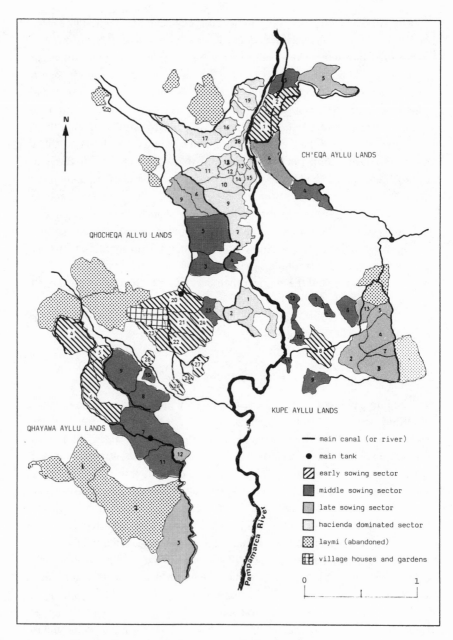

CH'EQA AYLLU LANDS

QHOCHEQA ALLYU LANDS

QHAYAWA AYLLU LANDS

KUPE AYLLU LANDS

Pampamarca River

— main canal (or river)
● main tank
▨ early sowing sector
▨ middle sowing sector
▨ late sowing sector
▨ hacienda dominated sector
▨ laymi (abandoned)
▦ village houses and gardens

0   1

MAP 8. The planting and watering sequence in Pampamarca

result, irrigation frequencies are much higher here than in other local villages, nearly optimal for agriculture. The people of Qocheqa and Qhayawa water their fields every fifteen days and every seventeen days, respectively, even during drought years. This abundance is most remarkable because it gives us a window into the past. By "opening" it, which we will do before leaving the village, we can gain insight into social dynamics that were emerging in many other communities a century or more ago, during the era of depopulation and plentiful water.

Although Kupe and Ch'eqa ayllus, on the east side of the canyon, have their own water, their irrigation systems overlap significantly. Kupe's water has always come from springs fed by Lake Huansacocha, located in the puna about 15 kilometers away. The water is delivered by a stream that becomes a long canal, called Ch'uychu, and is collected at night in a tank, T'iwqa, that lies high above the ayllu's land. Ch'eqa territory, on the other hand, gets much of its water via two very short canals, one of which leads from the Pampamarca River—an unusual situation in the valley—and the other from two small springs. The remainder, a large amount that irrigates four sectors, comes from the Ch'uychu canal. The tank water is used continuously by the people of Kupe in a fifteen-day cycle, whereas the daytime canal water goes to Ch'eqa for a period of eight days, then returns to Kupe and combines with the tank water. The result is a two-week cycle in both areas. This is roughly the same frequency as in the other ayllus, showing that these supplies too are more than adequate under normal conditions.

In contrast to the springs on the other side of the canyon, the water filtering from Lake Huansacocha fluctuates markedly with drought. Nevertheless, the ef-

KEY TO MAP 8

Qochega ayllu	*[Qochega ayllu cont.]*	*[Kupe ayllu cont.]*	*[Qhayawa ayllu cont.]*
1 Waqaya	17 Tranka	3 Anchakani	4 Kunyapampa
2 Achqa	18 Molino	4 Qutanayu	5 Qochapampa
3 Chaqchaqlla	19 Aqo	5 Payanqa	6 Ismanqa
4 Walluka	20 Iskuncha	6 Tranka	7 Qurerqa
5 Qurpa	21 Ukraya	7 Aqupacha	8 Tuntisma
6 Llank'achu	22 Achqa	8 Wampu	9 Wankallpa
7 Qochaqoyu	23 Wichuqaya	9 Malawata	10 Llansa
8 Waychanchi	24 Chawallku	10 Pukuta	
9 Allawka	25 Ch'amaqa	11 Tawina	*Ch'eqa ayllu*
10 Qhaqsi	26 Iskaymirka	12 Qhaqsi	1 Siqsinkaya
11 Pachapaki	27 Lliwana	13 Qhutqhuta	2 Qhutqhuta
12 Llanka	28 Tuwaqa		3 Lluqipata
13 Laqsa		*Qhayawa ayllu*	4 Payanqa
14 Aqupacha	*Kupe ayllu*	1 Mishka	5 Atela
15 Wanka	1 Pullqusi	2 Kantanya	6 Lawara
16 Ucupalla	2 Takapu	3 P'achataqsi	

fect on the hydraulic system was not very significant until recently because the use of the terrain fit these conditions. This situation changed when irrigation was expanded on two occasions, as we will see below. Droughts increased in frequency soon thereafter, creating a problem that had not existed before.

The sectors in the four territories vary greatly in number and size. As shown in Map 8, there are six in Ch'eqa, thirteen in Kupe, twenty-eight in Qocheqa, and ten in Qhayawa. Their size depends on the local topography, which sometimes limits the expanse over which the canals above can feasibly distribute water. In a few cases, sectors also contain a secondary spring that assists in their irrigation. There are nine of these all together, six of which have tanks, but unlike their counterparts in Huaynacotas, few are fully independent. In most cases, their water is used jointly with main water in a kind of pulsating pattern, in the following way.

The two flows are first combined to speed the watering of the area lying below the tank. Then they are used separately, with the main water sent up above, and the springwater sent down to start the next cycle in the area below. Then, when the main cycle comes around again, they are recombined to bring the watering frequency in these sectors into conformity with the one prevailing in the rest of that ayllu's system. Most of these sectors are not independent, and they fall within the jurisdictions of the ayllu water distributors, the campos.

The vast majority of sectors are intensively irrigated maize lands, or *sara chakra*, just as in Huaynacotas, with significant exceptions in the ayllu of Kupe. Pampamarca has many dry-farmed lands, here called *laymis*, which formerly produced tubers and cereal crops for each ayllu. All of these have been abandoned for agricultural use because of the persistent droughts of the 1970's–80's, except for several privately owned laymis in Kupe, which are irrigated, as some of the t'ikras of Huaynacotas used to be. When the laymis were farmed, they were managed in the same communal manner as high-altitude lands (suni lands) in other parts of the Andes (Guillet 1981; Orlove & Godoy 1986; Fuji & Tomoeda 1981). Even though they are no longer cultivated, the laymis continue to be of considerable importance as grazing areas for cattle, sheep, and goats, and as virtually the only pasture lands that belong to the ayllus today.

While taking an inventory of Kupe lands, I was puzzled when the campo described all of the higher sectors on that side of the canyon to me as laymis. He seemed to contradict himself by also saying that most of these areas were irrigated and privately owned, as I had already noted. This seemed a total confusion of terms until I realized that, like the t'ikras of Huaynacotas, laymis are irrigated if they can be reached by water and enough is available. What I had not understood is that it is not just the altitude that determines how these lands are used, but also the water supply.

The change in land use in Kupe during the last fifty years illustrates the importance of water supply. Until the early 1930's, only the maize-growing sectors below the tank could be irrigated because much of the water had been expropriated by the owner of a nearby herding estate, one not affiliated with the community. The landlord, who considered the water to be his property, would constantly interrupt the flow to irrigate his pasture on the puna. This meant that the laymi sectors could only be dry-farmed, and that irrigation was precarious at best on the maize lands down below. In 1932, however, the allyu members took legal action in Cotahuasi and managed to establish their exclusive rights to the water. This event, the first of what would be the comuneros' continuing resistance against the landlords, enabled the Kupe allyu to expand irrigation. Watering was increased in the maize-growing sectors, and five laymis were added to the cycle for the first time. A large area, originally *sara chakra*, which had evidently been abandoned during the colonial period, was added as a sixth laymi sector, called Malawata.[10]

The system was altered again in 1965, when an improvement project was carried out with materials provided by the state. The members of the two ayllus on the east side of the gorge, Ch'ega and Kupe, were able to line the Ch'uychu canal with cement in places where it leaked, greatly adding to the flow. This made it possible to increase irrigation in all the sectors, including the ones that had previously received water for the first time. Although the higher sectors are still called laymis, all of them are now worked much like maize lands: Qotanayu, Phaspa, Takapo, Tranca, and Anchakani. The fallow period has been shortened to two years, and they are no longer rotated in the traditional coordinated fashion. Each plot is now essentially privately owned, and some maize and alfalfa are grown there, so that irrigation occurs throughout most of the year. Malawata, the sector cultivated for the first time in 1932, is now truly *sara chakra* and is no longer fallowed at all. It lies at a much lower altitude than the others and has obviously been restored to its original use.

These events show that the three forms of land use so common in the Andes—laymis, watered laymis *(laymi yakuyuq)*, and *sara chakra*—define a continuum of intensification. Land use, even at high altitude, is therefore not static; people can switch from one form to another when enough water is available. Clearly, an upper limit exists beyond which this cannot be done, where some kind of fallowing regime is always necessary, but that lies high in the suni zone. Although the irrigation of fallowing lands has been reported in other communities on the western slope (Gelles 1986: 114–15), this kind of adaptive shift in land use has not, to my knowledge, been described before (but see Mayer 1985). It has probably happened in other valleys in similar situations.

The droughts that began to occur more frequently in succeeding years virtually negated the benefits of all these improvements by repeatedly stretching the water supply thin once again. The present system of distribution is less able to cope with these fluctuations than the old one, and there is a moderate shortage in drought years. During the late 1970's, an attempt was made to correct the problem by building a new canal leading from the river to the lower sectors in both ayllus. But the project, which received foreign assistance, was soon paralyzed by technical and financial problems and will probably never be completed.

The water supplies on the other side of the canyon, in Qocheqa and Qhayawa, are abundant and remarkably stable for two reasons: first, the springs originating in the mountain of Wit'u evidently come from "fossil" groundwater and are not directly dependent on rainfall; and second, the springs lie close by and the main canals are short, only 3–4 kilometers long, so that they do not allow much filtration and evaporation. These systems include no irrigated fallowing lands; all sectors are maize lands because they are accessible to water and there is enough to go around. The fallowing lands here, in Qocheqa and Qhayawa, are located higher up the mountainside, out of reach of any major springs, like the non-irrigated t'ikras of Huaynacotas. All of them are now used only for herding.

Two improvements were made in these systems in the twentieth century. Parts of Ispanqa, Qocheqa's main canal, were lined in an intermittent project that began in the late 1930's; and the tank and the lower part of Ch'eqa, one of Qhayawa's main canals, were improved in the 1950's. These efforts gradually increased the supply in both areas by fixing leaky sections, which were eventually lined with cement, but they did not lead to any major intensification, other than slightly faster cycles in the two areas. Here, just as in the other ayllus, people irrigate more than twice as often as in Huaynacotas.

Hierarchy and Inequity in Water Use

As in Huaynacotas, the campos who oversee the four ayllus' water systems normally volunteer for the job and are appointed with the approval of the members. The campo position used to be one of the most important posts in the civil-religious hierarchy around which ayllu life was centered. The office could only be held by an elderly man who knew the system well and who commanded respect, as in Huaynacotas. But several factors have since caused the office to lose some of its appeal and prestige, including increasing out-migration (both seasonal and permanent), advancing education, and a decline in the central importance of agriculture with the growth of cash-earning activities. This trend is part of a more general decline in *cargo* participation within the village. Today, the post is usually held by young men, who often choose it in lieu of the otherwise obligatory military service. This change in the nature of the position has contributed to an erosion of the campos' authority.

The campos' responsibilities are essentially the same as in Huaynacotas: storing the water, releasing it at dawn, dividing it. The distribution systems are more complicated, though, in that more factors interact to govern the movement of water within and between sectors. In some cases, microclimatic variation within the ayllu territories creates a more complex planting sequence, so that the order in which sectors are irrigated is less strictly determined by altitude. At the intrasector level, considerations other than conservation, such as the status and prestige of the landowner, determine the sequence of allotment. It is hardly surprising that in Pampamarca, a colonized community, water distribution is hierarchical, the first of many basic contrasts with the Huaynacotas system.

DISTRIBUTION BETWEEN SECTORS

Again, the order in which sectors are irrigated depends on the order in which they are planted. In each of the four canal systems, field preparation and sowing start the cycle, which is then repeated numerous times until the rains begin. But here the community's lands are oriented north-south, and this, along with the convoluted terrain, produces marked differences in exposure to the sun and wind. The planting cycle is attuned to these conditions and divided accordingly into three short phases, each covering about ten days: *ñawpa tarpuy*, or early sowing, *chawpi tarpuy*, middle sowing, and *qhepa tarpuy*, late sowing.

These phases are based on the time it takes for maize plants to sprout in each sector, but the whole sequence takes place in about half the time that it does in Huaynacotas, finishing by the end of September. Crops other than maize—potatoes and other tubers, barley, and wheat—can be sown any time thereafter, so that the late planting phase theoretically extends on into the year. The laymis in Kupe are planted during this period, being phased in at the appropriate point in the cycle, and the dry-farmed lands were formerly sown last of all, in late December.

If maize plants sprout in the normal eight to twelve days throughout the canal system, then the "best" lands are the first to be sown. Certain fields have priority because they lie close to the pueblo and the hamlets and are therefore the most easily tended and guarded. They receive the most fertilizer (dung) and the greatest investment of labor, and are the most productive. Such fields are the earliest ones sown in Qocheqa ayllu, where household gardens and pampas adjacent to the village itself are first in the order. This is also true in Kupe, where west-facing lands near the bottom of the canyon have priority. In both cases, the next-lowest sectors are then planted, and the schedule proceeds systematically upward, similar to the pattern in parts of Huaynacotas. Kupe ayllu's irrigated laymis are planted during the middle or late phase if the crop is maize or alfalfa, rather than potatoes or other tubers. Otherwise they are added later on, in December, as the cycle proceeds, just as the t'ikras were in Huaynacotas.

In areas where there is limited sun exposure, the sprouting of maize can take up to twenty days. In these cases, the sequence is modified by putting the sectors first in order, to give them a head start and protect them from frosts coming at the end of the year. This is true in Qhayawa, where the first sectors planted are the higher, colder ones. In Ch'eqa, certain sectors near the bottom of the canyon, which are cold because they lie in shadow much of the day, are planted first, followed by the others in a contiguous sequence. This parallels the procedure in K'uchqocha in Huaynacotas, where the more frost-prone sectors are sown first. Maize germination is more uniform in Huaynacotas, however, because sun exposure is less variable; there, frost vulnerability due to wind conditions determines how the altitudinal sequence is modified.

The watering cycle of Qhayawa ayllu is anomalous and seems inverted: it begins at the top and moves down. But that is actually the order found in most other parts of the Andes (see Mitchell 1976). The colder upper sectors are the first to be sown, followed by the well-sunned lands in the middle of the territory, and the warmest lands of all, which lie well below the others, come last. Since maize plants in this last zone sprout and develop faster than anywhere else, one might expect them to be planted sooner, perhaps in the middle of the order.

In fact, this large sector is sown even earlier, in July, shortly after the harvest. This is the only place in Pampamarca where double-cropping is possible. For that reason, the sector is called Miska, a term referring to lands sown early because of precocious crop development (Beyersdorff 1984: 62). Provided that fast-maturing plants like broad beans, garden vegetables, potatoes, or barley are planted, one crop can be grown between July and November, and another between December and June. Nonetheless, much of the sector is actually planted in maize, which yields only a single crop, but one that comes long before the main harvest at a time when household food reserves are low. All of this is possible because Miska is a very steep sector at low altitude that faces the prevailing winds and avoids frosts.

In both the territories on the west side of the canyon, water distribution is complicated by the fact that, as in Huaynacotas, their main tanks are located within the cultivated area, so that they divide the irrigation system into upper and lower parts. These areas can be watered separately, one with the daytime canal flow and the other with the water stored at night in the tank, as we saw in Huaynacotas. Or the two flows can be used together to water the lower sectors as quickly as possible, then separated into two slower cycles, and then later re-combined, which is the case in Qhayawa. A third alternative occurs in Qocheqa ayllu, where the lower sectors are sown first. Here the two flows are combined to speed the early planting as much as possible, after which the use of the tank is interrupted. All of the water then passes up above during the middle and late phases, so that the sectors there can be finished quickly by irrigating both day and night. This entire cycle takes only sixteen days, and the water even lies out of use for a short period thereafter because maize plants should not be watered again until almost a month has passed. After that, the tank is refilled, and the two-week sequence is repeated continuously. This cycle takes roughly the same amount of time we saw in Kupe and Qhayawa (fifteen and seventeen days).

Note that Ch'eqa, Qhayawa, and Qocheqa each have a second canal that leads from another major source, which complicates their structure (see Map 7). In the first two instances, the canal serves several sectors covering a large ex-panse of 10–20 hectares. All three canals produce very large flows, but in Ch'eqa and Qhayawa the range over which the flows can be diverted is restricted by the topography, so that a super-abundance is created within a limited area. Conse-quently, the water does not have to be stored and can be used without supervi-sion. The campo does exercise his authority in these areas to intervene in dis-putes and punish infractions, but he does not physically control the water. Ch'eqa's short canal brings water from the river; Qhayawa's brings it from the same spring that supplies the other main canal, whose volume is greater than one canal can handle. In both cases, the water runs continuously, so that it can be used both day and night. Here it is possible to irrigate more often than in the other sectors, but in practice people rarely do so more than twice a month, roughly the same frequency that prevails elsewhere. Under normal conditions, this is considered ideal for plant growth, not only in Pampamarca but in the rest of the valley as well.

ESTATE AND COMMUNAL WATER

Qocheqa ayllu is distinctive, one of only two places in Pampamarca where major hacienda properties lie within an area controlled by a campo. And here we see the typical hierarchical arrangement. By custom, estate lands that are planted in food crops are watered first, but the alfalfa fields come at the end of

the order so as to give priority to the campesinos' subsistence plots. Traditionally, the landlords had some of their best pasture fields in these sectors, and they
had separate days of water that came at the end of the cycle. This arrangement
apparently dates back to the late eighteenth or early nineteenth century, when
these estates were founded, but it conforms to a pattern that was widely instituted in the highlands during the colonial period (Villanueva & Sherbondy
1979: ix–x). Although it may have been established in compliance with colonial
decrees, its benefits for the landlords are obvious. Since they needed the labor
of ayllu members on their lands, they could hardly afford to shunt the comuneros aside altogether when they acquired property in community territory.
Instead, they placed themselves at the head of the regular cycle, claiming the
first few days of water as theirs, regardless of how much land they actually had
in production. They then took what was left over after crop irrigation for their
pasture and livestock.

Today only one area in Pampamarca is fully autonomous in water use, and
this is where some of the biggest hacienda properties are found. Four sectors in
the northern part of Qocheqa territory—Uchupalla, Tranca, Molino, and
Aqo—have an independent supply that runs from the ayllu's main springs
above and passes downward through a ravine. These areas were the original
mining estates of the colonial period. In all four sectors, water use is unsupervised because it is privately owned. Each landlord uses all the water on specific
days of the week that are his by long-standing customary arrangements, which
is to say, each has de facto private rights (Schlager & Ostrom 1992). This situation does not create any conflict because the supply is adequate for the landlords' needs, and campesinos do not have any land in these areas. The estates
thus form an entirely separate irrigation system.

For a long time, the nearby canal of Pampa Yarqa was used in a similar manner, even though it is one of Qocheqa's main canals and serves a huge area of
twelve sectors covering roughly 50 hectares. A lot of hacienda properties are
found there, including many alfalfa fields, but members of the ayllu have land
there too. The arrangement that was worked out for sharing this water has
changed in recent times, at the comuneros' insistence, and is worth discussing
in some detail.

Originally, the campo had no authority in this area. Again, the water was
abundant relative to the area served—seven to nine people could irrigate at the
same time—and its use was not supervised. Except for the smaller areas noted
above, this is the only major portion of any of the ayllu territories that had an
"acephalous," or first-come, first-served, type of organization. Traditionally, the
mistis were essentially the sole owners of this water, having simply pronounced

themselves as such when they founded their estates. By custom, they alternated with the ayllu members on a weekly basis, taking however much they wanted the first week, but they often had their fields watered only in the daytime and allowed the comuneros to use whatever was left when they were finished. This left the comuneros with two choices: to irrigate at night or to await their turn. As it worked out, during the week that they were supposedly free to water their fields in the daytime, they had to put up with frequent interruptions because the landlords would often take the water whenever they cared to, especially for their alfalfa. Although there was more than enough to go around, this was a big inconvenience because ayllu members could not count on a regular time for their watering, as they could in other areas.

The problem was alleviated in 1954, when an extraordinary thing happened. The comuneros confronted the landlords, refusing to work for them unless a distributor was appointed and a regular cycle—a *mita* or *turno*—was established. The landlords acceded to these demands, but the successful confrontation was something of a Pyrrhic victory, since the landlords' privileges were institutionalized in the process. A campo was appointed, and the same arrangement was set up as in other parts of Qocheqa territory. The estate properties remained at the head of the order, during the first week of the irrigation cycle, with each landlord having his own day of water, but only crop fields could be watered at that time. During the next week, the campo gave the comuneros water in a standard sequence, after which the flow was the landlords' again for several days for their alfalfa. When the food crops needed moisture again, the cycle was renewed; and the whole process took roughly twenty days.

Interruptions by the hacendados reportedly continued much as before, but order was at least established among the comuneros, who gained a degree of stability and security in their rights. Previously, when their use of the water had been unsupervised and it had been catch as catch can, there had apparently been a lot of conflict because they habitually interrupted each other. This system is still in operation today, even though the state theoretically became the owner of all of Peru's water in the agrarian reform of 1969.

The "acephalous" kind of distribution system now exists in Pampamarca in only one context: where the topography makes it impossible for water to be distributed over its full potential range, so that there is a great abundance in a limited area. Thus it occurs only in unusual situations where the normal condition, that of a supply adequate for existing conditions, is not just lessened but completely relaxed. Were this regime to be imposed in other areas, it would immediately lead to scarcity and conflict even in their well-endowed systems. The water supplies of Pampamarca are by nature unusually stable, but in most cases their adequacy is a technological and social achievement, one that is dependent on the cooperation of the users and, most of all, on the management and authority of the campo.

DISTRIBUTION WITHIN SECTORS

One of the most striking differences between the traditions of Huaynacotas and Pampamarca is the way water is distributed to individual parcels. Here it is the social structure that determines the order, rather than the lay of the agricultural land. Within each sector, water is given to households, not fields, in a hierarchical order based mainly on civil and religious service to the community in the well-known *cargo* system. Households are then free to distribute water to their plots in any order they like. This is a feature of all of the ayllu sectors, not just those where the mistis have land.

Within each sector, the landlords, if any, come first in the order, each having his own day of water at the beginning of the cycle. Otherwise, the campo gives priority to users in descending order through the status hierarchy, beginning with the man who has served the most *cargos* and financed several fiestas. New households headed by young men who have not yet begun community service are put toward the end of the order, and the few mature men who have never participated come last of all. These latter individuals are viewed with some contempt by the other ayllu members, and it sometimes happens that they are even skipped in the order, although this is rare.

The ranking is not formal or precise, but rather is subject to the campo's interpretation. Everyone in each ayllu knows who has held the most important posts and has a general idea of how much a person has contributed altogether in his or her lifetime. Nonetheless, because several people usually occupy roughly the same position, and no written list of the ranking exists, the campo simply follows the order as he perceives it. This naturally means that people try to influence his decisions, since he can and does use this discretion to favor some individuals by putting them before others.

Nevertheless, the custom is simply a manner of paying respect to those who are thought to have earned it, and it does not affect anyone's right to water. Regardless of the specific order, every landowner in a given sector receives his share during each cycle of the system, so that the frequency of irrigation is uniform, just as in Huaynacotas. Distribution is thus hierarchical in practice and in symbolic terms, but egalitarian in principle and effect, at least among comuneros. The odd act of discrimination against unranked members is strictly symbolic and never jeopardizes their welfare, since they always receive water once they protest.

This hierarchical pattern in irrigation, which has been noted in several other parts of the highlands (Gelles 1986: 123–24; Mayer & Fonseca 1979: 29; Mayer 1985: 63; Montoya et al. 1979: 85), might easily be ascribed to the influence that the landlords have exerted on the community during more than a century of living there. After all, they are the village leaders and the top members of the status hierarchy; in sponsoring religious fiestas, they set the standards by which others are judged. Indeed, since they claimed first place in the distribution order, probably when they arrived, one might be led to think that they imposed or somehow created this kind of system in the ayllus. Unlikely as it may seem, however, it appears that, like the contiguous system of Huaynacotas, this tradition has prehispanic roots. The Inca system of water management was evidently a dual one, where the rules and principles of use depended to some extent on the state of the water supply. At times when the supply was plentiful, or perhaps in places where water was always plentiful, as in Pampamarca, some kind of hierarchical system was probably originally in place, as we will eventually see.

From a hydraulic point of view, the most important feature of this kind of arrangement is that, because plots are not watered in contiguous order, a certain amount of water is wasted through greater filtration, but unless the sector is a large one of, say, more than 10 hectares, the quantity is probably fairly small. In any case, no one is concerned about the waste because it is customary, and because the supply is usually adequate in all the ayllu territories. Another important feature is the system's flexibility. Because of absences and time conflicts, the order in which households ask for and receive water often varies between cycles. As a result, the exact sequence must be determined and communicated to the sector members each time. This is done in small meetings called *reginas*, which are held at dawn on Sundays and Thursdays at some designated site, such as a tank. There the campo publicly announces the order for water use. In principle, anyone who is not present will be put last in the order, or perhaps even miss his turn. In practice, however, a high-ranked person will be accommodated if he does not attend the meeting and cannot irrigate at the designated time. Typically, it is the low-ranked people who must press their demands on the campo and take their share when it is granted. This is the most common kind of favoritism in irrigation.

The regina is a clear expression of the differences between the Huaynacotas and Pampamarca systems. In Huaynacotas, as we saw, no formal meeting is necessary because the distribution sequence is fixed; the campo simply reminds upcoming users that the water is about to pass to their canal or section thereof by passing the word the night before, not necessarily even in person. In that case, a scarce and precarious supply requires a fixed schedule, about which communication can therefore be rather casual. In Pampamarca, by contrast, an ample and stable supply allows a more flexible and less conservative schedule, but one that requires a more rigid mode of communication.

Finally, because shares are given to households, rather than to adjacent fields, irrigation does not have the transparency that the Huaynacotas system has. A user often has only a vague idea of where the water should be when he or she is not using it.[11] This feature, and the obvious problem that it creates for the detection and punishment of infractions, will be discussed later, when we look at problems that have recently emerged among ayllu members over water use.

Despite all of these basic differences, the rules that govern water use are much the same here as in Huaynacotas, at least for ayllu members: all must prepare their fields for irrigation, must participate fully in maintenance work, and must not take water out of turn. People's rights are also much the same: the right to one share of water during each distribution cycle at the same frequency as all other ayllu members. The landlords, of course, simply considered themselves to be exempt from some of the rules until recently. Another issue, however, is more troublesome, that of proportionality among water shares.

TERRACE DESTRUCTION AND CHANGES
IN WATER USE

As in Huaynacotas, flat terraces, or *andenes,* cover most of the local landscape, and they are generally watered by the atu pooling method. The only difference worthy of note is that the atus here are shallower, typically built to a height of only 15–20 centimeters, so that they hold less water, as one would expect given the adequacy, even abundance, of the resource and the higher frequency of irrigation. The amount accumulated—which again is directly proportional to plot size, creating a basic equity among the rights of people who use the technique—is sufficient to keep the subsoil humid for three weeks, the longest time that ever passes between waterings.

Again, new terraces are rarely built, but they have to be constantly maintained and repaired. The construction technique as shown to me was precisely the same as in Huaynacotas and needs no further discussion. It is the exceptions in the landscaping and irrigating tradition that are of interest. In a small number of sectors, a different watering method is used, one that, at the time that I did my fieldwork, was apparently not to be found in Huaynacotas. Locally known as *qhosqay,* it differs markedly from the more prevalent one, referred to as *qarpay.* An identical procedure has been described in many other communities in the highlands (Fonseca Martel 1983: 64; Mayer & Fonseca 1979: 27; Guil-

let 1987: 14–15, 1992: 58–59), but I doubted for a long time that it was prehispanic, native to this region or any other part of the Andes.

I know now, years after my fieldwork and even years after writing the first
version of this book (Trawick 1994b), that it is prehispanic; indeed, it almost
certainly predates the pooling method. It is much simpler to carry out, involves
less labor, and does not require the constant leveling of the landscape. I am sure
that it even predates terracing, which after all is a sophisticated, labor-intensive
technology. However, like so many other basic elements of Andean life, qhosqay
was appropriated by the landlords during the colonial period and was thereby
fundamentally altered or distorted in terms of its functional significance. This
is a theme to which we will return again and again in the chapters that follow,
but it is important here to explain exactly what I mean.

Qhosqay involves simply releasing water at the top of a series of terraces and
allowing gravity to draw it over the surfaces below, including the walls where it
spills over from one plot to the next. No scratch canals or other structures are
built to direct the water, except for a single horizontal canal running across the
top of each *anden* (terrace). The irrigator simply uses a shovel to open breaches
in the canal wall and to unclog any areas of soil that become blocked down below. When properly done, it takes about three hours for the water to saturate
the surface and subsoil of 1 topo of land, but that of course depends on the volume and velocity of the water. The larger and faster the flow, the less effective
the technique is and the longer one must irrigate, a process that has no definite
or obvious endpoint.

This technique, which I call the top-down or inundation method, and which
is essentially a matter of slowly washing the soil, has the obvious advantage of requiring less labor than the atu method; it can be done reasonably well by a single
person working alone. Once water is flowing over the whole parcel, the irrigator
can even leave it for a while and attend to other tasks, such as guarding against
canal blockage and water theft higher upslope. A certain amount of water is inevitably wasted, but, at least when it is used on terraces, the campo will usually
try to minimize this by cutting each allotment in half and having two people irrigate at the same time, thereby preventing the water from rushing too rapidly
and causing serious erosion. Essentially the same procedure is used on ordinary
maize terraces at the beginning of the year in preparation for planting, although
that is referred to as *phaspay*, meaning a light or superficial watering. Phaspay is
also practiced in Huaynacotas and in fact begins the main watering cycle.

The comuneros practice the top-down method on only a small minority of
their maize and other crop fields, whereas the landlords use it on nearly all of
theirs. Pampamarca, it should be noted, is not the only local village where the

method is used, nor is it the only one where we find this Quechua name. Locally, the verb qhosqay means "to release water from the top of a field to the
bottom." But, significantly, in the Cusco region, immediately to the east,
qhosqay refers to something else, seemingly contradictory, which may indicate
where and how the technique originated. According to Margot Beyersdorff
(1984: 93), there the verb qhosqay means "to sow in dry-farmed lands," and the
noun *qhosqa* refers to "non-irrigated lands and/or the late sowing thereof" (also
see Lira 1970: 191). One might expect, therefore, the method to be used on fallowing lands that are irrigated, like the t'ikras of Huaynacotas, and that is indeed the case here.

Interestingly, the only such lands in Pampamarca are the ones in Kupe that
received water for the first time after the court action in 1932. Qhosqay is used
predominantly, though not exclusively, in these sectors. The reason is simple:
most of the plots are not terraced in the same manner as other areas under intensive irrigation. They have sometimes been leveled slightly, flattened at the
extreme upper and lower ends, and given retaining walls, but minimal work
was invested in them, and most were left with a steep slope in the middle, extending over most of the surface. They are identical to features that, in other
parts of the highlands, have been called "crude terraces" or "semi-terraces"
(Mayer & Fonseca 1979: 21–23; Brush 1977a), and generally accepted as components of the original indigenous technology. They cannot be watered through
the pooling method without investing a considerable amount of labor in landscaping.

Taking this into account, as well as the fact that the top-down method did
not seem to be a part of the tradition in Huaynacotas, I thought at first that
qhosqay was an entirely new technique, adopted when these lands were put
back under irrigation after a long period of abandonment during the colonial
period. I now know that it is these eroded and sloped terraces that are new, the
semi-terrraces, not the watering technique, since the method is in fact used in
certain circumstances in Huaynacotas, as we will see below. The sloped landforms on which it is carried out have changed the very nature of the practice,
however, one that corresponds closely with the way the landlords use it. It has
become much more wasteful and less well controlled when used on these
sloped surfaces, which are not prehispanic but rather colonial and post-colonial
features.

Besides the etymology of the term qhosqa itself, there are several reasons
why I think this is the case. First of all, the laymi fallowing lands on the other
side of the canyon, in Qhayawa and Qocheqa, which have never had water and
now lie out of use, are not in the same condition. The terraces are fairly flat and

virtually identical to ordinary maize terraces, despite the effects of erosion and lack of maintenance for the last few decades. They do sometimes have slightly more of a slope than ordinary andenes, and this is in fact true of most dry-farmed lands in the valley that have recently been abandoned. But other areas that have clearly lain abandoned for a much longer period, ever since the population collapse, are severely eroded and have the same slumped, sloped profile as the laymis in Kupe. This is true throughout the valley in the abandoned areas previously described. It seems unlikely that less labor was originally invested in the Kupe lands, long before the Spanish arrived, than in those of the other ayllus, especially if they were irrigated in prehispanic times, which they clearly were because they lie within the Kupe canal network. A long period of abandonment in the past seems a much more plausible explanation for the difference.

Second, the ayllus of Kupe and Ch'eqa have grown very little during the last two centuries, and even today they have only about twenty families each. These kin groups have had reason historically to put abandoned lands back into production, like everyone else, but with so little labor to invest in the effort, they have also had reason to do that more slowly and even in a different way. This probably explains why a puna hacienda owner was able to expropriate much of their water during the late nineteenth century: much of it must have gone unused, along with the land, for many years. We have seen that Malawata, one of Kupe's prime maize-growing sectors, was not returned to cultivation until the lost water was regained in 1932. It therefore seems likely that at least some of the laymi sectors had lain out of use because of depopulation for a very long time.

Third, note that the irrigated laymis in Huaynacotas—the t'ikras—are generally quite level. This characteristic seemed conclusive to me for a long time, even though the lands had been abandoned for twenty years and I had never had a chance to see them irrigated. I simply assumed that they were watered in the same way as other terraces, by the pooling method, and I was told this was true when I asked. But I have since learned, on my return trips a decade later, that the answer to my question should have been no. They were instead irrigated through a procedure identical to qhosqay, although there it is simply called phasphay, the same light irrigation used at the beginning of the year on ordinary maize terraces. Formerly, the terraces were irrigated once for planting in this way, to give tuber crops a head start before the rains began. But the campo would cut the water flow in half, just as in Pampamarca. And any pooling structures, if used at all, were quite shallow and served mainly to keep the water from spilling over the terrace edge.

The use of qhosqay on the sloped terrain of Kupe ayllu has changed the technique for the worse, introducing an element of waste and inequity in water use that apparently did not exist before. When used on ordinary maize terraces, as it is in a few sectors belonging to the other ayllus, qhosqay is a light and superficial irrigation, identical to phasphay. But here in Kupe the water is allowed to rush over the surface with little control over either the flow, the amount of time that plots are irrigated, or the amount of water used, all of which would be difficult because the "semi-terraces" are quite large and the slopes are steep. What this means deserves emphasis: semi-terraces and this kind of wasteful slope irrigation, features that are found closely associated in many other parts of the sierra, are probably not original components of the local technology, but rather products of land abandonment, erosion, and, ultimately, population collapse. Here, at least, they seem to be of relatively recent origin.

Finally, note that some parcels in the Kupe laymi sectors have been thoroughly leveled and are watered using the atu technique. These plots are located mainly in the steeper areas, and they are surrounded by sloped plots irrigated in the other manner. Yet one also finds some rather level terraces that are irrigated from the top down. This mixed pattern, I think—mixed in terms of both landscaping and watering technique—reflects the fact that certain families invested more work in reclaiming abandoned land and landscaping than others, so that they were able to continue to use the more water-saving technique. But the predominance of qhosqay in these sectors suggests that because of the abandonment, erosion, and a continuing scarcity of labor in that allyu, the newer method has largely displaced the traditional one and the landforms associated with it. Again, one can see the history in the landscape itself.

As for the landlords, they clearly adopted qhosqay, carelessly and without the necessary controls, in places and contexts where it was not originally practiced. The main reason is simple: long ago they began to destroy the terraces on their properties, replacing them with *potreros* or *canchones*, the large sloped alfalfa fields (corral-fields) that are typical of the hacienda landscape (see Montoya et al. 1979: 77–79; and Mayer & Fonseca 1979: 29–30). Because of their size and slope, these fields can only be watered by the top-down method. In some cases, however, the big terraces on the haciendas have been left intact; yet these too are irrigated in the same manner. In contrast, adjacent ayllu lands, which also remain in their original leveled condition, are watered in the other way. This, I think, clearly indicates that qhosqay was not the method originally used in the areas where the estates were established. It is obviously something new, which has displaced something older.

The rebuilt fields cannot be watered in any other way, but again, it is striking that no effort is made to curtail the amount of water used on them. With no campo to control the use, the landlords simply have their workers open the canal gates and flood the fields, one at a time, which usually results in a large buildup of water at the lower end of each parcel. This water is sometimes drawn off to another field farther downslope, but usually it is just allowed to escape into the canal system as waste. Soil erosion does take place, especially when the fields are sown in food crops rather than alfalfa, yet the estate owners are as unconcerned about this as they are about the lost water.

Because the top-down method does not allow the water to be pooled on the surface and accumulate, as in the atu technique, it encourages users to prolong irrigation, often quite excessively, to ensure that the soil is deeply saturated. This variant of the practice is sometimes called qhosqay, but it is clearly a Spanish way of doing things. Although I cannot offer any proof of this hypothesis, I think that the landlords were the first to use the method in this way, without the necessary precautions— that they introduced it, and that ayllu members later adopted it in areas where they found it practicable, rather than the reverse.

The very fact that this technique is used exclusively on the haciendas but on only a small (though growing) percentage of comunero land indicates where this version of the practice originated, where it spread the fastest, and where it has been adopted in recent times. Its use is clearly linked with the destruction of terracing and the rebuilding of slopes, a process that has been promoted by two agents: the estate owners themselves and the erosion that has come with the passing of time. Today, one sees it used mainly in areas where these two factors have been most at work, but the hacendados were obviously rebuilding fields and watering them this way long before the people of Kupe put their abandoned lands back into production. In any case, it bears repeating that the technique seems to have emerged and spread toward the end of the era of depopulation, when water was even more plentiful than today, and labor was more scarce.

Although seemingly mundane, the emergence of top-down irrigation was a significant event in the history of Pampamarca and most other villages in the Cotahuasi valley. As a method that uses much more water than the bottom-up technique, it had the capacity, not only to waste a lot and reduce the available supply, but to destroy the proportionality that is so central to the tradition in Huaynacotas and other similar communities. Because it requires less work, it must have been appealing in an era when labor was still scarce, and when comuneros were becoming involved in cash-earning activities outside the community. For a long time before that, this advantage was probably outweighed by its many drawbacks. In recent years, however, the method has spread, along with the practice of tearing down terraces, to some extent into a few of the other maize-growing sectors within the ayllu territories. This change reflects a widespread trend that began much earlier in other parts of the valley, one that in many cases has resulted in the virtual elimination of the more water-saving technique.

Here, just as elsewhere, the shift is associated with alfalfa production and the destruction of terraces, but a small segment of the peasant population is mainly responsible for it, namely, the *medianos propietarios*. These men, who are more heavily involved in the cattle trade than most village members, have recently acquired new lands by various means, and they are slowly moving into a dominant position as the landlords leave the community. In many ways, these ayllu members have begun to conduct themselves like hacendados, particularly with regard to water. Their use of top-down irrigation is just one of several practices that now distinguish them from their neighbors, as we will see below. Fortunately, the effects of these changes have not yet become so drastic as to seriously disrupt the traditional system of distribution, and probably will not for some time. But they are causing problems that, by all indications, did not exist in the ayllus before.

Adapting to Drought

Droughts are coped with in an unusual way in Pampamarca, simply because the water flows remain stable despite the reduced rainfall. Of course, precipitation is just as vital to crop development here as anywhere else, and it must be replaced so far as possible. But since most of the springs do not decline in flow, this can be done more effectively than in Huaynacotas and other villages in the valley.

Once it becomes obvious that a serious situation has developed, the campos call a meeting of all the users and recommend that emergency measures be implemented. Upon approval, the procedures immediately go into effect. With regard to distribution, only one adjustment is made: the irrigation of alfalfa plots is suspended until about a month before the harvest, so that food crops can receive all of the water. Just as in Huaynacotas, the amount of alfalfa grown by ayllu members is relatively small, accounting for perhaps 10–15 percent of the land, but production began to increase in 1960, when cattle sales became a more important source of income and seasonal wage work declined, and it has grown slowly ever since.[12]

Theoretically, the landlords are also subject to this restriction where their land lies in an area under the campo's authority. But until recent years, most of them continued to do what they liked with their "private" water.[13] Thus it was largely up to the comuneros to absorb the impact of droughts. Today, the landlords tend to be more cooperative, but they usually ask for, and get, one watering for their alfalfa during a dry spell.

The most important adjustment to drought occurs in the realm of technique: atus are only filled about halfway, so that the amount of water consumed in each cycle is reduced. This procedure was reportedly tried in Huaynacotas, but never worked very well. There, however, the objective was to maintain the frequency of irrigation and prevent it from declining any further. In Pampamarca, the goal is to speed up the cycle so that everyone can water more often.

The campos here do not have to struggle to get people to cooperate, as their counterpart in Huaynacotas did. There, the system is over-extended even under normal conditions. During droughts, people had to be watched, and to watch each other, to ensure that all complied when this kind of adjustment was attempted.[14] Pampamarquinos know that the lighter irrigation will be effective based on past experience, because the flow of water will not dwindle. Qocheqa and Qhayawa ayllus reduce the mita at these times from every sixteen or seventeen days to every eight or nine days.

The same measures are implemented by Kupe and Ch'eqa, but on their lands the cycle eventually stretches out to about a month because the water supply is vulnerable and continues to decline. Also, several sectors are laymis irrigated by the top-down method, which cannot easily be adjusted. Nevertheless, this frequency is still much higher than what prevails in most other villages in the valley, even during normal years. In general, Pampamarca remains the least affected of all local communities by drought, despite the loss of land and water to the estates and all the changes in practice that I have outlined here. This does not mean, of course, that the impact of drought is eliminated altogether. Irrigation can never fully replace daily precipitation, and the harvest is always reduced substantially when the rains fail.

Canal Cleaning and Ritual in a Context of Domination

The campos are responsible for directing the yearly cleaning of the canals and tanks, which here too happens during the festival of Yarqha Aspiy. This fiesta, held on three consecutive days in late August, is one of the most important events of the year, but it does not coincide precisely with a saint's day celebration. The four officials coordinate their planning so that each ayllu's canal cleaning and the associated rituals will occur in sequence.

In many Andean communities, the primary canals are maintained in sections called *suyus*, each of which is worked by a separate group under the direction of a leader or *capitán*. In Pampamarca, the water users in each ayllu ter-

ritory, both members and nonmembers, pitch in together in a more spontaneous manner. Most of the primary canals are fairly short, and work parties
leapfrog past one another in a competitive sprint until the job is finished. The
secondary canals are cleaned in smaller assigned groups.

Everyone participates in Yarqha Aspiy except the estate owners. Just as in
Huaynacotas, the event is primarily a men's affair, and women generally do not
participate in the work itself. Women who have no male head-of-household
available to fulfill the obligation will usually hire someone or have a male relative do it for them. Of course, they make the crucial contribution of cooking
and serving all the food for the big event. Attendance is noted in an opening assembly, so that families can later be fined for nonparticipation. In all the ayllu
sectors, including Kupe's and Cheqa's, where the water comes from quite far
away, the entire canal cleaning is accomplished in a single day. There, however,
the two ayllus combine to clean the upper part of the system, that is, the stream
and the portion of its course that is canalized, as well as the tank, before dividing into separate groups to clean the main canal within their own territory.

The campos are responsible for financing much of the celebration. And it is
they who, in a ritual called *t'inkachiy*, must ask the main spring (*pukyu*) to
continue supplying water to the people whose lives depend on it. Accompanied
by other ayllu officials and a three-piece band that they must hire and pay for,
they climb to the head of the main canal, where they chant a ritual prayer as
they make a burnt offering, called a *q'osnichiy* or *pago*, of llama fat, coca, in-
cense, maize of three colors, and numerous other items in a prepared bundle.[15]
They also pour liquor and chicha into the spring. The campo must then drink
a huge portion of aguardiente from a special cup called a *q'ero*, which he passes
to the other members of the party. The drinking continues until the participants have consumed all of the alcohol brought for this purpose, including two
or three large urns of chicha, which the campo has prepared and brought to the
spot about a month beforehand. The party then descends the canal to the village, stopping along the way at the gates of secondary canals (*tomas*), where
more drinking and benedictions take place. This is almost precisely the same
ritual carried out in Huaynacotas.

Today the landlords, who have always felt themselves exempt from the task
of canal maintenance, do at least make the gesture of contributing bottles of alcohol or sending along a hired wage laborer, a *peón*, to work in their place. They
did not feel obligated to do so during the height of the hacienda era. The
change arose out of the challenge to hacendado power and authority mounted
by the people of Pampa Yarqha, among others, beginning in the 1950's, which
soon culminated in the appointing of a campo and the establishment of a reg-

ular cycle in that area. According to people who witnessed the event or participated in it, the confrontation expressed the comuneros' growing intolerance for the landlords' abuses and their increasing resentment toward traditional forms of labor service and patron dependency. The hacendados were forced to begin to contribute something to the canal cleaning, and the change in attitude made them shift thereafter toward slightly more equitable terms of wage and exchange labor. This was Pampamarca's agrarian reform, a change in which outside influences played a crucial role.

Reciprocity as Servitude: Exploitation and Resistance in Agricultural Work

Ayllu members here work their fields and help one another in much the same manner as in Huaynacotas. Ayni and yanapakuy are used in the same situations and have the same significance. Again, ayni partners are sought not only among kinfolk and affines, but also among friends and neighbors. Ayni here, no less than in Huaynacotas, does not rely on kinship to hold it together or make it work, contrary to what most studies of reciprocity suggest. The only difference I could see was that Pampamarquinos seemed to more often become spiritual kin, or compadres, because they cooperate in this way.

Unfortunately, the focus on kinship has given the impression that ayni, the main form of cooperation in subsistence work, is not common in communities that are not densely integrated by blood relations. It has also, I think, reinforced the notion that indigenous people are primitive, that they live in a kind of social universe that became obsolete long ago. This is clearly not the case, as we will see when we examine work exchange in the lower valley.

As one would expect, it is work relations between large and small landowners that here show a form and content different from those in Huaynacotas. In this case, the estate owners have a higher socioeconomic status than the smallholders, but ethnic and cultural differences help to create distinct dynamics between the two groups. The mistis, of course, are in a position of power, based mainly on their control, or potential control, over essential resources. Consequently, the smallholders have been able to impose fewer constraints on the terms under which the wealthy minority operate. They have struggled to do this, like their counterparts in Huaynacotas, and they have made significant advances in recent decades, but many of them remain vulnerable to forms of coercion that keep them subordinate and dependent on the landlords.

Traditionally, on the three largest haciendas (10–15 hectares)—Uchupalla, Pachapaki, and Waqalla—most of the routine tasks were done by a full-time manager, a *kamayuq*, or mayordomo, who was paid a cash wage and given the use of a subsistence plot. These men, who were usually outsiders, watered the alfalfa fields and tended the livestock. Land-poor members of the ayllus worked a few other plots under sharecropping arrangements. The remaining land, the landlords' own crop fields, was worked by ayllu members through a combination of mink'a, for the larger tasks, and wage labor, for routine jobs such as irrigation. Today, only two of the three haciendas are still being worked in this manner. Both are smaller than before because some of the fields have been sold, a process that reflects the landlords' gradual withdrawal from the community.

The other estate properties are worked in a similar manner, but, being smaller, they have no mayordomos, and most have few, if any, sharecropped fields. Here minoristas who, a few decades ago, were paid a cash wage of only twenty to thirty *centavos* a day, water the alfalfa and tend the livestock (the exact amount depended on the cost of a bottle of *pisco*, or aguardiente, to whose price the wage level was traditionally pegged). And, as on the large estates, they also work the crop fields through a combination of mink'a and wage labor.

Not surprisingly, a mink'a in Pampamarca is rather different from one in Huaynacotas. Again, the work party is composed of two distinct groups: one that comes early and works the entire day, and one that comes later and grows in size as the morning proceeds. The core group consists of any sharecroppers who work on the estate, as well as numerous ajihados, compadres, and other people who are indebted in some way to the landlord. Traditionally, these workers did not receive special compensation; there was no institution of wak-llay here, in which mink'a partners receive the use of a piece of land on the parcel being worked. All of them worked in exchange for good food and lots of drink for themselves and their wives and children, just as the other participants did, plus a small share—a shawlful—of the eventual harvest. Today, they earn a token cash wage as well. The other workers, if they come early in the day, also receive the cash wage, about the same amount as in Huaynacotas. They are other comuneros who may or may not have a special relationship with the landlord. Invariably, many villagers eventually arrive, along with their families, so that a mink'a here is a much larger event than in Huaynacotas.

The most striking difference is that the landowner and his wife do not participate at all in the work. They are strictly the hosts and masters-of-ceremonies, who spend most of their time directing the work and serving alcohol, chicha, and food to the participants. Just as in Huaynacotas, they converse and joke—mostly in Quechua, which the mistis speak fluently—but they will not hesitate to demand that people work harder or be more careful. Landowners in Huaynacotas control the work by participating and setting an example, by using a tool to set the pace or show how they want things done, and they apparently never give orders. Another crucial difference is that the landlords' own children and kinsmen are typically not even present, so that the host family does not contribute to the physical effort in any way. This, of course, means that the ayllu members provide all the work done at a mink'a event, and this has reportedly always been the case.

The conditions of work that prevailed on Andean haciendas have been described in many studies (e.g., Cotler 1968; Keith 1976; Caballero 1981; Skar 1981; Fuenzalida et al. 1982), and even though the estates here were small and their owners relatively poor, labor relations were much like those that were common elsewhere before the agrarian reform of 1969. But the reform, which broke up many of those haciendas, never had any direct effect in Pampamarca because the estates were too small to be affected by the law.

A striking difference in the two communities' mink'as lay in the comuneros' obligations toward the landlord. Nearly everyone in Pampamarca had their own subsistence plots, often ample ones, so that few people were dependent on cultivating estate fields through sharecropping for their survival. According to my older informants, these ayllu members were not obligated to accept invitations to mink'a events or to work for wages on estate land, but it was necessary to do so occasionally in order "to maintain friendly relations." It is quite clear that they regarded the wage work as exploitative, and that they considered mink'a, especially, to be a form of labor servitude: "*hina mita*" (like the *mita*) and "*trabajo gratuito*" (free labor) were phrases they typically used in describing mink'a. They clearly did not see this as assistance or mutual aid, as in Huaynacotas, but rather as a form of tribute or forced labor. Why, then, did these relatively self-sufficient comuneros provide both unpaid work and token wage labor for the landlords? The following were the concrete reasons they gave for their participation:

1. To gain the use of a plow and oxen. Until the 1950's, the landlords were the only people who had plows, which could be used to sow a field in much less time than was possible with the native *chakitaklla*, or foot-plow. The hacendados rented their tools and animals out to comuneros for a small fee, but they would only do this for people who worked for them.

2. To protect their livestock. When other people's animals wandered onto the landlords' fields, they would usually slaughter them whether or not the animals had done much damage to crops. This was less likely to happen to someone who helped them.

3. To protect their land. The hacendados would sometimes demand an extortionate amount of cash as mitigation for damages done by animals, in order

to force a smallholder to give them a piece of land instead.[16] More important, they usually held the fields of some campesinos in usufruct as collateral on loans (an arrangement known as *prenda*), property that they could take posses-sion of at any time. These things were less likely to happen to a "good *peón*."

4. To avoid problems with water. The mistis frequently interrupted irriga-tion by ayllu members to water their alfalfa, but they would usually pick on someone who did not work for them.

5. To ensure the availability of loans. Loans of cash were very useful, though not essential, in financing fiestas, the sponsorship of which was virtually oblig-atory for ayllu members. The landlords lent money or liquor to people who were cooperative, sometimes even on favorable terms.

6. To work off debts. Landlords set and manipulated the interest rates on loans of money, as well as the monetary value of borrowed items such as trago or tools. This kept many people in a continuous state of debt, which motivated them to work on the estates so they could keep their land.

7. To avoid legal problems. The mistis sometimes falsely accused people of stealing livestock so they could get their property. Since they were the political leaders of the community, the comuneros were helpless against this kind of ex-tortion, but helpful people were rarely chosen as victims.

8. To gain legal protection. Poor people depended on the hacendados for as-sistance with any legal problems they had, which were always settled in Co-tahuasi. The cost of these cases could be enormous, depending on the whim and greed of provincial officials and pseudo-lawyer advisers, but it could be re-duced substantially if a patrón acted on one's behalf.

9. To gain the favor of one's godparent or that of one's child. Every landlord was typically the godparent of many ayllu members (perhaps thirty or more), a relationship that involved all of the above favors and forms of dependence. Ahi-jados were obligated to work in the fields of their padrinos; and compadres (the child's parents) would work too in order to strengthen the patron-client rela-tionship and encourage good treatment of their child. This was expected of them, and it typically continued throughout their lives.

It is important to note that, although the hacendados did acquire some property through these means, especially by foreclosing on loans to fiesta spon-sors, the mere possibility of such action seems to have kept the ayllu members in line. The main difference with respect to Huaynacotas is that some of the functions the landlords fulfilled here—assessing penalties for damages, giving loans, setting interest rates—are regulated by custom there. In Huaynacotas, village and ayllu authorities appraise damage done to crop fields, according to standards that are traditional and considered fair. Interest rates too are regulated by custom, and they reflect the fact that there are many more mayoristas capable of giving loans, so that a few men do not enjoy a monopoly. Perhaps most important, households rely mainly on the help of their kin in financing fiestas, and though borrowing does take place, there is an explicit prejudice against putting up land as collateral or accepting it as such. Huaynacoteños mortgage their livestock, rarely their land, when they need money; everyone seems to recognize that to do otherwise would jeopardize, not only their own welfare, but eventually that of the entire community.[17]

The mistis have lived in Pampamarca for more than a century, and their power over the ayllu members obviously extends quite far back in time. No doubt several things brought about the changes in the terms of labor between them, but the most important influence seems to have been the comuneros' first-hand contact with the world outside the valley. These experiences made people aware for the first time that they had some alternatives to dependence and servitude.

During fieldwork, I spent a great deal of time interviewing the three oldest ayllu members, all of whom were at least sixty-five years of age. They told me that people rarely traveled outside the province until the 1930's, when several pivotal changes took place. Before then, men had occasionally migrated to the mines of Kalpa and Cerro Rico in the neighboring province of Condesuyos or to the plantations in Camaná and the Majes valley, but only to work long enough to make what they needed to finance their *cargos*. This was, quite obviously, a continuation of a tradition extending all the way back through colonial times, when men had no choice but to migrate to acquire money for tribute payments and to serve in the mita. Once those burdens were abolished by the government, migration seems to have become less common and to have remained so until the 1930's. Not only were great distances involved, but *paludismo*, or malaria, was endemic in the lowlands of Majes and seriously threatened the workers' health.

Both impediments were removed in the mid-1930's, when the road was completed as far as Chuquibamba, cutting the travel time in half, and a government spraying program finally eradicated the disease. But though migration during the agricultural slack season then became a feasible option for everyone, for most people the world beyond the village was still a very large unknown. Fortunately for the comuneros, around that time an outsider came to work in the community: a mestizo schoolteacher from Arequipa named Valdivia. By all accounts, the impact of this *indigenista* was enormous. During his three years of service, he taught Indian children that they could leave the valley to work on the outside, that there was no reason why they had to be so dependent on the mistis.[18] He made no secret of his dislike for the landlords and gave no special treatment to their children, an unprecedented situation whose impact extended far beyond the classroom.

Two other factors reportedly encouraged seasonal migration. The first was military service, which was supposedly obligatory and did, in fact, take many young comuneros outside the province. This experience gave them training in new skills, instilled a sense of empowerment and pride, and familiarized them with other valleys and the city. The other factor, historically speaking, was the worst drought of the twentieth century, which struck in 1939 and lasted for five years. Virtually no rain fell during this time, so that the cattle either starved for lack of pasture in the hillsides or had to be killed. Even the crops were affected severely enough that hunger drove many men outside the province. The impact on other local communities was truly disastrous, resulting in a massive temporary exodus of people to the mines and the plantations of Majes and Camaná. A final factor, of course, and ultimately the most important one in encouraging migration, would be population growth.

By the end of the 1940's, seasonal migration had become an integral part of the subsistence strategies of some households. Wages acquired on the outside were used to buy clothing, alcohol, tools, and other goods that the families could not produce themselves. Migration would not become the norm until the 1960's, when population growth accelerated, rice production expanded on the sugarcane plantations of Majes, and the road was finally completed, but by mid-century the trend had reportedly been established. Migration had, however, already made one dramatic change: it was now the favored means of acquiring money to finance fiestas. Work in the mines of Cerro Rico and Kalpa was especially lucrative, but other activities earned a hefty profit. This alternative to borrowing and debt servitude loosened somewhat the landlords' grip on the community.

Migration had another effect: some comuneros began to go into petty trade themselves, acting as middlemen in the exchange networks that linked the valley with surrounding regions. For example, ponchos and leather goods purchased in Parinocochas could be sold quite profitably to campesinos in Castilla Alta; the money could then be taken to Majes and used to buy alcohol and other items for eventual sale in Pampamarca. Other forms of trade were available to anyone with a few burros and a taste for travel and entrepreneurship. Such small-scale business was quite lucrative and gave quick yields. Those profits could be used, not only to finance *cargos*, but, perhaps more importantly, to buy additional land in the village.

It was this kind of activity, along with the mine work, that led to the emergence of the first middle proprietors.[19] In this, Pampamarca was catching up with a development that began much earlier in peasant communities in many parts of the highlands, sometimes for different reasons. In areas closer to major urban centers and places where transportation was not such a problem, in communities where population pressure on the land was more severe and began to be felt at an earlier point in time, petty trading had long since become a crucial addition to the survival strategies of most peasant households, and this sort of differentiation among comuneros had emerged (see Mitchell 1991a, b).

My three oldest informants were among the new middle proprietors. It is striking that all of them attended the village school and were students of Sr. Valdivia, that two of them served in the military, and that all of them began to migrate, initially to help finance *cargos*, at an early age. Without exception, they pointed to these outside experiences as pivotal, not only in their own lives, but in the history of the pueblo. According to them, by the 1950's the new influences had led to a change in attitudes toward the hacendados: a "loss of respect" that was expressed in several ways. First of all, people ceased to tolerate the abuses that had often been a part of wage labor. Comuneros who had worked for the landlords had often been driven very hard and sometimes physically mistreated. They now refused to work under those conditions and would simply walk off the job. Just as important, they began to demand a higher wage, equal to the going rate in the lower valley. When I first visited the pueblo in 1986, the wage, though still quite small, was the same in both areas—10,000 *soles* or ten *intis*—but for a long time it had been considerably less. Once these precedents had been set and the point had been made, there was little the hacendados could do about it.

Second, people who worked for the landlords in mink'a began to ask for more compensation. Here I am referring to workers in the core group, not those who came later in the day. No longer so dependent on the landlords for loans and special favors, they began to ask for money alongside the food and drink they got, if they were to do most of the work. The amount actually given was small and largely symbolic, but at least it acknowledged the vital role that these clients played in mink'a work. In 1988, workers got eight intis, or only about one-fourth of the going rate in the lower valley. The wages for this work are still extraordinarily low today, not only because the workers receive other compensation but because the landlord is still a padrino or compadre of theirs.

Third, the campesinos in Pampa Yarqha, the main area in which the mistis had land, demanded that order be established in the irrigation system, and that the landlords contribute to maintenance work. The canal had reportedly become clogged several times because the faenas were poorly organized and some smallholders were no longer participating. In 1954, a meeting of all users was called, at which a campo was appointed and a standard distribution sequence—a hierarchical one—was established. Although these changes had little effect on the landlords' water rights, the ayllu members declared that they would no longer maintain the system unless the mistis contributed something to the effort. The landlords responded by sending several bottles of alcohol or a hired laborer—often their mayordomo—to work in their place, which has been the custom ever since. The comuneros are no longer satisfied with the arrangement, as we will see in a later chapter, but at the time it was considered a major breakthrough in relations with the landlords.

Finally, and most significantly, many comuneros simply refused to work for the landlords anymore and distanced themselves entirely. In the early 1960's the members of Qhayawa, the largest ayllu by far, began to move their main residences out of the village into a new hamlet within their own territory. They have lived there, in Qochapampa, ever since 1964. On several occasions I questioned residents about their reasons for moving, and they made it clear that they had wanted to get away from the mistis, that they were tired of the hacendados' interference in their lives. Although they also pointed out the convenience of being closer to their fields, they emphasized a desire to remove themselves physically from the landlords' sphere of influence.[20] This, I think, was the real turning point in the decline of the mistis' power in the village.

Today, only a handful of comuneros are dependent on the landlords and still work for them. It is hard to see this when one is in the pueblo because the hacendados are still so prominent there, but their clientele is now actually rather small. This is the main reason, though not the only one, why the mistis rarely take water out of turn anymore, why they no longer harass and threaten people, why they contribute to faenas, and why they are slowly leaving the area.

Class Differentiation and Inequity in Water Use

Soon after I began visiting Pampamarca in 1986, I became aware that certain problems were emerging within the traditional system of water distribution. I occasionally heard references to water theft and to people defying the campos, and I got the impression that such actions were relatively new or more common now than they had been before. People spoke of a breakdown of authority, of a "loss of respect" for the campos and other ayllu officials, but they never identified the source of the trouble. At first, I assumed the hacendados were the guilty parties, given the way they had often behaved in the past. But it turned out that certain ayllu members were responsible, namely, the middle proprietors.

Several characteristics distinguish these families, which number only eight altogether, from the other comuneros. They have an average of 2–3 hectares of land, though two have as many as 4. All of them raise some cattle, as the minoristas do, but most of the household heads are part-time ganaderos or cattle buyers. In addition, three families, like the landlords, sell alcohol within the village, which they purchase from wholesalers who frequent the lower valley. Several of the men also engage in other petty trade, selling such merchandise to herders on the puna and using the profits to buy cattle or small amounts of wool. As I have already pointed out, the middle proprietors tend to be more educated than other people, several have served in the military, and most of them got involved in migration and trade at an early age. Without exception, they have held important *cargos*, typically the religious ones, and are high-ranking members of the village hierarchy.

Other differences are evident in the way they work their land. Because of the importance of cattle in their livelihood, at least half of their fields are planted in alfalfa; otherwise they have about the same amount of land in food crops as the minoristas. Like other comuneros, they do a lot of their own farming, but unlike them, they often make use of wage labor too. Although there is some use of ayni among them, jornal is their main form of extra-household help. As one might predict, no one in this group has anything to do with mink'a; the custom is so closely associated with the hacendados, and with the notion of exploitation, that people will not work for them on that basis.

The families often hire other ayllu members, at the going rate, to do any of the common agricultural tasks for them, including irrigating their fields, practices that are rare at best in Huaynacotas, where irrigation is hardly ever turned over to anyone else, and where an employer works alongside anyone he may hire. The middle proprietors are the only people I have seen in Pampamarca, other than the hacendados, who will stand by and watch while peons do their work or who will send a wage laborer to do a task that they do not feel like doing themselves. Although they are very hard workers, they perceive labor as a commodity that can be bought, in addition to being a way of life and a service that can be sold, which it is for most other village members. To the middle proprietors, wage labor, unlike ayni, is essentially a way to accomplish two things at one and the same time. Typically, it allows them to have a field tended while they look after their cattle or go looking for animals to buy, but they sometimes turn things over to others simply to give themselves some free time.

The practice of having other people irrigate for them does not cause middle proprietors problems, as it would in Huaynacotas, in part because the hacendados set this precedent long ago. The landlords backed up their water rights with force, by giving extremely harsh punishments for theft. For someone to steal their water was almost unheard of, and a similar cautious respect is shown to the *medianos propietarios* today. They are rather aggressive men for the most part, people with enough economic power to intimidate fellow village members. No minorista would think of challenging or interfering with their water rights because, like the mistis, they can protect them themselves, without the help or the consent of the community.[21]

These families typically hold land in several sectors, roughly half of which is planted in alfalfa. These rebuilt, reclaimed, or purchased *canchones*, pasture fields, are watered by the top-down technique. Most of the families also have some terrraces, on which they may use the other method, but in general they prefer qhosqay because it requires less labor. Although the families are only a few, they have rebuilt fields and planted alfalfa in several sectors, including ones where little or no pasture had been grown before. It is from this constellation of practices, and from the nature of the cattle business, that the problems they are causing in irrigation arise. There are many reasons for their behavior, to be sure, but the most basic one stems from the characteristics of the alfalfa plant itself. Pasture production not only motivates people to destroy terraces, to build corral-fields, and to irrigate in a new manner. It also causes them to need water, or to want it, on an irregular basis and on short notice.

The problems in irrigation were difficult for me to investigate, not just because people were reluctant to say who was responsible for them, but also because the explanations they offered did not really make sense. In explaining water theft, which usually amounts to a user taking his share out of turn, people spoke of a lack of respect for the rights of others and for the campo, of a "me first" attitude, and of a propensity by a few individuals to take advantage of the humility or timidity of the majority. These were stereotypical accounts, portraits of the "*campesino vivo*," the peasant who has become bold and adopted the calculating, exploitative behavior of mistis and members of the dominant society (see Poole 1987). Others pointed out that the campos nowadays were young men, rather than respected elders as they traditionally were, and that, being rather poor and new to community service, they were more vulnerable to pressure and bribery. All of these observations were valid, providing a perfectly good explanation of what was apparently going on. Nevertheless, I found it hard to believe that the problems arose simply from selfishness, from a desire of some people to set themselves above others, or from a taste for status and power—in other words, from purely symbolic and social concerns.

But until I asked certain specific questions, no one ever gave me a concrete, material reason why, in a community where landowners irrigate their parcels roughly twice each month—a frequency considered optimal in every other village in the valley—some people would want to bring trouble on themselves by going against tradition and watering more often or precisely when they chose. The root of the problem, as it turned out, lay in the families' desire to exploit their pasture land to the fullest. Alfalfa is a perennial plant, a very thirsty one, which produces several crops a year. Whenever someone exhausts a plot after fattening cattle on it, he or she has a strong incentive to water it again immediately in order to speed up the regeneration of the plants. The new crop will reportedly benefit even if the plot has recently been irrigated. More important, consistent watering can produce four cuttings a year instead of the normal three, especially on the lower-altitude lands. But because the plant's blooming period is fairly short, a delay of even a few days now and then can make a big difference.

This, of course, means that pasture fields are on a completely different production schedule from food crops, one that impels people to speed it up, to maximize it, through frequent but irregular irrigation. For this reason, the cattlemen often pressure the campos, in private, to put them where they want to be in the order. When their request for such flexibility is denied, they sometimes take other people's water.

If someone wants a theft to go unnoticed, he will steal the water at the beginning of a person's turn, rather than in the middle or at the end, which would cause an obvious decline in the canal flow. Minoristas are sometimes guilty of this most common kind of thievery, called *pushkuy*, which is done only to benefit maize or garden vegetables. But stealing just a little of an allotment never provides enough water for a pasture field. Outright theft, which is often merely a fait accompli masked as a campo's last-minute change in the order, almost always has to do with alfalfa.[22]

As for the middle proprietors, they probably do not even consider what they are doing theft, since it is simply a matter of pushing someone else down in the order. Their explanations for the practice were much the same as other people's; they portrayed it as a form of "*vivesa*," of boldness and arrogant disregard, but, according to them, what harm did a delay of a morning or a day do, especially if it involved someone's maize plot? This was their way of accounting for other people's complacency about the problem, but to me it showed that these "new rich" believe they have a special need, which in a strictly material sense, they do.

This kind of behavior has been tolerated, under some protest, by the community as a whole for several reasons. Most of the comuneros are intimidated by people who have some economic power, to whom they may be indebted because of past favors such as credit. But the most important reason by far is that the irrigation frequency is high to begin with and there is more than enough of the resource to go around. Even though these breaches of custom do cause inconvenience and resentment, the delays they create for others are only brief and do not consistently fall on the same households. Consequently, few victims ever perceive their rights as truly threatened.

The final crucial reason is that most of the infractions occur unobserved, behind the scenes. Because distribution is hierarchical and the watering order is dispersed and somewhat flexible, the system is less transparent than in Huaynacotas. Only the campo knows exactly where the water should be at every given moment, and irrigation, being more dispersed, is a less public activity. As a result, vigilance by the users themselves is much less systematic and effective. Theft and favoritism can occur more easily because the controls on them are not so strong. Of course, everyone knows who is stealing water from time to time, but since deviations from the proper sequence are not immediately obvious, people have to go to a lot of trouble to prove it and track the water down. That is the impact that hierarchy has had.

In the other villages in the valley where elite minorities reside—Puica, Huarhua, and Toro—people complain today about this same breakdown of tradition, and the process seems to have been under way for some time. In places like Cotahuasi, however, where landlords achieved their dominance much earlier and in greater numbers, these kinds of changes began to take place long ago. That is why Pampamarca has a special historical significance. As the only local community where water is plentiful today, it reflects hydrological conditions that must have prevailed throughout the valley until the early part of the twentieth century, before indigenous populations had fully recovered from collapse. It was during this period, when pressure on resources had remained relaxed for centuries and land and water were abundant, that the transformation of Andean traditions began in the hacienda-dominated communities. Thus Pampamarca provides a unique glimpse at some of the dynamics that must have been at work.

Basically, the negative impact of practices introduced by the Spanish—pasture cultivation, terrace destruction, slope irrigation, and hierarchy and inequity in distribution, elements that were introduced within a depopulated system—was not strongly felt until later, when resources became scarce because of rapid population growth. This, I think, was the context in which some comuneros first began to depart from custom and adopt the practices of the landed elite. Because water was abundant, the consequences of all this for others, particularly the resulting waste of the resource, did not become disruptive until a substantial number of people adopted them and the total population grew large enough to stretch the water supply thin. Pampamarca, being uniquely well endowed, has not yet reached this critical point, and will not for some time into the future. But, as we will see in the next chapter, Cotahuasi and its annexes reached this pivotal threshold long ago.

FIVE

Cotahuasi

Domination and Social Decline
in a Hacienda District

To look down on the town of Cotahuasi from the puna above at Allway is to see perhaps the most spectacular view in the valley. From there, at more than 13,000 feet, one gazes down over a vast irrigation system stretching into one of the deepest chasms on earth, a dazzling landscape whose most striking features, other than the extreme depth, are its size and complexity and, above all, the fact that it is artificial, a product of human work and intent.[1] Many shades of green spread out below like a huge patchwork carpet, looking fluorescent in the thin air against the dry brown scrub of the surrounding mountains. One is aware that this landscape is thoroughly domesticated and has been for a very long time, an ancient thing created out of soil, rock, and water. Springing from sources in the suni herding zone, immediately below, the water forms three streams that descend in different directions, dropping down toward the river in long cascades, to form gardens that perch on the mountainsides at different elevations.

Several features made the district especially attractive to the Spanish, who settled here earlier and in greater numbers than most other parts of the valley. Being the largest expanse of cultivated terrain by far, the place was destined to become a major population center, but other chararacteristics, such as its topography and hydrology, helped to make it the natural hub of the commercial economy. Today, the district is made up of a town and three outlying villages that share the largest canal system in the province, serving roughly 600 hectares. The community territories are contiguous and span two ecological zones, the suni and theqheshwa,[2] including extensive flatlands that lie along the valley bottom. Their gentle gradient and warm climate made the latter ideal sites for haciendas, which is one reason why pueblos like Cotahuasi, Taurisma, Tomopampana, and Alca, the major district capitals, were established at low elevations.

The outlying villages sit fairly close to the capital, less than an hour's walk

away, proximity that is quite unusual in the valley. This, along with other factors, encouraged especially close relations between the indigenous and Spanish
populations. Partly because of it, Cotahuasi became a district thoroughly dominated by haciendas, one whose annex communities were, for a long time,
much like the ayllus of Pampamarca.

The necessity of sharing canal water also fostered this close association. During the eighteenth and early nineteenth centuries, the water was divided up between the major haciendas and the local ayllus, under arrangements similar to
those that were emerging in Pampamarca. Here, however, where the estates
later expanded and multiplied, a growing share became privately owned, essentially belonging to the landlords, leaving the adjacent indigenous communities,
the ayllus, to make do with a steadily dwindling supply. Ultimately, this parasitic relationship was encouraged, or at least made easily possible, by the location of the alpine springs themselves.

Rather than being widely separated, as in Huaynacotas and Pampamarca,
the district's major sources all lie in the same area, a large expanse of pasture
land in the suni zone called Huambo. In the middle of the nineteenth century,
one of the principal merchant families, the Loayzas, somehow took ownership
of these prime herding grounds, the only ones belonging to the local ayllus,
which enabled them eventually to lay first claim to the water.[3] More important,
they also ensured that these water rights could not be disputed legally or negotiated later on. By taking control of the land itself, the Loayzas established a sort
of bridgehead that settled the matter of rights before many of the smaller estates in the district were even established, and long before Peru's first water law
was passed. Eventually, this move would benefit other wealthy families as they
gradually appropriated much of the flow of each spring.

In many respects, the sharing arrangements were similar to those in Pampamarca, but here over half the supply was ultimately privatized. Furthermore,
water was scarce to begin with, and the springs were quite vulnerable to
drought, factors that helped set the stage for further change and inevitable conflict. As we saw in Chapter Two, the haciendas continued to expand as the wool
trade flourished during the late nineteenth and early twentieth centuries, moving out from the pampas into the remaining community territory at a moment
when the native population was growing rapidly for the first time in centuries.
The water to irrigate these new properties came, not from the private supply of
the major estates, which had long since been established, but from the communal shares of the expanding ayllus. The growing scarcity resulted in conflict, not
just between landlords and peasants but, more importantly, among the peasants themselves.

PHOTO 4. View of Cotahuasi

In this district we see the effect of the same set of new practices that we examined in Pampamarca—alfalfa production, terrace destruction and a new way of irrigating, water privatization, hierarchy and inequity among water rights—but here they were introduced under different hydrological conditions and carried to an extreme. Another new element entered the equation when the Peruvian state became involved, initially in 1902, by passing legislation that, in one way or another, encouraged estate expansion and directly benefited the landed elite. Because the encroachment occurred in a context of rapid demographic growth, it created a hydraulic relationship between the estates and communities that was essentially parasitic and that steadily worsened with time.

By the middle of the twentieth century, the expansion had undermined ayllu life at its very foundation, unleashing a struggle over water within each village as the supply tightened. Rights to communal water came under more and more dispute as previously abandoned lands were put back into production. With the frequency of irrigation declining, many comuneros became dependent on the landlords for water, which they had to purchase—water that had been taken from the communities in the first place. One cannot understand the subsequent turn toward mestizaje, toward the widespread abandonment of "Indianness," without taking these developments, and others that followed soon after, into account. This tragedy of the commons would continue to worsen, with the landlords and the state playing complementary and ultimately destructive roles. The end results are evident in many places throughout the highlands today, generally wherever these two agents or agencies have long been in control. All of this indicates that Hardin, in his now classic analysis of the famous tragedy, got the story backward, at least in the case of water, mistaking causes for solutions to a problem that immediately changes face once the history of the region is known.

Hydraulic Structure and Land Use

Throughout the early part of the twentieth century, most of the population was concentrated in the four major settlements, plus the tiny hamlet of Reyparte. The rest was dispersed in homesteads scattered throughout the irrigation system. In 1940, at the height of the wool trade, the district's total population was 3,353, or slightly greater than the 1981 level. Of these, 1,354 people (40%) lived in the capital, and 1,005 (30%) in the annex communities. The other 994 lived on the estates in the "rural" sector (DNE 1940: 120). Hacienda expansion had brought a near doubling of the rural population, including the annexes and

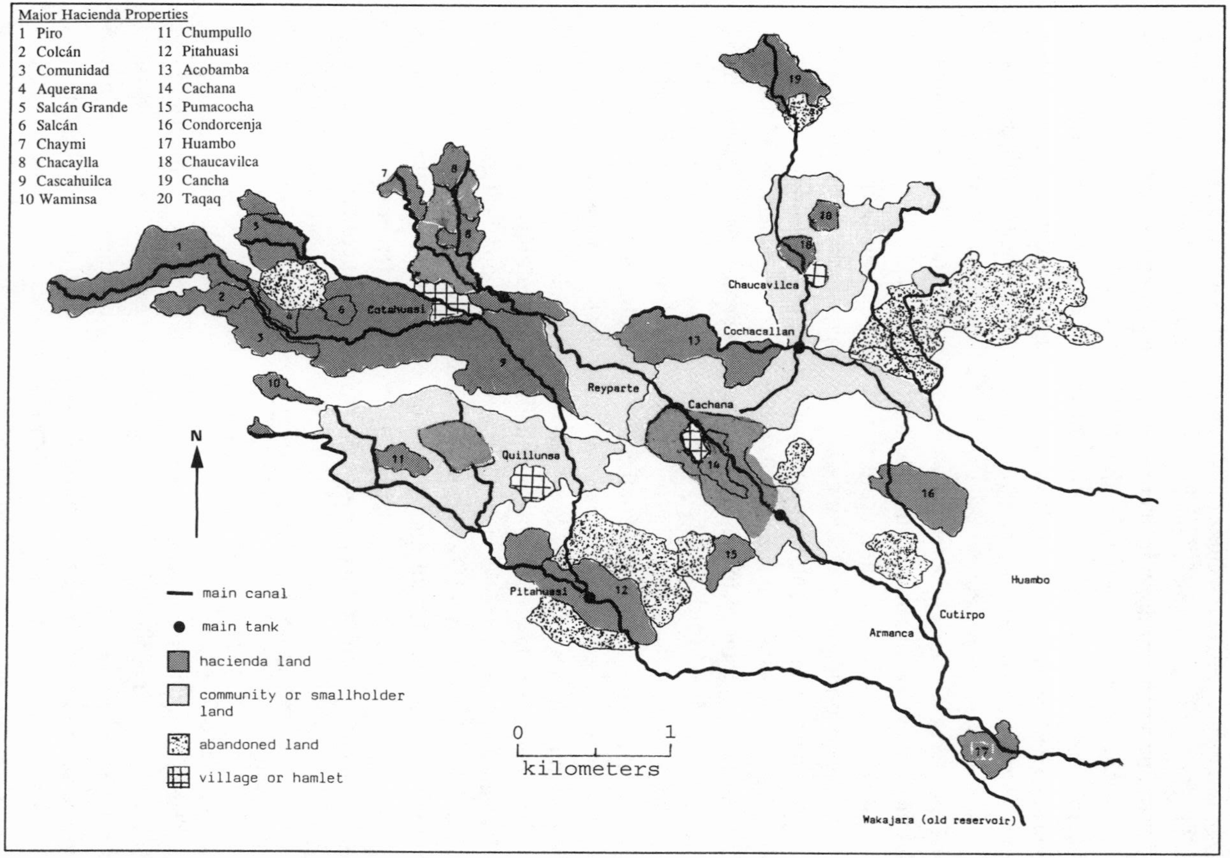
Major Hacienda Properties
1 Piro
2 Colcán
3 Comunidad
4 Aquerana
5 Salcán Grande
6 Salcán
7 Chaymi
8 Chacaylla
9 Cascahuilca
10 Waminsa
11 Chumpullo
12 Pitahuasi
13 Acobamba
14 Cachana
15 Pumacocha
16 Condorcenja
17 Huambo
18 Chaucavilca
19 Cancha
20 Taqaq
Cotahuasi
Chaucavilca
Cochacallan
Reyparte
Cachana
Quillunsa
Pitahuasi
Huambo
Cutirpo
Armanca
Wakajara (old reservoir)
N
main canal
main tank
hacienda land
community or smallholder land
abandoned land
village or hamlet
0
1
kilometers

MAP 9. The irrigation system of Cotahuasi

former ayllus, since 1876. Meanwhile, Cotahuasi itself had declined 29 percent. The district as a whole had grown only slightly, by 13 percent, but the peasant population had expanded steadily at a moderate rate, roughly 1.4 percent a year, growth that was much stronger in certain areas than in others (Table 1).

Quillunsa, the one ayllu that the estates had only recently penetrated, had doubled in size since 1876, growing to 426 people. The annex and hacienda community of Chaucavilca, some of whose land had also remained intact, had grown 51 percent, to 302, but Cachana, most of whose territory had been absorbed by the estates long before, had declined 19 percent, to a total of 277. The former ayllu of Reyparte, also established in the colonial period, had shrunk to only 130 people, a fall-off of 20 percent. It appears that all these groups had actually expanded to some degree, but that the excess growth had been absorbed by haciendas in the now-enlarged rural sector. Since 1876, this segment of the population, including all workers who resided on the estates, forasteros as well as land-poor members of the communities, had increased 223 percent. The latter, who were sharecroppers, came not only from the annexes that had declined in population, but also from the two that had grown substantially, Chaucavilca and Quillunsa. As for the haciendas themselves, their numbers had increased by fifteen since 1876, and many of the owners now lived in the annexes of Quillunsa and Cachana, rather than the district capital.

In the 1940 census, 66 percent of the rural population identified themselves as indigenous people, rather than mestizos (DNE 1940: 120). But it is clear that the turn toward mestizaje had begun by this time.[4] Some of my older campesino informants confirmed that their parents were fully bilingual, wore clothing of store-bought fabric, had a year or two of elementary education, and already considered themselves to be *gente mestiza*. My ethnography of the district begins at this point, around 1940, the earliest period to which the processes of change can be traced through reliable accounts. Although the traditional system of irrigation had already been modified significantly, elderly people were able to provide information on these changes, as well as the impact that they had had by then.

The district is composed of three major canal networks, as shown in Map 9, each of which originally belonged to a different ayllu. They are fed by a group of springs, twelve in all, that join together in three large flows to form separate hydraulic units. In addition, there are two smaller networks fed by three secondary springs that emerge farther downslope and are too small to be shown on the map.

One of the major flows spills over a waterfall into a canal called Cutirpo, which serves the eastern part of the district, beginning at about 3,600 meters. These lands originally belonged to the ayllu of Antamarca, which eventually became the annex and hacienda community of Chaucavilca. A second flow passes over another waterfall called Armanca and drops into a canal of the same name, which now serves various lands in the middle and northern parts of the terrain below. This water initially belonged to Collana ayllu, whose territory took up the whole central portion of the district. Owners of the estates in Piro and Cachana expropriated all of it for themselves, along with the land, during the seventeenth and eighteenth centuries. The third flow, the largest by far, passes through a long canal called Wakajara down into the southwestern part of the district. Before the agrarian reform of 1969, this canal watered the haciendas of Huambo and Pitahuasi, all of the lands belonging to the annex and former ayllu of Quillunsa, as well as many estate properties in the vicinity of Cotahuasi itself.

The two smaller canal networks lie adjacent to the capital in the central part of the district. They bring water from three secondary springs, each of which has its own tank. Even though the canal of Armanca passes through this area, the comuneros of the hamlet and former ayllu of Reyparte had no rights to the private water and were forced to depend on these local sources. Evidently, this situation dated back to the seventeenth century, when the estate of Cachana was established on part of Collana ayllu's land, causing some people to be resettled and a new ayllu, namely Reyparte, to be formed. The other network serves Chacaylla, which borders the town of Cotahuasi. The water again comes from two minor springs, called Iskaywayqo, and is stored in the reservoir of Señorpa. All of the land in this area belonged to hacendados and other members of the elite community, so that the outflow of Señorpa was part of the private supply of the estates.

Within most of the major hydraulic units, which today are called sectors (*sectores*),[5] there are some small areas irrigated by minor springs, each of which also has a tank. This independent supply helped to create many of the smaller hacienda properties, established during the period of estate expansion. Although not large enough to be represented in Map 9, they are listed in Table 3, which shows the district's hydraulic system in 1988, including the amount of land served by the primary and secondary sources. One source is not listed in the table but is shown in Map 9: the easternmost canal in the district, which leads from an isolated spring to two large parcels on the upper margin of Chaucavilca sector. This tiny alpine source, serving tracts of smallholder land, has always been independent of the rest of the system and will not be discussed here.

TABLE 3

Spring and Tank Capacities in Cotahuasi, 1988

Spring/tank	Flow (lt./sec.)	Capacity	Hectares	Turno (days)
		Quillunsa		
Pitahuasi	214.96	7,012.67	186.10	28
Kuchuqocha	1.44	141.64	2.50	15
Wallaqocha	4.20	320.52	10.00	30
Chumpullo 1	3.00	73.84	1.00	20
Chumpullo 2	2.99	282.84	6.00	26
		Cotahuasi		
Pitahuasi	214.96	7,012.67	161.55	28
Cascahuilca	5.92	246.28	2.54	15
Animas	2.58	186.75	2.00	12
Senorpa	6.96	556.62	12.22	18
Cozo	2.61	112.63	0.34	8
Rinconada	2.81	128.11	2.54	15
Aytinco	2.55	251.11	3.82	15
Oqara	6.52	212.55	7.47	22
Choco	4.63	292.24	8.15	24
Wallpawaqaq	3.31	347.42	6.79	20
		Chaucavila		
Qochacallan	100.04	3,813.90	86.60	40
		Cachana		
Pumaqocha	6.00	427.33	6.36	25
Armanca	79.76	2,662.05	61.60	22
		Reyparte		
Pisqe Grande	13.63	966.05	10.18	22
Pisqe Chico	4.24	208.68	1.27	15
Wawaqocha	13.84	311.58	2.54	15

SOURCE: Ministry of Agriculture office, Cotahuasi.

Map 9 also shows the areas formerly occupied by the major haciendas, but several points should be made about the actual distribution of estate land. First, by the middle of the twentieth century, most of the older estates, such as Cachana and Piro, had expanded and been subdivided among more than one owner. Second, the major properties around the capital were surrounded by many smaller ones owned by small and middle proprietors; most were tradespeople or professionals such as schoolteachers who lived in the capital. Third, within this large domain of estate land, campesinos did own some scattered plots, most of which were without any water rights. Finally, there were some important estate properties scattered within the community land, especially in Quillunsa and Chaucavilca, that were too small to display accurately.

The haciendas and communities were spread out over an area of approximately 580 hectares (1,433 acres) of irrigated terrain, ranging in altitude from 2,300 to 3,600 meters.[6] Within this expanse, water was distributed from the three main canals, called *canales matrizes* or *canales madres*, through a system of twenty-eight secondary canals, or *tomas*, and a great many tertiary ones, called *acequias*. Strangely enough, there were no reservoirs to store the major spring flows of Cutirpo, Armanca, and Wakajara until 1942, when the first of three big tanks was constructed. Consequently, irrigation traditionally occurred both day and night over roughly 85 percent of the terrain. Among several possible reasons for the failure to build tanks is the fact that all three flows are quite large. Wakajara, which is more than twice as big as the others, now fills a truly massive structure, one much bigger than the ancient tanks of Huaynacotas, Pampamarca, or any other village in the valley.

The canals appear to be prehispanic, though it is not possible to say whether any modifications were made during the colonial period. Another important feature distinguishes this network from most others in the province. The main canal conducting the water of Wakajara to Quillunsa and Cotahuasi follows the course of a natural stream and gully for about 7 kilometers. It has not been modified structurally along most of its length, a fact that allows a huge amount of water loss through filtration. This waste contributes to social conflict during periods of water scarcity, a problem that, for this reason as well as many others, is more prevalent in Cotahuasi than anywhere else in the valley.

Given that the hacendados owned such a great amount of water, it is not surprising that the pattern of land use in the district differs markedly from the pattern in Huaynacotas and Pampamarca. Both the nature of the production zones and their configuration are different, continuing to reflect conditions established during the hacienda era. Most of the "dry-farmed" lands are scattered throughout the system as isolated plots located in the maize-growing zone. As we saw in previous chapters, unirrigated or abandoned land is rarely found within the canal systems of peasant villages, since land in the qheshwa zone is at a premium and has been put back under irrigation wherever possible. This process was never completed in Cotahuasi, either in the area around the capital or in the annexes, mainly because so much water was expropriated by the estate owners so early. By 1940, although the total district population had long since recovered to, and even exceeded, its precolonial level, a great amount of land that had once been irrigated had been left without any water rights. Technically, these were *eriazos*, or dry-farmed lands, but, as we will see shortly, they were not entirely without access to water at that time, as they are today.

It is also striking that no fallowing lands are under irrigation here, nor were they during the hacienda era. The lands lie out of use, apparently abandoned long ago, for the same reason. There are two large expanses of at least 80 hectares each on the steep slopes above Chaucavilca and Quillunsa, as well as several smaller ones (see Map 9). These consist of eroded terraces located in the upper qheshwa and suni zones, but the largest area lies close to a main canal, Wakajara, and is connected to it with feeder canals. According to local people, this area has not been cultivated in recent times. It was apparently abandoned during the nineteenth century, probably because so much water was lost to the estates during that time. The other areas have never been irrigated, but the condition of this one, which originally was, deserves mention because of what it reveals about the history of the district. These abandoned fallowing lands in the suni zone, like the dry-farmed plots in the qheshwa, are visible evidence of the prolonged struggle that has taken place in Cotahuasi during the last two centuries, and is still going on today. Historically, it has been both a class struggle, between landlords and sharecropping tenants, and an ethnic one, between Andean people and their Spanish overlords, or bosses. But now we will see into the heart of it: a conflict over water.

Estate and Community Water

As elsewhere in the highlands (and in all the Spanish colonies), the hacienda system was based on legal titles certifying the private ownership of estate land, acquired through means, both licit and illicit, whose scope we can now better appreciate from what we learned about mink'a and the *cargo* system in Pampamarca. But it is not widely known that, in most cases, these also included titles to water, without which land is of little use. Deeds to properties acquired before the turn of the nineteenth century specified the days of the week, or of alternating weeks, during which the estate owners had exclusive rights to the main water supplies. These lands were referred to as having "*agua propia*," their own water.

For example, the owner of Salcan Grande, a big hacienda below Cotahuasi, controlled all of the flow of Armanca every Thursday. Higher up, in Chaucavilca, the owners of two smaller estates had sole rights to the water of Cutirpo on alternating Thursdays. The basis for this private ownership was referred to in property deeds as the "*usos y costumbres del pueblo*," the customary system of water rights established during the colonial and early republican periods, which was codified and legally ratified by the Water Code of 1902 The shared irrigation water of most districts in this valley had long been divided into two distinct cycles, one for the estates, referred to as the *agua de las haciendas*—or, appropriately enough, the *agua de alfalfa*—and one for the communities, the *agua de las comunidades.*[7] Being privately owned, the estate water was used on an individual basis without supervision. The communal water was under rule-based management, just as in Huaynacotas and Pampamarca. From a legal standpoint, the village lands were said to be "*sin agua propia*," without their own water, which meant that each plot was entitled to a share during every cycle of the community's distribution system.

On the surface, this dual organization looks much like the arrangement in Pampamarca, where the landlords also had their separate days for irrigation,[8] but here they truly owned much of the water and used it on fixed days of the week. They did not depend on the ayllu distributors, the campos, for the storage and release of their water. The communities then got to use the water on the remaining days. But this relationship changed significantly after the 1902 legislation because the estates continued to expand thereafter into community territory.

Before the passage of the Water Code (also known as the Spanish Water Law), two arrangements governed the division of the two kinds of water. Where the estate and community lands were contiguous and lay within the same original ayllu territory, as in Chaucavilca, the landlords and the community alternated in using the flow of the main source. In contrast, where the two kinds of land were separated by a considerable distance, a weirlike structure called a *yut'a* permanently divided the source into two roughly equal flows, so that irrigation took place continuously on both estate and community property at the same time. Both estate owners and community members are said to have watched the weir constantly in order to keep anyone from tampering with it and to protect their rights. This was the traditional arrangement between the community of Quillunsa and the haciendas of Huambo, Pitahuasi, and upper Cotahuasi for sharing the water of Wakajara, which irrigated most of the district.

The 1902 code ratified these arrangements by granting ownership of a given source to the holder of the property where the spring was located, provided that he had actually been using the flow (Pasapera 1902: 130–32). If the remaining water passed through other private land as it descended, it became the property of the next landowner downslope, provided that he too had been using it, and so on throughout the canal system. Anyone who had been irrigating continuously for a period of twenty years was authorized to continue, a right that could not be interrupted or diminished, even by someone whose land lay farther upstream along a canal. This provision made all the water of Armanca private property, as well as half the flow of Wakajara and more than half that of Cutirpo. Since the Loayza family now owned all the pasture lands in Huambo, where the springs were located, and also cultivated some land there, they had first claim to each flow, followed by the other elite families with whom they had come to share these sources during previous decades. They got legal titles, clearly expressed in their property deeds, to all the water on the day when they had traditionally used the flow.

As for the rights of the villagers, the law declared that whatever water was left was public property, to be used collectively or communally by Communities of Irrigators (Pasapera 1902: 166–69). Where this "excess" water was already being used, in villages such as Chaucavilca, Cachana, Reyparte, and Quillunsa, the use was legalized and officially recorded. But the established rights of users were not to be disturbed or interrupted; no new allotments were to be granted if this would tread on existing rights.[9] Thus the intent of the law was to freeze established rights, communal as well as private, as custom had defined them by the beginning of the twentieth century.

It is important to note that, by the time the Water Code was passed, the local hydraulic traditions were probably like those of Pampamarca in nearly every way. The landlords of Cachana and Chaucavilca had long since claimed their private water. Even in Quillunsa, the biggest annex and the last one penetrated, some estate properties had already been established within community territory. The water to irrigate these new lands had come from, and was still part of, the community supplies, and this would also be true for properties acquired by the landlords later. In theory at least, the rights of these landlords were to be no different in essence from those of comuneros.

Of course, few people are alive in Cotahuasi today who are old enough to know much about any of this.[10] But my informants' recollections, based on first-hand experience and on what their parents and others had told them, defined two distinct periods, before and after 1940, when several pivotal changes reportedly took place. Their very general account of irrigation in the annexes in the early part of the century marks that as a period of gradual decline in the communal tradition, a story that, although not empirically or historically precise, made a great deal of sense in view of what I was learning during that same period about Pampamarca.

First of all, "Spanish" families had by then been living in the annexes, including the ayllu of Quillunsa, for some time. They were the major landowners, with at least 5 hectares each, and were the leaders of those communities. Even in Quillunsa, the last ayllu to be penetrated, they usually held the office of *teniente gobernador*, or mayor, and were often the sponsors of lavish Saints Day festivals. Although considered hacendados, some of these people were actually middle proprietors by provincial standards.

Second, the "communal" tradition of the annexes was hierarchical, with a prestige ranking based on participation in the *cargo* system. The landlords, as the highest-ranking people, were the first to irrigate, having their own customary day or days of water. Most of those in Cachana, Chaucavilca, and Cotahuasi had titles to these days, but even in Quillunsa, where the resident landlords lacked them, they controlled all of the communal supply during two days of the week.[11] By law, the rights of those landlords were no different from those of comuneros, but in practice their rights were equivalent to private ownership in nearly every way. Everyone seemed to agree that water traditionally came to a given estate property on particular days, once every fifteen days, during which all of the land would normally be serviced. The frequency reportedly was the same on estate properties within community territory, as in Quillunsa.

When the misti landowners acquired property within Quillunsa territory, they demanded that their water shares be very generous, and that they be inserted into the watering order in such a way that the shares would be chronologically fixed, like those of the older, larger estates. Essentially by force, the hacendados took control of the entire supply for Sundays and Mondays, leaving the rest of the community to wait to begin, or to resume, the communal cycle.

This routine two-day preemption imposed a real hardship on the comuneros. It reportedly took twice as long, roughly a month under normal conditions, for all the community members to water their land during the rest of the cycle. The comuneros would simply continue to irrigate, with weekly interruptions, until they were finished, however long this took, and then start their cycle over again. Thus, although the fields of the Quillusana hacendados were by law "*sin agua propia*," their water rights were in fact equivalent to the private rights of the major estate owners.

This is the sort of de facto conversion in resource tenure that the liberal decrees of Bolívar, during the previous century, had ultimately made possible, by establishing the alienability of "Indian" community land.[12] The change was incompatible with, and disruptive of, the traditional system of water management in the annexes. It interrupted and prolonged the distribution cycle and, just as in Pampamarca, divided the user community into privileged and nonprivileged members. More important, it made communal water even scarcer and caused the comuneros, whose numbers were growing steadily at the time, to compete more and more with each other for access to that vital resource.

Privatization and the Decline of the Communal Tradition

As new estates continued to be established, the resulting contraction in the water supply unleashed a struggle among the members of each annex community. At some point after the Water Code was passed, individual comuneros began to seek certification of their communal rights in order to protect them, not just from the hacendados, but also from other comuneros. They acquired legal titles to their lands, which verified that they were privately owned and that they had been irrigated before the law was passed. These deeds confirmed that the properties were "*tierras con riego*," irrigated lands, but that they did not have their own water.

As we have seen, there were many eriazos, lands abandoned during the colonial period, scattered throughout the irrigation system, as there still are today. In theory, the Water Code left these without any water rights, but it appears that the law was not enforced for some time after it was passed. Indeed, in this isolated valley, the full extent of the law may not even have become known to comuneros until they had some need of it, until the emerging threat to their rights became real and perceptible. In any case, although the legislation did ratify existing patterns of use, some of its provisions, such as the prohibition on expansion, were obviously ignored. According to the information I was given, a certain amount of new (i.e., reclaimed) land was put under irrigation by the comuneros, with community permission. Naturally, this expansion stretched the communal water even thinner, so that the frequency of irrigation declined even more, at least for comuneros. This problem was perhaps inevitable in communities that were growing rapidly at the time.

Apparently, the acquisition of titles to irrigated land was, at least in part, a response to the growing water scarcity that estate encroachment, and the expansion of irrigation among the villagers themselves, induced during the early part of the century. This was the only means that individual comuneros now had of protecting their rights. Since the hacendados had already penetrated or colonized the annexes, the communities could not seek recognition of their land and water as communal property, unavailable to outsiders, when that became possible under the Peruvian constitution of 1920 (see Davies 1970: 68–95).

Instead, the comuneros sought recognition that their holdings were private property, as they already were in practice, with established water rights. In this valley, no village took advantage of the legislation enacted by the Leguía government (1919–30) for the protection of communal resources until well after mid-century. For people in the hacienda-dominated annexes, the only option was land privatization. And the main reason was clearly a concern for the security of communal water rights.[13]

Since the land titles indicated whether a given property had traditionally been irrigated, that should have settled the issue of who had rights and who did not. As with so many legal matters during this period, however, this did not turn out to be the case. Many of the people watering newly reclaimed land simply purchased false titles from a *tinterillo*, a kind of corrupt judge or pseudo legal specialist who was all too common in the highlands during this time. It is not surprising, therefore, that the comuneros' titles began to be disputed almost as soon as they were acquired.

People mentioned three other sources of conflict in the annexes in this period: water theft, favoritism on the part of the campos, and defiance of the campos' authority. All of these must have been responses to water scarcity, at least in part, and all were symptomatic of the decline of the communal tradition. Certain people managed to get allotments for land not irrigated before, and as the watering frequency declined, others struggled to get water more often, to get it out of turn. One group, however, had a particularly strong motive for getting water illicitly: the arrieros, whose muleteering business and involvement in long-distance trade required them to produce a certain amount of alfalfa.

These peasant arrieros were actually middle proprietors, having roughly 3–4 hectares each, enough land for family subsistence as well as the cultivation of pasture for a few cargo animals—typically three to six burros, since mules were generally too expensive and out of their reach.[14] They were regularly hired by the hacendados to transport goods over the altiplano. There were probably just a few in each community, as there would be later on, but the occupation itself clearly dates back to the late nineteenth century, when the wool trade began to flourish and expand. In all probability, like their counterparts in Pampamarca, this small group, with its special need for water, was responsible for much of the internal conflict.

The rest of the community members, of course, also had need of more water. They got it from the only people who had plenty to spare: the hacendados. Although it is not widely known, the buying and selling of private water was common during this period, not just here but throughout the highlands in general (see, e.g., Mitchell 1994). Most people did not have the wherewithal to buy it, however, and had to turn to sharecropping instead. Probably the main advantage of this relationship was that it enabled them to cultivate usufruct land that was extremely well watered and productive. But in addition, estate water was occasionally given as a sort of wage for work or sometimes even as a reward for good behavior, for use on a tenant's own crop fields at home. Sharecropping, which is said to have existed before this time, would eventually become a local institution. But for many comuneros, access to estate water would become the primary reason for turning to sharecropping in the first place.

Such was the state of irrigation in the annexes before 1940. I have said nothing about landscaping and watering practices, because I know nothing about them except that they must have already been differentiated in a manner similar to the pattern existing today in Pampamarca, and for the same reasons. The comparison is appropriate at this point and may be helpful in overcoming the limitations of data on a period that ended long ago. One can see, after a moment's reflection, that most of the conditions described above would have arisen at this time in Pampamarca, had two circumstances been different. If the estates had expanded there during the early part of the century, and if water had been relatively scarce to begin with, the same kinds of hydraulic relationship would undoubtedly have emerged. The problems that afflict irrigation today would have developed much sooner, and then intensified, and the cooperative tradition would have undergone an early decline. Moreover, if the water supply had been quite vulnerable to drought, as was the case in Cotahuasi, the breakdown would soon have become a crisis.

The 1940's: Drought and the Intervention of the State

The 1940's were a turning point in the district, when several pivotal changes took place. The first was the worst environmental disturbance of the twentieth century, the five-year drought that began in 1939 and lasted through 1942. The desiccation was so severe, even for the hacendados, that alfalfa production had to be reduced to a bare minimum, for mules only, and all cattle had to be sold or slaughtered. For campesinos, the effects on crops were so devastating that large numbers of men were driven out of the valley to seek work in the mines of Cerro Rico and Kalpa or on the big sugarcane plantations of Majes and Camaná. For many young indigenous people, this was the beginning of their migratory experience, a natural disaster that forced them into the outside world for the first time. Men had migrated before that, but only individually or perhaps in small groups, and it was done in order to finance fiestas or cargos, the same pattern that we saw in Pampamarca. This, however, was a massive group exodus that affected the lives of everyone and changed the whole tradition of peasant livelihood in the valley. Agricultural work was left in the hands of wives, children, and kinsmen, as it would be later during seasonal migration. And for those who stayed behind, especially in the annexes of Cotahuasi, the struggle for water intensified, reaching new heights.

Water theft reportedly became rampant, affecting even hacendados and other members of the elite community. Aside from the dire scarcity, the core of the problem lay, again, in the existence of false titles, which had also emerged in the use of private water and now became a serious disruption. But outright theft of private water did occur as well, despite the difficulties involved and the harsh punishments that inevitably followed. Gradually, over previous decades, modest shares of estate water had been sold to small and middle proprietors such as shop owners, tradesmen, and schoolteachers within the elite community of Cotahuasi. These people, too, had titles, but so did others who had deeds that had been altered by the tinterillos. This kind of fraud was evidently possible because there had also been a lot of selling and swapping of purchased rights among the smaller landowners themselves. In this confusing situation, where parts of a given day's ration of water were routinely being diverted and transferred to someone else, the hacendados were hard put to keep track of what was going on.[15] As the drought persisted, even the large and small landowners in the Spanish community came into increasing confrontation.

The state of affairs was even worse in the annexes, because comuneros were constantly having their water either stolen altogether or having their turns interrupted. Apparently, in the face of a scarcity that was devastating food crops, people had more reason than ever to question each other's rights and take matters into their own hands. My informants described a chaotic situation in which theft, favoritism, and other infractions became so common that all semblance of order was lost and traditional authority broke down. As one of them explained to me, "The situation was so bad that someone had to come from the outside and establish order."

In 1941, the national government stepped in, at local request, to try to remedy the situation. A decade earlier, in 1932, the first official procedures for rural water administration had been established, and a bureaucracy had been created to oversee the country's water resources, primarily the management of "public," rather than private, water (Costa y Cavera 1934). Gradually, official directives extended the state's jurisdiction to include certain parts of the highlands, namely, the headwaters of the coastal rivers. Apparently, this new authority was asserted slowly at first, mainly in communities that were in need of it. In hacienda districts like Cotahuasi, where private and communal water coexisted and were intertwined, and had been ratified by the Water Code long before, some sort of central authority was clearly necessary as the drought took its toll.

The government created such a position during the third year of the crisis. In compliance with the new legislation, public water was taken out of community control and put in the hands of an administrator appointed by the state bureaucracy. This appointee (Administrator was his official title) was required to be an outsider, but he did not have to have any technical training other than familiarity with the new procedures (Costa y Cavera 1934). A local man from the village of Puica was chosen, a well-known landlord who did not own any land in the lower part of the valley at the time, and so was qualified.[16]

The Administrator took immediate action, beginning with an inventory of lands that had legitimate water rights, both private and communal, under the Water Code. For the first time, all properties were officially registered in a list of irrigators, the Padrón de Regantes. The Administrator ordered irrigation to be restricted to those lands only and to be conditioned on the payment of a small tax by each household, based on the amount of land the family owned. He also appointed new water distributors in each annex community. Significantly, these men were hired and paid a small wage, and even allowed to stay in the position for several years, rather than serving voluntarily, out of a sense of duty, and in rotation, as campos always had in the past. All of this changed the very nature of the office and was required by the new legislation (Costa y Cavera 1934).

These changes had profound consequences, but they fell almost exclusively on the peasant population. State policy had little effect on private water use among the major estates. The false titles were eliminated, and the hacendados continued to irrigate just as before, without charge or supervision. They did this by simply refusing to pay the water tariff. The state sought only to clarify the rights and customs that had traditionally been observed in each highland valley and to establish a neutral official who would administer them according to certain minimal requirements (Costa y Cavera 1934: 13). It did not question the wisdom of those practices or try to change them, so that the estate owners got away with this tax default. Largely because of it, the landlords in the annexes were also able to preserve their privileges intact, by asserting their power over the new "communal" authorities.

Even though the system lasted only a short time, it had a complex impact on the rights of community members. Their allotments obviously increased in frequency because the lands that had been receiving water illegally no longer got it. For the people of Quillunsa, however, that benefit was negated by another action taken at the same time. In 1942, at the very end of the drought, the area's biggest reservoir, Yawarcocha, was built to store the flow of Wakajara overnight—water used by Quillunsa, on the one hand, and the haciendas of Huambo, Pitahuasi, and upper Cotahuasi on the other.[17] This, too, would have been entirely beneficial had the old system of sending two separate outflows, one to the hacendados and the other to the villagers, for simultaneous and independent use, been retained. Instead, in compliance with official procedures, they were forced to alternate in using the entire outflow of the reservoir. The big estates were to get their private water for three days, after which it was to be passed to Quillunsa, to be allotted by the new distributors. In principle, with a combined outflow providing twice as much water as before, both parties should have been able to water twice as much land each day in half the time, so that the net effect ought to have been nil. But as noted, the hacendados living in Quillunsa continued to get water on their traditional days in the communal cycle just as before. Under the old arrangement, their portion had been only 28 percent of the weekly water supply, but now, with twice the flow, they consumed a full 40 percent. They managed to do this simply by taking their water and asserting their power over the communal authorities and the other village members. In any case, as a result, it now took significantly longer for everyone in the village to irrigate his land than before. The watering frequency improved after the drought ended, but it never returned to what it had been previously. It now took six or seven weeks for all the village lands to be serviced.

In fact, the amount of water the comuneros lost was actually somewhat greater than indicated, since under the old arrangement, like their counterparts in Pampamarca, the hacendados had tried as far as possible to water only during the daytime. Nighttime irrigation was considered unpleasant, difficult, and inefficient. But they had often allowed the villagers to use estate water after dark, and this was no longer an option. Ironically enough, then, the construction of the tank, a major improvement that relieved everyone of the burden of irrigating at night, actually caused an erosion of people's communal rights. This change was extremely significant, since it set the stage for a struggle between the people of Quillunsa and Cotahuasi that has been going on ever since. The alternating arrangement was later modified, and the tank of Wakajara was moved farther downslope and rebuilt with state help, but the basic pattern persists to this day. It continues to be the main obstacle to just about every change that would be beneficial: improving the irrigation system, reducing corruption, and resolving conflict within the district.

The decline in the watering frequency in Quillunsa reinforced and strengthened the existing pattern of labor relations, that is, the dependency of comuneros on hacienda water. By making subsistence even more precarious, the new arrangement can only have facilitated the ongoing extraction, by the hacendados, of peasant labor. As the annex populations continued to grow during the next two decades, landholdings were subdivided and fragmented through inheritance, producing the kind of *minifundia* that prevails throughout the highlands today. In this situation sharecropping became an option much sought after, a means of gaining access to additional land and a secure supply of water.

Under such conditions of scarcity and hardship, it was inevitable that serious problems would emerge. The new system of administration was not among them, for it lasted just two years, shut down soon after the drought ended. Evidently, since the hacendados' rights were private and recognized as such under the law, there was no legal basis for forcing them to pay anything for their water. Thus, after this short interlude, the landlords returned to using the resource just as they had before.

The people in the annexes also resumed irrigating under the traditional hierarchical system. At first glance, then, one might think that nothing had changed much under state administration. But in fact the state, in this short spell of time, had succeeding in changing the role of campo, the central authority in irrigation and in communal life, dramatically and irreversibly. Even a brief lapse was apparently enough to accelerate the declining power of these officials.

The new policies had divorced the office from the civil and religious hierarchy of which it was a vital part, changing its ritual nature and deeming it that of a purely secular water distributor, or *rondador*. Instead of a position of service involving considerable sacrifice and expenditure for the benefit of the community, it had become an appointed and salaried post open to almost anyone, without any ceremonial or prestige dimensions.[18] In fact, people had been required, if only briefly, to pay a fee for a service that campos had always provided before free of charge. The campos had become mere technicians who worked for the Administrator, men who collected the water tariff and who were ultimately accountable only to him. And unfortunately, two years were sufficient to make the break with tradition a serious one indeed.

Over the next two decades, the prestige hierarchy, of which the campo had been such an important part, went into decline in each annex community as fewer and fewer comuneros became willing to serve in that and other posts. The most important celebrations, like the top political offices, came to be financed exclusively by the wealthier members of each community, mainly the hacendados, and the position of campo was at some point divorced from the hierarchy altogether. Increasingly, it came to be held by young men, often in lieu of military service, just as in Pampamarca. Consequently, the fiesta of Yarqa Aspiy was soon reduced to little more than a drunken faena: the Escarbo de Asequia, or Canal Cleaning, as it came to be called, in which no offerings were made and drinkers brought their own liquor. These circumstances still prevail today, but it seems clear that the most significant change affecting the social and ritual life of the community, the one in the campo's role, occurred a long time ago. It appears to date back to the decade after official management policies were implemented for the first time.[19]

Elderly people speak of the "loss of respect" that ensued, the same kind of decline in authority occurring today in Pampamarca. Evidently, once the distributors ceased to be highly regarded, they became more vulnerable to pressure and bribery. Traditionally, the village status hierarchies had determined the watering sequences, but as the landed elite gradually took over community leadership, the order apparently fell open to debate and negotiation. Increasingly, comuneros struggled to gain the distributor's favor so that they could get an advantageous place in the sequence, as people continue to do today. When they could not get it, some of them simply took the water.

As the hierarchical tradition became distorted and corrupted in this way, watering patterns must have become more dispersed and irregular, just as we see happening today in Pampamarca. Under these conditions, vigilance and accountability among neighbors ceased to be strong features of the hydraulic system, and the problems already existing in irrigation—theft, favoritism, and conflict—must have become more common, just as my informants said. As we saw in Pampamarca, when the allotment sequence is flexible and subject to change from one cycle to the next, detecting and punishing infractions become much more difficult. The only people who know where all the water should be at a given moment, and who know an infraction when they see one, are the distributors, who are more easily swayed or influenced under these circumstances. This is a basic flaw in any system of management that is too highly centralized, where power and authority, as well as monitoring, are concentrated in just a few hands, and it has caused serious problems, even bloodshed, in Cotahuasi ever since the government first became involved in local irrigation.

The Use of Private Water

As I have already noted, the new procedures, far from damaging the hacendados, either did not affect them at all or actually improved their position in terms of the quantity they controlled. On the big estates, they continued to use their private water without charge or supervision. This of course meant that they had to protect those rights themselves, through the threat and use of force, just as they always had before. In order to understand why this was necessary, we need to look more closely at the nature of those private rights.

We have already seen why the hacendados felt they could not do without water shares that were grossly out of proportion with the amount of land they owned. Their motives went beyond simple greed or a desire to deprive people of water in order to exploit them. Although privatization did ultimately work to the hacendados' advantage in this respect, they had a concrete need for more water, just as their neighbors in Pampamarca did, which is why it was first expropriated. The cultivation of alfalfa formed the very core of their livelihood, the fuel that made long-distance travel and the transport of cargo possible. To achieve maximum production, water shares had to be large and frequent enough to allow an entire property to be irrigated at least twice a month. However, this often was not necessary because the demand varied cyclically throughout the year. A nearly constant surplus enabled the hacendados to boost production in the short term and on short notice to feed herds of mules and cattle that fluctuated markedly in size, according to the rhythm of the wool and cattle trade. Mule teams had to be fattened for a full month before long trips onto the puna, and cattle were prepared for the overland journey to Chuquibamba and Lima in the same way. During the period in between, however, when the animals were absent or idle and the owner's needs temporarily lessened, the surplus water could be sold or bartered for peasant labor.

For example, the owners of the hacienda of Pitahuasi, which covered roughly 30 hectares altogether, usually had only about 10 hectares under irrigation at any one time. Yet this family owned three entire days of water, enough to service three times that area. This privilege may have begun with the original seventeenth-century owners, the Pérez family, who owned three of Cotahuasi's four early haciendas (Villanueva 1982 [1689]: 319–20). The surplus left the later owners, the Loayzas, free to increase or decrease irrigation as they wished, while giving them a great deal of bargaining power. Before the agrarian reform, they normally used only one day of water and employed the other two in negotiations of various kinds, bartering or outright selling.

Note that only truly private water was traded in this manner. The hacendados of Quillunsa did not use their shares of communal water this way, even though they too were generous ones. In numerous cases, the hacendados even had a duplicate supply because they owned a secondary spring, courtesy of the Water Code of 1902. The landlords monopolized this water, using it as much as possible for routine irrigation, so that their private shares of the main water of Wakajara, Armanca, or Cutirpo could be traded or sold.

We saw that neither Huaynacotas nor Pampamarca ever permits springwater and main irrigation water to duplicate each other. But here both kinds were private, and both were used as a commodity to procure labor and maintain work relations favorable to the hacendados. Campesinos could acquire water by working for it, by purchasing it with money earned from the previous sale of their labor, or by buying it on credit against future work. And, for them, a long-term sharecropping relationship with a patrón was, as much as anything else, a way of making these options as secure as possible. This kind of dependency was central to the landlords' relationships with their clients, so that sharecropping was based as much on a need for more water as on a shortage of land. Water-trading, and this kind of informal water market, may well have been common wherever private rights existed in the highlands, but, if so, with very few exceptions (Mitchell 1994), the practice has been overlooked in previous studies.

Naturally, in a situation where estate water was highly valued and sought af-

ter, it was constantly in danger of being stolen. The hacendados prevented theft
by riding up and down the main canals on horseback while their land was being irrigated, always with rifle in hand, protecting their liquid property. They
were feared and respected for good reason: the punishments for theft were extremely harsh and were entirely up to their discretion.[20] All of this reveals the
main reason why the system of private rights could be sustained at all: it was
based on the threat and the use of force, on a power of the local elite that had
no institutional or legal restraint.

The system of water control on the haciendas was thus an acephalous one;
there was no central authority to whom the landlords were subordinate, nor
were there any specialized irrigation roles. In effect, each hacendado, along with
his tenants, simply took the water that belonged to him on the appropriate day,
when the rights were legally his. At first glance, it is hard to imagine how such a
system could have functioned smoothly, but apparently it did when the supply
was adequate. Armed confrontations between landlords are said to have happened, but those incidents were rare and only seem to have occurred during
droughts.

In recent years, similar forms of organization have been reported in communities elsewhere in Peru, even indigenous ones, as investigators have tried to
define the different forms that irrigation traditionally took in the Andes. The
first detailed studies revealed a surprising amount of variation, and some re-
searchers have attempted to sort this out, in effect by trying to establish the
minimum level of organization necessary to sustain hydraulic life. On the basis
of two rather ambiguous case studies, some authors have argued that acephalous or individualistic systems of control and "informal" distribution patterns
may have been common in prehispanic times (e.g., Guillet 1987: 16, 1992). Their
suggestion is that hacienda-like structures, lacking any effective central authority, may be adequate for the running of small-scale systems, at least under certain conditions (but also see Guillet 1994).

The evidence from the Cotahuasi valley clearly shows that in the indigenous
communities, water is centrally managed according to strict rules and procedures, with only one exception. Only where water is extremely abundant, where
the topography makes it impossible for a supply to be distributed over its full
potential range, is a first-come, first-served type of organization viable, as we
saw in the previous chapter.[21]

The Cotahuasi annexes and the other villages in the lower valley, however,
have been transformed to varying degrees by depopulation, hacienda domination, and the various influences of the state. Indeed, these extrinsic influences

have produced much of the variation documented in the literature, especially among centralized communities, as my findings in the Cotahuasi valley also suggest. Thus the effort to specify the different forms that local hydraulic traditions have taken must be based on detailed studies of the processes of change, rather than being focused simply on their outcome. Because of their failure to do this, anthropologists have been unable to settle the issue of whether a widespread Andean hydraulic tradition ever existed. Even more important, they have had little or nothing to say about how irrigation can be, and should be, improved in many places, given the way that history has unfolded.

It is clear that, in most cases, acephalous systems are partial ones, as in the case of the haciendas, which relied on legal titles backed by the state and were components of a larger structure including the more complex communal organizations of the annexes. Or they are perhaps recent phenomena indicative of communities in the process of transformation or even disintegration. Although such systems may emerge and even persist for some time under certain circumstances, decentralization is not a viable basis for hydraulic organization in this environment. Where there seems to be far less than enough water to go around, a situation in which people simply help themselves cannot persist for long without resulting in conflict and significant inequities in people's rights. Wherever such systems exist within the arid zone, except in rare cases where water is superabundant (see Paerregaard 1994), they are of recent origin and are clearly in the process of changing into something else. Recent claims that they date back to Inca times in some communities simply are not credible.

We have seen that, by expanding, the haciendas displaced and disrupted the hydraulic tradition in the annexes, eventually bringing about its transformation. Aided and abetted by the state, hacienda growth set in motion an internal struggle over water in which comuneros began to fend increasingly for themselves and compete with one another, sending community traditions into a tragic decline. What emerged in Cotahuasi district was a corrupt system in which village members pursued their own interests by manipulating or even defying the water distributors. From there, it would have been only a short step to a total breakdown and loss of authority, to a situation in which the strong won out over the weak, to a truly acephalous, almost anarchic system. The historical and ethnographic evidence from Cotahuasi shows that such systems are degraded ones, products of either a dominant hacienda tradition or the misguided policies of the state, or both. In such communities, the indigenous system of management has been virtually lost, as it had been in Cotahuasi by the time of the 1969 agrarian reform.

Landscape Modification and Watering Technique

As we have seen, the major haciendas were established on all of the pampas in the district—in places like Piro, Cancha, Cachana, and Pitahuasi, where the natural slope of the terrain cannot have been more than about 5 percent. As in Pampamarca, this pattern was due to the high priority that the hacendados placed on growing pasture in large fields, or canchones. Big fields have several advantages over smaller terraces. They make it possible to pasture several animals at once on the same plot, without damaging terrace walls; they can be watered more easily than terraces, by a smaller number of people, as we saw in Pampamarca; and they can be plowed and sown relatively quickly, with a yunta, or ox-drawn plow, rather than with the chakitaqlla, or foot-plow. But because few areas in Cotahuasi have relatively flat topography, landlords could only turn to the surrounding slopes as they built more and more of these fields. This is a process that spread during the hacienda period and is still under way. Today, large pasture fields cover at least 60 percent of the district and are the diagnostic feature of the hacienda landscape.[22]

The building of these fields was, and continues to be, of great significance because it reversed the modifications that local people had always considered necessary for efficient water use in sloping terrain. Consequently, as we saw in the previous chapter, it altered local irrigation techniques as well. Ultimately, the effects of this simple change ramified throughout the system, affecting everything from the water balance to soil erosion to intercommunity relations. The new watering method that it promoted was, and is, extremely wasteful in comparison to the one that was displaced. We saw this in Pampamarca, but here the process of terrace destruction, and the adoption by farmers of the new technique, have proceeded much farther.

Today, almost everyone in the district (that is, all of the fifty small, medium, and large farmers formally surveyed, as well as nearly everyone I asked about the subject) seems to have rebuilt and consolidated at least some terraces into bigger fields. Nowadays there are even more reasons for this alteration than there were before 1940, but the technique and its basic logic remain the same as they were for the early hacendados. The technique as such is simple, a mere matter of flattening a group of terraces into a single sloping field, as shown in Figure 5.

Since the fields are usually steeply inclined—slopes of 6 degrees, or 10 percent, are common—they cannot be watered by the traditional method used in the native communities. Instead, essentially the same top-down procedure employed in Pampamarca is used, although it is not known here as *qhosqay*. Again,

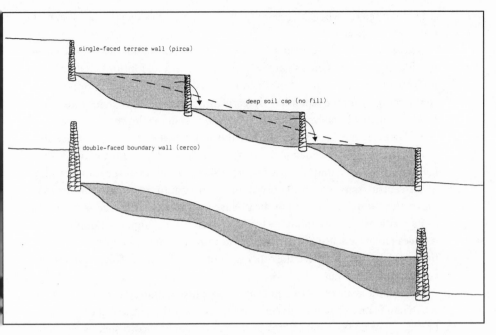

single-faced terrace wall (pirca)

deep soil cap (no fill)

double-faced boundary wall (cerco)

FIG. 5. Terrace destruction and corral building

it involves releasing the water at the top of the field into a temporary canal running across and slightly downslope, and allowing gravity to draw it continuously over the surface below. However, in a big pasture field, the surface is divided into horizontal strips, each with an earthen canal and barrier forming its upper border. Called *melgas*, these sections are irrigated singly or in pairs, starting at the top of the field and working slowly downward. The feeder canal bordering the field is first blocked with a temporary dam of sod and stones (a *champa*), forcing water into the uppermost canal or pair of canals. The irrigator then begins at the far end of each strip, opening breaches in the canals and allowing water to wash over the expanse below for ten or fifteen minutes. He then repeats the process, portion by portion, till he has worked his way to the other end. Note that essentially the same technique is employed when the parcel is planted in food crops.

After the field has been covered from top to bottom, the whole process is usually repeated one or two times, until the irrigator is satisfied that all parts have been well saturated. Inevitably, a great amount of water collects in the bottom part of the field, as in Pampamarca. If the person has another field down below, he will usually let a little of this excess soak in and direct the rest to that field. But often the whole lot is simply left to drain off through the canal, so that much of it is wasted.

The amount of time required varies among farmers, but it typically takes much longer per unit area than the bottom-up method, four or five hours per topo. Again, the technique is one of continuously washing a field, as opposed to submerging it, but the repetition is clearly unnecessary and extremely wasteful. It occurs mainly because no effort is made to curtail the flow of water arriving at the field in the first place, so that the water rushes over the surface too quickly to be well absorbed. According to Enrique Mayer and Cesar Fonseca (1979), a similar technique is used in several communities of the Cañete valley of the central coast (see also Fonseca 1983). These authors seem to assume that the method was a component of the prehispanic technology, but certain aspects of its relationship with another, clearly indigenous technique of flooding level terraces remain unclear. It cannot be determined from their accounts whether the one technique displaced the other with the proliferation of sloped fields devoted to alfalfa production.

Both authors are of course quite aware that production systems in the valley are dynamic and evolving; indeed, that is precisely the focus of their ground-breaking work. Nevertheless, this particular oversight is consistent with a tendency on the part of other authors to treat differences in watering technique as if these simply reveal the multiplicity of native Andean ways of doing things. It seems to me that such diversity instead reveals a history of change. For example, the top-down watering method has been documented throughout much of the Colca valley, where it is often employed on terraces and in some cases seems to be the predominant one in use today in Quechua-speaking communities that are extremely rich in terms of native dress, myth and folklore, and other Andean traditions (Valderamma & Escalante 1988; Gelles 1994; Guillet 1987, 1992). But in the traditional community that Treacy studied (1994b: 268), pooling structures are also widely used (*chakas*); he was able to show, among many other things, that this method is actually the far more prevalent one in that particular village. Furthermore, another nearby community also seems to use the pooling method widely (Valderamma & Escalante 1988: 79). This mixed pattern, I think, indicates that "traditional" irrigation has changed in the Colca valley during recent times, in at least one key aspect that has not been considered.

Everywhere in the Andes, the current configuration of hydraulic and landscaping practices is the outcome of two processes: a de-intensification in land and water use as the population collapsed and a gradual re-intensification with the demographic recovery and dramatic changes in the political economy of the last two centuries. Though the specifics may vary in each case, these processes are part of the history of all highland communities, and they both must be taken into account if the significance of contemporary practices is to be understood. It seems certain that some changes must have taken place during the era of depopulation, when water was abundant and labor was scarce, and it is possible that some were retained even as conditions later changed. A watering technique that economized on labor would seem to be a likely candidate, especially in a valley such as the Colca, where demographic recovery has been so slow that, as late as 1982, the population was still only about half what it was in Inca times (Cook 1982: 81–88).

If the method was adopted so widely that it largely displaced the original technique, then its use of more water would eventually have had significant consequences. At some point, the supply would have become inadequate to cover the full expanse of land that had been irrigated in Inca times, resulting either in some abandoning of fields, or, if it occurred early enough, in preventing a certain amount of long-abandoned land from being put back into production as the population grew. The latter is exactly the state of affairs in most parts of the Colca valley today, where the labor-saving technique seems in some cases to be the only method used (Guillet 1992: 95).

Changes in climate have clearly had little to do with this (Treacy 1994b). Furthermore, Spanish people have never lived in most of these villages in significant numbers, so that haciendas were never widely established there (but see Gelles 1994, 1995), and alfalfa cultivation reportedly did not begin until the 1960's (Manrique 1985; Guillet 1992). Watering techniques have been described only very briefly in some of the villages (Guillet 1992: 58–59; Valderamma & Escalante 1988: 79), but it seems possible that more than one method might still exist, as in the community where Treacy (1994) did his groundbreaking work. If that is not the case, then the labor-saving method has probably displaced the other one completely, simply because it is easier to carry out. I suspect that where the wholesale change did occur, it happened relatively recently, and that the technique is responsible, not only for the abandoned land, but along with the spread of alfalfa production, for much of the conflict now taking place within the local communities.

The top-down technique has not spread as far in Cotahuasi as it apparently has in certain parts of the Colca valley. It is largely confined to areas where terraces have been destroyed and where alfalfa has been inserted into the crop-rotation cycle. But those areas now constitute a huge portion of the terrain, and it is clear that the practice spread mainly during the last half of the twentieth century. Several factors promoted this change, as we will see shortly, but for now only the economic ones will be considered.

Although statistics on land use in early times are hard to come by, it is clear that the expansion of pasture occurred in three distinct phases. Up till the 1930's, the only people who grew alfalfa in the district were the hacendados and smaller "Spanish" proprietors (mistis), plus the handful of comunero middle proprietors (arrieros) in each of the annex communities. The cattle business was still small scale, sporadic, and restricted to the few landowners who were willing to move their herds overland to the coastal port of Chala, a long journey in which pasture had to be purchased for the animals along the way. Hacendados were the only people who could afford the trip and who had the necessary connections with other alfalfa-growers along the route. Furthermore, the business was quite risky and not very profitable. According to the ganaderos I know, cattle drives back then were more of an adventure than anything else, a part of a man's lifestyle rather than a major source of his livelihood.

The whole route changed in 1930, when the road was completed as far as Chuquibamba, connecting it with Arequipa, with coastal ports to the south, and with the new Pan-American highway being built along the coast. This road reduced the time for the cattle drive from two weeks to only three days, greatly cutting the costs involved. Despite this improvement, the business grew slowly over the next two decades because the wool trade continued to be so much more lucrative. Apparently, the rise in cattle demand, and in beef prices, corresponded roughly with the postwar expansion of the urban population in Lima, where the majority of the animals were sent.

Consequently, the number of comuneros who produced alfalfa increased slowly during the 1940's and 1950's, the height of the hacienda era. Most of them just planted a small plot to feed a dairy cow or fatten a bull for sale, as most campesinos do today. Some comuneros did begin to grow alfalfa on a larger scale so they could rent their fields out to cattle-buyers at a fairly good profit. But this usually required the purchase of additional land, and few campesinos had the necessary capital.

The best evidence we have of these developments is the first agrarian census, which was carried out nationwide in 1961 (DNE 1968: 234–46). The information was recorded only a few months after the road was completed, so that things had not yet had time to change very much. Compiled for the province as a whole, rather than by district, the census showed that approximately 28 percent of the irrigated land in the valley was planted in alfalfa, including villages like Huaynacotas and Pampamarca.[23] Of this total, 42 percent was grown on major estate properties of more than 5 hectares. The vast majority of the smaller units (85%) were medium-sized holdings of 1–5 hectares, dispersed fundos that were probably owned mainly by landlords, as most of them still are today. Peasant households with less than a hectare of land accounted for only 9 percent of the pasture grown in the entire province.

Consequently, until the 1960's, watering techniques must have been rather clearly differentiated between the estates, where the top-down method predominated, and the annex communities, where the pooling method still generally prevailed. Cotahuasi district, however, is somewhat distinctive in the way that the pooling method is is carried out. Here, the atus, also known as *pozos*, are even shallower than in Pampamarca, built to a height of only 10–15 centimeters. Another difference is that, after people have irrigated their terraces, they return to top the atus off again when some of the water has had time to drain, something that is prohibited in both Huaynacotas and Pampamarca. The most important reason for this repetition is simply that the water distributors allow it to happen. In general, people are allowed to irrigate until they are satisfied that they are finished, just as with the other method, and this has clearly been the case for a long time. Because the atus are so shallow, however, the repetitive method still takes roughly the same amount of time as in other places, about three hours per topo of land, depending on the state of the supply.

This is the customary way of irrigating a terrace in the district, the way that such things have "always" been done. It does not do any great harm—indeed, it obviously uses less water than the pooling method in Huaynacotas—but the procedure is distinctive. Although I cannot prove my hypothesis, I think that this practice began during the decline of traditional authority in the 1940's and 1950's people told me about, and that it spread widely during a later period of state management, beginning in 1960. Things may have always been done this way, as most local people say, but the technique seems to fit with the other basic changes in practice that took place during this same time.

History of a Typical Hacienda Irrigation Unit

The nature of work on the haciendas—landscaping, water distribution, the division and allocation of labor, and the social relations of work—can be best understood by examining, in retrospect, of course, a typical landholding unit, or fundo. Figure 6 depicts the former hacienda of Iskaywayqo (Two Ravines). Although smaller than most estate properties in the area—it covers just 2 hectares—I chose it for study because it is one of the few clusters of plots in the district that forms a discrete, easily mapped unit and that remained under single ownership until the late 1960's.[24]

According to the former sharecroppers who now own most of the land, the terraces (Fig. 6, units 3 and 5) were the usufruct plots of their parents, who worked them mainly on a family basis. The bigger fields were of three types: the owner's alfalfa fields (units 2 and 6), which were tended by a mayordomo and

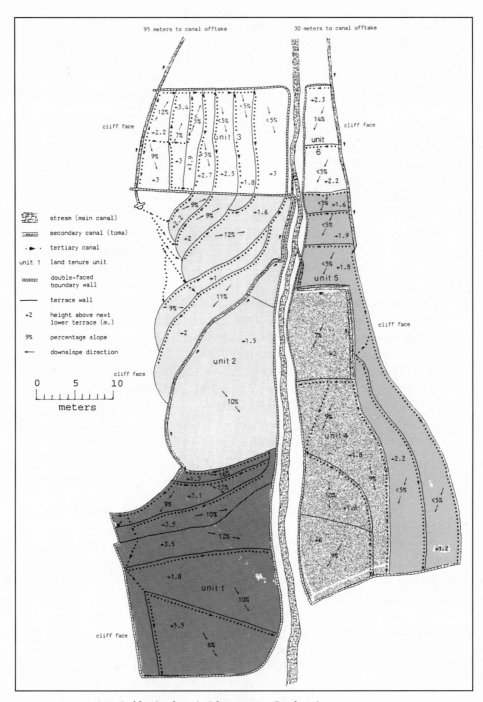

FIG. 6. A typical hacienda unit: Iskayawayqo, Cotahuasi

his family; the mayordomo's subsistence plot (unit 1), worked under usufruct by him and his family; and the landlord's own subsistence plot, or *wayka* (unit 4), which was worked cooperatively by the sharecroppers. All of the fields were used in a long-term rotation sequence, with the crop fields being planted periodically in alfalfa to enrich the soil through nitrogen fixation, just as they are today.

The estate had its own local source of water, two springs lying above the main canal, which is merely an unmodified stream that passes down the ravine through the middle of the estate. Although the springs do have a tank, it is located well below the property, so that the water is used both day and night, just as it was in the past. The secondary canals, which appear to be prehispanic, have simply been excavated and reinforced with low retaining walls. Stratigraphic examination of the terraces revealed that they were built using the same techniques employed in the indigenous communities; thus they, too, are probably prehispanic.

Regarding landscape modification for alfalfa production, three things are worthy of note. First of all, the natural slope of the terrain limited the degree to which terraces could be consolidated and enlarged into corral-fields. The steepest gradients of the fields (units 1, 2, 4, and 6) are 10 to 15 percent. Where two terraces adjoin at very different levels, as in units 1 and 4, further consolidation would require a great amount of labor and produce a field so steep that it would hardly absorb water at all. To overcome this problem, the alfalfa plots may be separated by narrow strips that resemble terraces but have a pronounced slope, as in the upper parts of units 1 and 2.

Second, terraces often collapse from erosion, especially during flooding after a downpour or after the shock of an earthquake, and many owners prefer to just leave them that way. An example can be seen in the upper part of unit 3, where the wall of the canal above the plot collapsed several years ago during a rainstorm, spilling down over the three terraces immediately below. Little was done to repair the damage. The canal border was rebuilt in makeshift fashion and, as the rainy season proceeded, the terraces had continued to erode until eventually the middle of all three collapsed. With time, the disturbed soil and rock were naturally redistributed, until the surfaces became steeply inclined in various directions.

According to the owner of that plot, the same thing had happened many years earlier in the adjacent part of unit 2, where the canal continues downward and ends abruptly. The canal and the upper part of the first four terraces collapsed and eroded, and, when the sod was later broken up for replanting in food crops, the disturbed soil was simply smoothed out, without any attempt to

level the surfaces or thoroughly repair the walls. As a result, the terrace became
sloped strips of land.

Finally, perhaps the most important reason why terraces were (and are) being torn down is an invading element, the grama mentioned earlier. The constant advance of this weed, the kikuyu, directly promotes the creation of sloped
fields. The grass (*Pennisetum clandestinum*) is an extremely hardy plant native
to east Africa. It was brought to Peru in the early 1940's by a hacendado of the
neighboring department of Apurimac, who deliberately introduced it on his estate, thinking that it would be good pasture for the Arabian horses he had also
brought back with him from overseas.[25] Unfortunately, it is not, but it successfully competes with and displaces alfalfa.

The grass produces enormous amounts of seed that spread rapidly in irrigation water and animal dung. Consequently, within a few years of its introduction, it invaded Cotahuasi and adjacent provinces that were linked to Apurimac
through the cattle and mule trade, and eventually took over most of the Andean
countryside, as all Peruvian farmers are painfully aware today (see Montoya et
al. 1979: 69). Throughout the lower valley, where alfalfa has been inserted into
the crop cycle on the vast majority of plots, the grass has become a menace that,
among other things, continually invades terrace walls and weakens them with
its long, penetrating roots.

The battle against the weed is constant; indeed, this has come to constitute
the single-greatest labor input in the cultivation cycle. If the grama is not continually removed from walls as it sprouts, they will crumble and eventually collapse if they are not rebuilt. Five years is said to be the maximum amount of
time that an untended wall will last.

This is another reason, actually the primary one, why the terraces in the upper part of unit 3 were allowed to collapse. The entire plot had been too thoroughly taken over by the grama to make the repair worthwhile. Like an increasing number of his neighbors, this farmer preferred to consolidate his unit
into one big sloped field. Consolidation reduces the total surface area of walls,
and thus the overall amount of work required to weed out the grama. In cases
where someone is repairing a given series of walls anyway because of structural
collapse, the change in landscaping requires little additional effort. If this is not
done, and the invasion is simply left to take its course the next time it gets a
start, the end result will often be the same in any case. Climatic or geologic
events, or even routine irrigation, will eventually collapse the terraces, and if the
damage is not repaired, as in the case of unit 3, the person will eventually end
up with a sloped surface.

This situation presents people today, as it did for the hacendados before, with a constant dilemma. The continuous erosion processes have greatly elevated the labor cost of maintaining indigenous practices, not just terracing, but also the original watering technique, thereby adding to the many other pressures that favor the adoption of the Spanish alternatives. The significance of this predicament with respect to irrigation and "the water problem" can hardly be exaggerated.

RECIPROCITY AMONG SHARECROPPERS

The vast majority of work on Iskaywayqo and the other local estates was done by sharecroppers, just as on the similar haciendas of southern Ayacucho (see Montoya et al. 1979; and Montoya 1980). Under this arrangement, called *al partir*, the owner supplied the land and water, the *partidario* (sharecropper) supplied the labor, and owner and worker split such costs as seed and tools, as well as the eventual harvest. Most other services regularly performed for the landlord, such as building field walls, were paid for in money. Recall, however, that the sharecropper was expected to perform several major chores, such as providing firewood for the landlord, without pay, if he wished to maintain the relationship. And his spouse had to similarly take turns working as a domestic servant in the landlord's home. Only the work that involved irrigation will be discussed below.

As on any estate, the partidarios were responsible for irrigating their rented fields (Fig. 6, units 3 and 5), as well as the hacendado's own crop field (unit 4), with the estate's private water. Where the water was collected in a tank, as in the case of the secondary springs, someone had to climb to the tank and fill it the night before (a task called *estancar*), opening the proper gates along the way and closing all others, and then release the water at dawn. This was not necessary in Iskaywaycco, since no tank was used, but where it was done, all the sharecroppers who used the water on a given day took turns carrying out the task.[26]

Even where storage and release were someone else's responsibility, or where there was no tank, the sharecroppers still had to climb up the main canal at dawn on every watering day, closing the mouths of any gates that might be open, and then follow the water down to the fields. Again, the tenants working a given property would do this in rotation. Cooperation of this sort was routine, since cultivation on the haciendas was based on a series of labor exchanges among sharecroppers, various forms of ayni. The vigilance had to be carried on constantly throughout the day, but the task (*vigilar*) was usually taken over at some point by the landlord.

The hacendados never got their hands dirty or wet, but they typically spent much of the day protecting their water from theft. They knew what their own rights were, and those of their neighbors, and on the appropriate day, they "sent their people" to go and get the water that belonged to them, which normally occurred without event. A sharecropper's son might do this in his father's place, but the male members of the household would then normally work together to actually distribute the water. The wife might do this instead, but only if her husband or sons were unavailable. But the landowner was strictly a guard and enforcer who of course never participated in the work itself.

Two unrelated families who lived close to Iskawayqo, in Reyparte and Cachana, irrigated and cultivated the rented or usufruct terraces (units 3 and 5). Each household had approximately 1 topo of its own at the time, located within the community. In addition, one family worked a second plot on another property belonging to the same landlord (about 0.75 topo), and the other rented two fields (1.75 topos total) owned by someone else. By all accounts, this was a typical arrangement; it was unusual for a sharecropper to cultivate more than 6 topos all together (2 hectares). The greatest number worked by anyone I know is 7 (2.3 hectares), but there were reportedly a few cases where a family cultivated more than 10 topos belonging to various "patrones."

Most of the sharecropped plots on this hacienda were terraced, planted in food crops (maize, potatoes, wheat, or barley), and irrigated by the pooling method. For the most part, the families cultivated the same crops and used the same technique on their land in the annex communities. As on most estates, the partidarios were sometimes given portions of the owner's water for use on their own property. These parcels were located in Reyparte and Cachana, adjacent to the main canal of Armanca, where the landlord had private rights. According to my informants, this was done under three kinds of circumstances.

On rare occasions, the landlord gave the water without request, as a reward for good work or commendable behavior, such as the prompt payment of a debt. At these times, he might simply say, "Papito, qarpa yakuyta chakraykiman apakuy" (Take my water to your field), and that would be that.[27] But usually a supply was granted in exchange for work done beforehand or afterward. For example, this particular owner usually made the stipulation, "Kambyanakusunyakuypaq, killantin llapan waykaykunata qarpanki" (We'll swap: for the water, you will irrigate all of my crop fields for a month). Finally, when it was urgently needed, the partidarios sometimes bought the water on credit for a specific sum, which was added to their running account with the landlord. Because of purchases of alcohol and other store merchandise, they were nearly always heavily in debt, a bill that they continually paid off through wage work, all without any money actually changing hands. Indebtedness, like servitude, was basic to the hacendado-partidario relationship, the bond between patron and client, and water was one of the main commodities involved in maintaining it.

The sharecroppers considered the granting or sale of water a great favor because it could make a significant difference in their crop, but the price, whether in cash or work, was always high. In a year of normal rainfall, this might happen once at most, but during the height of the dry season, when communal water came only every two months, it could mean the difference between a mediocre crop and a good one. In a drought year, when the community cycles would stretch out even longer, the water might be given two times and could be a lifesaver. This illustrates a crucial fact emphasized repeatedly by the former partidarios: access to water was an essential part of their relationship with the landlord, one of their primary reasons for becoming sharecroppers in the first place.

For the routine tasks of irrigation and cultivation, the work force of the household was normally sufficient. For the heavier tasks of plowing, sowing, weeding, and harvesting, help was, again, first sought through yanapakuy, from any married sons or daughters living nearby in their own homes. They were expected to help, along with their spouses and children, if they resided in the same district.[28] The other partidarios working on the same fundo were nearly always the second source of assistance. Sharecroppers typically cooperated in all the major cultivation tasks, again by practicing ayni. As an arrangement strictly between comuneros and/or campesinos, ayni did not undergo any drastic modification on the haciendas, but it did have one feature worthy of note.

Repeated ayni exchanges tended to create a relationship in which the sharecroppers were inclined to work together each year if they possibly could. The people working a given fundo usually formed these relationships out of mutual convenience, because they had roughly the same amount of land, and thus virtually identical labor needs, and because their plots were adjacent to each other. Such partners were the first people to be asked for help every year; they anticipated the request and counted on the labor being returned. The exchanged work was sometimes merely that of the household head or a mature son, but for the biggest tasks ayni would involve the whole family.

These relationships ensured the rapid completion of key tasks, but when the need arose, the partners would look after each other's plots in minor ways, just as in Huaynacotas and Pampamarca. Where the partners were close kin, the bond might be an especially strong one and involve many other forms of assistance. But the primary basis for the relationship was the necessity for workers on a given fundo to cooperate; kinship was, again, a secondary consideration. Frequently, related households had to make sharecropping contracts with different landlords, so that kinship was not usually a factor in labor relations and patterns of cooperation on the estates.

Today, the ayni tradition is still quite strong among Cotahuasi's former sharecroppers, even after the major changes in land ownership brought about by the agrarian reform. In this sense, the indigenous custom did change because of its use on the estates. In selecting regular partners, criteria such as possessing roughly the same amount of land as oneself and the proximity of the other person's fields to one's own came to outweigh any preference for kin. Here, where the kin-based ayllus disappeared long ago, where rented plots were often located far from a man's own fields and those of his relatives, and where rates of seasonal migration grew rapidly during the last decade of the hacienda era, so that the presence of kin was less assured, reciprocity came to be based primarily on a balanced mutual interest. Thus, the essential elements of ayni, the same ones that we saw at work in the other communities, came to the foreground, while factors such as kinship receded.

THE MAYORDOMO

Throughout the year, the sharecroppers' work had to be coordinated with that of the mayordomo, also called the *kamayuq*, who was responsible for watering the owner's alfalfa fields (Fig. 6, units 1 and 6) and tending to his animals. At least once a month, the mayordomo and his family irrigated all of the fields using the top-down or inundation method. The canchones were always the first plots to be serviced; on big properties that did not have use of a tank, where distribution was round-the-clock, they would usually be tended during the day, and the partidarios' fields watered at night. The mayordomo of this hacienda was also in charge of 10 topos (3.3 hectares) of pasture on a nearby fundo, where the hacendado and his family lived. Typically, a man took care of 5–10 hectares of land, so that, even with the help of his wife and children, irrigation would take up one to two weeks of every month.

The bulk of the family's work consisted of moving the mules and cattle about so that no section of land got overgrazed. Iskaywayqo had only a small amount of pasture land, and only two to four grazing animals at any one time, but on a larger property, where at least 50 percent of the plots were always planted in alfalfa, the task might involve controlling a team of twelve mules (a *piara*) and a lesser number of cattle. The main requirement was that the animals be rotated at appropriate intervals, between fields and between properties, so that the proper ratio of animals per topo (ideally 1:1) was maintained. Although the work demanded the constant attention of a whole family, it was not very labor-intensive and normally required no outside help. Nonetheless, the mayodomos and their families had to be present at all times, which is why they were always landless people, undistracted by the labor demands of other plots. They were usually forasteros, outsiders; this particular family was originally from Puica, at the eastern end of the valley, where the father had been orphaned at an early age and left without any inherited land.

The invasion of the grama in the late 1940's greatly complicated the mayordomos' work, making it necessary either to attack the weed constantly with pick and shovel or to cut the alfalfa by hand and feed it to animals kept out of the fields in corrals.[29] Consequently, during the last two decades before the reform, landlords increasingly resorted to hiring sharecroppers as wage laborers to assist in the task. For his work, the mayordomo received a substantial cash wage and the use of a plot of at least 1 topo (unit 1 in Fig. 6) to support his family. Eventually, he might be given the field permanently as a reward for years of service. The parcel was worked by the household members, who rarely had recourse to yanapakuy because, as outsiders, they had few if any kinsmen in the district.

Although mayordomos were commonly responsible for overseeing sharecroppers elsewhere in the highlands (see, e.g., Montoya et al. 1979; and Skar 1981), in this district that was primarily the landlords' task. Since the mayordomos' assignments did not involve any basic conflict of interest with the partidarios, relations between the two were not ordinarily antagonistic, as they usually were in other regions. In fact, on this hacienda, they cooperated in an arrangement that the landowner had made with each of his sharecroppers. The mayordomo, who was an experienced *guián*, or plowman, did the plowing, while the sharecroppers and their families took care of the sowing and other tasks, both with the free use of the owner's oxen and plow. This cooperative work was done on the subsistence plot of each worker in succession, as an even ayni exchange.

WAYKA: EXPLOITATION THINLY DISGUISED

In Chapter Two, we saw that labor relations on the haciendas changed through time, that they moved away from servitude toward sharecropping and wage labor during the late nineteenth century. Insight into this process can be gained by considering the manner in which the landlord's own crop field, the wayka, was usually worked, as on this fundo. A practice that has not been described in the Andean literature before, it is significant because, like mink'a, it reveals how estate owners manipulated and distorted indigenous traditions in an attempt to keep certain remaining forms of servitude acceptable to their workers.

According to native Quechua-speakers in the province, wayka, or *waykilla*, is a form of emergency assistance in which members of a person's kindred and ayllu are obliged to join him, en masse, in the rapid execution of some task. It commonly refers to the defense of a kinsman in a dispute or conflict where several people gang up against one person. This might occur during a feud, especially between members of different ayllus. But the term also denotes massive, spontaneous aid in planting or harvesting a field, in repairing a collapsed terrace, or in any urgent task that must be completed quickly. Nothing is expected in return.[30]

When people in Huaynacotas and Pampamarca explained the concept to me, the question of returning such a favor did not arise. When pressed on the issue, they pointed out that such help would definitely be given back by the beneficiary were a similar emergency to arise. Here, the element of kinship or ayllu membership is implicit, but the idea of reciprocation is strained; wayka simply denotes a favor that one would automatically do for a relative or neighbor in an urgent situation.

As with so many aspects of indigenous tradition, this practice was appropriated by the estate owners and manipulated so that it was fundamentally distorted. The name wayka was given to parcels of land where the landlords' own food crops were grown, and where an analogous kind of "help" was obligatorily provided by the sharecroppers. They were expected to pitch in together to carry out all the major cultivation tasks, at times chosen by the landlord, just as if they were helping a relative and fellow village member. They also took turns watering and tending the field on a routine basis, but for that work they usually received a small wage.

In almost every respect, the group work was like mink'a as practiced in Pampamarca, and in fact the two terms were often used synonymously, as they still are retrospectively today. The owner was not obligated to reciprocate, however, either with alcohol and food or with a share of the harvest, though he usually did so in practice. In this sense, wayka on the estates was rather like yanapakuy: an unreciprocated gift of labor, but one given simultaneously by several people to a mutual patron or guardian, rather than a kinsman or neighbor. Significantly, in this case the beneficiary was not necessarily even present, and he certainly never participated in the actual work.

As practiced on the haciendas, wayka (often Hispanicized as *waykita*) was in fact a form of free labor service, similar to mita, but without the idea of a turn or rotation. In colonial times, hacienda serfs had to work the landlord's subsistence plots without pay during the entire year, in mita-like fashion, a form of rent paid on their usufruct fields.[31] Although they did not have to divide their crop with the landlord, as in sharecropping, the rent actually took up most of their time, so that their own fields were neglected, and their harvests often poor. Wayka was essentially just a vestige of this feudal tradition dressed up as an indigenous practice.

By employing the notion of wayka in an idiom of fictive kinship, of paternalism and even more fictive neighborliness and commonality of origin, the hacendados apparently sought to transform constant labor service into a series of special favors done only periodically. This probably occurred as they converted all but a few of their plots into sharecropped fields. We have seen that, in order to attract a labor force as the estates expanded, the landlords had to reduce traditional forms of servitude and eventually eliminate them altogether, in accordance with early republican law. The persistence of the "waykita" down to the time of the agrarian reform shows that the landlords drew this transition out over more than a century, a fact that they tried to obscure, or de-emphasize, by manipulating tradition.

Of course, these mystifications did not fool anyone, but they stuck all the same. Wayka, like the distorted practice of mink'a, came to express differences of ethnicity, status, wealth, and power, rather than symbolizing a fundamental equality, a sameness and commonality of origin. Like mink'a, it became a form of exploitation, rather than of mutual aid, and continued to be just that for a very long time.

In the 1950's, things began to change on this and other local estates the same way they did on estates in Pampamarca, and for the same reasons. Increasingly, comuneros began to resist these forms of exploitation and demand a small wage for wayka and mink'a work. The terms they negotiated then with the landlords were the same ones that came to prevail in other districts: the wage was small, less than half the going rate for jornal, but it was given in addition to food and drink and a share of the harvest. This arrangement spread widely, and, by the 1960's, it had become the customary form of group work on the haciendas. In some cases, however, especially where a landlord had always been abusive, sharecroppers would no longer participate in this kind of exchange at all. They refused to work on the owner's crop fields for anything other than cash wages. For the valley's most notoriously abusive landowners, this was the only way that they had ever been able to get the work done, but more and more found themselves in this predicament as the 1960's drew to a close.

The new peasant activism here was spurred by the same forces we saw at work in Pampamarca. During the last two decades of the hacienda era, the peasants in the district came into much closer contact with the outside world than they had been before, and many of them became much better educated than their parents. They began to travel routinely to other provinces, to work on the outside, and, perhaps most important of all, to have cash of their own, which they could save and spend as they liked. It came as a shock to me to realize this, but having appreciable amounts of money or money actually in hand was a rather new experience for campesinos, and it obviously caused them to appreciate the potential value of their captive or indentured labor.

Admittedly, money was not such a novelty for some of them; the muleteers and their hired assistants, the *arriero-peónes,* had been traveling outside the valley and earning cash from the landlords for a long time. Many campesinos I met had worked as muleteer peons at some point in their youth, and like their neighbors in Pampamarca, they described these experiences as pivotal in their own "awakening." But many others, even at this late stage, were still unaccustomed to using money, having lived their entire lives in debt.[32]

"No nos pagaban nada" (They didn't pay us anything), "Nos pagaban una miseria" (They paid us a pittance), and "No teníamos plata" (We didn't have any money) were phrases that I heard repeatedly in my conversations with former sharecroppers. At first, I thought they were merely referring to the meagerness of the wage they got for work on the hacienda. But as it turned out, they were speaking specifically of the fact that most of them had to render these services to the landlord in order to cancel, a little at a time, debts for goods they had bought on credit. I knew about this kind of servitude, to be sure, but it had not occurred to me that it kept sharecroppers unfamiliar with the use of money and somewhat mystified by the way that debts could grow. They rarely received any bill or coins and did not often have any on hand to spend.[33]

The opportunity to travel to new areas, to work for wages and to actually have money and use it, came much earlier for peasants in many other parts of the Andes, places closer to roadways and major cities than this remote valley, especially those where population pressure on the land began to be felt more strongly at an earlier point in time (see Mitchell 1991a). It was only in the 1950's, as the road to Cotahuasi came closer and closer, that the local peasants got their chance to learn the potential value of a day's labor. Other things also contributed to a growing awareness of options to dependency and servitude—education, military service, radio communication—but the experience of having money was probably the most important one. Population growth was probably also critical in the shift, since it accelerated the parcelization, or splitting up through inheritance, of the already small landholdings that the comuneros had (ibid.). This, too, must have impelled peasants to resist the hacendados and demand a wage to supplement dwindling agricultural production and declining real incomes.

Canal Maintenance: Cooperation as Servitude

We have seen that the landlords, who had their own water, were able to neglect most of the requirements for running an irrigation system, to shun all forms of conservation and cooperation, especially in maintenance. As in Pampamarca and most parts of the Andes, Cotahuasi landlords left the cleaning and repair of tanks and canals—not to mention roads, bridges, and public plazas—entirely to their sharecroppers and other annex community members. Exemption from all forms of communal work was one of the most tangible expressions of the elite status of people of Spanish descent, and many former landlords continue to consider it their prerogative even today.

Until sometime around the middle of the twentieth century, the comuneros and partidarios continued to carry out the majority of the maintenance work in the customary manner, during the celebration of Yarqa Aspiy. Each annex community held the event on the same day every year, one that marked the beginning of the agricultural season and coincided with a saint's day fiesta—Santa Rosa in Chaucavilca and Cachana (August 30) and San Exaltación in Quillunsa (September 8).

Before these rituals degenerated into mere civic chores, they were reportedly identical to those in the other two villages, including the offerings to the springs that supplied the communities with water. As there, each comunero household had to contribute one person to the maintenance task in compensation for the use of communal water and the service of having it delivered by the campo. And again, the biggest landowners, the major beneficiaries of the water system, always exempted themselves from the work.

The hacendados of Cotahuasi were famous for not ever attending Yarqa Aspiy at all, even when they owned land in the villages. By their own admission, they felt no obligation to do so; at best, they would send along a bottle of cane alcohol or a partidario who was not a community member to work in their place. Utter indifference to the event was the behavior that comuneros expected of the hacendados, but this expectation gave some landlords the opportunity to demonstrate that they occupied a special category within the elite community: the *gente buena* or "good people." Patróns who showed a paternalistic concern for the welfare of their clients and the communities were held in high regard, and enjoyed extraordinary loyalty from their tenants. This bond commonly endured over several generations in both families. Nevertheless, when landlords showed up at communal work events, they were always careful to express their privileged status Their *brazos cruzados* (folded arms), their supervision or criticism of the workers, and their jokes, or sometimes their standoffish-

ness, were the behaviors that comuneros described to me as typical of the landlords.

The actual quantity of communal work involved in maintenance was considerable, though not so great as that which has been reported in some other
communities. The cleaning of the upper part of the canal system, the one used
by both the annexes and the haciendas, was completed in only two days. Quillunsa serviced the canal of Wakajara, all the way up to its source in Huambo, in
a single day, and Cachana and Chaucavilca combined forces to clean the canal
of Cutirpo in the same period of time. Shortly thereafter, in late August or September, smaller faenas (*huch'uy phayna*) were organized by each annex for
cleaning the secondary canals and the storage tanks of the smaller springs, also
in a single day. Whenever necessary, other projects were mounted for emergency canal repairs.

The lower part of the system, used exclusively by the estate owners and independent smallholders, was cleaned in separate events organized by the landlords and manned by their sharecroppers. Called simply faenas, or communal
work projects, these did not have a fixed date, were not ritualized, and did not
necessarily even happen every year. When they did, each landowner would send
some of his partidarios (or a hired peón, in the case of a smallholder), each
with a bottle of liquor, to join one of two groups: one that cleaned the canal of
Armanca from bottom to top, and the other that cleaned the part of the main
canal in upper Cotahuasi. The tanks of the smaller springs did have to be
cleaned every year, but the landlords organized small groups on separate days
for this task.

This was essentially all that was done in the way of routine maintenance on
the estates. Feeder canals were not cleaned or repaired on a regular basis, as they
were in the annexes, but rather as the need arose. Hacendados would organize
parties to work on them only when it became absolutely necessary, as, for example, when a canal became blocked. Although such blockages were common,
hacendados rarely had to cope with them because partidarios carried out small-
scale maintenance in their own interest as a matter of course.

Thus, within the district as a whole, keeping the irrigation system in good
repair took just two days of ritualized community labor a year and two more
for the estate faenas. Adding the smaller group tasks on secondary canals and
cleaning the small spring tanks brings the total total to six workdays, and to
seven after the Wakajara tank was built in 1942. Removing that tank's yearly accumulation of silt was done mainly by the comuneros of Quillunsa as part of
their Saint's Day fiesta.

According to my informants, maintenance actually amounted to only about four days of labor a year for a given campesino household because sharecroppers participated only in the faenas of their own communities and their landlord's estates. Although it is difficult to compare different cases, these figures are somewhat lower than those reported for other communities on the western slope, ones where maintenance is largely a ritual affair (see Gelles 1984, 1986, 1994; and Valderama & Escalante 1986, 1988). Two factors probably account for Cotahuasi's lower figure. First, its main canals, those cleaned in the fiestas and faenas, are relatively short, only about 12 kilometers long from the main sources to the lowest extreme of the system. Second, roughly half the secondary canals, those servicing only estate lands, were not always maintained by formal groups. Thus not only was the physical infrastructure itself more compact, but in this thoroughly hacienda-dominated system, the community members had to carry out much of the maintenance work on their own throughout the year.

After the communal organizations were reorganized in 1941, the fiesta of Yarqha Aspiy, as previously noted, degenerated into a massive faena, now known as the Escarbo de Asequia. No rites were performed, and the water distributors no longer sponsored the event, now merely organizing it. The work arrangements remained the same, but the comuneros became increasingly resentful of what passed as "communal" work. In their eyes, a large part of their maintenance work, like their work in the wayka fields, was a free gift of labor to the hacendados, one no different from the colonial mita. Although twice outlawed by early republican governments, and ultimately abolished, the institution of forced labor persisted in canal maintenance simply because the work had to be done. The landlords managed to get around the law and preserve the institution de facto, just as they did in the case of servile agricultural work, by continuing to shun all cooperative labor. Thus, the comuneros of Quillunsa, Chaucavilca, and Cachana had no choice but to go on bearing this entire burden, as they had since colonial times.

Even the most benevolent landlords never recognized the size of their debt to the communities in this regard. Local peasants still see this arrangement clearly for what it was: again, *"trabajo gratuito"* and *"hina mit'a"* are phrases they use in describing communal labor, just as in Pampamarca. When speaking in Quechua, they often insert the Spanish words to convey the idea. To me, this suggests that forced work, labor service with no form of reciprocation from the beneficiary, is a Spanish concept wholly alien to indigenous practice.

Such expressions reveal the contradiction that the hacendados introduced into the communal work tradition when they began to encroach on community lands. Phayna (faena) and mita, two fundamentally different concepts, became one and the same thing, at least in part. Cooperative work among comuneros for their own mutual benefit became a kind of tribute, a form of exploitation by the hacendados. As we will see later, this corruption of tradition has survived Peru's agrarian reform, and it continues to be very much resented by the campesinos today, forming a legacy that hampers all efforts toward irrigation improvement.

The 1960's: A Return to State Policy

The arrangement for doing maintenance work changed somewhat in 1960, along with other aspects of local irrigation, when another effort was made to reform the distribution system, again in compliance with state policies. This was one of many changes that took place soon after the road arrived, inevitable consequences of a more direct link with the outside world. This time, however, the reform was undertaken voluntarily by both the water users and the water owners, partly in order to take advantage of the availability now of state technical and financial assistance for community development. The district could hardly have turned to the government for help with its water problem, or for agricultural "extension," if it were not observing the laws and regulations that officially governed water use. Indeed, this is where the economic future of the province lay, in a closer and more dependent relationship with the state.

The same measures were put into effect that had been tried in 1940, but this time they stuck. A landlord from Taurisma was brought in as the administrator (now bearing the official title Jefe de Aguas y Riego, or Director of Water and Irrigation); a new land inventory was carried out; the water tariff was reinstated, for the use of both public and private water; and new distributors were appointed, people who served for longer periods than their predecessors but were not much better remunerated.

The new measures apparently brought about little change in the annexes, where water continued to be distributed according to customary procedures, such as they were. Community members had to pay the tariff again, but the rate was very low—two *soles* a topo—and they evidently did not put up much resistance. The fact that they now had to pay for water may have encouraged bribery and favoritism to some extent, but that kind of problem had existed in the annexes for a long time. The hacendados, who of course had to pay the tax too, apparently cooperated for two reasons: because the water continued to belong to them on their traditional days, just as before; and because the theft of their water had become a serious problem again, and it was clear that someone had to be paid to oversee the system and help them to protect their rights.

The increased incidence of theft was directly related to a gradual proliferation of private rights that had taken place. Many of the bigger properties had been subdivided through inheritance and sales, so that the original rights were now owned by more than one major landowner, each of whom would sell water from time to time in the informal water market, which was booming but causing serious problems. Because permanent rights had been sold to many smallholders within the elite community (i.e., professionals and shop owners), several people now owned a given day of water, often many, and small amounts were always being diverted, even on days that belonged to the major estates. Single shares were being sold to sharecroppers, too, as we have already seen. Water was reportedly "going all over the place," and another inspection of titles was therefore needed. The threat of force, on which the hacendados had always relied to protect their rights, was simply no longer effective in a situation where they shared and traded their days of water.

The new system of administration put a stop to the theft, or at least reduced it dramatically. The landlords, one of whom was now overseeing the system, saw to it that stiff penalties were given out to set examples for anyone who might be so tempted. Today, people in the town of Cotahuasi, members of the dominant families, tend to look back on the period that followed, the rest of the decade, as a sort of golden age of irrigation in the district. According to them, it was a time when order prevailed, when there was a "fixed *turno*," so that all users got their water twice each month. Many contrast the situation, rather nostalgically, with the much more chaotic state of affairs that prevails today. Of course, this is a case of selective memory, since the landlords were the only people who enjoyed this kind of security. The comuneros, by contrast, were now insecure about their rights, suspicious of each other, and, above all, resentful of the privilege that the elite familes enjoyed. Given all these symptoms of the "tragedy" that so often occurs in the commons, it is not surprising that repercussions were strongly felt in one vital area: maintenance of the canal system.

This is another reason why the landlords embraced the new management policies so readily: maintenance had begun to break down, especially in the lower part of the district, where many of the biggest estates were located. During the 1950's, the partidarios who had always cleaned this part of the network had begun to demand a wage before they would do the work. And the hacendados, who were reluctant to pay it, had allowed parts of the main canals to fall into disrepair. They were now required to contribute every year to the task, and were evidently relieved enough to turn the burden of directing maintenance over to a central authority that they were even willing to pay a price for it: sending a peón to work in their place. Still, the landlords did not have to contribute in proportion to the amount of land they irrigated, and they were just as averse as ever to doing any of the physical work themselves. Thus the new arrangement was still far from being equitable in any sense of the word. But a step had been made in the right direction, and the job consequently got done.

Mestizaje: Changing Identity and the Decline of Village Life

Communal labor thus joins the list of indigenous practices—landscaping and irrigation techniques, communal water management, and forms of reciprocity such as wayka and mink'a—that were fundamentally altered when they were appropriated and distorted by the hacendados. But what, it might be asked, does all of this have to do with the process of becoming a mestizo?

It is clear that, by the time the agrarian reform was imposed in 1969, the members of the annex communities no longer considered themselves to be runakuna, or *gente indigena*. We have seen that this re-identification process had already begun by 1940, and by the end of the 1960's, it was obviously complete. The term comunero had ceased to be used widely by then, and the villagers had come to refer to themselves simply as campesinos, peasants, as they do today. Even more significantly, Spanish had become their main language. Of course, many factors contributed to this change in identity, most of which had nothing to do with irrigation: again, public education and obligatory military service, seasonal migration and growing cash incomes, and the influence of radio and other means of communication with the outside world. These exerted a powerful influence and had a strong appeal.

But the process of culture change, like the related one of urban migration, is caused by some factors that "push" and others that "pull" people toward a new identity and a new way of living. The force that impelled the comuneros in this direction was the breakdown of the indigenous way of life; customary ways of behaving, both toward the environment and toward one another, had ceased to meet their needs and provide them with a secure livelihood. Population growth and shrinking landholdings were doubtless the two most important push factors. But irrigation was the source of peasant livelihood, and changes in it, largely exogenous ones, also pushed those communities into impoverishment and decline.

The changes had created significant inequalities between individuals in the relative amount of water they used and, in many cases, even the frequency with which they got it. The landlords had imposed these conditions initially, but inequities had eventually emerged among the comuneros too, in part because of the different methods they now used to irrigate and the differences in water demand. The new procedures the state had introduced in the 1940's invited still greater inequities. By imposing a highly centralized administrative structure that was easily corrupted, the government had opened the door for more favoritism and other abuses. This was especially true because water distributors were no longer village leaders and community servants, but rather technicians who were employees of the state.

This distortion and breakdown of tradition—which would continue and even intensify after the agrarian reform of 1969—obliterated the fundamental equality, or equity among water rights, upon which village life had once been based. Communal water had become increasingly scarce, but the shortage had not affected everyone equally or proportionally, or complicated their lives to the same degree. Under these circumstances, there must have been a strong incentive not to abide by customary rules so as not to share the same fate as other village members. Increasingly, water allocation had become a kind of free-for-all struggle—now a highly bureaucratized one, rather than a cooperative effort—a slowly unfolding tragedy. This occurred because there were now tangible rewards—systemic ones—for resorting to illicit means of getting more of the resource.

Every traditional form of cooperation had been distorted in a similar way, except one, ayni, which the peasants had been able to keep to themselves. Wayka, mink'a, and phayna, forms of group work that people had once engaged in for their own mutual benefit, had become blatant forms of exploitation. These institutions had come to express profound differences in wealth, status, and ethnicity, and to involve coercion, so that they directly contradicted the principles upon which they had originally been based.[34] Phayna, once a form of reciprocity between the individual and the community, a task done by everyone in return for the use of a resource vital to all (Mayer 1974: 55–62), had long since become, at one and the same time, a highly unbalanced exchange analogous to mink'a, in which sharecroppers did labor service for their patrons, the biggest water users.

Obviously, when customs become so thoroughly distorted, when traditional norms only contribute to a person's own oppression, then she or he has good reason to leave them behind. Under these circumstances, the honest and conscientious person, the humble one who accepts what seems to be his or her fate without seeking alternative ways of acting, is arguably a fool. This is the legacy that the hacienda owners and the state together created in the end: a "communal" way of life and a kind of social identity that no longer worked or made sense. Similar declines in the quality of peasant life occurred elsewhere, of course, for reasons that were also contributing factors here—population pressure, the declining value of farm production (Mitchell 1991a,b)—so that a downward spiral would probably have begun inevitably at some point in any case. Village populations throughout the valley declined after they reached their peak in the 1960's because of urban migration, indicating that this is true. But urban migration is not the issue here. The important question is, why did the change in ethnic identity occur in some villages and not in others?

Mestizaje would not have started when it did, and manifested itself so strongly in the very core of village life, if the hacendados had simply expropriated a lot of land and left the comuneros alone, without taking their water and interfering in their internal affairs, especially in that core activity of irrigation. It would not have proceeded so fast were it not for alfalfa, the only cash crop, with all the changes in water use that its cultivation eventually brought about. Nor would it have continued apace, even accelerating during the next two decades, if the state had not gotten more directly involved. In Cotahuasi district, where it was scarce to begin with and had to be shared, water proved to be the key to the landlords' success and to the indigenous communities' demise.

SIX

A Failure of Good Intentions

The Military's Attempt at Land Reform

The agrarian reform of 1969 was a remarkable effort, by leaders of the Peruvian military, to bring social justice to rural people by changing the structure of economic and political power in the countryside through "rational" planning. The impact of this ambitious program has been assessed in many studies, all of which have shown that the outcome fell far short of what the military junta, led by General Juan Velasco Alvarado, hoped to achieve when they seized control of the country in 1968.[1] In imposing the land reform, the military sought nothing less than to carry out a peaceful revolution, and thereby avoid the conflict and bloodshed that clearly lay ahead if they did not act. The reform failed to avert the impending disaster, however, in part because it was based on an outmoded perspective, one that ignored the massive transfer of property from landlord to peasant that had already taken place.

In most parts of the highlands, a diverse set of processes had greatly reduced the amount of land concentrated in estates by the late 1960's, loosening somewhat the landlords' grip on the rural economy. As a result, the peasantry in most places had become highly differentiated in terms of landownership. Because the military failed to perceive or understand these changes, their revolution ultimately only compounded the problem of rural poverty. Furthermore, by mobilizing and politicizing peasants while raising their expectations for real improvements in their lives, the military sowed seeds of discontent and conflict, which Sendero Luminoso would exploit effectively later on. The politicization of the peasants has been vividly illustrated by Linda Seligmann (1995) in her ethnography of communities impacted by the reform, and their social differentiation has been demonstrated statistically, and more abstractly, by José Caballero (1981) in his illuminating study of the state of affairs in the sierra as a whole before the reform.

As Caballero points out, the paucity of land in campesino hands was partly due to a proliferation of "rich" peasants and middle proprietors who had profited from the breakup of many estates in the decades leading up to the reform. In most provinces, the hacienda had long since ceased to be a profitable enterprise, and a great amount of property had been sold or rented to these smaller competitors. Nevertheless, the hacendados continued to hold the countryside in their grip. The virtual monopolization of land was not necessary for dominance in highland economic life, only a certain dominion over land, along with control over most commercial and financial activity—particularly credit— and a firm lock on the higher positions of political authority (Caballero 1981: 93).

In Caballero's view, the practice long considered to be most central to hacienda life, the extraction of labor rent for the use of land, was less significant than generally thought. Cash rent had become common by the late 1960's, and sharecropped properties now constituted only a small percentage of the total land under cultivation. Consequently, abolishing traditional forms of tenancy and servitude, a major objective of the reform, would have only a minor effect on the quality of campesino life. Under the circumstances, he contends, the breakup of the remaining estates in 1969, though certainly necessary, could not in itself alleviate the poverty of the peasantry. A more radical and comprehensive agenda for changing the rural power structure was required.

In some respects, conditions in the Cotahuasi valley just before the reform were consistent with these observations. There were important differences, however, that may be relevant to other parts of the highlands. First of all, as we have seen, the power of the local elite was never based on very large holdings of land. The haciendas here were fairly small production units, but they were highly profitable, and this was directly based on the extraction of rent, both in labor and in kind, rather than in money. These basic features arose from the scarcity of irrigable land, the ecology of the wool trade, and the logistics of long-distance transport. Since even a fairly modest property could be quite lucrative, the fragmentation of the biggest haciendas, a trend that continued throughout the latter half of the twentieth century, did not necessarily indicate the demise of the hacienda economy or any major decline in the landlords' power.

Moreover, though it is true that most of the estates were broken up into even smaller units as the reform drew near, it was the impending threat of reform, together with the other changes described by Caballero, that brought this about. The valley's economy did open up, quickly and dramatically, and a competing "campesino economy" did emerge. But those changes happened quite late, during the decade leading up to the reform, when the threat of it was quite obvious and real. The landlords' control over the provincial and regional economy was so tight that little differentiation among the peasantry was possible until they began to sell off some of their land, and this did not happen until the eve of the reform. In any case, as we have seen, the power of the estate owners was based, as much as anything else, on their disproportionate control of water, without which land is of little use.

Land Tenure and Hacienda Dominance

Of all the major hacendados in the province at the time of the reform, thirty-six families in all, only one had enough irrigated property—more than 30 hectares— to be subject to expropriation.[2] The other local families hardly merited the name hacendado by national standards; their holdings averaged only about 20 hectares and were usually composed of several dispersed properties. At first glance, this seems consistent with Caballero's finding that, in the last decades of the hacienda era, most of the sierra farmland had come to consist of "small" production units of less than 50 hectares, thanks largely to the breakup of the big estates. Within the setting in which these local families operated, however, they were not small proprietors, or even middle-size ones, but dominant *latifundistas*, whose control over the provincial economy was as great as that of big landowners in other regions. This power was crucial to their great success as *laneros*, or wool merchants, and it was based on the large amount of land and water they owned as a group in each community. The properties under their control were small only by national standards. According to my experience in many parts of the sierra, 50 hectares is a huge estate, and this fact casts a new light on Caballero's entire analysis.

To everyone in the valley, peasants and former landlords alike, the characteristics that defined hacendados are obvious. Local terms of reference identify them clearly as an elite class: "*los terratenientes*" (the landlords), "*los grandes*" or "*los ricos*" (the great or the rich), and "*los principales*" or "*los decentes*" (the principal or decent ones). People also speak of them as españoles or mistis, as they sometimes do themselves, suggesting a close correlation between ethnicity and wealth that does not stand up under close scrutiny. In this valley, being of Spanish heritage was traditionally a necessary but not sufficient condition for having a lot of land and being rich. Again, many poorer people lived in the district who were closely related to the landlords and who were tradesmen and professionals, rather than peasants.

The above labels are applied to residents and former residents who once had big properties worked by mayordomos and sharecroppers. They owned most of the irrigation water and had alfalfa fields, mules, and cattle; and many of them owned herding estates on the puna, as some still do today. They were *rescatis-*

tas, collectors of alpaca wool from herders on the surrounding plateau, and they ran the local stores, selling merchandise to poor people on credit. They were the only source of cash loans, and just as in Pampamarca, they were the patrons and godparents of the local campesinos.

Most of these people do, in fact, appear to be of European ancestry, being much lighter-skinned than any peasant, a result of marrying almost always within their own small group. But that of course has nothing to do with their behavior, their attitudes, or their way of life, despite what people, and often enough they themselves, say to the contrary. These are matters of culture and ideology, of ethnic identity, and the landlords, their kinsmen, and their descendants, who constitute roughly 90 percent of the population of the town of Cotahuasi, are culturally Spanish.

Although the extent of their power did depend on the amount of land they owned, these families were considered hacendados whether they had 10 hectares or 25. However, from the agrarian census of 1961, one could easily get the impression that their property had been reduced by then and their power had already declined. Estate properties of more than 5 hectares took up only 29 percent of the valley's total farmland and constituted just 9 percent of all land-holding units at that time. Most land was held in medium-sized properties of 1–5 hectares (54% of the total), which formed 44 percent of all production units. Smaller holdings of less than a hectare accounted for just 17 percent of the area under cultivation. Only 2 percent of the households counted were without any land at all (DNE 1968: 234–62).

The predominance of middle holders at this time is deceiving. For one thing, a family estate typically consisted of several properties, often located in different villages, and these medium-sized holdings appear to have been counted as separate units in the census.[3] For another, many of these may have been inheritances carved off of a larger property. Despite the legal change in ownership, these fragmented properties were often worked cooperatively by siblings and were still, for all practical purposes, one estate. Finally, if these properties did not belong to the wealthiest members of Cotahuasi society, most of them belonged to their close relatives, other people of Spanish descent.

Many of the former residents of the rural areas who had moved to the capital to make their living as tradesmen (blacksmiths, tailors, cobblers, woodworkers, etc.), professionals (schoolteachers, clerical workers, policemen), or petty merchants were mistis and were considered to be members of elite Spanish society. Like the hacendados, most of them had titles to irrigation water, and all of them relied on campesinos to work their land. Their numbers had increased during the middle part of the century, as both the population and the commercial economy grew, but this had only reinforced the landlords' dominant position. Indeed, most of these people made their living through business generated, either directly or indirectly, by the wool and cattle trades, and though some had recently come to the valley from elsewhere, most of them had not. They were kinsmen and affines of the landlords, descended from the same original stock; this, as any resident will readily acknowledge, was a basic fact of local life, and continues to be so today.

In these circumstances, the percentage of land owned by hacendado families was certainly higher than the 1961 figures suggest. Although the exact extent of their dominance at that stage is unknown, the data I collected in 1986 are illuminating. At that time, roughly 390 hectares, or 67 percent of the 576 hectares under irrigation, had once been owned by hacendados and other members of the elite community.[4] This percentage includes the small and medium-sized properties in the vicinity of Cotahuasi itself, nearly all of which belonged to them. Yet, judging by the earlier census, the families cannot have made up more than about 40 percent of the district population. This, of course, was a high degree of monopolization of land, even though it was based on relatively modest units.

Economic Change During the 1960's

By the time the military seized power in 1968, the province had gone through nearly a decade of change that had ended the hacendados' dominance, at least in its traditional form. Road development had greatly reduced the valley's isolation, bringing people under the influence of factors that, as Caballero and others have demonstrated, had already transformed much of Peru's rural economy. Travel elsewhere and contact with outsiders had become routine experiences for campesino men, rather than luxuries enjoyed mainly by hacendados, arrieros, and *cargo*-holders who migrated to finance their fiestas. The valley was now more closely integrated into Peruvian society, and its people were much more susceptible to outside influences.

For the hacendados, the arrival of the road from Chuquibamba in 1960 was the culmination of earlier developments that had signaled the beginning of the end. The most important was the declining profitability of the wool trade from the late 1950's onward, battered by competition from surrounding areas, something that was made possible only because those areas had already been reached by roads. It is ironic that the construction of the road should turn out to be the single-most-important factor in the hacendados' decline. The project was a monumental effort, a huge faena carried out by campesinos from throughout the valley, but it was financed mainly by the landlords and other members of the business community.

The completion of the dirt road immediately opened the valley to truck traffic from Arequipa, reducing the trip to one day and establishing a two-day direct route to Lima, via Majes, the main cattle market. Trucking firms were soon started by two local families, arrieros from Alca, who abruptly displaced the other arrieros and virtually monopolized the importation of merchandise (except alcohol) into the valley. Shortly thereafter, tri-weekly bus service from Arequipa was started by two companies, one of which was founded in the city by a local landlord.

These changes had three principal effects on the local economy. First, they made travel simpler and more affordable for everyone, so that migration and the development of economic ties with other provinces became important to all segments of the population. Suddenly, wage work in Majes and Camaná during the agricultural slack season became an activity upon which any peasant household could depend.[5] Elite families who had made their living through the wool business were able to compensate for its decline by increasing their involvement in the cattle trade, which in turn allowed them to further develop their economic links with the city.

Second, the road unleashed a flow of permanent migrants to the departmental and national capitals, a process that increased with time and ultimately affected all strata of the district society, shrinking the whole by some 17 percent by 1981. Never before had it really been feasible for campesino families to seek to improve their conditions of life by moving to the city; that option had been restricted to hacendados and their children (and the few campesinos who worked as domestic servants in the landlords' urban homes). The temporary and cyclical migration that accompanied it was extremely significant from the standpoint of the agricultural economy, in part because of the remittances family members sent back home to those who stayed behind.[6] But permanent migration, which seems to have been substantial, was even more critical, since it led to a substantial transfer of land between peasants, activity that was not controlled by the traditional elite.

Third, and perhaps most important, the arrival of the road broke the transport and commercial monopoly of the landlords in one swift stroke. Small business immediately became a feasible option for campesinos and other poor people, who could invest in the selling of alcohol and other cheap goods without having to buy additional land and water for mules. Commercial establishments in Cotahuasi and other pueblos of the lower valley began increasing rapidly as a result. By way of illustration, the number of shops and stores in

Cotahuasi district had swelled from sixty-five in 1961 (DNE 1968: 133) to ninety-three by the time I began my fieldwork in 1986. Today, mestizos, people of mixed cultural heritage and class origin, own most of these shops and even a couple of the stores.

For middle proprietors, especially those with access to capital, the road increased their involvement in ganadería, the cattle business, which soon reached a new magnitude and profitability made possible by truck transport. People could either become cattlemen themselves or make a living renting alfalfa fields for fattening steers for the market. Or they could combine the two. In either case, there was an incentive to plant more pasture and acquire more land.

Significantly, even though most of the biggest stores continued to be owned by hacendados, the proliferation of smaller stores and shops increased competition and drove prices down, thereby giving campesinos an option to labor tenancy and debt servitude. No longer was it necessary to work in wayka or mink'a, or to do household chores for a landlord, in order to purchase on credit or get a loan. Giving credit became a way to keep a customer, rather than a means of extracting labor; interest on loans thus became mostly monetary, and rates soon became more uniform.

Furthermore, campesinos could now get credit from someone of their own cultural heritage and background. During the late 1960's, two new businessmen arrived in Cotahuasi from Puno, on the altiplano, native Quechua-speakers who opened up stores and set new standards for commerce. The mistis, if they wanted to stay in business, had no choice but to follow suit. To this day, these original store owners express resentment toward "the Puneños" and, ironically enough, accuse them of having established their businesses by selling contraband from Bolivia. Few will acknowledge that they themselves were guilty of the same thing, trading illicitly on a large scale in cane alcohol.

By the time the military took control of the government, it was obvious that the hacendados' era had come to an end. The killing blow came shortly after the road arrived: the bottom dropped out of the wool trade in 1963 with the collapse of the international market. Prices reportedly fell from 2,000 *soles* per quintal to only 500 within the space of a year. The shock was not sufficient to force the hacendados to sell their land, but, together with the surge in retail competition, it did soon cause most of them to abandon their stores. Today, only three of the sixteen commercial establishments originally owned by hacendados remain in business. All of these changes were set in motion by the road, and they marked the beginning of the development of the rural market that the Velasco military regime would seek.

Military Intervention: Turning the World Upside Down

The military imposed the agrarian reform law in June 1969, a few months after seizing power in Lima. Although the program went into effect immediately, its implementation was a massive process that was slow to reach the more remote corners of the sierra. Not until two years later did officials arrive in the valley to direct the adjudication process: two land judges, who were to oversee the transfer of estate property to campesinos, and several agents of SINAMOS, the National System for the Support of Social Mobilization, who were to promote the program and encourage campesinos to take the necessary legal steps.

The reform decree (DL 17716) stated that the land would henceforth belong to the people who actually worked it (Bustamante 1974). Indirect forms of exploitation such as sharecropping were to end, as were all forms of tenure involving the payment of rent, whether in labor, money, or kind. Obligatory labor was finally to cease, even where a token wage had been paid for the work, as in wayka and mink'a. Wherever these tenancy relationships had existed in the past, sharecroppers and tenants had the right to acquire the fields they worked, regardless of the size of the property. Thus an estate did not have to be formally expropriated in order to be broken up and redistributed. The landlord in such cases would retain 5 hectares as his or her minimal share.

The biggest estates, those exceeding 30 irrigated hectares, were to be expropriated by the state and turned into worker-run cooperatives, with the landlords retaining just 15 hectares as their maximum share. In other regions, this limit, together with the obligation to personally work the land, proved to be the most important of the law's effects. In the future, no one in the highlands would have more than 15 hectares, and everyone would work his or her own property directly. To compensate the landlords for their losses, the state proposed to issue them twenty-year bonds based on the appraised value of the property. In theory, then, this was a truly revolutionary decree, mandating a massive transfer of estate property to campesinos, and under very favorable terms.

Unfortunately for the military, and despite their good intentions, the landlords had plenty of warning that a major upheaval was coming. The early 1960's had been marked by peasant uprisings, land takeovers, and an armed insurgency that had spread over much of the sierra, even touching Cotahuasi—movements whose suppression had, in some areas, involved considerable bloodshed and loss of life.[7] This political violence had intensified a policy debate already under way in Lima, one that had branded the haciendas as an obstacle to progress and led to mounting pressure for change.

The result was a law passed in 1964, during the administration of Fernando Belaúnde, Peru's first real attempt at land reform. Although its direct impact had been minimal and confined to a few areas of the coast and highlands (Matos Mar & Mejía 1980: 102–5), the obvious shift in the political winds was perceptible even at the local level.[8] Consequently, the landlords had devised a strategy to mitigate the effect of any new move toward reform.

By the time the land judges arrived, there was essentially no need for adjudication. Most of the hacendados had already taken steps to keep their estates from being expropriated. Two of the tactics they used were mentioned earlier: distributing chunks of land to heirs and other family members, in cases where this had not been done already, and selling other chunks to middle proprietors. To these they now added a third: evicting sharecroppers from whatever land they kept. Most of them took these steps before the 1969 decree was announced, and in many cases long before the military coup. Although this sort of thing happened in many parts of the sierra (Montoya et al. 1979: 232–35; Matos Mar & Mejía 1980: 115–17; Montoya 1989: 163–64), the strategy was particularly effective in Cotahuasi because the haciendas were so small to begin with.

The landlords' first way of getting around the law was to make a simple change in the property deed, transferring title to one or more children and heirs. Often, as we saw, this was nothing more than a ploy because the land continued to be worked in much the same manner as before, as a large family unit. Hacendados had begun selling some of their land to others, to nonrelatives, when their wool profits fell, but such sales accelerated after the 1964 reform and showed a spectacular rise as soon as the military seized power. Early on, before the possibility of reform became real enough to affect land prices, they were picky about who they sold it to, the salaried professionals and others in the capital who were members of their class and the only people who could afford it. These people typically bought several fields at once or even entire fundos. Later, during the middle of the 1960's, as it became obvious that a reform was coming, land prices began to decline and ultimately sank from 100,000 *soles* a hectare to only 50,000, at which point the landlords became willing to sell to anyone who would buy. The mid-1960's is when the majority of purchases reportedly took place.

At that point, campesinos who had made money in the wool trade (arrieros) or the shop business, in local services such as plowing, or in seasonal work in the mines were able to buy land too. But urban migration, which had grown steadily after the road arrived, also contributed decisively to the surge in land transfers and the lowering of prices. For the first time, parcels were readily available because smallholders were leaving the annexes and moving out of the valley, and the main people interested in buying these were not hacendados, but campesinos. For poor people and for those who were not members of elite society, this form of acquisition was much more important than the purchase of estate property.

The certainty of reform now called for a more radical step. Landlords evicted their partidarios and, planting alfalfa on the formerly sharecropped fields, turned most of each property over to the care of their mayordomos. On the remaining land, the part devoted to family subsistence, they began to rely exclusively on wage labor. A year of this tactic was sufficient to deprive the partidarios of their potential legal claims. Furthermore, the move fit nicely into a new economic strategy and shift in land use that was growing in popularity anyway because of the decline of the wool trade: the turn toward raising cattle. I know of only a few men who failed to make the change during the years immediately preceding the reform.[9] Middle proprietors who had bought estate property also employed the tactic in order to hold on to what they had acquired.

Such measures enabled most of the landlords to protect roughly half their land, so that they could sell whenever, and to whomever, they liked. After General Francisco Morales-Bermudez deposed Velasco in 1975 (with U.S. backing), and more conservative forces took over the Peruvian military, the reform came to a standstill, which allowed land prices to recover substantially. The final transfer of estate property took place then, but, just as before, most of these sales went to people within the elite society of Cotahuasi and the lower part of the valley.

Even though the reform was subverted and its impact minimized in this way, the significance of the program should by no means be underestimated. It did bring about an unprecedented redistribution of estate land that benefited a large number of campesinos. Furthermore, the military's intervention shocked Cotahuasi society in a profound way, standing it on its head both socially and politically for several years. During that entire time, the landlords were subjected to an intensive campaign of propaganda that defined them as the most backward elements of rural society, even as enemies of the people. The land judges and SINAMOS treated them as a rural oligarchy worthy of contempt, and the few who had failed to take the necessary steps found themselves powerless to influence the adjudication process in any way.[10] This upending of customary relations astonished the campesinos, who even today tend to consider the reform, with all of its flaws, the most important event that ever happened in the history of the valley, and Velasco its greatest hero.

After the SINAMOS agents arrived in 1971, they launched a vigorous mobilization campaign, targeting the few major properties whose owners had not divested themselves of their holdings, especially the bigger estates on the puna. They explained the provisions of the law to former labor tenants, including herders, and urged them to take legal action wherever it was still possible to do so. Because the local haciendas were so small, there were few cooperatives to be organized and overseen, a major responsibility of SINAMOS in other regions. In Cotahuasi, the organization thus played a direct role in promoting the adjudication process and in spreading the news that the era of the hacendados was over.

How the Landlords Circumvented the Law

In some sense, the agrarian law was its own undoing. It was poorly designed to achieve its goals, especially in a valley where the estates were so small. The ceiling above which expropriation was to take place was simply too high for the law to have a significant effect. Only Lancaroya, in the district of Pampamarca, with 60 hectares, exceeded the 30-hectare limit. That property was taken over by the state and redistributed, benefiting a large group of campesinos, who formed a cooperative, but the remaining estates were only subject to the piecemeal adjudication of estate workers' rights, a lengthy process that the sharecroppers themselves had to initiate.

In Cotahuasi district, where the biggest haciendas were broken up by this process (Salcán Grande, Pitahuasi, and Colcán), the sharecroppers, who had rented about half the total irrigated area of each, were the only workers who benefited from land redistribution. Salaried mayordomos, and the pasture fields they tended, were largely excluded from the adjudication process.[11] So were wage laborers, the peasants who had cultivated the smaller properties in Cotahuasi. Because the work was always temporary, and the turnover rate high, the owners could claim that they had worked the land themselves (see DL 17716, Art. 20).

As we have seen, most of the landlords were astute enough to protect themselves from sharecroppers' claims by evicting them well before the reform. Where that was not done, each worker was to be granted a *unidad agrícola familiar*, or agrarian family unit, the target landholding of 3–5 hectares that the government considered necessary to support an average rural family. According to this criterion, reform beneficiaries were to become middle proprietors, even if an entire estate had to be broken up to achieve this end, as happened with Salcán Grande. Given the modest size of even the largest properties, this made the consequences of not evicting partidarios potentially devastating, which is why few landlords failed to do so.

The tactic was simple and effective, and did not require extraordinary foresight, since it was based on the provisions of the earlier Belaúnde law. Yet the Velasco reform decree did not take such an obvious form of evasion into account. No provisions nullified changes in labor use that took place before it was announced, that is, before June 1969. That was far too late in Cotahuasi, since most of the landlords had already acted. Landlords in other parts of the highlands probably took the same action as well, but, to my knowledge, it has not been reported before.

Note that on the biggest estates—Salcán Grande and Pitahuasi—only a portion of the land was routinely irrigated, half of which was planted in alfalfa and overseen by a mayordomo, so that it was protected. Unfortunately, many of the sharecropped fields, which were ultimately redistributed, were eriazos with no water rights.[12] Under the terms of the new water law (which we will come to in the next chapter), most of these were deprived of the supplementary water the sharecroppers had formerly gotten from the landlords from time to time. The soon-to-come drought (or any drought, for that matter) made these lands virtually useless, negating many of the benefits of the reform.

Clearly, then, whether the land reform actually provided benefits was inextricably tied to the accompanying water reform, specifically in the matter of how the estate water was to be redistributed. Since farmland was nearly useless without irrigation, it was access to water that determined how much useful land people ended up with at the close of the reform decade. In many cases, the fields acquired by campesinos turned out to be worthless and were abandoned—an ironic consequence of a program intended to stimulate and expand agricultural production.

All of these points reveal a basic problem with the reform. Although it did set off a major redistribution of land and increase the number of small and medium-sized properties, as intended, many factors served to limit the extent to which campesinos could benefit from the process. One of the most important was the evasive tactics of the landlords, but there were others, some of them inherent in the law itself, that made it difficult for poor people to rise to a higher economic level. Perhaps the most significant of all the law's flaws was the failure to take account of the man-land ratio. In order for every household to have at least 3 hectares, as the military would have liked, the district would have had to contain four times as much irrigated land as it did, or to have one-fourth as many people. In the end, the program simply did not reflect the reality of life in the sierra at the time. Inevitably, this meant that the reform created opportunities that some people, those with money, were much more able to take advantage of than others.

The program had a similar impact on the puna, though there it was even less substantial. SINAMOS targeted herding estates bigger than 1,000 hectares, but only two were that large, and here again the landlords were able to circumvent the law. The district of Puica, one of the province's main herding areas (see Inamura 1981, 1986), was selected for intervention in order to set an example. But by the time the land judges and the SINAMOS agents were in a position to start any legal action, they found that the haciendas there had been almost totally decapitalized and abandoned by their owners.

For example, a man named Carbajal, the premier lanero in the valley and owner of the first estate targeted (some 2,000 hectares), liquidated his property immediately after the reform was announced in 1969. After passing word to prospective buyers in the adjacent provinces of Cusco and Arequipa, he had his entire alpaca herd, reportedly more than 2,000 head, brought down to the end of the road at Alca, completely filling the streets with animals. Over the next three days, he sold the whole lot to throngs of buyers, whereupon he retired to his home in Arequipa and devoted himself to running a small tourist hotel, purchased with his profits. The caretakers, who had worked the estate in a manner analogous to sharecropping, took over the estate, and they received title to it after the reform agents arrived in 1971, but unfortunately the land was all they got.

The other landlords in the area quickly followed suit. All had reportedly reduced their herds to only fifty or sixty animals by the time a second Puica estate was expropriated late in 1972. Again, the family who had overseen this hacienda for decades, without pay, was given control of it and eventually received legal title. Apparently, the reform agents sought to make an example of these big estates and cause other landlords in the area to take flight, hoping that herders would then make use of the legal procedure for asserting their rights to shares of properties below the official ceiling for expropriation.

That hope, however, proved to be groundless. Few of these estate workers ever dared to take legal action without the prompting and backing of SINAMOS, so that the adjudication movement never got off the ground. The hacendados in the district of Huaynacotas, the second major herding area in the province, decapitalized their estates so thoroughly that they were able to avoid adjudication entirely. They had only to liquidate their herds, abandon the area in apparent defeat, and wait for General Velasco to fall from power. When Morales-Burmudez deposed him in 1975, the reform came to a halt, allowing the landlords to reassert their ownership and manipulate the herders into working the estates in much the same manner as before (Inamura 1981, 1986).

In the end, then, the reform program on the puna was only momentarily successful and had only spotty effects, since most of the haciendas were too small to be subject to expropriation. More than half the province's 28,000 hectares of pasture land remained unaffected, lands where tenants went on paying a labor rent. The landlords remained dominant on the plateau until Shining Path guerrillas moved into the area in 1988.

A final point must be emphasized. The reform had no legal impact on any of the annex communities above the valley, except for those in Cotahuasi district. In Huaynacotas and the few other communities like it, no one had more than 5 hectares of total land. Permanent migration continued to generate land transfers and led to some swelling in the ranks of what would elsewhere be considered middle proprietors, but the reform itself was never a factor.

In the other hacienda-dominated annexes, no estate properties were expropriated, and none were broken up through adjudication either. Perhaps the program's greatest weakness was that, in these remote communities—Pampamarca, Puica, Achambi, Toro—comuneros never took any legal action without the prompting of government officials. In villages such as Pampamarca, where the few estates were small even by provincial standards, a vigorous promotion campaign would have been necessary to start the adjudication process, something that was well beyond the capacity of the few reform agents, who clearly had their hands full in the lower valley.

This is not to say that the program was a total failure. In fact, its indirect effects were quite significant, as we saw in Pampamarca. They seem to have been essentially the same in all the pueblos where elite or misti families had historically been dominant. The reform, and the accompanying mobilization effort, led to a rejection of traditional labor relations on the estates throughout the entire valley. Well before 1969, comuneros had increasingly shunned the old forms of dependency and refused to work for any landlord without some payment in cash. The reform law endorsed this resistance and caused it to spread, even though servitude was not eliminated entirely. As the dominant families responded by selling their land and withdrawing gradually to the city, these properties were bought by the wealthier comuneros in each community, people who are now emerging as the new leaders, as in Pampamarca. Thus, in those hacienda-dominated annexes not directly affected by the reform, the program set off a redistribution of estate land nonetheless. Moreover, certain peasants were able to acquire this land and, by all appearances, move into positions of leadership and power that the mistis were vacating, a transfer of power that did not occur in the lower valley. This happened, of course, because the landlords were such a small elite minority there. There were no poorer people of Spanish descent to buy their property, only comuneros.

Why the Reform Failed

The pattern of landownership in the district in 1981 is shown in Tables 4 and 5. Anyone looking at the district's total acreage for the pre-reform year of 1961 would conclude that little had changed. But in fact a lot of land had changed hands in those twenty years. Large proprietors now controlled only about 25 percent of the total land under irrigation, whereas middle holders with 1–5 hectares owned roughly 45 percent. Since the combined holdings of these two groups was roughly the same in the two years (70 percent in 1981, compared with 67 percent in 1961), it seems clear that most of the redistributed land went to a relatively small group of people, swelling the middle ranks of the tenure hierarchy (Trawick 1994a: 417–40).

Although the vast majority of people quite obviously benefited only a little from the reform—smallholders, 73 percent of the population, still owned only about 30 percent of the land, roughly the same amount as in 1961—the picture is less bleak than it appears to be at first glance. The population figure for smallholders is significantly inflated. It includes many landowners who do not really belong there: women who had a field or two of their own, but whose husbands also had land, often a lot more. Since the source on which I built Tables 4 and 5, the List of Irrigators (Padrón de Regantes), is a record of the actual title-holders of property, not households, the number of smallholders listed is obviously much higher than a family count would show.[14] Because of the fragmentation of landholdings through inheritance, the total number of peasant households with a hectare or less may have grown somewhat despite urban migration, but the number who had only a topo or less was certainly far less than 73 percent and had probably decreased substantially since the reform.

The statistics do not reveal the reason: the membership of all strata changed substantially after the reform. Hundreds of people left the district permanently—621 between 1961 and 1981, a total decline of 17 percent—including a large number of campesinos, and they had in many cases sold all their property. Partly for this reason, many other campesinos were able to acquire small amounts of land during the reform decade. Although this enabled them to become more independent with respect to food production, a significant enough development, few of them had the capital needed for moving up into the middle strata, into the commercial domain.

Ultimately, most sales of hacienda property were made in response to either the threat of reform or the reality of it, and were therefore induced by General Velasco's program. The other economic changes previously discussed weakened the hacendados' position and contributed to the pressures for further change,

TABLE 4

Landownership in Cotahuasi District by Hectares, 1981

Amount of irrigated land	Cotahuasi		Quillunsa		Cachana		Chaucavilca		District	
	Total	Percent	Total	Percent	Total	Percent	Total	Percent	Total	Percent
<0.35	18.32	6.6%	7.13	4.2%	6.93	14.3%	9.76	6.5%	42.14	6.7%
0.35–1.0	50.5	19.7	48.14	28.4	17.36	36.1	51.00	33.6	144.45	23.0
1.0–3.0	54.30	21.2	67.75	39.9	12.62	26.2	61.09	40.5	195.76	31.3
3.0–5.0	53.4	20.8	13.41	7.9	11.30	23.4	8.75	5.8	86.85	14.0
>5.0	79.2	30.9	3.3	19.6	—	—	42.7	28.3	155.20	24.9
TOTAL	255.72	100.0%	169.73	100.0%	48.27	100.0%	150.75	100.0%	624.40	100.0%

SOURCE: Padrón de Regantes, 1981, Ministry of Agriculture Office, Cotahuasi.
NOTE: According to my count, the total amount of irrigated land in the district is 624 ha, not 576 as stated in the source. I cannot account for the difference.

TABLE 5

Landownership in Cotahuasi District by Number of Owners, 1981

Amount of irrigated land	Cotahuasi		Quillunsa		Cachana		Chaucavilca		District	
	Total	Percent	Total	Percent	Total	Percent	Total	Percent	Total	Percent
<0.35	101	33.7%	30	21.5%	37	49.3%	51	33.6%	219	37.8%
0.35–1.0	118	39.4	63	45.0	28	37.3	60	39.5	269	40.4
1.0–3.0	56	18.7	39	27.9	7	9.3	35	23.0	137	20.6
3.0–5.0	14	4.6	4	2.8	3	4.1	2	1.3	23	3.4
>5.0	11	3.0	4	2.8	–	–	4	2.6	19	2.8
TOTAL	300	100.0%	140	100%	75	100.0%	152	100%	667	100.0%

SOURCE: See Table 4.

TABLE 6

Land Acquisition in Household Sample

(50 households from all strata)

Means of acquisition	Holdings in hectares	Percent of all holdings
Inherited	28.65	26.3%
Bought from hacendados	48.59	44.5
Bought from migrants	28.38	26.0
Agrarian reform	3.45	3.2
TOTAL	109.07	100.0%

NOTE: The total holdings account for 17.5% of all the irrigated land in the district.

but by themselves they were not sufficient to impel many landlords to begin selling their property. Thus, in order to assess the reform's impact on land tenure, the effects of estate liquidation have to be distinguished from those of sales of smaller properties belonging to urban migrants, whose departure began shortly before the start of the reform decade (1964–75).

I attempted to sort out the trends in land transfer, both before and during the reform, through an economic survey of fifty households in the district, stratified by property size.[15] Before proceeding to the results, let me note first that Table 6 merely summarizes my findings, and that the following analysis goes into details not shown in the table. (For a separate breakdown for each group, see Trawick 1994a: 417–40.)

I should also point out that the survey had another and perhaps more important purpose. It was a way to examine current patterns of labor use and document any changes that had occurred because of the reform or for other reasons. By questioning people about these matters, I hoped to see whether the use of ayni had changed as campesinos became more involved in commercial activity, and to find out exactly how the bigger proprietors now worked their land. Since forms of obligatory work such as wayka and mink'a had been eliminated, mayoristas now had to recruit labor on a different basis. Here I was especially interested in any changes that had occurred among the few campesinos who had bought land and moved up into the middle stratum.

It ultimately became clear, even from such a small sample, that most of the estate property transferred in the district went to members of the elite community, to people who were not of campesino background. Sixty-eight percent of the land that was purchased from the haciendas (63 percent of all purchased land) was bought by members of the dominant families, ones whose inheritance or other acquisitions had only been large enough to give them small- or middle-holder status. The reform provided these people with an opportunity to pursue their ambitions and, in several cases, it enabled hacendado heirs to ascend nearly to the level of their parents. Two other important avenues to the middle ranks were also now open to them: many of the younger generation who moved to the city and sold their property usually did so to a sibling or two who stayed behind. It also enabled elites from pueblos like Taurisma and Alca who had never been able to afford any of the choice land in Cotahuasi proper to extend their operations to the provincial capital.

The rest of the estate land purchased, 32 percent, was bought by peasants, who were able to benefit from the reform roughly in proportion to their economic capacity. The breakup of the haciendas contributed to an expansion by certain households, but this process was already under way because of the road and the resulting emigration. In fact, campesinos ultimately bought 65 percent of their land from other peasants who were moving permanently to the city.

As for the impact of the reform law itself, only 6.7 percent of the total land transferred from estates was acquired through adjudication, amounting to just 3.2 percent of all property in the survey, a sample that is clearly too low to be representative of the district population. Numerous properties were redistributed in this way, both medium and large, so that the true number must be significantly higher, though I do not think that it could exceed 20 percent of the total land in the district.

The reform did reduce the average size of landholdings by breaking up estates bigger than 10 hectares and forcing the sale of many medium-sized properties that were part of those estates, but since the landlords were able to control the process to such a great extent, it did little to change the nature or the composition of the dominant class. The fact is that, despite all of the changes flowing from the reform and the decline of the wool trade, the bigger properties continue to be of great economic value today. To be sure, these "haciendas" are smaller than before, covering only 5–10 hectares, and they are not so numerous, but they continue to take up roughly 25 percent of the irrigated land. Thanks to alfalfa and cattle production on these lands, some members of the traditional elite have managed to maintain comfortable incomes and hold on to much of their influence in the political domain.

The reform did, however, bring about some positive change in politics by making the campesinos more of a force to be reckoned with. Nevertheless, after democracy was restored in 1980, the wealthier families (including many middle proprietors) were able to reassert their dominance within the three major parties; and today they run the district, and indeed the province, in much the same way that their parents did. The individual players have changed, and the game itself is now more complex, as we will see, but the mistis continue to have a firm lock on the higher positions of authority at the district and provincial levels.

Thus the reform did bring about a "changing of the guard," but one that was essentially limited to a transfer of land and power to a younger generation of the elite. Campesinos were not among the members of this new provincial elite. Significantly, nearly all have become more independent, and some have even become middle proprietors, but they remain in a subordinate position today, both economically and politically. Throughout the lower part of the valley, the people who wield power and influence tend to be the sons or other legitimate descendants of hacendados; foremost among them are the larger landowners, still the wealthiest people in the province. Although their power to coerce has been greatly reduced, and they do not have as much land as their parents and predecessors had, these families are still very much in control. Cotahuasi, like the other district capitals, is still a "misti pueblo."

Peasants and Capitalists: The Basic Division
Within Local Society

The reform, and the other economic changes of the last two decades, have had one other effect that must be discussed. They have altered, and yet somehow clarified, the basic division within local society. The district has been composed of two classes of people ever since early colonial times: peasants, subsistence farmers who are highly self-reliant in work and in food production, and commercial farmers, whose agriculture is oriented primarily toward external trade and relies mainly on the labor of others.

Despite the social and cultural changes that have taken place since the road arrived, particularly in the annex communities of Cotahuasi, the members of these two classes still see themselves as distinct kinds of people with separate and often opposing interests. Since the 1960's, ethnicity and cultural heritage have become somewhat less critical in defining the classes than before, though the differences are still important. To the campesinos, who spoke mainly Quechua and considered themselves to be *gente indigena* until not long ago, it is a person's behavior, attitude, and life-style that determine which class he or she belongs to, and these qualities are expressed most clearly and tangibly in the performance of agricultural work.

In the simplest terms, each community in the district is now composed of campesinos, or peasants, who till the soil themselves, primarily in order to provision their households, and *empresarios*, or businessmen, for whom agriculture is mainly a money-making pursuit, usually one of several (Fuenzalida et al. 1982). The members of the second group are essentially gentlemen farmers or, most often, cattlemen who rely mainly on hired laborers to cultivate their fields, so that they can devote themselves to other activities and do as little of the physical work as possible. As we have seen, this shunning of manual labor has always been a central feature of provincial Spanish culture and identity, a fundamental expression of elite status. The peasants' reliance on family labor and reciprocity, however, extends even further back in time, back to the origins of the indigenous tradition. During an era when many aspects of the native heritage have been lost, particularly in the domain of ritual, this basic continuity has come to define the life and culture of the campesino.

This is not by any means to say that, in their self-reliance, peasants are all satisfied and healthy; that clearly is not the case in Cotahuasi. Here as elsewhere in the highland, to be a peasant means, in all too many cases, to be malnourished and underfed and to have to work much too hard. Population pressure on resources and depressed prices on the domestic and international markets have palpably worsened their quality of life in most places (Mitchell 1991a), and that has clearly been true in this valley, even though there is no cash-cropping and the valley has steadily lost population with the out-migration of entire families. I do mean to say, however, that peasants see their capacity for work and their self-reliance in this regard as virtues, ones that distinguish them clearly from members of the dominant society.

In this setting, where campesinos do not produce crops for the market, and where opportunities for them to earn cash locally and buy additional land have been relatively limited, the process of differentiation within the peasantry has been slowed and, because of the limitations of the reform, truncated to a great extent. However, there is another difference, an ecological one having to do with how the land is utilized, that corresponds closely with the class division being discussed. Businessmen may be store-owners or salaried professionals, and they may engage in a variety of money-making pursuits, but most of them rely on cattle-raising or dairy farming as a major source of income. Thus, from an ecological perspective, local society is composed of campesinos and ganaderos. A businessman can be, and typically is, a ganadero, whereas a peasant, I would insist, cannot. But what exactly does this mean?

Here I should point out that because most local campesinos have a cow, to provide the family with milk and to produce a calf periodically for sale, they do grow a little alfalfa as feed. Some of them grow a more substantial amount to "rent" as a source of cash income. Furthermore, it is quite clear that money has long been essential to campesinos, and that they now engage in a wide variety of activities, including petty trade, in order to acquire it—not only in this valley but throughout the highlands in general (Figueroa 1982; Sánchez 1982; Gonzalez de Olarte 1984; Mitchell 1991a, b). Thus there is actually a continuum of variation, along a number of different variables, that distinguishes the businessman from the peasant. The important questions are, which differences are most salient, and at what point do people cross over the line? When does someone cease to be considered a peasant, and for what reasons? The answer, according to my understanding, lies in the person's engagement (or lack of it) in agricultural work.

Some peasants in the district have managed to buy enough land to qualify as middle proprietors. A few of them still have recourse to reciprocity in agricultural work because they are still considered to be peasants, but most of those who have moved up in the tenure hierarchy have to hire wage labor. From my experience in the district, the crucial thing that distinguishes the few from the many, providing insights into the process of class differentiation, is that they continue to do most of their own work, including irrigation, and to depend on other people as little as possible. They expand the household labor force periodically through mink'a, a necessity that reflects the local scarcity of labor, but such help takes the form of assistance in a family task, and as in Huaynacotas and in most households in Pampamarca, it does not replace household members who are busy with other things or unwilling to work themselves. It is festive group labor in which everyone present participates.

When, on rare occasion, replacement labor is sought, it is provided by wage workers, as is always the case, regardless of the status of the landowner. But even then, just as in ayni or mink'a, the employer and his or her helper(s) always work together. Aside from being the most efficient way to get the job done, this labor relationship expresses a fundamental attachment to work, and affirms the notion that campesinos, unlike hacendados and other empresarios, do not rely on others to do their work for them. That is a capitalist way of doing things, seen as antithetical to peasant life.

Letting others do the work seems to be the principle distinguishing the form of mink'a being practiced by some of the district's wealthier campesinos today from the old form practiced on the haciendas. Of course, it is the same principle that we saw respected by the larger landowners in Huaynacotas, and, in the case of jornal, sometimes not respected by the middle proprietors in Pampamarca. People who routinely hire others to do their work for them and who assume the posture of being "worked for," as the wealthier comuneros in Pampamarca sometimes do, are seen as mistis, people who behave like landlords. They therefore have no choice but to purchase that wage labor. The law now requires this, of course, but where the landowners are former campesinos, the law is irrelevant.

It would be useful, in this connection, to know how many local people the participatory work ethic now applies to, which is to say, how many still rely on reciprocity. We can quickly exclude most of the larger landowners in the district, middle and large proprietors with 3+ hectares, who no longer have recourse to mink'a, but most of those people are members of the "Spanish" families and have never participated in reciprocal exchanges. As for those of peasant background, if my small sample is any indication, the number who have forsaken reciprocity for wage labor must be rather small. Of the thirty-two peasant families in the sample, only two rely exclusively or even heavily on wage labor, and both of them are middle proprietors. This figure may be highly unrepresentative, but it serves to support my very strong impression after almost three years in the district that the number of campesinos who do not use reciprocal labor is still quite small. The majority of people in the annexes are still considered to be peasants, and they continue to practice reciprocity, because they still do most of their own work.

The survey turned up only three families that practice mink'a (6 percent of the total, 14 percent of the middle proprietors). Although I was not able to determine how widespread the practice is today, this low frequency appears to be characteristic of the district as a whole. Indeed, for a while, I did not suspect that mink'a was still practiced by anyone, since most people (especially in Cotahuasi itself) insisted that "*yá no hay mink'a*," that the custom was a thing of the past. It was only when I began the household survey, rather late in my research, that the truth was revealed: mink'a has persisted because what was once an exploitative custom or tradition has been redefined as a mutually beneficial arrangement between and among certain peasant families. It is now essentially a symmetrical exchange between equals, a form of "unbalanced" reciprocity (Sahlins 1965, 1972) that may not have existed in the district before. Mink'a— like ayni and, for campesinos at least, even jornal—is now based on a fundamental equality or commonality: the notion that campesinos' lives are centered on agricultural work, and that all are equally tied to it. Otherwise, the terms of the exchange are quite similar to those we observed in Huaynacotas: labor is given in return for good food, corn beer, cane alcohol, a share of the harvest, and a party afterward.

As for the peasants' use of jornal, I cannot say definitively that they always work alongside their peons, as they invariably said they do when I asked. That, like much else in this domain, awaits further research. Even so, my findings, however tentative, may help to clarify some of the most fundamental issues that have long been disputed in Andean studies. Those issues have to do with the nature of the so-called Andean community and the significance of reciprocity.

The major debate in the literature has always boiled down to a simple question: whether village life in the highlands is still based on any meaningful continuities with the distant past. More specifically, scholars dispute whether certain widespread forms of economic behavior, and a supporting ideology, still really differentiate comuneros and campesinos from other people who live in the highlands. One side of the debate holds that, at least in some of the more remote and "traditional" areas, such differences exist, and that they constitute a separate sphere of exchange within the economy, based on a significant degree of self-reliance and forms of reciprocity dating back to the Incas and beyond— but at the same time one firmly linked to the market, the monetary sphere of exchange.

This position, known as the "moral economy" position, has been most extensively argued by Enrique Mayer (1974a, b, 1977, 2002; see also Mayer & Zamalloa 1974). Mayer contends, following Karl Polanyi (1957) and others, that some peasants in the region, like primitive agriculturalists, really do act, at least within a certain domain, according to a distinct logic, one concerned primarily with subsistence and food security, and only secondarily with cash acquisition and profit, with getting ahead. Based on their attachment to the land and their reciprocal exchanges with each other, they have a distinctive identity and way of life, which they seek to protect and preserve by resisting or even rebelling against the many forces that threaten them (Scott 1976, 1985, 1990).

The other side insists that, in the majority of places, no such differences exist, that peasants act out of the same motives as all other people, to maximize their income; it is only that their options are limited by their poverty. According to this view, known as the "political economy" position, poor peasants in the Andes rely on ayni only because labor is scarce and they cannot afford to pay wages, and wealthier peasants who practice mink'a do so only to acquire scarce labor (Sánchez 1982; Figueroa 1982; Painter 1992). The more extreme advocates of this position claim that mink'a is simply a form of exploitation, even among peasants, one no different from the kind practiced on the haciendas. In using it, wealthy peasants manipulate tradition in order to accumulate capital at others' expense, just like any hacendado (see also Orlove 1977a; Mitchell 1991b for cases where this is in fact clearly accurate).

According to those who take the more extreme position, no real continuity with the distant past is possible because the circumstances in which reciprocity is practiced today are so different from those in the prehispanic era (Painter 1992). Peasants are no longer self-reliant in any meaningful sense; they are highly dependent on cash for a wide range of essential goods, including much of their food (Figueroa 1982), and they rely on purchased chemical inputs for both subsistence and cash crop production (see Mayer & Glave 1999). In sum, according to this view, campesinos are just as dependent on the market economy as everybody else, and their motivations are basically the same: to maximize the income, both monetary and nonmonetary, they generate from their meager resources. They are just poor, even the "rich" ones, as people on the margins of the capitalist system.

There is still a third, middle-ground position, which holds that factors such as population growth and land pressure, coupled with the declining value of cash crops in the face of imports of subsidized grain from the United States and other countries, have forced peasants throughout the Andes to migrate and turn to other activities such as petty trading, or to increase their production of cash crops, simply in order to maintain the peasant way of life (Caballero 1981;

Mitchell 1991a, b). Many peasants have come to recognize, these authors argue, that self-reliance no longer works, that the only way to maintain their standard of living is to pursue various other activities, including cash-cropping, to stem the decline in nutritional standards and maintain the quality of life.

Let us now look more closely at some of the wealthier campesinos in my sample. The three "rich" peasant families who practice mink'a are on the whole indistinguishable from their counterparts who do not. They appear to have only a few things in common. For example, they all have a hectare or more of surplus land. But the commonality stops there. Two of the three plant the land in alfalfa and have several head of cattle. The other family has no cattle and sows the extra land in wheat or barley for household subsistence and to produce a surplus.

The first two families are relatively comfortable; both possess fairly decent homes, with a full array of kitchen utensils and tools. The third, a direct beneficiary of the reform, is quite poor and lives in a disheveled shack, only partially roofed. The more affluent families get their cash income from occasional cattle sales and the rental of their pasture land, the poorer one from a small bakery or *panadería*. The wealthier heads-of-household are not particularly active in politics, whereas the other man is a sort of informal campesino leader, an avowed Communist who has never held office but who commands a lot of respect among poor people in the district.[16]

One of the most obvious commonalities among the three families, besides doing most of their own work, is that they grow nearly all of their own food. With the exception of such staples as sugar, cooking oil, and bread, they only purchase processed and imported foods—rice, macaroni, and other wheat products—for use on special occasions or to bolster meals when the household larder is low. They may also buy fresh meat from time to time, to serve to guests on festive occasions, but only when they cannot slaughter animals of their own. The most frequently bought item by far is aguardiente, cane alcohol, something they have always had to purchase. But they are highly self-reliant with respect to food and to work.[17]

Obviously, I cannot prove on the basis of three cases that these commonalities explain why a "rich" campesino's friends and neighbors are willing to assist him in mink'a, or why he is still considered to be a peasant. But I can say that the hypothesis is consistent with what I observed and was told. When I pointed out that the host family seemed to be fairly well-off, and asked why people were willing to do mink'a with them, mink'a partners usually answered by pointing to, among other things, the commonalities of work and attachment to the soil.

As one man put it: "Son campesinos como nosotros. Sí, tienen su pasto, sus vaquitas, tienen plata. Pero su vida es la chacra. Trabajan la tierra, ellos mismos. Por eso les ayudamos no más." (They are peasants like us. Yes, they have their pasture, a few cattle, they have money. But their life is in the fields. They themselves work the land. Therefore, we help them.)

In such cases, I would suggest, exploitation is often only in the eye of the beholder, the anthropologist or economist. I do not consider a day of work for good food, plenty of drink, a sizable share of the harvest, and a drunken fiesta afterward to be exploitative when everyone concerned takes full part in it, especially taking into account the fact that mink'a is much more expensive for the host than wage labor (Mitchell 1991b: 206). Nor did any of the participants I talked to about mink'a think so. Sharing in the work makes all the difference. I do not wish to deny that mink'a can be exploitative, especially when a great number of godchildren and compadres are involved (Orlove 1977a; Mitchell 1991b), and I think that arrangement has been common historically in places where differentiation within the peasantry has been rapid, which has not everywhere been the case. But there are at least two varieties of mink'a, and one has to look closely at the circumstances involved before making judgments about the nature of the exchange.

The patterns of labor use that seem to prevail in the district today, not to say remarks like the one cited above, suggest that the political economy argument, when pushed to an extreme, leads to certain errors and distortions. The first is a failure to distinguish campesinos from other people who live in the highlands. In the literature, the term campesino is used vaguely to refer to peasants, on the one hand, and used generically on the other, to refer to people who live in the countryside, which of course is its literal meaning. Local people themselves, however, are quite clear about the correct meaning of the term: campesino means peasant, as I have defined it here.

This discrepancy reflects a lack of agreement among anthropologists on a clear and useful definition of the term peasant itself (see Mintz 1973; Orlove 1977b; Silverman 1979; and Kearney 1996). Following campesino usage, I would suggest an ecological definition based on energetics and their relationship with the land: peasants, like primitive agriculturalists, are people who do most of their own work—the essence of what M. R. Trouillot (1988) calls the "peasant labor process"—and grow most of their own food. They are invariably involved in various kinds of commercial activity—typically labor migration, if nothing else—and they may even sell surplus crops for the market (though not in Cotahuasi), but as long as they remain fairly self-reliant in these respects, they are still considered to be peasants.[18] I suspect that in some of the published studies, some people who are classified as "rich" campesinos, on purely economic grounds, are not really considered to be peasants by their fellows.

The second confusion is a failure to distinguish clearly between the different forms of group labor and labor exchange. Sánchez and Painter, for example, quantify and categorize the various forms—family labor, ayni, mink'a, and jornal— as if they were comparable in function, when in fact they are not. Ayni, the reciprocal lending of labor, does not reduce the amount of work a family has to devote to subsistence at all, making it equivalent to family labor in some ways, but fundamentally different from mink'a and jornal, both of which are forms of additional labor or even family labor replacement. Mink'a is not closely described in their work (or its equivalent for Painter), but these authors nevertheless give the impression that only the asymmetrical, exploitative type exists in the communities they studied.

I suspect that, if more attention were paid to who actually works and who does not, they would find that the symmetrical type does exist, and that it is practiced by some of the larger landowners in their communities. Furthermore, I predict that they would find the practice to be correlated with high levels of use of family labor and relatively low levels of wage labor. Indeed, I strongly suspect that today, during the post-reform era, the symmetrical type is the predominant one in many parts of the highlands, if not the only type that exists.

Another problem with these studies is that most of them were completed in the 1970's, during the reform decade, and we have no more recent data for comparison. In Cotahuasi district, one could probably have found the old type of mink'a still being practiced by some of the dominant families back then, but it is nowhere to be found today, because campesinos have universally rejected what they knew to be an exploitative relationship. Today, in an era when they have new access to essential resources, they are no longer vulnerable to the old forms of coercion, and they will not engage in this form of reciprocity with someone who is not a peasant like themselves. This is clearly how they have wanted things to be for a long time, as we saw in the previous chapter. What the campesinos have done is to take mink'a back from the landlords, redefining it and making it what they thought it should have been all along. Unfortunately, as Joel Jurado (1989: 67) has pointed out, we anthropologists have often lagged far behind the campesinos in adjusting our ideas to the realities of social change in rural life.

Another basic error can be found in some studies of household economy (e.g., Figueroa 1982; Sánchez 1982). There, family income and expenditure are categorized and quantified in such a way as to obscure the significant degree of self-reliance upon which peasant life is based. Certain so-called food items are grouped together with real foods, then quantified and multiplied by their market value, in order to show that a large percentage of peasants' total consumption—measured in monetary terms—is purchased. The impression is thereby given that campesinos buy a significant amount of their food.

But the fact is, these purchased "foods" consist almost exclusively of alcohol, coca, and cigarettes, products that peasants have always had to buy or get from elsewhere, two of which are not food at all, but drugs (Figueroa 1982: 147; Sánchez 1982: 186). As Gonzalez de Olarte notes, in the only comprehensive regional studies that have been done to date (1984: 132–33, 1987: 98), peasants in communities throughout the Cusco region produced, during the 1980's, roughly 80 percent of the total calories they consumed. Unfortunately, he did not fully explore the implications: that campesinos in many areas are still highly self-reliant, and that the growth of the market in some parts of the highlands is, in this and other respects, under constraint. In many places, peasants still eat the same kinds of food they have always eaten, despite all the other changes that have taken place in peasant life. No one would deny that, because of the population growth that has been so marked in most places (though not in Cotahuasi, which has steadily lost population since the 1960's), peasants have had to tighten their belts, and that total calorie intake has probably declined (Mitchell 1991a, b). But it is clear that the pattern and degree of self-reliance in food, at least in remote areas like Cotahuasi, has not changed much at all. Some areas and regions have obviously changed more (see Kearney 1996), others much less, in this regard, and opportunities for cash-cropping, or the lack thereof, have a lot to do with this variation.

The relevant issue in the debate is food, not alcohol, cigarettes, cooking oil, or industrial goods such as fuel, fertilizers, pesticides, and other supplies that must be purchased. No one would deny that campesinos have been buying these items, even their clothing, for a long time and have had to acquire cash to get them. The point is rather that they avoid depending on the market as much as possible for their sustenance. This is a major continuity with the past, and this is the basis of peasant life, as Mayer (1974a, b, 1977) originally insisted. Peasants hold on to this self-reliance, not just because they see it as a virtue, a character trait with intrinsic value (especially when seen against the dependency and exploitation typical of the landlords), but mainly because time and again it has protected them from the vagaries and fluctuations of the market economy.

Much has been written in the literature about peasant "differentiation," the widening of differences in wealth within campesino communities, and about "de-campesination," the process of becoming something other than a peasant.

Based on what I have observed, the two terms describe a fairly simple transition. Certain people are able to acquire surplus land for producing crops or, more commonly, raising cattle for the market. Where the amount of land is fairly small, this does not necessarily change their work habits or their patterns of food consumption. In Cotahuasi, where the extra fields are nearly always devoted to pasture production, these people may begin to hire wage laborers to assist them, but their way of doing things will probably not change much.

Once they acquire even more land, however, and become more engaged in cattle-raising and other commercial activity, they necessarily begin to distance themselves from the work itself. With limited time and energy, they use more wage labor as a replacement for their own effort. Furthermore, as their cash income increases and they are able to buy processed or imported foods, which take much less time to prepare, they often become less reliant on their own food production. Past a certain point in this process, they are perceived as being less attached to the land and to agricultural work than other campesinos, and to be more concerned with making money than anything else. A threshold is crossed that differentiates them from their peers—a subjective one, but one that, for campesinos, has certain clear indicators or markers. Let me emphasize again that the vast majority of the "peasant" middle proprietors in the district have apparently indeed crossed over it, and thus they only have recourse to wage labor.

According to my understanding, the most important of those behavioral indicators lie in the carrying out of certain kinds of work: routine chores such as irrigation; larger group tasks such as sowing and harvesting; and communal activities such as the upkeep of the irrigation system. As families distance themselves more and more from these tasks, hiring other peasants to do the work for them, they cross the line and become empresarios and ganaderos in other people's eyes and ultimately even in their own. Or, in other Andean valleys, they become *agricultores*, commercial farmers. These "new rich" families continue to live in the community, of course, often playing a prominent role in local politics, but their relationships with other village members invariably change.

What, then, is the nature of those relationships? This too has been the focus of a lot of discussion. Rodrigo Montoya (1980, 1989; Montoya et al. 1979) and others have tried to explain why, after all the campesinos' years of resistance and even revolt, they have not solidified more as a class and a political force against the empresarios who are supposedly a threat to their very existence in the long run. The peasants in Cotahuasi can hardly be said to be unaware of this conflict with the landlords, and they have acted accordingly at various times throughout the years. But it is true that they have not expressed this opposition politically, in a unified manner as a class and a society.[19] Commenting on this situation in Puquio, Montoya (Montoya et al. 1979: 160–71) notes that many factors reinforce a widespread perception that "everyone now has land," and that anyone can acquire more property if he is willing to work hard enough. The flurry of sales that occurred because of the reform has created an illusion of free access, softening the opposition between classes and concealing the little social mobility that really exists today for campesinos.

One often hears such statements in Cotahuasi too: "everyone now has land" or "we are all landowners now." To me, however, this merely indicates that what peasants value more than anything else is their independence, and in this regard they have made significant advances. Most people now own at least a small amount of land; the situation is not nearly so bad as the landholding figures for the 1980's suggest, for reasons already explained.

More important, few peasants if any now depend on the empresarios for their subsistence, at least not through sharecropping, which has fallen out of practice. And though many campesinos still work as wage laborers, they can go elsewhere for such employment and usually do so, which is why one hears so many complaints about the local shortage of peons.[20] Since the campesinos value this independence so much and have struggled so hard to attain it, they can hardly be said to lack a form of class consciousness.

From my point of view, the statements reveal something else. When campesinos point out that everyone now has land, they are indicating that the shortage of land, or the difficulty of acquiring more, is not their primary concern. They need something else even more, something that has actually become more scarce because of the reform, and that of course is water. This need is so obvious and so frequently stated that it almost goes without saying. Montoya (Montoya et al. 1979: 162) emphasizes that this is, and long has been, the main preoccupation of peasants in Puquio too. Since campesinos express this concern so readily, it is their lack of political action in the hydraulic domain that would seem to require explanation. We have seen that they have long been involved in a struggle over water rights, and that their main antagonists have always been the larger landowners. Why, then, have they not been able to act together politically to put an end to this conflict and force the landlords to meet their demand for a fair share of the resource? The answer turns out to be very revealing, but quite complex.

SEVEN

Failure Again

Water Reform, Drought, and the Legacy of Class Conflict

Within months of announcing the agrarian reform law, the military issued another revolutionary decree that abolished private water ownership and, at least theoretically, brought all of the irrigation systems in the country, and all water users, under one system of administration. But for twenty years or more, the impact of the General Water Law of 1969 (DL 17552) was little discussed in the anthropological literature, in part because ethnographic studies tend to be done in villages like Huaynacotas and Pampamarca, where the law turned out to have little or no effect.[1] Yet the state's intervention must have had a profound impact on many highland communities, especially along the western slope, where control over water was basic to the socioeconomic and political power of the provincial elite. In hacienda-dominated districts like Cotahuasi and in the villages along the valley bottom, some kind of water reform was necessary if the land reform was to be significant, and the rural power structure changed.

The law and the attached regulations (DL 17552; CEPES 1984) called for drastic modifications in rights, duties, and procedures. All water was to become the property of the state, to be administered locally by an employee of the Ministry of Agriculture, the so-called Technical Administrator. Hacendados lost their rights of ownership and now had to use water as directed by that official under the same conditions as everyone else. The administrator was to work with a hierarchy of user groups in carrying out the law and planning the irrigation schedule for the agricultural year. Each local community elected its own irrigator committee (*comité de regantes*) to represent it at the district and provincial levels. The top bodies there were called the Irrigator Commission (*comisión de regantes*) and the user group (*junta de usuarios*), respectively.[2] To get the program off the ground, all spring flows were to be measured, taking into account their seasonal fluctuations. The water was then to be divided up to service all the lands that had previously had water rights, whether communal or private. Although new rights could be issued under certain conditions, none were to be granted in times of scarcity.

The state called for a system that was efficient and "rational," in that it would be adjusted precisely to the needs of specific crops and the various local soil types and micro-climates present within the irrigation system. This variation was to be studied empirically in order to identify areas with similar water requirements, so that water could be allotted according to the pattern and rhythm of "demand." Ultimately, the administrator would set a list of priorities in conjunction with the user groups to adjust this schedule, or Plan de Cultivos y Riego.

Finally, in times of drought, water use was to be curtailed, with food crops given priority over pasture for animals, in accordance with an emergency plan to be agreed upon by the administrator and the user groups. At these times, and all others, people were required to use water efficiently and economically, as de-fined by the administrator, under penalty of fine or the eventual loss of their rights. Thus the spirit of the law demanded a certain uniformity in use, but in a system based on the assumption that water "requirements" varied widely, the letter of the law was another matter. People's rights were left poorly defined in relation to each other.

The water reform was a bold attempt by the state to eliminate a primary source of conflict and hardship in the countryside, but unfortunately the pro-gram failed to achieve its goals. Despite the expropriation and redistribution of private water, the state of irrigation declined in the district after the new law was implemented, a slowly unfolding "tragedy of the commons" that had reached a crisis point by the time I began my fieldwork. Interestingly, a better system was set up initially, one similar to the type found in Andean communi-ties like Huaynacotas, but several factors caused it to come unraveled after only a few years: defects in the law itself, a basic flaw in the distribution system, ef-forts by certain people to subvert the program, and, most important of all, re-current drought.

Shortly after the new system was installed, drought years struck in close suc-cession, causing a massive contraction in the supply. Because of certain loop-holes in the law, some people could get more water than others in this situation, and many people did, typically the wealthier landowners with power and influ-ence. This obvious inequity thereby introduced into the systen then reverber-ated throughout the district in a self-reinforcing manner, setting off a struggle over water that further exacerbated the scarcity. The result, as I found when I arrived in late 1985, was a profoundly divided society, rife with inequity, cor-ruption, and conflict, whose people were incapable of working together to solve problems that needlessly affected the lives of everyone. The situation was tragic indeed, and soon became even more so.

The Initial Success of the Reform

The Technical Administrator quickly set to work to carry out the law with the assistance of newly elected officers of the Irrigator Commission, whose president, a member of the APRA party, would later serve as governor of the province (Subprefect) during my fieldwork. As a first step, he diverted the water of Armanca, a flow that had belonged exclusively to the landlords of Cachana and the lower part of Cotahuasi sector, and rerouted it to Cachana, Reyparte, and Chacaylla sectors, plus the small, largely campesino hamlet of Reyparte. To make distribution more efficient, a new cement reservoir was built at Cachana in 1972 under SINAMOS direction, using state funds and local faena labor. Because the Armanca flow was so large, big enough to have provided the estates with a sizable surplus, this change promptly made Cachana-Reyparte-Chacaylla the best-watered part of the district. Significantly, the president of the Irrigator Commission and a few other people on its board of directors (the *junta directiva*) just happened to own land in Chacaylla at the time.

To compensate for this diversion, the water of Wakajara, which before had served all of Quillunsa sector but only the upper part of Cotahuasi, was re-allotted to cover the estate lands in the lower part of Cotahausi formerly served by Armanca. This water, too, was stored at night in an essentially new reservoir, Pitahuasi (it dated back to 1965 but was rebuilt with cement in 1970 under SINAMOS direction). Although this tank is the biggest in the entire province, the flow was only sufficient for the vast area served under normal conditions. When the drought struck, that area proved to be the most poorly watered part of the system.

The second step of the reform was to establish new distribution patterns for each major tank and water source. This was initially done by installing a contiguous sequence like Huaynacotas's, an arrangement known as *de canto a canto* ("from one side to the other"). Wisely enough, the Ministry of Agriculture strongly promoted this pattern as the basic model for an irrigation plan (Gelles 1994: 254; Guillet 1992: 104, 1994: 179–81) and continues to do so today. But as we have seen, the law recognized that certain areas within an irrigation system have special water needs and instructed administrators to accommodate to them in devising a schedule. Thus, a contiguous sequence did not have to be strictly followed—indeed, should not be—throughout the entire expanse being irrigated. Nevertheless, the ministry did promote the arrangement as a way to minimize water loss, apparently unaware of its other benefits.

In any case, a truly contiguous pattern was established and strictly adhered to during most of the period of military rule. For each major source, irrigation began at the lower end of each sector, or community territory, and proceeded upward, canal by canal and field by field, to the next sector higher up. This sequence was always repeated, so that all sectors were on the same schedule and received water with the same frequency. Landowners had to plant their fields at the appropriate time at the beginning of the year, when water was available to them, or wait until their turn came around again in the next cycle. Since this pattern was much more systematic than the previous one, a lot of water was saved.

Side by side with this step, the administrator ordered distributors to limit watering time to three hours per topo. This requirement immediately affected the many people who had spent as much as five hours irrigating their land, which is to say, those with alfalfa fields, where only the inundation technique could be used. Clearly, a large percentage of the district's crop fields had already been converted to pasture, and, if the proportion approached the ministry's 1981 estimate of 55–60 percent, the new controls would have had the effect of reducing the time needed to complete the entire cycle by 20 percent.[3] The savings may actually have been closer to 30 percent, since, at three hours a topo instead of five, three sets of allotments could be given out daily, rather than two.

These new arrangements made for a relatively uniform system of distribution to all users of the system, both former landlords and peasants, who had paid the required water tariff. Significantly, all of this was accomplished without the precise measurement and control of canal flows that were required by law, since the ministry office, like many of its kind throughout the highlands today, had neither the equipment nor the manpower to comply with that provision. This was not necessary for major improvements in the system, a primary reform goal, or to establish a reasonable degree of equity and uniformity in water use, an objective that was not included in the legislation.

Another critical change was the "sectorization" of the secondary springs, which had been a source of surplus for many of the hacendados. This was accomplished by determining how long it took to water a topo of land with the outflow of each small reservoir and dividing the figure into the number of hours in a tank day, that is, the number of hours that it took for the stored water to drain out. The result was then used to calculate the expanse that could be served by the flow over a period of seventeen to twenty days. An area of this size was then designated and given exclusive rights to the springwater, but was deprived of main irrigation water and taken out of the *turno*, or cycle, of the main system. Meanwhile, the fields expelled from the spring sectors were added to the main watering cycle. The springs were thus now entirely separate mini-systems, run in the same manner as those of Huaynacotas. Each of the areas had its own small *comité de regantes*, which appointed a distributor and a delegate to represent it in the district user group.[4]

Finally, to ensure compliance with the new law, the water authorities began dishing out severe penalties, called *multas*, for theft and other infractions. For a while, some former landlords reportedly continued to take water to which they were no longer entitled. Within the first few months of the program, three of them had to pay fines equivalent to about thirty U.S. dollars each, an unprecedented amount. The only multas that hacendados had ever paid before were token sums for not having sent workers to the canal cleaning and other maintenance faenas. According to the governor of the province, who had served as the president of the Irrigator Commission during this transition, the lesson was quickly learned, and the hacendados' abuses soon stopped.

Although the effects were only temporary, these measures were successful in establishing a stable and "rational" order for the first time. Many people, including the governor and two men who served as water distributors during this time, agree that in Cotahuasi and Quillunsa sectors, a fixed cycle of seventeen or eighteen days for the two communities together was maintained throughout most of the period of military rule. This ample frequency was remarkably similar to the one the hacendados had enjoyed before, and it now included everyone. Significantly, this had been accomplished, quite unknowingly, by installing most of the basic features of "indigenous" irrigation, as practiced in Huaynacotas and the other autonomous communities, including a rough proportionality in water rights. Thus the water reform was at first a great success.

The things that later caused the system to unravel and slide into inequity and corruption will be discussed below, but a primary reason was that the cooperation of many users—especially the hacendados and middle proprietors, who had just lost all of their privileges—was enlisted successfully only because the prevailing conditions were unusual, if not unique. For one thing, rainfall was adequate or abundant throughout most of the period of military rule (as we saw in Chapter One), and water supplies were at fairly high levels. Just as important, the new regime was installed by an unelected military government that ruled by force. The greater district community had always been divided, a situation that the reform made even worse, and only stiff sanctions backed by the threat of force could sustain measures whose impact fell mainly on the wealthier and more powerful residents. The new law, in other words, worked well at first mainly because it was implemented in an atmosphere of dictatorship and revolution.

Through its action on behalf of the campesinos, the reform exacerbated a political struggle within the elite community that had been going on for thirty

years. During the late 1930's, several of the sons of hacendados and middle proprietors who had been educated and employed for a time outside the province
had returned to the valley as committed reformers, part of the growing tide of
national discontentment with the power of the landed oligarchy. These men
had joined the American Popular Revolutionary Alliance (the APRA party), and
on their return, they had founded a local chapter that steadily grew in strength.
Because of its anti-oligarchic stand and its advocacy of rural commercial and
industrial development, APRA appealed mainly to less affluent members of the
Spanish community, especially those middle proprietors who had been left
without a large inheritance, locally referred to as *los aspirantes*. As in many parts
of the countryside, these men had established the local party in opposition to
the landlords and in favor of economic reforms that would loosen their control
over the valley.

Significantly, all the men elected to assist the administrator in reforming the
irrigation system were members of this Aprista group.[5] Not surprisingly, the
landlords saw the effort as a plot by these men to manipulate the situation for
personal gain, a perception that may have caused them to resist measures they
might otherwise have found unobjectionable (or at least would not have objected to so strongly). Their suspicions were not unfounded. As noted earlier,
the president of the Irrigator Commission and other prominent Apristas had
land in Chacaylla, the area that became the best-watered sector because of the
reform.

Some re-allotment of Armanca was clearly necessary to improve the system,
as were all the other measures put into effect. What the diversion accomplished,
however, in hydrological as well as sociological terms, was to pit the campesinos
and former sharecroppers of Quillunsa against the former landlords and middle and small proprietors of Cotahuasi in a competition over a water supply
that would shortly thereafter become highly unstable and insufficient because
of recurrent droughts. Meanwhile, the leaders of APRA were able to watch this
conflict from the relative comfort of Chacaylla, the area least affected. Whereas
the big landowners had always been the people least affected by drought before,
many of them now suddenly found themselves bearing most of the burden of
water shortage. And the people who had done this to them, in their eyes, were
the Apristas.

If later events are any indication, the action did in fact reflect the party leaders' political strategy, which was to manipulate the opposition between the
land-rich and the land-poor in order to gain approval for policies that cost the
leaders themselves nothing, and that even helped them to rise to the level of
their aspirations by filling their pockets. The comments of several former land-

lords indicate that they saw the water reform strictly in these terms, as a program that would not really benefit the campesinos much, but only enable the Apristas and other "false Communists" to prosper and rise to power, so that they could swindle and steal from the campesinos thereafter.[6]

As we will see, had all the users cooperated, the newly instituted system probably could have provided them with adequate water even through the drought years that struck toward the end of military rule, from 1978 to 1984, or at least much more than they ultimately got. The system did have certain weaknesses or defects, but the problems that emerged could have been avoided, given the willingness and full participation of the entire community. Instead, after the military's class alignment changed under Morales-Bermudez in 1975, bringing the land reform process to a standstill, some of the landlords and middle proprietors were able to undermine the program by reclaiming certain privileges. This was done in defiance of the Apristas, who lost their control over the Irrigator Commission soon after the change in military government.

Unfortunately, the drought began at about the same time, putting the system to its first real test and giving the landlords a tangible and compelling reason to seek special treatment, to corrupt the system. The subterfuge had a ramifying effect throughout the district, which only made the community less able to adapt effectively as the drought took hold. Corruption weakened cooperation and adherence to the rules, which further increased the scarcity, which further weakened cooperation, and so on. No one described the drought years to me in precisely these terms of cause and effect and positive feedback. But I do know that both factors—the various forms of subterfuge made possible by defects in the law and the frequent years of drought—ultimately helped make the situation of most people in Cotahuasi and Quillunsa more precarious than before the reform, even under normal rainfall conditions.

The New Era of Drought and Its Impact

Drought in an arid agricultural zone is not just an environmental phenomenon, but also a social one. Since water demand is always "socially constructed"— determined by people— the supply is only deficient relative to the quantity they consider necessary for irrigation, and the severity of a shortage depends entirely upon this assessment, as well as the means that a community employs to cope with the crisis. Consequently, any shortage, whether long- or short-term, requires careful analysis. One must find out what a drought is, as local people define it, what its effects on the community are, and to what extent the local response to it either mitigates or heightens the problem.

During the 1980's, the recurrent failure of the rains and the shortage of water were a central preoccupation of nearly every person in the province. Everyone seemed to express concern over a recent increase in the frequency of drought years, one of the few things on which people of all backgrounds seemed to agree. They referred, not to a general desiccation, but to a new pattern of irregular rainfall that some said had begun twenty years before, others thirty. Overall, there seemed to be a consensus that the normal precipitation pattern had first begun to vary during the 1960's, and that the trend that had intensified in the late 1970's and had now become chronic.

A drought is locally defined, not as a virtual absence of rainfall during a given year, but as a major decline in both the amount and the frequency of precipitation, in this case during the wet season of late December through March. Here the standard for comparison is what people consider to be the "normal" pattern: sporadic rain beginning in late December, becoming daily from January through March, and then tapering off in April. Everyone claims that this was the prevailing pattern throughout most of the twentieth century, and that, with the exception of the long drought of 1939 and another brief one in 1953, dry years used to be sporadic and never came in close succession as they do now. For the local people, then, it is not so much a matter of individual years of shortage as a sustained unpredictability of the water supply. Rainfall was formerly much greater than today because it fell more regularly over a longer period, and because it rarely failed.

According to them, a normal wet season would see almost steady rain throughout each afternoon, evening, and night, followed by clear sunny mornings. I can verify their description, having been there during what was said to be the normal year of 1986. The pattern is considered optimal for plant growth because it provides abundant moisture and enough sunlight for crops to thrive and allow excess water to evaporate and drain off.

A drought can take any one of several forms. In some years, there is a general scarcity of rain because, even though it may cloud up every day and threaten to rain, little actually falls, as in 1982 and 1983. Or, heavy rains in January may be followed by clear skies for the rest of the season, as happened in 1987. A third pattern is that of heavy but very irregular rainfall, with alternating wet and dry spells of one to two weeks extending throughout the season, as reportedly happened in 1989, after I left the valley. All of these were considered drought years by local farmers, regardless of the total amount of rain that fell. There were five such years all together during the decade that bracketed my fieldwork, 1978–88 (see Fig. 2).

It is important to understand, however, that a drought is basically a two-year phenomenon. When the rains fail, that year's crop may be damaged, but it will usually not fail entirely because the water supply may not dwindle all that much if precipitation was abundant during the previous year. The effects will not be fully felt until the planting season in September of the following year, when irrigation will be less frequent than normal. But here again the loss may not be too great if the usual amount of rain falls thereafter. The harvest will be strongly affected during both years, but at least there will be something substantial to harvest. Two dry years in succession, however—such as occurred in 1978 and 1979 and again in 1982 and 1983—will have a disastrous effect on the water supply, ruining three growing seasons and producing a real emergency.

The rainfall data for the province show just such a strongly fluctuating pattern, as we have already seen. However, since we have no historical average, data gathered during what has supposedly been a long-term decline in the supply cannot be assessed empirically. The average precipitation in Cotahuasi over the twenty-four years of record was 261.6 millimeters, with a large standard deviation of 110.9. The average during the rainy season proper was only 236.6, with a similar deviation of 93 millimeters. These averages may in fact be significantly lower than the previous historical mean, however, since they appear to approximate a critical threshold. With only one exception, the years in which rainfall dipped more than 50 millimeters below these levels during the 1980's, a decline of only about 20 percent, are remembered as droughts.

If one applies this criterion to the entire quarter-century of record, it appears that seven years out of twenty-four, or nearly one in three, were environmental crises. These dates correspond well with local farmers' recollections, which naturally become less precise as they extend further back in time. Because people refer back to the year that the rains failed to come, and because a drought lasts for at least two years, the true number is more like fourteen, and the percentage roughly half. In fact, the entire 1978–84 period was one long drought, just as the local people say.

Other evidence seems to support their perception of a long-term decline, namely, the frequently noted desiccation of natural pasture and other vegetation in the mountainsides surrounding each village; and the abandonment of high-altitude fallowing lands, which occurred throughout the province during the period in question. It is important to recall, however, that most of the fallowing lands in the district were abandoned long ago, and for a different reason. Many other lands fell out of cultivation only recently, during the long dry spell of 1978–84, but again this occurred for reasons unrelated to the drought. The distribution of abandoned land is not so much a record of what has recently happened to the climate as a record of what has happened in irrigation.

The largest abandoned areas are found in the upper qheshwa zone at the southeastern end of the district, above Pitahuasi and Chaucavilca, extending upward into the suni (Map 9). These are vast stretches of eroded terraces covered with scrub vegetation that elderly people insist have been in this condition from at least their parents' lifetimes, if not before. The most likely explanation might therefore seem to be that they were abandoned during the population collapse. But on closer inspection, that seems unlikely because the terraces are in relatively good condition. They can easily be distinguished from more recently abandoned ones, but they are not nearly so badly weathered as the terraces in Pampamarca (in Kupe) and elsewhere in the valley, which clearly have been out of use for hundreds of years. It is obvious that they were originally fallowing lands, and that some were irrigated periodically, like the t'ikras of Huaynacotas, since they have the remains of canals. I suspect that they were abandoned sometime during the nineteenth century, probably because so much water was privatized and diverted away from the ayllus, the original annex communities. If the lands have in fact been in this condition for only about a century, then that must surely be the reason why. These are the first areas that would have been abandoned in response to a contraction in the supply.

The other type of abandoned land (the remaining areas shown in Map 9) fell out of use shortly before the long drought began in 1978. These are the dry-farmed terraces and fields, or eriazos, that lack water rights. Located in the maize-growing zone, they cover the slopes surrounding the two largest former estates, Salcán Grande and Pitahuasi, but a great number that could not be shown in Map 9 are interspersed among the irrigated fields of Cotahuasi, Reyparte, Cachana, and Chaucavilca sectors. They cover about 140 hectares, a figure equivalent to 24 percent of the area being watered today and 20 percent of the arable land in the qheshwa zone.

The higher lands were originally used for growing potatoes and other tubers, wheat, and barley in a fallowing cycle, but they were not communally controlled as in the native communities. The lands became private property long ago, and some of them were formerly sharecropped by the landlords, who owned a small percentage. The ones farther downslope were sometimes used to grow wheat or barley without irrigation, but most of them were irrigated and planted in maize. Those fields were occasionally irrigated with water acquired from the hacendados before the reform; they had to be abandoned when the new law put an end to the buying and selling of water. Although the drought would have caused this to happen anyway, it was the reform that initially brought about the abandonment of perhaps one-fifth of the arable land in the district.

Unfortunately, I cannot say what percentage of this expanse was actually cultivated before the reform, only that it was a large one. But it is important to note that the scarcity of land in the district is more apparent than real, and that many people, especially the campesinos, have fields they would like to cultivate but cannot in the present circumstances. These terraces, like those higher up, will obviously lie abandoned until the amount of water available in the system can be increased. Dry as they are, they will have to be irrigated intensively if put back into production,[7] and this would require at least 20 percent more water.

Although irrigation has been used periodically to maintain the total area under cultivation, it can never completely counteract the effects of drought. Irrigation was not developed to replace the rains, and we have seen that, in a heavily populated region like the Andes, it cannot play such a role very effectively. The amount of springwater available cannot eliminate the impact of a dry spell even in well-watered communities like Pampamarca and Alca; this is why everyone is so preoccupied with irrigation improvement. Despite the somewhat better years of the 1990's, the ups and downs of the 1970's and 1980's may signal a long-term change in the climate, making the need to do something soon all the more urgent. Any measure that will increase the supply will heighten irrigation's effectiveness in the ultimately impossible task of drought mitigation.

Table 7 compares the distribution of irrigation water in the dry season of 1988, a year of "normal" rainfall, with the distribution in 1987, which was considered to be a drought.[8] Tank capacity and outflow are presented for each of the three primary water sources and the secondary springs.

One of the most significant things that the data reveal is the theoretical sufficiency of water entering the system under normal conditions. According to the Ministry of Agriculture technician who helped me collect the data, it takes roughly 31 liters of water a second to irrigate 1 hectare in five hours, a benchmark that is thought to adequately cover any crop and soil type. Accepting this figure merely for the sake of argument, this means that, barring much evaporation and filtration, the total system flow of 506.24 liters a second is enough to service 32.6 hectares per day, a volume that would permit a district-wide cycle of eighteen days during the driest months of a normal year— and that was indeed the case during most of the period of military rule. Unfortunately, the theory does not match reality because a great amount of internal water loss occurs in the unlined canals.

According to the local administrator, the outflow of Pitahuasi, when full, is enough to irrigate 35 topos a day in the area immediately below the tank, but by the time the water reaches Quillunsa, it can only irrigate 24, and by the time it reaches Piro, in the lower part of Cotahuasi sector, only 12. I was able to calcu-

TABLE 7
Decline in Springwater Flow During Drought, 1987 vs. 1988

(Flow in liters per second)

Springs (tanks)	1988 flow (normal year)	1987 flow (drought year)	Decline (percent)
	Primary springs		
Wakajara (Pitahuasi)	214.96	174.12	−19%
Cutirpo (Cochallan)	100.04	83.04	−17
Armanca (Cachana)	79.76	63.01	−21
Average decline			−19%
	Secondary springs		
Cascahuilca	5.92	4.68	−21
Animas	2.58	2.10	−19
Senorpa	6.96	5.57	−20
Cozo	2.61	2.04	−22
Rinconada	2.81	2.14	−24
Aytinco	2.55	1.99	−22
Oqhara	6.52	5.02	−23
Chocho	4.63	3.89	−16
Wallpawaqaq	3.31	2.65	−21
Average decline			−21%

late roughly the total amount lost over the entire route by comparing the flow at Piro with the tank outflow at Pitahuasi on a day when no water was drawn off in between; the difference was 62 percent. This is a worst-case index, however, using very approximate methods (the flotation technique) at the two extremes; had I measured the flow higher up in Cotahuasi sector, the fall-off would probably have been substantially less. Even so, there is certainly an enormous loss, which implies that the average amount actually used per unit area must be much smaller than the administrator's benchmark figure, as in fact it is. No one has ever measured the exact loss or calculated the optimal quantity of water needed for the prevailing conditions, but local practice clearly shows that the amount required even for generous watering is much less than the official standard.

The effect of drought, of course, is to lower the dry-season springflows even further. In Cotahuasi, as in most other villages, the effects vary for each source, but a substantial decline occurs in nearly all cases. During October of the dry year of 1987, I estimated the reduction in storage at Pitahuasi by measuring the difference between the existing water height and a line that the tank operator, the *estancador*, told me was the "normal" dry-season level. This turned out to be roughly 1,680 cubic meters, or 24 percent lower, implying a reduction in tank outflow of the same amount. I later tested this figure by having the tank outflow measured with a current-meter, borrowed and brought from Arequipa, and the result turned out to be 19 percent less than the outflow in the following, normal year. Despite a certain amount of variation, the average difference in the tank outflows of most of the secondary springs in Cotahuasi sector was comparable, at 21 percent.

It is important to point out that 1987 was by no means a typical drought year. The total amount of rain was actually normal for the period of record (1965–88); it is just that nearly all of it came in January. The year was definitely considered a drought, but the decline in the supply cannot have been nearly so large as in an ordinary one, when total rainfall is at least 20 percent below average. I therefore think that the usual decline in spring flows, certainly in the main water sources, must be 30–40 percent after a truly dry year. This agrees with a figure of 30 percent that the administrator claimed to have actually measured at some point in the past. I can only attribute the substantial decline in 1987 to the effects of two months of sunshine (February and March) when it normally would have rained.

During the first year of drought that struck after the reform, in 1978, the administrator and the Irrigator Commission declared an emergency and, in compliance with the water law, contracted the area to be irrigated in the next planting season. Strictly speaking, each landowner was supposed to reduce the expanse under irrigation 30 percent, approximating the shortage that droughts are thought to induce. But the local authorities decided that this rate would be unfair to smallholders with 1 hectare or less and applied it only to landowners who had more than that.

By all accounts, the plan failed badly. Several people told me that the law was regularly flouted because of favoritism and non-enforcement. I have no reason to doubt their word, since favoritism was common at the time in other areas of the system. In addition, the contraction was done separately for each sector, and many of the middle proprietors had small plots of land in various sectors, so that the expanse they actually had to stop watering was reduced, if not eliminated. And of course the majority of landowners, the peasants, were not affected by the emergency regimen at all. Thus the amount of land actually taken out of cultivation in the district at this time was probably far less than 30 percent.

Furthermore, another adjustment the authorities made at this point counteracted the other measure to a great extent. Supplementary water was given to the sectors of the secondary springs, so that they were reincorporated into the main cycle and were no longer independent. The springflows continued to be used separately as well, but this was supposed to be coordinated with the main cycle in the same syncopated fashion as in Huaynacotas and Pampamarca, so that there was no overlap. In addition, although the area covered by the springs was supposedly reduced when they were brought into the main system, the authorities recognized that, in times of drought, the dwindling flow from their small tanks rapidly evaporated as the water was used, so that unless the area they served was cut back to almost nothing, a dose from the main canals was needed. The result was the re-emergence of the system of dual water rights typical of the haciendas. It persisted after the springflows returned to normal, in 1984, to become one of the main sources of resentment and conflict within the district.

Interestingly enough, this problem only developed in Cotahuasi sector, where the majority of the small springs are located and where the landlords had held a virtual monopoly on the water. In Quillunsa, three important local springs, all relatively small, were never under hacendado control. They are now well managed by the community on the same plan the administrator originally imposed: they contract without overlap during droughts, to within a very small area below the tank, then expand again when it is over. Never has there been any duplication in Quillunsa, or in Cachana and Reyparte sectors, which each incorporate one or two rather large springs in the same way. In the management of these springs we find a vestige of the communal system, which has otherwise broken down in so many ways. The return to normalcy is possible because the spring-watered fields do not have, and never have had, rights to main water under any other circumstances. Duplication only developed where hacendados had broken the customary use of the springs in the past by establishing private legal claims to the water sources.

Thanks to this double dose of water, forty-nine hectares of Cotahuasi sector's irrigated fields (30% of the total) are some of the choicest land in the district. Their special status is a source of a great deal of friction today between the user groups of Cotahuasi and Quillunsa, a conflict essentially between former landlords and peasants.

Adjusting the system during the first drought emergency had several other negative consequences, which will be examined below. Because of them, serious problems arose in connection with the irrigation of crop fields and the watering of alfalfa. For complicated reasons—and paradoxically enough—the first years of drought, by creating scarcity and thereby increasing people's natural desire for more water, caused the previously established controls on irrigation time to be relaxed. One can easily see how this happened, simply by looking at the way things are done during droughts today.

Tragedy in the Commons: Social Causes
of an Environmental Crisis

Several features of the military's reformed system actually heightened the impact of the ensuing scarcity, helping to create a state of disorder and conflict. The first lay in the realm of technique and had been a prominent feature of local irrigation ever since the colonial period: the top-down inundation method itself. Because alfalfa had been integrated into the crop-rotation cycle long before, and a large percentage of terraces were destroyed to accommodate this change, the method is now used to water a majority of the food crops, particularly in Cotahuasi. More than 60 percent of the fields in that sector have been consolidated and expanded for pasture production, and the percentage in the annexes is substantial too, though clearly less than 40 percent.[9] This has obviously been the case for some time, since alfalfa production expanded rapidly soon after the road arrived.

We have already seen that the inundation technique, as practiced in Cotahuasi, encourages people to irrigate for longer than necessary and is extremely wasteful of both water and soil. Since nothing indicates saturation, people tend to continue watering for four or usually five hours per topo, just to make sure. Of course, the amount of waste and erosion depends on the volume of the water flow and the slope of the plot (see Treacy 1990: 172). But in this district the tendency to prolong irrigation has little or nothing to do with slope (many of the fields are actually fairly flat), and the water flow is not curtailed in any way.

Many people returned to this habit of excessive irrigation during the drought, especially the larger landowners who grew the most pasture. Consequently, one of the key accomplishments of the water reform, the standardization of irrigation time, was nullified. Ultimately, this had the effect of again reducing, by as much as 30 percent, the total area watered in a day, since, at five hours per topo instead of three, there was often only enough for two allotments a day, rather than the anticipated three. This is an astonishing thing to have happen during a drought, but it is not hard to see how it happened, and why the water distributors were powerless to stop it.

To begin with, a three-hour-per-topo limit was not written into the General Water Law. The administrator was authorized to set standards affecting the quantity of water use. He supposedly had the technical ability to decide upon them based on agronomic and hydrological data, but the administrator who instituted the reform in Cotahuasi, like every other man who has served in the post since then, had neither the instruments nor the information needed to do his job—not even a current-meter. Nor did he have the equipment needed to mete the water out precisely—adjustable canal gates. This situation probably prevails throughout most of the highlands even today (Hendriks 1986).

Instead, the administrator, in consultation with officers of the Irrigator Commission, quite rightly imposed a local standard, based on the amount of time that was thought to be sufficient under local conditions. Here I should point out that many people in the district will acknowledge that three hours per topo is enough under normal conditions, and everyone seems to be aware of this. But naturally, when the drought hit, people thought that a different and "longer" standard should be set to compensate for the decline in flows. The only technical standard that the administrator apparently had for reference was the benchmark mentioned earlier—five hours per hectare flowing at 31 liters a second—which he probably found in some ministry guideline. I heard this figure cited repeatedly in conversations and several times in user-group meetings as an official policy. But this flow is extremely large by district standards; it would be a substantial part of the maximal flows of the three main reservoirs, and only three of the secondary springs even reach this level (Table 7). Like most of the state's official agronomic standards, which seem to be based on the conditions typical of the coast, where the irrigation systems are more "advanced" technologically and much bigger in scale, this one is inapplicable to the local situation. It is equivalent to using 10 liters of water a second for five hours per topo, a flow that is, according to ministry data, roughly comparable to the volume of many of the secondary canals.

The result, in any case, was that five hours a topo became an unofficial rule-of-thumb that people could cite whenever the distributor pressured them to stop irrigating at the appropriate time. And if it supposedly took five hours to water a topo with a large flow, then logically it should take at least that long with a smaller one. Three hours is actually enough, even during a drought, and the administrator tried to get people to stick to that amount. But he had no official policy statement to back up him up; indeed, the only standard that he had indicated that people should be allowed to continue for much longer.[10]

Nothing has since come along to change things. Lacking official data to show that less is indeed enough, distributors are not inclined to take water away from people before they are ready. They fear the social consequences—of enmity, charges of favoritism, forms of retaliation—that would arise from forcing some self-restraint on people. But there is another, more important reason: distributors do not have the authority to curtail irrigation under the General Water Law. All they can do is report infractions to the administrator, who alone has the power to impose any penalties. Moreover, those penalties now consist solely of monetary fines, or multas, which at best are given long after the fact and require a formal bureaucratic procedure on the adminstrator's part. The crucial power to withhold water or shut it off during irrigation is not written into the law.

The function of distributors today is simply to divert the water wherever they are told it is supposed to go and to report any problems to the water officials. They open the appropriate gates, without exercising any control over volume, and tell people the order in which the flow is theirs to use. If the resource is to be used efficiently, as the law requires, other conditions besides the time limit should be met, but these have not been clearly defined either, and the distributors have no power to impose them. For example, when the inundation method is used, scratch canals should already be in place on the surface to direct the flow when it arrives or water will be lost, as commonly happens. More important, feeder canals should be cleared of the grama, which continually chokes them and absorbs great amounts of water if left in place. Landowners usually fail to make these preparations, which are widely acknowledged as necessary but require extra labor on their part. Distributors can do little about it, since by law the administrator is solely responsible for regulating water use. And the control that he actually exercises, in practice, is virtually no control at all.

Overuse was further encouraged when, during the drought, water ceased to be distributed in the orderly sequence originally imposed. This emergency measure is where the problems really began. In conformity with the law and the desires of most water users, crop fields were given priority over alfalfa fields and now irrigated on a different schedule. A supplementary watering for cropland only, called an *auxilio*, was inserted into the main cycle of each sector as needed and was lengthened thereafter as the supply continued to decline.

The way this works can be seen by taking the example of Cotahuasi and Quillunsa, which alternate in using the Pitahuasi tank. During the planting season of 1987, a drought year, the share for each sector was fourteen days of water for both crops and pasture, plus five days of auxiliary water for crops only, which came directly after its normal turno, or cycle. In this way, all the remaining crop fields could be watered after the end of the regular cycle. Meanwhile, the irrigation of alfalfa was delayed until the main cycle resumed again, when it took up where it had left off before.

The result was an overall cycle of thirty-eight days for food crops and approximately eighty days for alfalfa. Because such a large percentage of each sector was planted in pasture, at least two full cycles would pass, with the auxiliary waterings in between, before all the alfalfa could be irrigated. Subsequently, the auxilio was slowly lengthened for each community until the time between waterings extended to forty-eight days for food crops and over a hundred for alfalfa. Although no one seems to remember it today, this was more than twice as long as the cycle in the early days of water abundance and military rule.

As one might predict, the auxilio does more harm than good. It gives water to roughly half the number of fields and puts food crops and alfalfa on completely different schedules. Inevitably, because the irrigation of pasture lags far behind and is interrupted, the main cycle separates into two waterings that are going on in completely different areas of the sector, often several, at the same time. This dispersal, in turn, has two negative effects: it increases water loss through filtration and evaporation, negating some of the savings that the prioritization policy is intended to produce; and, because a contiguous sequence cannot be followed and the order turns out to be rather flexible in practice, the door is wide open for theft, favoritism, excessive watering, and other kinds of abuse. The regimen is much less transparent, almost opaque, to the individual water-user and even to the distributor himself.

Consequently, when the auxilio was introduced in 1978, it actually increased the prevailing scarcity and caused the Cultivation and Irrigation Plan to fall apart. Soon there was no plan at all, other than to have a turno and an auxilio, and to start the whole sequence at the bottom of each sector at the beginning of the year. Undoubtedly, some attempt was made to water both crops and pasture in orderly sequence, consecutively according to field location along each canal, as still happens today, but exceptions were allowed, and this often took place in two or more parts of the sector at once, and in any case the fields no longer bordered each other. As a result, the entire burden of monitoring and control now fell on the distributors, whose task quickly became an impossible one.

Consider, for example, that Cotahuasi sector alone covers 161 hectares, or roughly 400 acres, within which there is a 500-meter gain in elevation, or 1,640 feet, a vertical rise greater than that of a lot of ski areas in the United States. It is quite obviously impossible for a man, even in the best physical condition, to patrol such a large expanse all day long, running up and down constantly to inspect the water route and observe irrigation taking place, as I learned by accompanying one extraordinarily fit and conscientious distributor in his work on several occasions. Few people are able to make a decent attempt at this assignment, and fewer still are willing to try, since the rewards are not great. Distributors received the equivalent of only twenty-five cents a day while I was in the district, or about half the going rate for wage labor. Because their pay did not reflect the importance of the service they provided to the community, they were not motivated to take their job very seriously, although this man did—a leader within the campesino community, and one of the peasant middle proprietors who still use mink'a.

Thanks to the emergency measure, waste and inequity soon prevailed. Water use became so dispersed and irregular that vigilance and accountability ceased to be strong features of the hydraulic system. And because the new system completely unraveled during the drought, scarcity persisted thereafter and became generalized, so that the auxilio soon became an integral part of the normal distribution regime. Only after years of truly abundant rainfall is the main cycle now extended so as to cover all of each sector in one rotation.

Again, these conditions prevailed throughout the district during most of my fieldwork, and they continue to do so today, despite a more "normal" rainfall pattern. Even though there was a drought going on, water was being wasted everywhere because its use went virtually unrestrained, with people watering a topo of land for five hours. It is important to note, however, that this problem was much more serious in some sectors than in others, and that the problem of favoritism, at least in its most detrimental form, was largely confined to sectors where the big landowners, the former hacendados and their heirs, still had land. Not surprisingly, this kind of corruption emerged primarily in Cotahuasi sector, where these people had recently lost the privileges they had always enjoyed before. Thus flaws in the law and the irrigation system did not create the problem, nor did the drought. They merely gave these former hacendados (and everyone else) a compelling reason for using more water than they were entitled to, and perhaps twisting arms to get it.

Yet the larger landowners, the empresarios and ganaderos, had an additional reason not shared by everyone else, as they still do today. At the beginning of the agricultural year, these families often have difficulty planting at the designated time because they rely on wage laborers, who can be hard to find during that busy season, especially now that campesinos have many ways of acquiring cash. The problem was especially acute during my time in the valley, but it has generally been common ever since the agrarian reform, for obvious reasons: most campesinos at this critical time are busy sowing their own fields every day, right through the first watering cycle. Even the ones with the least land, who need the work and the money, have to attend to their own fields and are busy part of the time. And this is true throughout the lower valley, since planting is going on everywhere at roughly the same time.

One of the main effects of the agrarian reform is that the big properties lost their resident labor forces and much of their local ones too. Today, most peons who work on the bigger properties come from communities in the upper valley, like Huaynacotas and Pampamarca, where planting begins a week or two

later, in early September. And even there, the large landlords have difficulty re-
cruiting workers because the comuneros can and do go elsewhere to find work,
like the local campesinos. Worse still, from their point of view, most of the comuneros they do manage to recruit work only long enough to get the money to
move on to better paying, temporary jobs in Majes, Camaná, and beyond.

Because of this problem, the landowners often exert pressure on the administrator to grant their allotments when they need them, when they have found
the necessary labor. And since planting sets the schedule on which later irrigation should take place, requests for other "emergency" allotments generally follow. For those who can pay, crop fields require an investment in fertilizer and
insecticides, to say nothing of labor, and no one who plants his field during the
early days of the auxilio is going to willingly watch his crops dry up until his
next turn comes around.

Not surprisingly, special allotments are also frequently sought for alfalfa, as
in Pampamarca, especially when pasture is needed for upcoming shipments of
cattle, where truly large investments have been made. The rental of these fields
is big business in Cotahuasi today and has been for a long time. Alfalfa does respond well to frequent watering, but this "need" is especially great when a lot of
money is at stake. And, at the lower altitudes in Cotahuasi district, one can get
a maximum of five cuttings a year if the water comes often enough, rather than
the four that are possible in Pampamarca. Naturally, with so much on the line,
the requests of wealthy people with power and influence carry a lot of weight
with the administrator. And he is authorized, under the law, to change the
schedule at his discretion, to accommodate to a significant variation in water
needs.

Even under normal conditions, when no auxilio is in effect (as in 1985 and
1986), the main cycle will begin at the bottom of a sector and move upward
canal by canal, but very often some people with special permission will also be
watering fields higher up, so that the sequence is constantly truncated and
spread out. When the auxilio is added, chaos ensues—as I discovered when I attempted to measure the main canal flow at the very bottom of Cotahuasi sector
in Piro, on a day when the distributor had told me all of the water would arrive
there intact.

After measuring the flow, I walked upslope along the canal to the pueblo,
only to find water being drawn off at four different points along the way. In
each case, a secondary canal had been opened, with official permission given at
the last minute to water one field of perhaps a topo, three of which were located
far off the main canal. Totally exasperated for having wasted so much work, I
estimated that this diversion added about 1.5 kilometers to the original canal

distance of 7.5 kilometers, increasing correspondingly the water lost through filtration and evaporation, all in order to service fewer than two hectares of land. The three distant fields, it turned out, belonged to friends of the governor, the administrator, and a member of the Irrigator Commission.

Now I could make sense of an earlier experience. When I had arrived in Piro that morning, four of the twelve people who were waiting to irrigate had been told by the distributor that they would not get water until the following day. Their resentment and frustration on hearing this had been obvious, but it was also clear that the news came as no big surprise, even though the distributor had not given any explanation. Indeed, he himself did not know why or exactly who had benefited from the change; he had simply been told to open the various canal gates on his way down to Piro.

Later investigations confirmed that such last-minute changes in order were a common occurrence, as people had often told me. On several occasions, I heard people complain about these unexpected disruptions at user-group meetings and argue that at least the reasons for them should always be explained to the affected people, but nothing was ever done about the problem.

The Irrationality of the Current System

All of these problems reveal the fundamental irrationality of the official system of management and show how unsuitable it is for communities in the highlands today. First of all, the model that the law presents, which calls for the precise calculation of water requirements, is based on the assumption that those needs are known, and that there is enough water available to meet them. But crops have no water "requirements"; rather, they respond differentially to a wide range of frequencies of irrigation, just as people do to varying amounts of food and nutrition. In fact, the standards used by the Ministry of Agriculture are merely optima based on an assumption of sufficiency—clearly inappropriate for use in the sierra, where water is scarce to begin with, where droughts are common, and where irrigation frequencies are generally far from ideal.[11] Scarcity is in fact the normal state of affairs.

The law fails to present a workable model for use in the region, in which both the prevailing scarcity and the periodic crises should be absorbed equitably on the same schedule by everyone. Any other arrangement inevitably causes conflict and, being more opaque and less transparent, it encourages violations, as we have seen. Astonishingly, nowhere in the legislation is it stated that people's water rights must be comparable to each other in any way. Obviously, highland communities could not afford to abide by such a law, even if they had the necessary equipment and infrastructure. Under conditions of scarcity, the General Water Law is simply a recipe for waste, inequity, and corruption.

As things stand now, the power to determine people's water rights—that is, how much water they get and how often—is concentrated at the top, in the hands of the administrator and leaders of the user community, people who are rarely present when irrigation is actually carried out. The people who are routinely present, the distributors, play only a minor role at best in determining the watering order, and they have little power to control use or enforce conservation standards, which are not even specified in the associated regulations. As for the users themselves, they are very much aware that favoritism and waste are common, but they are equally aware that they are powerless to do anything about it. Typically, the resentment and suspicion of others that this causes discourage cooperation and result in poor maintenance of the system, a problem that has been widely documented (e.g., Hendriks 1986), and that further exacerbates water loss.

Under these conditions, it is almost impossible to get people to conserve water by improving their own methods of utilization, at the cost of a small amount of additional work, because they have no rational reason for doing so. In their eyes, unless everyone undertook the same conservation measures (something they see as highly doubtful, based on past experience), the resulting savings would only pass on to someone else, and would not benefit them in any way. This "free-rider" problem (Erasmus 1977; Ostrom 1990, 1992) appears to be endemic in communities where irrigation is overseen by the state, and Cotahuasi is no exception. From what I have seen, that kind of behavior is extremely common in the district, as local people will often quite freely admit, even volunteer. Indeed, in many people's eyes, the whole country of Peru is one big nation of free-riders, one huge corrupt system. The ramifications of this view, whether it is really accurate or not, are felt in every domain of social and political life, as anyone who has spent much time in the countryside is aware. The interesting question, to me at least, is whether anything can be done about it.

The corruption has become endemic and pervasive, but in a sense, it begins at the most basic level, in irrigation, and that is where a start could be made. So far as the reform itself is concerned, though, it has accomplished nothing at all beyond its early success in clearing up a similar mess in its thirty or so years of operation.

Attempts to Solve the Water Problem

As an ethnographer, I naturally wanted to understand how people in the district perceive the water problem, its history, and the whole legacy of conflict over the resource. Getting at their perceptions turned out to be rather easy, since several plans had been proposed for resolving the situation, whose relative merits were continually being disputed during my time there. Formulated by outside agencies in response to local requests for assistance, the proposals reflect differing views on how the apparent shortage can best be alleviated: by increasing the supply, by improving the infrastructure, or by eliminating the corruption and waste in the distribution system. Although most of the plans ran into serious difficulties and were never fully implemented, all of them deserve close attention. Even the failures provide insight into the hydraulic nature of Cotahuasi society, into how its most basic divisions and conflicts are constructed in both a material and a social sense, and how these rifts are represented and interpreted at the cultural level. On a more practical note, they show clearly the folly of making invalid assumptions about, and having inappropriate models for, irrigation, ones that in this case have been promoted by the state and are quite common in the "developing" world.

Most of the projects ultimately foundered because they did nothing to change the existing mode of organization, which forces separate communities to share water and compete for it. Plans for increasing the supply had the effect of intensifying the rivalry between user groups—particularly Cotahuasi and Quillunsa, the two biggest villages in the district—and making cooperation all but impossible. They failed to take into account both local history and social reality, merely intensifying an ongoing struggle that continues to exacerbate the scarcity of the resource while preventing any unified and constructive action.

Some of the plans distorted people's perceptions of the water problem by focusing their attention on aspects over which they have no control, and by fostering the notion that any viable solution requires outside help. This was consistent with the basic assumption underlying the state's model—that irrigation is far too complex for local people themselves to oversee. The model is basically technocratic and agronomic, treating irrigation as a technical problem rather than a social one, a matter of meeting the water needs of crops rather than those of people. No doubt it, like the law itself and the similar laws of Ecuador and other neighboring countries, originated in land-grant universities in the United States. In any case, the model reinforced the popular view that the prevailing scarcity is real, and that people do not really contribute much to it. This, in turn, hampered efforts to correct problems in distribution and use, problems that almost everyone is aware of and over which people do in fact have some control. During my time in the district, the government's involvement in the water problem merely reduced the communities' ability to cope with the crisis and furthered an agenda of making Cotahuasi a client of the state in nearly all of its affairs. The situation posed a real challenge to my understanding, ultimately forcing me to see that, even in matters of basic ecology, in one of the more unstable and rigorous environments in the world, seemingly insoluble problems turn out to be largely socially and historically constructed. The good news is that they are therefore capable, at least in theory, of solution.

DREAMS OF FINDING MORE WATER

It is only logical that, in a situation where rainfall had recently become unpredictable, people tended to give first priority to the aspect of the problem over which they have the least control: the relatively "closed" or circumscribed nature of the hydrological system. A large majority of those that I talked to were mainly concerned with increasing the amount of water entering the system; thus they favored large-scale construction projects to tap distant water sources. This approach is exemplified by the oldest and most ambitious proposal, which aims to divert a tributary of the Cotahuasi River far up in its headwaters: the Choccocco Project, initiated in response to the drought emergency of 1939–44.

The idea was to build a 30-kilometer-long canal to bring water from the Choccocco River high above Alca into the upper part of Cotahuasi's irrigation system at Huambo. With government support, construction was begun on the canal in 1953, using local faena labor, and it advanced several kilometers before being stopped by technical and financial problems. New studies followed in 1962, but, despite enthusiastic public support, the proposal remained shelved until 1980, shortly after the end of military rule. At that time, it was reevaluated by a state and departmental organization, the Development Corporation of Arequipa (CORDEA), which concluded that the project was not economically feasible. The cost of diverting a great amount of water over such rugged terrain was said to be too great for the expected benefits. Another, similar proposal encountered the same difficulties.

Despite this negative appraisal, most Cotahuasinos continue to hope that the project will be revived, and that the government, or some international organization, will someday simply give them the necessary money.[12] After more than half a century, they still see this plan, or something like it, as the only solution to their problem. Although many people know that much of the water they have is going to waste and could therefore be saved, most of them consider the social and historical obstacles to that solution more insurmountable than the daunting challenge posed by the rugged landscape itself. They also express doubt that a conservation plan would lead to any truly equitable outcome, conveying an exasperating sense of inertia and pessimism.

Still, given this widespread perception, we can well understand why local people, most of them former hacendados and sharecroppers, should cling to a hope of benevolent patronage. Traditionally, this kind of dependency was the campesinos' only recourse in solving problems beyond their control. Moreover, the province, like many others in Peru today, has in fact been a beneficiary of international development philanthropy. The rejection of the Choccocco plan, and other proposals like it (e.g., tapping alpine lakes, as in Huaynacotas; pumping water up over 1,000 meters from the river), is therefore difficult for people to accept. Given the limitations imposed by the environment, there is no great reserve of water that can be tapped to make the district invulnerable to drought. No foreign patron, still less the state, can be expected to support a costly project that would not, in any case, overcome the natural limits of the resource, yet people keep hoping against hope. Since leaders of the major political parties have been promising to get this done for so long, in an effort to get elected—especially those of APRA, who consistently promoted Choccocco and other similar schemes—the fantasy will be difficult to eliminate.

Surprisingly little support existed for a more modest plan that is actually the only viable scheme for augmenting the water supply. This is the Tomepampa-Piro Project, which proposes to import river water into only the lower part of the system. Part of the problem is that it requires a great deal of cooperation between villages with respect to labor and the sharing of the resource. The user community as a whole seems to be receptive only to large-scale proposals like Choccocco that would directly benefit all groups and all individuals in the district. A strong element of intersector jealousy and rivalry, one that has a long history but for which the reform itself is partly responsible, prevents the majority from embracing the best alternative.

The Tomepampa-Piro plan was originally proposed in 1980 by a French-Peruvian development consortium (CICDA-PRODAPU) that worked in the valley from 1979 through 1985. Here the idea is to tap the mainstream of the Cotahuasi River far upstream at a point where it is not too deep and divert the water through 16 kilometers of canal into the lower part of Cotahuasi sector. Because of the gradient, without extensive pumping the canal would not be capable of irrigating more than 90 hectares, equivalent to 51 percent of the land in Cotahuasi sector but only 16 percent of the district total. The point, however, is that this would free up about half the lower sector's main water for use in the rest of Cotahuasi and in Quillunsa as well, a benefit that would supposedly be shared evenly, like the work responsibilities.

In 1982, CORDEA, the departmental development agency, then under the leadership of the Popular Action party of President Belaúnde, carried out a feasibility study, and it even began constructing the canal a year later. This effort, financed entirely by the state and manned by faena labor, was paralyzed by serious problems in 1984. When the plan was reevaluated in 1987, CORDEA, then under APRA leadership, judged it to be unfeasible for both technical and economic reasons. In reality, these problems could have been solved fairly easily with another government grant, but that was clearly an impossibility with the state in virtual bankruptcy under Alan García and APRA.

During my fieldwork, continuing the project was favored only by those landowners who would benefit from it directly, especially the former sharecroppers and reform beneficiaries of the barrio of Santa Ana in Cotahuasi, all of whom were willing to work in the necessary faenas.[13] Many more workers were needed, however, and Quillunsa users, in particular, were firmly opposed to participating because they would not receive any of the river water themselves. Based on past experience, the Quillunseños understandably suspected that they might not receive the promised share of main water. These were the objections voiced at assemblies of the Quillunsa Irrigator Committee, where participation was considered and voted down several times. But there was another important reason for their resistance to the plan.

On a more significant but less obvious level, this community, composed mainly of campesinos, rejected the idea that lower Cotahuasi—historically the demesne of the hacendados—would again become the best-watered part of the district. Even though numerous campesinos would have received water from the canal and enthusiastically supported the project, most Quillunseños saw the plan as a ploy on the part of certain Cotahuasi mayoristas to dupe the rest of the people in the district. This aspect of historical class conflict was not obvious to me at first, and without seeing it, the rigid opposition of the community appeared irrational. It seemed to exemplify, in almost stereotypical fashion, the difficulty that campesinos sometimes have in working together for their own benefit, a problem that biased observers tend to attribute to ignorance, lack of education, or some other alleged symptom of rural poverty. The plan was clearly the only feasible one, with only the minor problem of adjusting the main water shares.

The logic of what was happening only became clear when I took a closer look at landownership in the area to be affected. At first glance, it seemed that most of Piro and the lower part of Cotahuasi sector had been divided up thoroughly by the reform, into small properties owned by businessmen and peasants of every social standing. But nearly all of the remaining hacendado families in the district have modest holdings there. After looking closely at the List of Irrigators, in the process of selecting my stratified sample, I remembered that the conflict between landlords and peasants had been mentioned briefly but repeatedly in the Quillunsa meetings. It became obvious in private conversations thereafter that this was the crux of the problem.

On principle alone, the people of Quillunsa dismiss any suggestion that they should provide labor for a project that would benefit these big landowners, both former and current, more than themselves. Yet there was an even more significant historical factor at work, an element of intercommunity jealousy and rivalry. Recall that the water of Wakajara and Pitahuasi had been diverted into lower Cotahuasi only recently, during the reform, in compensation for rerouting the formerly private water of Armanca. Even though this diversion initially left the Quillunseños with a small surplus, they justifiably felt that the reform had denied them additional water that was rightfully theirs, and given it to former landlords who traditionally had had no rights to it. They refused to contribute labor to a project that would now give those same people even more water.

This position, in turn, reinforced the Cotahuasinos' belief that that Quillunsa had received an over-generous share of water from the reform, that it had left them with a surplus and enabled them to expand irrigation—an opinion that was not unfounded. The Quillunseños' apparent lack of interest in increasing their own water supply tended to be explained in this manner. Neither the provincial authorities nor the various development agencies evaluating the proposal understood that, to the people of Quillunsa, the Tomepampa-Piro Project would merely have returned to them water that they should have gotten back in the reform. The most significant thing about the proposed canal was that it would have put the landowners of lower Cotahuasi sector in the unprecedented and unacceptable position of nearly total hydraulic security, giving them abundant water and making them much less vulnerable to drought.

Because of this huge benefit and the privileges that the Cotahuasinos already enjoyed, Quillunsa voted that they should bear the entire labor and financial cost of the project themselves. This was the conclusion and formal recommendation that the committee members arrived at almost unanimously. At the same time, they cited Choccocco as the preferable alternative because it would directly and equally benefit all sectors in the district, and urged that efforts be intensified to get state or foreign financing for that project.

Although significant opposition was also mounted by people in other sectors and communities who would have had to give up land for the canal right-of-way, Quillunsa's attitude was the main reason why the project remained at a standstill. To be sure, CORDEA judged it to be both technically and economically unfeasible, but that was clearly not the case. The only real barrier was a so-cial and historical one, a longstanding conflict that had both material and ide-ological dimensions.[14]

IMPROVING THE INFRASTRUCTURE

The first improvement of the canal and tank system came in 1970, when SINAMOS sponsored the re-construction of the cement tank at Pitahuasi, which had been built in 1965 to store the water of Wakajara and replace the old reservoir in Huambo. Shortly thereafter, two other major tanks were built, Cochacallán and Cachana, to store the waters of Cutirpo and Armanca, respec-tively. The tanks of the district's twelve largest secondary springs were supposed to be rebuilt next, but the project was postponed for lack of funds until 1975, when plans were drawn up for doing that work.

CORDEA had initially sponsored the rebuilding of some of these tanks, but another organization, the Peruvian-German Pact for Food Security, or CO-PASA, took over most of the effort in 1987, after the national election that swept APRA into power. At that time, COPASA, an organization financed and super-vised by the West German government, entered into a cooperative agreement with CORDEA, which had been completely restaffed with APRA members. It was under COPASA's direction and sponsorship that the remaining tanks, as well as a long portion of the main canal of Cutirpo, were lined with cement. Other canal improvements were planned but were never completed because of the political violence of November 1988, which forced COPASA to withdraw from the valley.

All these projects were designed, financed, and supervised by outsiders; the actual work was done by faena labor parties manned by the respective user groups. The strong element of patronage and dependency was obvious enough: "engineers" designed the new water-control features, set the conditions and the timetable for the work, provided the expensive materials (concrete and iron) that were touted as the solution to the water problem, and even gave the people food rations as incentives to work. Even though COPASA took steps to maxi-mize the workers' participation in managing the project, the arrangement con-tradicted the principle of mutual self-help that is the essence of faena, commu-nal work. It also reinforced the notion that the most serious hydraulic problems are beyond the local people's capacity to solve.

All of this was unfortunate because, in this district, as in many other districts throughout the highlands, the communal work tradition was weak to start with. We have seen that the tradition had already degenerated well before the reform. Thus a truly communal tradition had to be built, much like a tank; and, for the government and the development organizations, the improvement projects were to be the start of this effort at institution building. Apparently, beginning with SINAMOS, the organizations expected that cooperation in improving tanks and canals would somehow generalize to other situations and permanently strengthen communal organization, thereby leading to better maintenance of the irrigation system.[15]

Instead, these organizations, with the important exception of COPASA, only fostered dependency. They failed to address the fundamental conflict of interest between peasants and businessmen, cattlemen, and other people heavily involved in the commercial economy. The lesson learned from all my experience with such construction projects, in Cotahuasi, Pampamarca, and Huaynacotas, is that the major problems with which they are typically plagued —the slowness of the work, the absences and frequent halts, the tendency of assemblies to turn into shouting matches where issues end up unresolved—are all really symptoms of a single malady. They express the smallholders' resentment of, and resistance to, the large landowners, who work or contribute as if they were just any ordinary participant, when in fact they benefit more from the projects because they have more irrigated land. Montoya (Montoya et al. 1979: 175–83) has observed that the comuneros of Puquio, in Ayacucho to the northwest, clearly recognize and resent this contradiction. They tolerate it, however, because they do not really expect businessmen, in this case people of Spanish heritage, to act in any other way. In Cotahuasi, indeed throughout the entire valley, the campesinos keenly resent this inequity, too, and have expressed that feeling throughout the years in various ways, as we have seen.

Curiously, the most that SINAMOS and CORDEA ever tried to do was to get the landlords and other large proprietors to contribute one person, typically a hired worker, to communal work projects. They succeeded mainly because the law required it, with predictable results. However, in several cases, in both Cotahuasi and Pampamarca, I saw projects that were ridden with conflict run smoothly once an agreement had been reached that, as in Huaynacotas, labor duties would be proportional to the amount of land that each person in the benefited area possessed. Interestingly, such proportionality was required by the Water Code of 1902, but only with respect to the cash contributions that people had to make to state-sponsored projects (Costa y Cavero 1934: 75), an arrangement that has persisted ever since. Even the General Water Law ignores the crucial issue of who is going to do the actual work, and in what amounts, and this is where the development organizations in Cotahuasi eventually had to intervene.[16]

COPASA alone among the various organizations did come to such agreements, initially only as necessary to overcome strikes and work stoppages. But these happened so often that it soon became an official policy. Even so, the arrangement would resolve the basic conflict only temporarily, always among one group of people working on a single task; and did not generalize to other situations as planned. By mediating only temporarily to defuse the conflict and ensure that a given job was completed, COPASA prevented the issue from being addressed in a wider sense or at a higher level. If the development organizations had really been serious about strengthening the communal tradition and improving maintenance, changing the law to address the pivotal issue of proportional labor contributions is the single most significant thing they could have done.

In faenas, the campesinos' resentment toward the big landowners, people who still intimidate many of them, is usually expressed only in passive forms of resistance, such as slow work and frequent absences. But on foreign-sponsored projects, they are brave enough to express their resentment through boycotts because they are bolstered by the power of outsiders who can threaten to withhold construction materials if the mayoristas do not comply with the will of the majority. This COPASA did more than once. Unfortunately, the confrontation seems to evaporate when the sponsoring organization leaves, and since the outsiders make no effort to bring about a change in local or national policy, the process will simply repeat itself the next time, when another organization sponsors a project among a different group of water-users. Meanwhile, resistance will continue in more routine community affairs; and, in places like Cotahuasi, where the communal tradition was corrupted long ago, the maintenance of the irrigation system will suffer. To far too many observers, campesinos will appear to be unable to work together for their own benefit, when in fact they are not the problem.

What is needed is for the state, and the development organizations, to back up the campesinos in their demand that mayoristas play their proper role in the physical work of projects, not just in their financing and supervision. A dramatic change would ensue in hydraulic projects in general, especially in maintenance work, and probably in many other aspects of community life as well. Until this happens, some mayoristas will continue to try to take charge of the projects behind the scenes, to minimize their own work quotas, and to exploit these situations for their own benefit, with predictable results: conflict and paralysis.

A CONSTANT DILEMMA: THE FAILURE OF
EFFORTS TO IMPROVE WATER USE

One plan that local officials have supposedly been trying to push through
for more than twenty years is aimed specifically at those who are partly responsible for the water shortage, the users themselves. On its face, it seems pretty
simple: to reorganize distribution in a way that brings water use into full compliance with existing law. They invited the public to discuss this possibility at
several meetings in the drought year of 1987, the result of which was a series of
recommendations offered jointly by Cotahuasi and Quillunsa. Logically
enough, the two communities recommended that a new land inventory be carried out, that the water shares of the sectors be adjusted equitably accordingly,
and that the distribution system be reorganized to eliminate duplicate shares
and other inequities. Thus they did in fact vote to solve the water problem at its
real source, to adopt the most feasible and practical plan.

Despite the consensus, they made virtually no changes. The amount of land
in Cotahuasi and Quillunsa was measured and found to be roughly equal, confirming the adequacy of the water shares, and nothing else was accomplished.
This outcome raises two puzzling questions that remain to be answered. How
can wasteful inequities, such as favoritism and dual water rights, endure in violation of the law and despite the professed determination of the authorities and
the community members to eliminate them? And what does their persistence
reveal about the structure and character of this society, and especially the local
role of the state?

The problem of favoritism would seem to be more intractable than the lack
of control over water use, since it is essentially a form of corruption, a failure on
the part of officials to abide by the General Water Law and the attached regulations. Yet, as we have seen, the legislation itself is a major part of the problem.
The law encourages requests for special treatment because it fails to assert any
uniformity or proportionality in people's rights, and because the model upon
which it is based is inappropriate for use in the sierra. This is an institutional
flaw, but another one is even more basic, contributing directly to favoritism,
wastefulness, and other problems having to do with water use. It is the way that
water is divided and shared between communities, the fact that they alternate
in using it rather than using it at the same time.

Now that major reservoirs have been built for each primary spring, most of
the user groups have to share water in the same manner that Cotahauasi and
Quillunsa have been doing ever since 1942. This kind of arrangement, which
seems to be found in many areas where the government has sponsored the construction of major tanks and is in charge of administering the resource, pro-

motes conflict by making irrigation a "zero-sum" game, in which one group's gain is the other's loss. Alternating use distorts people's perceptions and leads them to lay the blame for their shortages on their neighbors in the other sector. It creates the same kind of suspicions and doubts between communities that now exist within each community, in this case between communities that are distant from each other and separated by steep rough terrain. In so doing, it perpetuates and institutionalizes the water conflict, which of course has a long history.

As a result, each user group tries to increase its share by demanding that the irregularities in its neighbor's system be corrected, rather than attending to the problems in its own. During my time in the district, the struggle over water had reached a stalemate that obstructed all efforts to improve the system, affecting every practical proposal for change. It had also set the campesinos against each other, pitting the peasants of Quillunsa against the former sharecroppers and reform beneficiaries of Cotahuasi, who were now "united" with the principal families and the new mayoristas living there. Some of the wealthier landowners have been able to exploit this conflict quite skillfully, to gain still further advantage.

Favoritism only makes matters worse. In its least detrimental form, distributors favor friends by putting them first in order for the day's water, or sometimes get even with enemies by putting them last. These deviations from the schedule may not be conducive to the optimal functioning of the system, but since only a fairly small expanse of land is involved, not all that much water is wasted as a result. We have seen that the same thing is done in Pampamarca on the basis of prestige, and that water remains abundant there nonetheless. However, the practice does contribute to another major defect in the system, a lack of vigilance and accountability, of transparency, as we have already seen.

A second kind of favoritism is much more disruptive and does jeopardize the common welfare, as we have also seen. Local political authorities and irrigation officials use it as a way to reinforce their power bases, to gain favors in return, and generally to strengthen their control over the pueblo. Giving priority to friends and cronies is a common occurrence, as many people will quite readily admit, but under the present system of administration little can be done about it. To return to the Piro example I cited earlier, we saw that in every case but one the owners of the favored fields were relatives, friends, or compadres of important people, including the administrator himself. Only in the remaining case did the water appear to have been given strictly on the basis of emergency need. Similar investigations on other occasions confirmed what people, generally campesinos, had been telling me for a long time: that this kind of favoritism is common, especially in Cotahuasi sector.

Interestingly, when I questioned the administrator about this incident, he complained that orders to grant such favors always came to him from "higher up," and that he had no choice but to comply. Taking advantage of my feigned ignorance in the matter, he deliberately gave the impression that the governor and the district mayor had authority over him. But I knew very well, and of course so did he, that they had no legal power in water affairs. In fact, he was merely responding to subtle reminders from powerful people of the insecurity of his professional position.

Since the law allows the administrator to change the order of allotment in these situations at his discretion, provided that he thinks enough water is available, it is difficult for a victim to do anything about the problem. And few people formally complain about favoritism anyway, because being bumped in the order tends to be only a matter of a day's delay, which does not cause much harm to crops, except during droughts. It is also hard for people to detect these irregularities, and even harder to prove that they are infractions. No one expects a contiguous sequence to be followed anymore, strictly speaking, since the administrator has the authority to change the schedule and has been doing so for a long time, supposedly in accordance with the law.

By loose definition, we can also speak of favoritism at a group level. It consists of granting new rights to members of one group or sector of a system in which water is shared, a practice that is more significant because it is permanent, cumulative, and large in scale. The prime example is the conflict over water between Cotahuasi and Quillunsa, where we can single out three separate cases of this phenomenon. An understanding of those cases and of how they are related to each other, is crucial if one is to fully grasp the dimensions of the water problem. It is also critical for understanding social conflict in general and the current state of relations between the classes.

The three examples are (1) the granting, under the reform, of an equal share of water from the Pitahuasi tank to both communities, without adjusting them to the amount of land under irrigation in each one, as the law required; (2) the granting of new rights to Quillunsa when it widened the agrarian frontier to incorporate certain previously dry-farmed lands; and (3) the permanent granting of supplementary water to the spring sectors of Cotahuasi, which had been intended only as a temporary measure in a drought emergency.

When I began to study the irrigation system, these events seemed bizarre and unrelated to each other, and I assumed that each had its own explanation. Nearly three years of controversy and investigation, however, showed me that they were in fact closely linked and had emerged in a definite historical sequence. I ultimately came to realize that these cases of favoritism were expressions of a survival strategy on the part of successive water administrators, who sought to implement the reform on the state's behalf, to adapt the system to drought, and to meet the conflicting demands put on them by the two communities, all without losing their jobs. They illustrate the contradictory role of the administrator as both a vulnerable outsider and a powerful mediator in local social conflict, a role for which these technicians are poorly prepared.

The various administrators did try to implement the law properly, but considerations of job security and comfort of lifestyle caused them to yield to the pressures applied by leaders of the two communities. The examples of group favoritism are concessions that the first two administrators made in an attempt to appease both groups, while still carrying out some semblance of a reform. The changes then became institutionalized because later administrators could not afford to do anything about them, and because neither user group could take legal action against the other without precipitating a corresponding action against themselves. In effect, the illegalities endured because they had created a stalemate, co-existing in a balanced state that only became tenuous during periods of severe water shortage.

When the original administrator and the president of the Irrigator Commission re-routed the water of Armanca in 1970, they had to compensate by somehow dividing the outflow of the new tank at Pitahuasi between Cotahuasi, now including all of that sector, and Quillunsa. This happened not because the General Water Law required it, but because the people of Quillunsa, fearing that they would end up with even less water than before, brought a lot of pressure to bear on the top water officials. At several meetings, leaders of the community explained to the new water authorities and the agents of SINAMOS the history of the relationship between their community and the adjacent haciendas. They argued that, if part of the tank water had to be given to landowners in lower Cotahuasi, who had traditionally had no rights to it, then the flow ought to be divided in half between the two communities, in an arrangement similar to the previous one, rather than precisely allotted according to the amount of land in each sector. This argument must have been appealing to the reform officials, consistent as it was with the military's determination to redress campesino grievances, and their alignment with the interests of that class. The motives of the commission president, an Aprista, were explained earlier: reprisal against the hacendados, more water for himself and other landowners in Chacaylla, and probably a hope for some gratitude from the campesinos.

Other efforts to persuade the officials included at least one major fiesta thrown by Quillunsa in the new administrator's honor. Today, Cotahuasinos tend to cite several such events as evidence that the official was "bought," in typical Peruvian style, for the price of a barbecue, a night of heavy drinking, and a woman.[17] I do not know the facts of the matter, except that people in Quillunsa admit that one big party did take place. They defended this action to me as simply an effort to make an appeal in the customary manner, pointing out that Cotahuasinos did the same thing, and even worse.

In any case, the water was divided in half, into two alternating turns of the same length, even though the land inventory needed for proportional division had been carried out as part of the agrarian reform. The amount of land under irrigation in Quillunsa was reportedly significantly less than in Cotahuasi, so that Quillunsa was indeed probably left with a sizable surplus during the years of ample rainfall that followed the reform. In 1998, almost thirty years later, people in Cotahuasi still complained that this was the case. Although the old land-use figures from the inventory have been lost and are not available to verify the accusation, it is confirmed by the second example set out above: shortly after the equal division was decided on, several Quillunseños, backed by the leaders of their user group, successfully appealed to the administrator to allow them to begin irrigating a substantial area that previously had been without water rights. Landowners there insist that the expansion was negligible, supposedly restricted to one marginal area of 5 hectares owned by a single person. I was able to confirm, however, that many more topos were given water, and rightly so; these lie interspersed among traditionally irrigated lands and along the sector margins. All together, they probably amount to at least 30 hectares, perhaps as much as 40, which is to say 18–24 percent of the total area under irrigation in Quillunsa today.

Because I was studying an irrigation system in a state of crisis, I was not able to take an inventory of these lands, or even to identify them in the List of Irrigators. I lived in and was most strongly associated with Cotahuasi, so that my efforts to do this aroused suspicion that I might eventually intervene in the situation somehow, that I posed the threat of taking water away from Quillunsa. It was difficult for people to believe that I could be investigating the matter so closely for any other reason, and there was little I could do to overcome their mistrust.

Although I cannot say how big the expansion was, it is important to note that these lands were the only ones within the village territory, the maize-growing area surrounding Quillunsa itself, that were not being irrigated. These lands had never been put back into production after the population collapse because the expansion of the haciendas had left the community without enough water. What the community was trying to do, then, in appealing for an equal water share, was merely to restore fully the communal water that the hacendados had originally taken away by force, and to expand cultivation toward its original limits. Elderly members of the community were aware of this history, and reversing it was reportedly a concern of the leaders, as well as one of their justifications for the request.

The only way I was able to learn what I think is the true story of these events was to take the logical step of asking the few people who had land in both sectors and, as members of both user groups, had divided loyalties. One landowner in particular was instrumental in piecing out the details—an elderly man from Cotahuasi with 2 hectares in Quillunsa who claimed to have been involved in the discussions and to know exactly what took place. Although most Quillunseños maintained the fiction that no significant expansion or favoritism on their behalf ever took place, he and the others said this extension of the "agrarian frontier," as it is called, benefited large as well as small landowners. At any rate, it involved enough land to legitimize Quillunsa's claim to an equal share of water. In the 1980's, according to the Padrón de Regantes, the sector had only slightly less irrigated land than Cotahuasi (169 hectares vs. 186).

The change was perfectly legal at the time, and the administrator acceded to the Quillunseños' request. Seemingly in compensation and to balance off opposing interests, he simultaneously granted new water rights in Cotahuasi, on the former hacienda of Salcán Grande, to some beneficiaries of the land reform, campesinos residing in the barrio of Santa Ana. In any event, as the drought took hold later on, the more influential members of the Cotahuasi community began to question the legitimacy of Quillunsa's new use for its water and its expansion of the frontier.

The law states that any new rights are to endure only as long as there is sufficient water for all previously established uses (DL 17752, Arts. 29–32). As the drought set in, that provision gave the Cotahuasinos a strong case that the irrigation of the newly opened lands in Quillunsa was illegal, and that the rights should be revoked. But though I continually heard complaints about this issue during fieldwork, no formal action was taken, apparently because the Cotahuasi leaders were actually quite satisfied with the arrangement, of which more will be said below.

The second case of group favoritism, and a major bone of legal contention—duplicate water rights—reemerged in the spring sectors of Cotahuasi under drought conditions, as previously described. The temporary rights to main water that many people received initially were allowed to continue because, just as in the granting of individual favors, it was in the interests of some officers of the Irrigator Commission and the local political authorities that it do so. The various administrators who served after the reform were simply pressured into playing along.

The hydraulic situation in the district cannot be understood without appreciating the circumstances under which these outsiders and bureaucrats try to do their work. Like many schoolteachers on their first assignment, they are sent to the "high provinces" for a minimum period of obligatory service (in their case two years), which they must complete in good standing if they are to advance to a better post. Generally from urban areas, these officials tend to consider this a period of labor-in-exile, especially since the remote Cotahuasi post is regarded as the least desirable one in the entire department. Weekend visits to family and friends in Arequipa are not possible; they can only make the twelve-to-fourteen-hour trip a few times a year, which also means that they work in isolation from their professional colleagues.

This predicament has several negative effects on how they do their jobs. Supervisors from the ministry office in Arequipa rarely monitor their work directly, as they should according to the law, but rely instead on reports that the administrators themselves prepare, together with any input coming from the provincial authorities. Naturally, the ministry itself is exceedingly sensitive to the reactions of these authorities and other powerful local men because, like all other Peruvian bureaucracies, it is highly politicized. The administrators of the post-reform period, left without the support of SINAMOS and the military, could hardly afford to provoke any serious controversy or local opposition.

While I was there, three men held the position in rapid succession, and none of them attempted to disguise their sense of frustration and lack of pride in their work. All three complained of being grossly underpaid, of lacking essential equipment such as vehicles and hydrometers, and of having to please people who were not respectful and who undermined every constructive effort they made. By their own admission, they were little concerned with doing their job well or with seeking creative solutions to problems. As one administrator explained to me, "It wouldn't be worth the trouble because I don't have any support and these [local] people are so corrupt." The main priority of all three (beyond being assigned to another post as soon as possible) was to appease their most powerful constituents, the only people to whom they were truly accountable. Whatever their tendencies may have been before they came to the valley, for them, working in Cotahuasi meant to compromise oneself thoroughly, to sell out.

The granting of duplicate water rights was the work of the second administrator (1978–86), a concession he felt forced to make to the powerful landowners with property around the springs if he was to advance his career and live in reasonable comfort during his time in the valley. When he announced his intention to cut off their rights to the springwater after the drought ended, the landowners vigorously protested. They argued that these areas had always been irrigated more than any others because they lay in the lowest and hottest part of the district and had special water needs. Pointing to the illegality of the expansion in Quillunsa, they threatened to take legal action against the community and, what is more, to lodge formal complaints against him, if the arrangement was changed. The so-called Water Boss, now part of a civilian bureaucracy under the control of the ruling Acción Popular party, understandably caved in.

The same threat was brought to bear against the next administrator, who served in the post during the drought of 1987, and who recounted the earlier events to me. He also complained of other, more subtle pressures that were built into his situation, of which I was already aware: the fact that, in a subsistence economy with no local market, an outsider has to rely on the availability of food surpluses that can be purchased, mainly from the big landowners (here milk, cheese, and fresh meat are powerful incentives); a person's need for credit in the stores, as well as other financial favors, when his salary is low and paychecks are often late; and the desire of professionals to be accepted and have some prestige within the more respected segments of local society, for the sake of their own comfort and self-esteem. For all of these reasons, both he and his successor allowed the duplication to continue, on the rationale that this compensated the Cotahuasinos for the earlier expansion of the frontier in Quillunsa, which had happened so long before that it now seemed irreversible.

MORE ON THE STALEMATE

The dispute between the two communities was constantly discussed at group meetings throughout my time in the valley, but nothing ever came of this. By the revised arrangement, the Cotahuasi landowners got a total of about 54 liters a second from the secondary springs under normal conditions, equivalent to about 25 percent of the main water as it leaves the reservoir in Pitahuasi. Even before drought struck again, the people of Quillunsa complained that Cotahuasi's allotment should be reduced accordingly, and their own increased. The adjustment was never made, however, even though the administrator had the necessary hydrological data. The result was a stand-off, in which each party threatened to take legal action against the other but had too much to lose to follow through on their threats—the Quillunseños their expanded frontier, the Cotahuasinos their double irrigation. In both cases, the legality of current use was highly questionable, but, as we have seen, the law is so vague on the issues involved that a formal appeal would have been a complicated and lengthy procedure. More important, any action would probably have resulted in a revision of the entire distribution system, which members of both sectors had reason to avoid.

Although Cotahuasi's was the weaker legal position because of the clearly preferential nature of duplication, Quillunsa was unable to take advantage of the situation since Cotahuasi, a much larger community, was always able to garner enough votes in the elections to win and maintain control of the Irrigator Commission. Some of the more powerful Cotahuasinos, who had friends on the board of directors, simply used the threat of legal action to keep the people of Quillunsa at bay. Publicly, they presented themselves as benefactors of the community and supported proposals that would actually be detrimental to them, while behind the scenes they acted to protect their privilege by undermining the change that they most opposed: eliminating duplication. Many smallholders were aware of this hypocrisy, but the configuration of interests and alliances within the Cotahuasi user group allowed the leaders to maintain majority support.

Here it might be asked why the other members continued to support these officials, when nothing changed, and to tolerate a gross inequity that heightened the general scarcity of water. The answer lies in their belief that not all that much water was at stake, in effect buying into the beneficiaries' arguments. When questioned on the matter of duplicate rights, people who enjoyed the privilege tended to claim that it was merely a supplement involving a small amount of water—often calling it a "*yapita*" (a little extra), which it definitely is not—that it did no harm, and that the heat sometimes made it necessary.

We have seen that the law is very strong on adjusting to local variations in water needs. The landowners no doubt pointed to this provision in pressuring the administrator and the commission officers to allow their dual rights to persist. Although no climate data were ever gathered to substantiate the claim, the law provided the officials with a legitimate excuse, first for originally granting the water and later for not acting after the user group voted twice for its elimination. Some peasant smallholders, I should point out, also have land in the spring sectors, and they naturally agree with their neighbors' views. The others are largely indifferent to whether the rights are retained or not because they understand that the duplication does not deprive them of water. For them, the arrangement is an unfair privilege, mainly of the big landowners, that is to be resented but can be tolerated because the water savings would only go to Quillunsa if it was abolished.

This again reveals the most significant and detrimental flaw in the attempts at water reform in the valley. By sanctioning an arrangement in which the outflow of the Pitahuasi tank is spread over a much larger area than before, the administrators created a situation in which, even in times of severe shortage, Cotahuasi users have no motivation to correct the inequities and forms of waste within their own community. Since the water is used in rotation, they tend to focus exclusively on preserving their own share while denouncing the irregularities of the Quilluseños. They focus on gaining new water at the other sector's expense, rather than on conserving and redistributing what they already have.

Under the existing arrangement, if the Cotahuasinos would undertake any of the conservation measures available to them, such as limiting watering to three hours a topo again, cleaning the grama out of their canals, implementing a fixed irrigation plan, or eliminating favoritism and duplication, then they would simply finish their own turn sooner. But the water savings would go to, or at least have to be shared with, Quillunsa. The only way to ensure more frequent irrigation is to implement these measures in both sectors, something that, considering the profound mistrust in both communities, is unlikely to happen any time soon.

Furthermore, one fact of life in the district changes this whole scenario: water practices are more orderly and efficient in Quillunsa than in Cotahuasi, something that many of the water officials must have known. Thus the water savings from improvements in distribution and use not only would be modest there and have to be shared, but would result in a loss of privilege for numerous people in Cotahuasi and only a small increase in the watering frequency for everyone else. Water use is also more efficient in Reyparte and, to a certain extent, in Cachana and Chaucavilca as well. It is far from perfect in any of those communities, and they all contribute to the water problem. But the Cotahuasinos are by far the worst offenders, and since they have such a strong influence on the way decisions are made and policies are implemented, they pose the main obstacle to a solution.

Quillunsa, like the other annexes, has changed a great deal since the agrarian reform. It is more homogeneous now and more united in its struggle against Cotahuasi. With only one exception, the big landlords have sold their land and left the village, and their replacements are poorer people, middle proprietors who live there full time and have no strong ties with the elites in the capital. Because of the exploitative behavior of landlords in the past, and the history of conflict between Quillunsa and its dominant neighbor, they seem to have made an effort to distinguish themselves from the traditional elites, in their attitudes as well as their behavior. The other village members, most of whom are campesinos, have simply had enough of the abuses of the past.

According to the residents, the larger landowners in Quillunsa do not seek special allotments for themselves or any other favors from the administrator, even in cases of real emergency. The distributor there perhaps favors the mayoristas at times, but there seems to be no consistent pattern. The mayoristas do irrigate excessively, since they grow a lot of alfalfa, but so do other people. Even the campesinos, who still cultivate terraces for the most part, usually irrigate their plots twice, topping off the pooling structures again in the manner previously described. Thus waste is definitely a problem, but it does not reach ridiculous extremes, even on the bigger properties. I have never seen water running freely over terraces in Quillunsa, on anyone's land, the way it so often does in Cotahuasi.

Like most people, the mayoristas neglect to clean their canals on a regular basis, and they are sometimes not ready to irrigate when the water arrives. They may occasionally resort to theft, but I have never heard anyone point the finger specifically at them. Perhaps most significantly, the families not only contribute to maintenance faenas but actually participate in the work itself, just like everyone else. I know because I have been there working alongside them; their participation clearly sets them apart from their counterparts in Cotahuasi.

Thus, serious problems do exist in Quillunsa, but the most chronic and disruptive ones, corruption and privilege, do not. That kind of favoritism seems to occur only in Cotahuasi and in other places like Cachana and Chaucavilca where former landlords living in the capital, or their heirs, still have fairly large tracts of land. In reality, Cotahuasi is responsible for most of the water problem, and as long as it holds sway over the Irrigator Commission, it poses the main obstacle to a solution. The other communities merely fight to hold onto the water that they have, and they will not move in a positive direction until the Cotahuasinos do.

What does this situation, and this history, show us about water management? Where communities do not have their own water sources, where they have to alternate in using the resource, the problem of conservation and hydraulic improvement is made much more complex than it need be. Appropriate measures have to be forced on the population because the arrangement robs them of their logic. People can have their own obvious and rational motivation to use water efficiently, but only if irrigation is continuous within their community, so that both the rewards for conservation and the negative consequences of waste and other misuse are felt locally and immediately, rather than being passed on to another user group. One can clearly see this mechanism at work in the irrigation systems of Huaynacotas and Pampamarca, and even in the autonomous spring sectors of Quillunsa and Reyparte, where water use is more uniform and conservative than in other parts of the system. In the Andes, a strong incentive for conservation can be found in the link between the efficiency and orderliness of water use and the duration of the irrigation cycle. But that link is only a direct and obvious one to the water-user if a community has its own water sources and, just as important, if the frequency of irrigation is uniform within the area served by each one, the same for everyone. That, of course, is why things are done this way in other places.

The outflow of the Pitahausi tank must be shared, but it should be divided, permanently and equitably, between Quillusna and Cotahuasi, so that watering occurs daily in both sectors. This could be done either by diverting the whole flow into two canals down below the tank of the same size or by building two separate out-takes of the same size. Either way, in light of the long history of conflict, the only fair thing to do is to divide the water in half, since both communities now have about the same amount of land under irrigation. Beyond just establishing a rough proportionality in their water use, this approach would not reward the Cotahuasinos for having wasted so much water. Although the partitioning itself would result in some increase in water loss, by spreading irrigation over a wider area each day, the savings eventually achieved through conservation would probably offset this loss with plenty to spare.

This is the solution that the various administrators should have arrived at, rather than allowing themselves to be thwarted by the impossibility of managing the system according to the law. In places like Cotahuasi where administrators do not have the equipment needed to dispense water precisely by volume, and where the resource is scarce to begin with, the sole function of the law and the official guidelines is to provide a justification for favoritism, and they should be abandoned or changed substantially. The water does not have to be precisely measured in order to improve the system dramatically; it simply needs to be divided into fixed daily flows for each community, and to be used in a more uniform and conservative way, as it was during the years just after the reform.

If this simple step were taken, the campesinos and other smallholders of Cotahuasi would cease to focus on Quillunsa and instead move to eliminate the duplication and other privileges that some of the landowners in their own sector now enjoy. They would then come to see that these infractions do, in fact, deprive them of water by lengthening the irrigation cycle. They would also have a strong motivation to improve their own methods, for the same reason. The current sharing arrangement prevents the campesinos from seeing this connection, and perhaps from allying with campesinos in other sectors to form a voting bloc that might challenge the Cotahuasino landlords' control over the Irrigator Commission.

In my opinion, giving hydraulic independence to each community, or at least to the two largest ones,[18] would change the whole political dynamic in the district. It would alter the balance of power between former landlords and tenants or, perhaps better said, between businessmen and peasants, and change the nature of relations between the land-rich and the land-poor. It would encourage peasants in all the villages to become united, rather than preventing unity as the current arrangement does, by allowing them to recognize the common interest that they share with their neighbors in other parts of the district. Presumably, they would then vote accordingly in electing officials and deciding on matters of policy. If this simple change were made, all of them would probably see the water conflict for what it is and always has been: a struggle against the former landlords and their descendants, a "class struggle." As it stands now, many of the campesinos and smallholders in Cotahuasi sector perceive the main conflict as one between communities, a perception that is self-serving but ultimately self-defeating. They are opposed to the mayoristas in many respects, and resent them in many ways, but they do not really see them as depriving other people of water.

Solving the Problem: An Outsider's Proposal for a Second Reform

Many things—the periodic droughts, the post-reform distribution pattern, the Ministry of Agriculture's inappropriate irrigation model, the social configuration of user groups, and the self-interested agendas of some of the larger landowners—work together to support the illusion that Cotahuasi's water supply is inherently inadequate. Despite the early success of the water reform, "*no hay agua*" seems to be the view held by all but a small minority of people. The water problem, though, and even the drought crisis are in reality largely self-induced. The impact of droughts could clearly be reduced significantly if all of the defects revealed in this study were corrected.

First of all, by returning to the early reform's standard of three hours a topo, including in times of scarcity, the total area irrigated daily could be increased as much as 15 percent in both Quillunsa and Cotahuasi. Three sets of allotments could then be given out each day, resulting in an overall water savings of as much as 30 percent, even during droughts. Second, the elimination of duplicate rights in the springs areas of Cotahuasi sector, which would augment the main water supply by about 25 percent under normal conditions, would make 18 percent more main water available for use in the rest of the sector and in Quillunsa during droughts, taking into account a 30 percent reduction in spring flow at these times. If this savings were shared equally, then each sector would have 9 percent more water. When combined with the previous savings, this would theoretically yield a total savings for the two sectors of perhaps 23 percent, which alone is nearly enough to cover the deficit induced by most droughts. Third, the establishment of strict standards for field and canal preparation—especially the removal of the grama—would significantly reduce water loss and provide a further savings, though I cannot say exactly how much. Considering the grass-clogged canals I have seen everywhere, this and other changes would almost certainly boost the overall savings to 40 percent or even more, which would entirely cover almost any drought shortage and allow the auxilio to be eliminated entirely, with all the problems that it creates.

A necessary precondition for all this would be the establishment of a fixed and contiguous distribution sequence in which no exceptions are allowed. In systems like this, where water is almost always scarce and irrigation is by turno or cyclical allotment, a uniform frequency would have to be mandated, so that any scarcity, and any benefits of conservation, are shared proportionally by everyone. If this were done, the larger landowners would simply be forced to cooperate, and when they cannot plant at the designated time, they would have to wait until their turn comes around in the next irrigation cycle, as they did for a while after the reform. Of course, the establishment of a stable cycle would in itself produce still further water savings, and probably a substantial amount, by minimizing the surface area in use and the resulting filtration, and because infractions could be spotted. Once these measures were in place, hardly anyone other than those who miss their turn for some reason would have any cause to commit infractions.

As for past expansions of the agrarian frontier, I do not consider these to be a part of the water problem, in Quillunsa or anywhere else. The lands in question were probably irrigated for hundreds of years before the Spanish arrived, and under a system of "rational" distribution and use, there would be enough water to irrigate them even during droughts. In fact, under normal conditions, all of the 140 hectares of eriazos that still lie within the maize-growing zone could probably be reclaimed and irrigated. That would require only about 25 percent of the 40 percent or more of water savings and leave enough to allow a higher frequency of irrigation for everyone—a uniform one, of course.

I have made the point before, but I want now to put it more forcefully. There is enough water available to allow an expansion of irrigation and still provide everyone with water much more often than they now get it, especially during droughts. There is enough to put an end to the water problem. Some of the wealthier Cotahuasinos, especially those who have land near the secondary springs, would simply have to be forced to swallow the losses that would come with the mandated changes. But I firmly believe that there is enough to be gained that even they would end up better off than before.

To be sure, the General Water Law would have to be changed in several ways—or replaced entirely—to accomplish all this. And the state would have to show a lot of foresight in revising the legislation and showing the way. The local people can manage the resource themselves, and they can do so in an equitable fashion, but only with a well-designed law that at once mandates the simple condition of equity and makes the communities autonomous. With local communities forced to decide on explicit requirements for water use, the state could get out of the business of managing water altogether, which it is trying hard now to do. Its local representative could then concentrate instead on assisting the communities to settle any future disputes and improve their infrastructure. These measures would change the letter of the law but not its spirit, merely closing loopholes that now allow certain individuals to manipulate the regulations in their own favor.

It is clear that only a comprehensive reform could put an end to the water conflict and restore the communities' capacity to manage their own affairs. The problems that the state has helped to create in irrigation are complex, as we have seen, and the user organizations cannot be expected to solve these problems on their own. A piecemeal effort would not have much effect, and neither would simply turning administration of the water system over to the communities without making changes in the law itself, as the government in fact did several years ago. In order to see this, one has only to look at what happened— or, more correctly, what did not happen—after I was forced, along with many other people, to leave the valley because of the political violence of 1988.

The events that occurred during the last few months of my fieldwork were unfortunate and tragic, and showed quite clearly that the roots of the class conflict are complex and deep. Sendero Luminoso's violent actions were explicitly directed against the large landowners and the political leaders of the community, and when these men and the water administrator were forced to leave, the local people temporarily regained control over the resource. A year later, in 1989, the government effectively sanctioned this change, turning responsibility for the operation and maintenance of irrigation systems over to user groups.[19] This shift in the balance of power created a unique opportunity, a kind of social and political experiment, whose outcome at this writing is still far from certain.

EIGHT

Water into Blood

Irrigation Improvement, Corruption, and the Coming of the Shining Path

During my time in the district, the government's involvement in the water problem seemed to be part of an agenda for making Cotahuasi a client of the state in nearly all of its affairs. For purely political reasons, ones of "national security," the newly elected APRA regime of Alan García began to invest heavily in the province soon after I arrived, especially in irrigation development, but also in other efforts to improve somewhat the quality of life. This was done in answer to the growing threat that the Shining Path guerrillas presented in their stronghold in the sierra, Ayacucho, a large department that borders the valley on the north and west. Regrettably, the local APRA party, whose founders had apparently been full of enthusiasm and good intentions initially, was now riddled with corruption. The infusion of large sums of development money led to a foreseeable outcome, one that nevertheless so outraged the local people as to ultimately push them to the brink of violence, of uprising and revolt. It was at that very strategic point that Shining Path made its presence known.

When I began my fieldwork, in late 1985, the "dirty war" in Ayacucho—the effort to stamp out Sendero Luminoso—had been going on for nearly five years and had not been at all successful. Tens of thousands of peasants had already been killed, sacrificed by both the guerrillas and the military, and their numbers would continue to mount over the next few years as the blood bath spread. Despite the violence, the guerrillas had steadily expanded their influence in those years, and by 1988, they had become a potent force in more than half of the country (Gorriti 1999).

In provinces where Sendero was highly active, states of emergency had been declared. These so-called Zones of Emergency, or Red Zones, were killing fields, where the guerrillas and the Peruvian army played a gruesome game of hide-and-seek. Peasant villages would become places of temporary refuge, and then became the sites of disappearances, murders, and even massacres as the army moved in and delivered its punishment. The Senderistas were just as ready to do the killing whenever they encountered any form of resistance or defiance of their authority by the campesinos. By late 1987, virtually the entire sierra had been touched by the conflict, except for the departments of Arequipa and Tacna, in the southwestern corner of the country. That whole region remained relatively free of political violence until the Shining Path made its first move south and east out of Ayacucho, onto the puna above Cotahuasi, in June 1988, six months before my departure.

Another extraordinary event on the political front had occurred during this time, whose effects had reached the valley almost immediately. The elections of 1985 had swept APRA into power, and its leader, Alan García, into the presidency. The Apristas had waited fifty years to govern the country and rule in the provinces, and despite the terrorism that was wracking Lima almost daily and the genocide going on in the countryside, the nation was generally euphoric and full of hope over their success when I arrived.

APRA, a populist party and always something of a personality cult, too, had long promised to carry out a revolution of its own: to extricate Peru from the web of imperialism and dependency so that the nation could devote its resources to developing its own productive capacity, its industry and agriculture. During the election campaign, García had vowed to stamp out corruption, particularly within the police and the armed forces, and to invest heavily in the countryside in programs that would benefit the rural majority. Improving the campesinos' quality of life was to be the government's new weapon against the Shining Path; the disappearances and massacres were supposedly going to end. All of these promises had been made with extraordinary passion and eloquence by a master orator and showman.

As the new government set to work on its assistance programs, certain parts of the highlands, including the Cotahuasi valley, were specially targeted for intervention. In an attempt to contain the armed insurgency within Ayacucho itself, La Unión and eleven of the surrounding provinces were designated as Emergency Development Microregions in 1985. These areas, part of a region known as the Trapecio Andino, or Andean Quadrangle—the most impoverished, isolated, and neglected parts of the sierra—were to receive massive infusions of state funds and teams of technical personnel.[1]

Almost overnight, Cotahuasi became a showcase for APRA's new programs, much talked about in newspaper articles and on television programs in Arequipa. The town itself was soon buzzing with activity: a swarm of outsiders arrived with heavy equipment and a fleet of motor vehicles, the first cafes opened, business was good in the stores, and a loudspeaker announced development projects almost daily. The road to Chuquibamba was going to be improved, new roads complete with bridges were to be built to Huaynacotas and Pampamarca, and a telephone center was to be constructed in Cotahuasi. Perhaps most important of all from my point of view, two major irrigation canals were planned, and the canals and tanks in several pueblos, including many in the district, were going to be lined with cement. A hydrological study of the upper watershed would be carried out in order to discover new ways to augment the water supply. The rejected plan to bring in water from the Choccocco River was put back on the table, and a small hydroelectric facility that had been planned for Alca was to be started up again. All these projects were announced by the personnel of the Microregion, a small army of engineers, architects, and other "technicians," who set to work building their headquarters in Cotahuasi. Nearly all of them were from elsewhere, and every one of them was an Aprista.

Signs of trouble right from the beginning cast a shadow over the positive atmosphere. The valley had a long history of political corruption, and many local people were skeptical, particularly APRA's chief opponents, members of the United Left party, who predicted a massive swindle. As it happened, their skepticism was wholly justified, for it soon became obvious that the only qualifications many of the "engineers" had was their party membership; yet they were being paid huge salaries. Several local men were hired, but only Apristas were eligible, and many highly qualified people who badly needed the work and who probably would have done it better were turned away.

For a great number of campesinos, though, the new projects were a blessing. They found plenty of jobs as temporary workers at the official minimum wage, an unprecedented amount. This drove up the going rate for such work and made agricultural labor even harder to find, something that complicated the lives of the larger landowners. Prices in the stores, which had already been rising at a fast rate, quickly jumped to levels that approached hyperinflation. The presence of a large group of outsiders who had so much cash to throw around began to have a disruptive effect on the local economy. APRA's takeover of the town, along with big promises but little actual accomplishment, bred resentment among the local people, which soon gave way to anger and a sense of betrayal.

As it turned out, the Apristas spent most of that first year building a lavish headquarters, drawing up innumerable plans, and, most of all, celebrating the party's rise to power. The staff—forty-six people in all, mostly young men— could be seen almost every night drinking beer in the stores or toasting someone's birthday in a private home. Eventually, however, they had to give some accounting for their activities, and that is when the confrontation with the local people began. In October 1986, at an open town meeting in the central plaza, the bosses of the Microregion and CORDEA gave a presentation on the projects and the budget, and tried to explain why only 10 percent of the total funds allocated for projects during that first year had actually been spent. When it became obvious that the Apristas had only spent money on themselves—on their salaries, facilities, and equipment, and their innumerable parties—the townspeople burst into an uproar. After a heated argument, led by members of the United Left, a vote was taken, and the outsiders were astonished to find themselves accused of incompetence and fraud, and declared to be "enemies of the pueblo." A notarized letter was drawn up to that effect, to be sent to the President of the Republic.

The matter was quickly smoothed over by the provincial governor, the local party leader, who promised that the projects would soon get under way, and so the letter was never sent. But relations with the local people deteriorated steadily over the next year and a half anyway as the Apristas' ineptitude and dishonesty became more and more apparent. After twelve months of planning and work, a new irrigation canal being constructed at Visve, just below Huaynacotas—one intended to replace the existing canal and take more water to the pampa of Collota—turned out to have been badly designed and, as a result, the out-take from the river would have to be rebuilt at enormous cost. Worse still, the other hydraulic projects, especially those in Cotahuasi district, had gotten so far behind schedule that they had had to be handed over earlier to COPASA, the West German organization, which had rapidly gotten them under way, much to the embarrassment of the Microregion and CORDEA. But most disturbing of all was the wholesale disappearance of construction materials, equipment, and project funds. Concrete for the new bridge to Pampamarca had long since been purchased and somehow dispensed with, but there was no bridge to show for it, a situation that would eventually lead to the arrest of the provincial mayor. Warrants were soon issued for the arrest of two prominent Apristas: the son of the governor, supposedly for stealing an expensive piece of surveying equipment, and the head of Popular Cooperation, the organization responsible for the temporary employment of campesinos, for embezzling thousands of dollars of development funds. Even the governor himself seemed to be guilty; his latest mistress, whom he had put in charge of dispensing food rations donated by the United Nations, was found to be selling them instead.

By early 1988, thirteen cases of theft and fraud had been discovered, a scandal that would ultimately cause two of the leaders of APRA to go into hiding. The district's water problem had not been alleviated in any way, despite the huge amount of money that had been spent in one way or another, and the same was true of all the other pueblos. The townspeople were outraged, and there was open hostility between them and the party members. This was the atmosphere that prevailed when Sendero Luminoso moved into the area.

The Shining Path Appears

The guerrillas initially passed through the valley on their way back to Ayacucho from the mine of Arcata in the neighboring province of Castilla, the same mine whose mita had brought local Indians to the brink of revolt during the eighteenth century. After attacking and looting it in June 1988, they stopped briefly at Huaynacotas, where they convened an assembly, shared some of their booty, and made a big impression. A small group came back a month later, this time to the villages of Chinkayllapa and Huacctapa, high up in Puica district, where they assembled the people and again delivered their message of communist revolution. As they would do in later visits to other pueblos, they then put local criminals on trial and executed them. Invariably, before leaving a village, the Senderistas would demonstrate who they were, and what their purpose was, quite emphatically, by finding out which members of the community were abusive and guilty of serious crimes against others, and in this instance, a drunk and wife-beater and a habitual cattle thief were put on public trial and killed when no one came to their defense. The guerrillas also declared that, henceforth, they would be the only political authorities and demanded that the mayor and the judge in each village resign. When the mayor of Chinkayllapa refused, he too was executed, and the point was made.[2]

The atmosphere in Cotahuasi grew increasingly tense over the next few months as the Senderistas let it be known that they were in the area and were a force to be reckoned with. Political authorities in all the pueblos received letters threatening them with death, as did the staffs of the Microregion and COPASA. An army patrol came to the valley briefly before proceeding on to investigate the higher villages; there they reportedly killed a few comuneros for giving hospitality to the guerrillas. Soon the province was said to be on the verge of being declared a Zone of Emergency, and that is when the chaos really began.

Certain members of APRA began to manipulate the situation and exploit it for their own benefit, mainly those who had something to hide. Should a state of emergency be declared, the salaries of all government employees would go up, in compensation for the risk they were now facing, and, more important, the crimes that were being discovered would be unlikely to be investigated. As rumors flew around, mysterious gunshots and explosions began to be heard occasionally at night, and revolutionary slogans appeared on the walls around town. The authorities soon received more threatening letters, phony ones as it turned out, which was obvious because, unlike the guerrillas' typically faceless death threats, they were signed "Sendero Luminoso."[3]

Some of the townspeople knew what was going on, and word of the emptiness of the threat soon spread. Meanwhile, the younger Apristas, partly because of their deteriorating public relations, had become a small army of thugs— "Buffaloes," as they were called—who were defensive, nervous, and insulting, even abusive, to the townspeople. More and more Cotahuasinos became convinced, as one of them put it, that "the only terrorists in *this* town are the Apristas." His interpretation seemed reasonable since I had invested a lot of time and energy in getting to know these people, and I knew they were capable of outrageous behavior. This widespread perception only worsened the already bad relations between them and the townspeople.

What the townspeople did not know was that some of the threats were really from Sendero, that two kinds of letters were being circulated. An ominous sign came in late July, when the police (the Guardia Civil) received a letter giving them until August 18 to lay down their weapons in the central plaza and get out of town, or they would be killed. News of this threat quickly spread, but most people just assumed that this letter too was a fake. And the theory seemed to be confirmed when the date passed and no attack occurred. Although people were naturally relieved, they became all the more incensed at the Apristas, since it soon became obvious that the hoax was working.

During the last week in August, a small contingent of "Sinchis," the Guardia Civil's crack antiterrorist force,[4] marched into Cotahuasi, which seemed to indicate that a declaration of emergency was imminent. But the troops stayed for only two weeks and returned to Arequipa without recommending any change. Meanwhile, unbeknownst to almost everyone, members of Sendero Luminoso, who may have anticipated the army's moves, had infiltrated the community and were waiting for the right moment to make their own.

Negative Identity, Corruption, and Their Implications

My understanding of the Shining Path, of its methods and what it wanted to accomplish, was heavily influenced by the events I was witnessing at the time and by local people's interpretations of those events. The guerrillas' goals, of course, were the same as those of the Khmer Rouge in Cambodia, of the Red Guard in China during the Cultural Revolution, and of all Marxist-Leninist regimes at early points in their histories: to tear society apart and rebuild it, to create a new kind of man, Socialist Man.[5] A lot was written about them while I was in the field, in newspapers and magazines, and I read as much of this material as possible whenever I was in Arequipa, but it was the reality of the state of affairs in Cotahuasi at the time that made the movement's goals comprehensible to me.

The Shining Path wanted to stamp out a basic kind of moral corruption, one that pervades many institutions in Peruvian society and is said to be found, by Sendero, in most people who try to be a part of it. The guerrillas, being Marxists, attribute this flaw mainly to the distorting effects of capitalism, to a history and a way of life focused largely on making money. But in the eyes of a great many local people, including most of the mistis I ever talked to about such things, this flaw is genetic or racial, inherent in all people of Spanish blood. I do not agree with them, of course. The largely negative and fatalistic image that many Peruvians have of themselves is a matter of culture and identity, but I think it has more to do with a government, a bureaucratic system, and an economy that have always rewarded corruption than anything else. These "structural" conditions have a long history in the Cotahuasi valley, like most places in Peru. Extremely low salaries for public employees and bureaucratic procedures that make no sense and serve as formidable obstacles rather than facilitating getting anything done—these are the institutional conditions that sustain and reinforce corruption. But as I have come to understand it, the source of the negative image is also deeply psychological, lying in a person's view of Self and of Society, of his or her own capacities and those of others. It is an intellectual and emotional perception, a very powerful image of the nature of the Peruvian elite. Campesinos, it should be noted, are prone to take the same view of the former landlords and other members of the dominant society (see Montoya et al. 1979 for a lengthy discussion of this "emic" point).

The most disturbing thing I learned during my fieldwork was just how fatalistic and self-defeating this image is, and how much it separated me, the ethnographer, from many of "them." I hasten to point out that this image, although pervasive and much talked about, has not been internalized by everyone by any means. I met many colleagues in academia who did not seem to share it, and there are many local people, even the sons of landlords, whose freedom of thought and spirit I admire.

It has often been said and written that Peruvians lack any kind of national identity, which is not really true. Many members of the "national" society, of the dominant society, have a strong sense of identity, but a largely negative one, particularly the traditional elites who still live in the countryside. One sees this clearly in remote places like Cotahuasi, where people of Spanish descent have lived alongside people of indigenous ancestry, and exploited them, over such a long period of time, living off their land, their water, and their labor. This being the case, the Spanish families in the valley are constantly confronted with their own history; they have to explain it and their predicament, the corruption that has "always" characterized the dominant class and, in their eyes, prevented the province and the country from advancing. They often do this by saying, and apparently truly believing, that it is in their blood, inherent in their nature as a people. I have heard this claim so many times that I cannot overemphasize its importance.

Such fatalism is clearly expressed in the elite's comments about themselves and about how they think a better society might be created. For example, I have been told many times, in reference to the difference between my country and theirs, that if Peru had been conquered by the British it would be a highly advanced country by now. Instead, it was colonized by *"la mala raza Espa- ñola"*—the bad race—who destroyed the great civilization of the Incas, en- slaved its people in a backward feudal society, and tainted them with Spanish blood. In these characterizations of the typical Peruvian, meaning a criollo or mestizo person, local elites, as well as many campesinos, invariably speak in terms of negative stereotypes, describing him in one or more of the following ways: lazy (*flojo*), greedy (*codicioso*), egotistical (*egoista*), deceitful (*engañozo*), backward (*atrasado*), dishonest (*mentiroso*), exploitative of others (*conchudo*), and shameless (*sin verguenza*), capable of any kind of betrayal.

During more than five years in Peru all together, I have heard these negative self-descriptions many times, in every part of the country, and heard very few positive ones. This is the most troubling thing about the ideology that explains, and to some extent justifies, corruption: the lack of any more positive side to balance out the negative image. A "Peruvian" is also supposed to be *macho*, a word that does have some positive connotations for men, but that is often used in association with these negative terms. The society has always been male- dominated and perhaps always will be, which is why the characterizations are invariably masculine. But the most commonly used term by far is *vivo*, literally clever or wide awake, which means all of the above and much more.

The word basically means smart but corrupt, yet it is also commonly used as a noun, to refer to a certain kind of person. In essence, the "vivo" is the quin- tessential free-rider, a rational self-interested individual, but one who exploits other people and resorts to illicit means of getting what he wants, who will bend or break almost any rule, norm, promise, or expectation. This is nicely ex- pressed in a bit of conventional wisdom that I heard countless times: "El vivo vive del zonzo, y el zonzo vive de su trabajo" (The *vivo* lives off of the fool, and the fool lives off of his work).

As far as I can tell, most people in the town believe that this is what a person must become, inevitably will become to some extent, if he or she is to join Peruvian society, the dominant national or urban society,[6] a view also commonly held by indigenous people (Poole 1987; Montoya et al. 1979). Mestizos, too, are wont to claim that "*vivesa*" is the only kind of behavior that is rewarded in Cotahuasi and in the cities, and that comuneros who leave home must change somewhat in this direction in order to survive. They also contend that many indigenous people (runakuna) are now becoming vivo, for example, the new middle proprietors. But like the landlords themselves, they believe that people of Spanish descent do not have to change in this regard, since they are that way innately. In fact, this supposedly inherent quality is widely seen as basic to the ethnic distinction between the Spanish and indigenous cultures. It is an essential aspect of the class difference as well, since campesinos hold the same view, although some seem to see themselves as tainted with vivesa to some degree by virtue of their mixed blood. Basically, in Cotahuasi, the more "Spanish" a person is, the more corrupt he or she is thought to be likely to become.

Local lore is rich in stories that are often cited as illustrations of this principle, although in a humorous way—and that supposedly distinguish the province as unusually corrupt and backward. The first motor vehicle arrived there in 1934, carried overland for three days from Chuquibamba, in pieces, on the backs of mules, to be reassembled in Cotahuasi's central plaza for a photo shoot. The pictures taken were sent to the President of the Republic in Lima to demonstrate that the road had finally reached the valley, and that the funds he had spent on it as part of his national plan for road development had been well spent. No one found out, but the road did not actually arrive until 1960.

Similarly, Cotahuasi is said to be the only provincial capital that has an airstrip from which no plane will ever land or take off, because none was ever intended to; it is far too short and cannot be made any longer. There is also the famous Polanco incident, referring to a con man who came to the valley shortly before I arrived in 1985, who presented himself as a representative of the Belaúnde government in Lima. He stayed for over a month, reportedly collecting tens of thousands of dollars for pork-barrel projects from carefully cultivated local cronies who, in their own type of scam, counted on profiting from the matching funds the government was supposedly going to provide. He then left and disappeared without a trace, leaving his friends holding a very empty bag. The moral of the story is seemingly that the local elites are so corrupt and inept that they cannot recognize one of their own kind, and cannot see that their own "vivesa" makes them vulnerable to the same treatment by others.

For most Cotahuasinos, this fatalistic self-image has some disturbing implications for people's behavior. First of all, since the tendency toward such behavior is thought to be inherent, people are not really expected to behave differently when confronted with a major temptation. People expect others to become corrupt upon acquiring power; they hope this will not happen, and they become indignant when it does, since everyone acknowledges that it is ruining the country, but they are not at all surprised. Second, since corruption is the only kind of behavior that is supposedly rewarded in Peruvian society, unless a person happens to be born rich, he really has no choice but to succumb to it, and he is thought to be stupid if he does not to some degree. Nearly all the institutions reinforce this ideology (the schools and universities being the main exceptions), and people are very much aware that the system works this way. The implication of all this, for many people, seems to be that there is no use trying to change things, much as they might want to. As is very often said by Cotahuasinos, in Peruvian society, "el honesto viene a ser un zonzo" (the honest person becomes a fool). A certain amount of corruption is therefore necessary, but the form and amount, of course, are up to the individual.

Finally, and most disturbing of all, I was told numerous times that, if people are inherently corrupt, they clearly cannot govern themselves democratically, and that they require an authoritarian regime and strong institutions to keep them in line. The number of people who expressed this idea to me in Cotahuasi during the 1980's was astonishing; there is hardly anyone I can think of, other than some members of APRA and perhaps a few of the United Left, who would dispute it. Even the campesinos seemed to feel that draconian measures were necessary to put the landlords and other vivos in their place. According to almost everyone, democracy did not and could not work in Peru, a fact that the Apristas were demonstrating through their behavior. APRA, the popular "revolutionary" party that had waited fifty years to come into power, was seen as the last hope for Peruvian democracy. And its government was rapidly becoming one of the country's greatest disgraces.

The nation, it was said, was left with two choices: to embrace some reactionary dictator, like Augusto Pinochet, the Chilean strongman, or to turn to an ultra-radical one, like Abimael Guzmán, the leader of Sendero Luminoso. To nearly everyone I talked to, these were the only alternatives. And by late 1988, the economic and political situation was so bad that it did not seem to make much difference to some people which of the two it would be. I was surprised to hear some of my friends, young people who were struggling to make a living in education or small business, say that they would join Sendero and give up their civil liberties if they had to, just to see the corruption end. Although I do not think that these young men, some the sons of hacendados, would have joined Sendero if put to the test, even their saying this shows the depth of people's despair at the disappearing funds and equipment, the failed development projects, and the other misdeeds of the Apristas, on both the local and the national level.

I did not talk much about Sendero with comuneros, or even with campesinos, because it would not have been wise to do so. When we talked about party politics, however, most of them expressed indifference, if not a total lack of faith in the political system, depicting voting as an obligation rather than a privilege. My impression was that they viewed the Shining Path, a political party too, with the same kind of skepticism. But it was obvious that their main political concern was corruption, throughout the legal and judicial system, the government and police force, and especially in irrigation, a problem that they obviously saw in class terms. For the campesinos, the struggle against the mistis, against the landlords and businessmen, whether in their own community or a neighboring one, was in essence a struggle against corruption, and eliminating it was a major concern. And that is what the Shining Path proposed to do, stamp it out, even if the guerrillas had to kill thousands of people in order to accomplish this end.

Even if Sendero had a special plan to solve the problems in irrigation, and so far as I know it did not, few of the local campesinos, if any, favored violence and bloodshed as a way to get the problem of corruption under control. And clearly they did not want to see massive executions of the local elites.[7] In fact, it seemed to me that the Shining Path never managed to garner much support even among campesinos or in villages like Huaynacotas and Pampamarca. Now, with the benefit of hindsight and some conversations, I can say that the guerrillas were a source of some fascination and perhaps even a little admiration, but they tended to be seen as outsiders trying to take away the campesinos' hard-won right to govern themselves and to impose on them a foreign ideology.

Blood in the Streets: The Attack on the Pueblo

The confrontation between the local people and the Apristas reached its peak in October 1988, by which time the town, like the whole country, was in turmoil. The corruption in Cotahuasi turned out to be only a small part of a massive betrayal by APRA of the public trust. The nation was now on the brink of collapse. The government in Lima had so badly mismanaged the economy, refusing to pay any interest on the foreign debt and cutting Peru off from its international creditors, that hyperinflation had set in months before.[8] With the economy spiraling out of control, the government had instituted shock measures in early September to curb the inflation rate: the first "*paquetazo*" (big economic package), which among other things doubled the price of gasoline, and consequently of most other commodities, literally overnight. So far as the province is concerned, perhaps the most serious effect was to cut off bus service to the valley, and most truck traffic as well.

Corruption was being discovered everywhere. The party, it turned out, had been rapidly pilfering the national treasury of what little foreign exchange it still had by allowing members to buy American dollars at an extremely low exchange rate. Alan García and APRA, appreciating that they were not going to be reelected, seemed determined to leave the country completely bankrupt for the next president. The townspeople, once aware of the wholesale corruption in Lima, and more to the point, of most of the crimes that had been committed locally, took action.

On October 21, they called a meeting of the Agrarian League, a district farmers' organization, which was well attended by people from Cotahuasi and all the annexes— campesinos and empresarios, everyone seemed to be there. The leaders summed up the mess and invited suggestions on what should be done about it. It was soon decided again, by unanimous vote, that the Apristas were "enemies of the pueblo," and that if the government did not remove the worst offenders within a month to the day, the townspeople would assemble whatever weapons they had and take over the Microregion headquarters. They were literally going to throw the Apristas out of town and confiscate their equipment, their vehicles, everything, on behalf of the people. It was an astonishing thing to witness—a local uprising, something right out of Bingham's 1912 account— not entirely unexpected but thrilling to see unfold.

Because the atmosphere in town was so ugly and downright dangerous by this time, I did not attend the meeting, but instead sat outside and listened to it being broadcast over a loudspeaker. The streets filled up with other people doing the same thing as the commotion inside grew louder and louder. I remember being acutely aware then of something that members of the police had told me a few weeks before: there were a lot of strangers in town. That was the moment when I became convinced that something bad was about to happen.

I decided to leave the valley as soon as possible, planning to come back to finish my work when the whole thing blew over. Because there was no bus service anymore, and very little truck traffic, I was not able to find a ride until almost a month later, on November 19, when a friend asked me to drive a pickup truck to Chuquibamba—someone who, I suspect, may have known what was about to happen and wanted to save me from it. It was during my flight back to the United States two days later, on November 21, the day the Cotahuasinos were supposed to take over the Microregion, that the guerrillas attacked.

A group of about thirty heavily armed men and women approached the valley from the northwest, stopping briefly at Huarhua, immediately across the valley. There they conscripted roughly eighty comuneros to accompany them. They attacked the capital at two o'clock in the morning, after the lights had gone out, entering the town in three groups from three different directions. According to several friends who were there at the time, lying facedown on the floor in their homes, the next four hours were one continuous hail of machine-gun fire and dynamite explosions, accompanied by the eerie sound of revolutionary chants.

The guerrillas shot up the place completely, blew up and burned some of the municipal buildings, including the telephone office and the electric generator, and looted all of the stores. Nine people were killed, including one Senderista by his own grenade, one policeman shot during a brief skirmish, and one young boy who was caught in the crossfire. A local storeowner was also killed when she refused to open the door and allow her store to be looted, cursing the Senderistas instead and—quite in character for her—pouring urine on them from a balcony above. They answered with a grenade, causing a huge cylinder of cane alcohol to explode and burning one whole square of the town to the ground.

Ironically, the primary targets of the attack, the Apristas and other political officials, managed to escape unharmed. As luck would have it, all of them were in a late meeting in the municipal theater, on the opposite end of town from where the assault began, and hearing the pandemonium, they took to their heels. The mayor was picked up by a truck driver a day later, far up on the puna, walking along toward Chuquibamba in his shirtsleeves, which is how news of the incident got out.

The Senderistas executed two people a few hours later, after daylight as the group was leaving the valley. One of them, a former hacendado with a history of abusing campesinos, was shot in the head when he cursed them for confiscating his favorite horse. As it turned out, his household had been infiltrated by a spy, a young woman from Ayacucho who had been hired as a domestic servant only two months before, who left with the guerrillas. Other infiltrators were later discovered, and two members of the community were found to have helped plan the attack, young men whom I would never have suspected.

The other man killed was the heir and owner of Lancaroya, once the biggest

hacienda in the valley, who was involved in a conflict over water with some beneficiaries of the land reform, a large group of campesinos from Huarhua and
Yanaquihua. He had recently filed a lawsuit over the disputed water, which he
was apparently going to win, taking back from the campesinos much of what
they had gained through the reform. The guerrillas, upon learning about this,
took him out into one of his fields, made him kneel down alongside a canal,
and then shot him through the head, letting the blood run out into the canal.
The body was left there, slumped over the canal, for several days.

The Aftermath

I did not return to Peru until after I heard about the attack three months
later. By that time, I felt it was safe to return, but only to Arequipa, where I
spent the next year doing interviews with migrants and other people from the
valley who came periodically to town. Luckily, my year in the city was very productive because many of the older and more knowledgeable people turned out
to be living there, and they were not hard to find. It was from them that I
learned much of the history I have presented here: details about life on the haciendas, about the water conflict, even a great deal about life in Huaynacotas
and Pampamarca. Finding out much about what was happening in Cotahuasi
at the moment was difficult, however, because bus service to the valley was still
sporadic and the telephone link had been cut. Even so, some details did come
out.

The most significant change was that many of the larger landowners had
fled to Arequipa, along with all the political officials and the water administrator. Every important government employee had left soon after the attack, including the staff of the Microregion, although most of the Apristas had since
returned to Cotahuasi. COPASA had closed its office for good and was gradually terminating its projects. The province had been declared a Zone of Emergency, so that the army had moved in and the number of police had been
greatly increased. The security forces had investigated the attack, found out
who the local conspirators were, and sent them to prison. Surprisingly enough,
they had not taken any action against the comuneros of Huarhua, even though
they had ended up with most of the loot from the stores. As far as I know, the
military accepted their explanation that they had been coerced into helping the
guerrillas.

The guerrillas had gone back into Ayacucho, accompanied by a few comuneros who apparently had reason to fear the army's retribution. During the
intervening months, however, the guerrillas had come back to the valley re-

peatedly, and they were now effectively in control of all the annex communities except those in Cotahuasi district. No political authorities remained in those villages. Somewhat later, the Senderistas briefly took over Alca and Tomepampa, overcoming the police and causing them to flee, but basically they stayed close to the plateau during this period. In effect, the valley's two ethnic zones—upper and lower, indigenous and Spanish—were occupied by two armed forces, the guerrillas and the military, who were at a standoff. Sendero nevertheless was emerging as the winner in the sense that, with almost all the wealthy landowners gone and no local authorities around, and with fear obviously widespread, it was able to exert a strong influence on the villages in Cotahuasi district, indeed on every community in the province.

Naturally, I expected this shift in the balance of power to affect the water situation, and there seemed to be good evidence that it had. A new president of the Irrigator Commission had been elected, a well-known member of one of the dominant "Spanish" families who was an avowed Communist—not a member of Sendero, but one of the few men in the province whose revolutionary credentials were impeccable, the real thing. With the more corrupt members of the community now in Arequipa, and the administrator out of the way, I thought that this man, a strong advocate of the campesinos, might be able to resolve the water conflict or ameliorate it in some significant way. It is now clear that he was not.

At first, I thought he had indeed succeeded in settling the conflict between Quillunsa and Cotahuasi, because I managed to get data indicating that the turns of both sectors had been shortened somewhat, but not by the same amount. This seemed to suggest that the duplication in Cotahuasi had been eliminated, and the agrarian frontier in Quillunsa restored to where it had been before the reform. But then I got other figures indicating that each community had the same number of days of water as before, and that nothing at all had changed. Things were still apparently at a stalemate.

Still, there seemed much reason for optimism when, after I finally left the country, I learned that, in the elections of 1990, the leader of the local Campesino Federation—a friend and one of my best informants—had been appointed mayor of the province, the first peasant to hold that office. The campesinos at last, I thought, were becoming a political force in the district. That optimism faded when I heard some months later that this man— an honest and well-meaning person—had been captured by Sendero Luminoso as he was traveling along the road on the puna and then executed publicly in Chuquibamba.

Despite this tragedy, many factors seemed to indicate that the campesinos were finally in control, to some extent, of their own destiny, and that major changes had taken place in irrigation. Admittedly, I wanted to think this was true, that a handful of powerful people and the administrator had been mainly responsible for perpetuating the water conflict, and that it would be resolved in some significant way once they were forced out. After my years in the valley, I wanted to believe in the people's capacity to solve their own problems, in their ability to govern themselves, at least in this one political domain or field. Only later did I manage, by letter and by telephone, to arrive at what I now know is the truth: nothing significant, in the way of improvements, ever happened.

Despite the occurrence of another drought, no major change in the water situation has taken place since I left the valley in 1988.[9] Since that time, several people have been killed, and the town virtually destroyed, in an assault directed specifically at the political officials and the larger landowners, who barely escaped with their lives. Yet the situation remains much the same, and the stalemate over the resource continues.

Recently I have become aware of another important factor in all this: the amount of influence that the landlords were able to exert from a distance, through occasional trips back to the pueblo. Nearly all of them have long since returned for good, but while living in Arequipa they did go back periodically to oversee their property, which had been left in the hands of trusted people. It turns out that they were able to look after their affairs pretty well, and that some of them are indeed rather bold people.

The other reasons for the lack of change have already been discussed, in these last two chapters, and I will not reiterate them here. Apparently, certain fundamental changes have to be made first, by the government or some other outside agency, before any real progress can occur. And ultimately, given the complexity of the water problem, I suppose that this realization is not so depressing. After all, the state helped to create the situation, and it must show the way now toward a resolution and a better way of doing things.

Where to Start Over: The Building of New Institutions

What do I make, then, of everything that happened in Cotahuasi in 1988 and during the next several years? This is not a rhetorical question, but one that Cotahuasinos have asked me several times since the attack. In effect, they want me to decide which side I am on, in which direction I think the country should go, and what should be done. Like any ethnographer, I presented myself as a neutral observer of events while I was in the valley, but after all that has happened, this position is no longer tenable, either to them or to me. Sendero Luminoso has since been virtually extinguished as a movement, but that has no real bearing on the matter, since the political choices, and the two sides, would seem to remain pretty much the same.

I have always insisted, however, privately in my own heart and mind, that a middle path could be found, and I think the country found such a path in the end. Peru got its dictator, but at least they elected him: Alberto Fujimori, who, among other things, disbanded the Parliament, which was supposedly too corrupt to function, suspended civil liberties, and rewrote the Constitution. However, it was not the path of dictatorship that Peruvians actually chose, and now that Fujimori has been forced out by electoral fraud and his own brand of corruption, we can perhaps hope for better things to come. The people, I think, chose the path that I have struggled to believe in all along and have tried to reveal in one small way in this book. They chose the building of new institutions, the hope of a peaceful revolution, under a strong but democratic government.

It is clear that the legal and political structure of the country has to be changed, and perhaps a return to democracy will make that possible. The challenge is to create new institutions that will not encourage corruption, preferably ones that will not even tolerate it. Having said so much about the nature of the problem, or Peru's specific version of it, I do not have to point out the enormity of the challenge. The first goal is obviously achievable, the second rarely if ever accomplished. But, based on all that I have learned and presented here, I would suggest that it must begin with the General Water Law and with irrigation. Everything that I experienced in the valley tells me that both goals can be achieved in that domain. The country must build new institutions and construct a new identity, a more positive one that includes everyone and embraces elements of the indigenous heritage, of the Andean way of life. In the highlands, at least, irrigation is the logical place to start.

The Story of Irrigation in the Andes

"Comedy" and Tragedy in the Commons

The story told in these chapters, which I will try to summarize here, was gleaned through ethnography of a particular kind—comparative, somewhat limited or selective in scope, and primarily ecological—research that was historicized as much as possible, but ultimately concerned with interpreting my experience in the valley. A similar narrative could probably be written about many parts of the highlands, long-time centers of regional commerce and the export trade, of merchant capitalism. I am by no means suggesting that the story has been exactly the same in all parts of the sierra, only that history and "development" have taken broadly similar trajectories in each place, because they all grew out of a single tradition, shared by communities at the outset. Furthermore, the same set of historical factors—sustained population collapse followed eventually by rapid growth, major changes in the ecology related to a new political economy, even basic changes in transport—provided the setting for a gradual transformation of that heritage in many places. Finally, the actors and agencies that played the dominant role in this long drama, the provincial elite and the state, in its changing and ultimately contradictory role, acted widely throughout the highlands in broadly similar ways. Yet it is possible to trace this history only in valleys like Cotahuasi, where several distinct kinds of hydraulic society still coexist in close proximity to one another.

"Comedy": Successfully Governing the Commons

The oldest of these traditions, represented here by Huaynacotas, is probably found only where people of Spanish heritage have never resided, an unusual situation in highland villages, and where the state has never imposed its water policies, which is not nearly so rare. The society is based on principles of equity and reciprocity: the right of everyone to a fair share of the most vital resource, strictly proportional to the size of one's property and given to all with the same frequency, provided that it is used responsibly and that corresponding duties to the community are fulfilled. The concept of proportionality is central and pervasive, since the duties of households to give back to the community, both within the hydraulic domain and outside it, through the sustaining activity of ritual, are measured against the material benefits that they derive from village membership. There are certain limits in Huaynacotas, constraints on social interaction and exchange, negotiated between the land-rich and the land-poor but very much determined, with some force, by the latter. And the power to impose those limits, to influence the terms under which the wealthier minority operate, is rooted in small-scale irrigation, in a basic accountability having to do with people's familiarity with the system and their ability to protect their own water rights.

This, to me, is the essence of the "moral economy" (Scott 1976, 1985, 1990), a general way of life and a distinctive kind of ideology that emerged in a number of specific forms among the world's primitive and peasant peoples. To those who will accuse me of "essentializing" here (Starn 1991, 1992, 1999; Kearney 1996), note that I am speaking, not just of an abstract morality based on lofty principles, but of a concrete ethic based on a well-defined set of practices, rules, and norms, and corresponding material relations. These have to do with the proper use of vital resources—land, water, and labor—and the ways that individuals should relate to each other, through the central reality of work, and to the community as a whole. Although the moral economy is primarily inward-looking, focused on internal social interaction, it is also a "political" economy, as any such ethical system must be by definition, and of course it does not exist in isolation.

It is hardly surprising, given the peculiarities of the Andean environment, that a special technology should lie at the heart of this particular tradition, one that probably dates back centuries to the Incas and their predecessors. That is what the early chroniclers, those voices from the distant past, have always said (Garcilaso 1966 [1609]; Guaman Poma de Ayala 1978 [1613]), although their words are texts whose possible biases we have rightly learned to question. Yet the full significance of this technology has been hard to recognize, mainly because it has been altered so widely and so variously by recent historical events.

I do not mean to imply that Andean society was based solely on irrigation, or that the moral economy did not exist in regions where the technology was not necessary; that clearly was not the case. Rather, my point is that irrigation communities formed the heart of Inca civilization, and that they have sustained the moral economy in the Andes and helped to keep it alive in Huaynacotas and other places, more so than any other institution. Furthermore, where the technology changed in significant ways, society changed along with it, undergoing a decline, Hardin's "tragedy of the commons," that took various forms but whose "essence," whose moral and practical significance, has been much the same everywhere. The symptoms of this decline—inequity, corruption, lack of cooperation, and conflict in general but particularly over water—can be seen widely throughout the region today.

Anthropologists have long sought to determine how irrigation has shaped the development of societies in relatively arid parts of the world like Peru. But as we ultimately learned, irrigation systems come in many shapes and sizes in various kinds of environments (Hunt 1988, 1989), so that, unless one makes certain initial assumptions, few interesting generalizations can be made in this regard. Without these, the most that can be said about the Andes is that a distinctive kind of hydraulic system—small-scale, vertically oriented canal systems fed by alpine springs—was constructed there in Inca times or earlier; that this was the only kind of system that could be built in most areas, because of their topography and climate; and that these small systems formed the basis of a certain type of society, a village society, or "micro-society" (Schaedel 1971), as they still do today —there and in many other arid and mountainous parts of the world.

It was the organization and operation of the systems that identified them as a distinctive tradition, and that helped to sustain a special, though not entirely unique, kind of community. And that technological and sociopolitical tradition, the one still thriving today in Huaynacotas, probably dates back at least to the Incas, who apparently endorsed it and may even have imposed it in some places. The most compelling evidence we have on irrigation in the remoter parts of the empire is the account of Garcilaso de la Vega, which I spoke of briefly in the Introduction.

What kind of water system was the Inca Garcilaso describing in his account? According to the ethnographic information now available, not just from my study but from many others done in different parts of the Andes, it appears to have been a dual system, with two modes of operation, one of which may live on in Huaynacotas and other places like it. This, I think, was the predominant one, employed during the normal state of affairs: water scarcity. Note that all of the basic principles of the Huaynacotas tradition are either mentioned directly in or can be inferred from Garcilaso's brief description, written so long ago: proportionality, uniformity (in the watering frequency, without which there can be no proportionality among people's shares, and even in technique, since, without that, how can the amount of time and water needed per unit of land be known?), contiguity, and regularity. All of these together imply the presence of the fifth principle, transparency, as well. To my mind, the same set of operating principles in two accounts in different times and places—mine and his—can hardly be a coincidence.

Having said that, it is highly likely, and quite consistent with Garcilaso's comments, that distribution took place according to different principles—hierarchical ones based on age and prestige—when enough water was available. This is the kind of arrangement, which comes down to distributing water to households and landowners, rather than to fields, that operates in Pampamarca. In the Andes, it is widely associated today with the *saya* system, a hierarchical moiety organization consisting of ranked upper and lower halves of the community, which is known to predate the Incas but to have been adopted by them for administrative purposes. It was continued by the Spanish and used largely to the same end. The moieties—usually called Hanansaya and Hurinsaya, respectively—still exist as social divisions in some communities in the Cotahuasi valley, but they are no longer spoken of in Huaynacotas or Pampamarca.

The dual social organization has been discussed extensively by many scholars (e.g., Zuidema 1964, 1986), and well analyzed ethnologically and historically by Gelles (1994, 1995, 2000). As for its hydrological dimension, the hierarchical basis for the watering order today is, almost without exception, gerontocratic, that is, based on a person's age and service to the community. This prestige principle is followed in a large number of Andean villages (Fonseca 1983; Mayer 1985; Gelles 1986; Treacy 1994a, b; Guillet 1994) and, as in Pampamarca, it is usually linked with the *cargo* system of ceremonial sponsorship, though in that case without moieties.

How are we to explain this striking kind of duality: the widespread existence of two apparently indigenous hydraulic traditions, both associated with the moiety system, that seem, at first glance, to contradict each other? I suggest that they grew out of an Inca practice of alternating periodically between strict equity and efficiency and a kind of hierarchy, in a sort of "gumsa/gumlao" arrangement, to use Leach's (1954) famous terms. More often than not, however, the moiety system is associated with contiguous distribution, the kind of system found in Huaynacotas, as Guillet (1994: 184) has noted.[1]

Since climatic and demographic conditions appear to have been roughly the same in Inca times as they are today (Thompson et al. 1985), I would suggest that the use of the hierarchical principle was intermittent in most places, rather than routine, and essentially symbolic, since a shortage would have been the normal state of affairs. That, of course, would imply something rather different from the permanent hierarchical arrangement that now prevails in Pampamarca and many other places. Furthermore, if each moiety originally had its own separate territory and canal system, as appears to have been the case (Mitchell 1976; Guillet 1994), then the difference between the two systems with respect to water conservation may not originally have been that great. When the moieties are distinct corporate groups—or the ayllus, if moieties are not present, as in Pampamarca—each with its own territory and hydraulic domain, watered without interruption according to a standard sequence, the difference is minimized.

If we accept, for the sake of argument, some degree of truth to Garcilaso's claims, how then were the Incas able to distribute the water proportionally, giving everyone the amount needed without favoring anyone? Surely they did not wear sundials on their wrists. The secret, I think, lay mainly in the method of landscaping and the technique of water utilization, in level terraces and pooling structures of uniform height, in watering every parcel of land in the same way. The standardization of irrigation time and of water consumption is an inherent feature of this technology. But another feature of equal importance was having everyone's land on the same schedule, as Garcilaso implicitly acknowledged.

These features together would have produced transparency and fostered a high degree of accountability, giving local communities a remarkable capacity for managing their own resources. Admittedly, Garcilaso is known to have exaggerated the wisdom of Inca governance, but based on my experience in Huaynacotas, these principles define a strategy that is highly effective in places where water is scarce and unpredictable. The arrangement provides people with a strong incentive to conserve water and abide by the rules, since by doing so they are directly maximizing the frequency of irrigation, a benefit that affects everyone in the same way. The principles create a feedback link between individual behavior and the common good that is direct and obvious to the individual farmer, and that cannot be achieved through any other kind of arrangement. Under this set of conditions—with vigilance dispersed among households and spread out all over the canal system, rather than being concentrated in the hands of the water distributor—people are confident of their ability to see what is going on and to protect their own rights, maximizing the amount of water they receive each year, and this has everything to do with their tendency to obey the rules and respect tradition.

I suggest that the Incas endorsed the tradition because of this, its superiority, and because, like the moiety organization itself, it had already emerged and become established widely throughout the highlands, probably in Huari times or perhaps even long before that.[2] Indeed, if Garcilaso's account is at all accu-

rate, the Incas may well have imposed it in the state surrogates or colonies—
mitmaykuna—and administrative settlements they installed throughout the
countryside, such as Cahuana in the Cotahuasi valley, where the tradition still
seems to be strong today.

It is hard to imagine any other way that equity in water rights could have
been accomplished in an Andean setting. There can be little doubt that this was
the central organizing concept, since the chronicler Guaman Poma, in his 1615
work, speaks repeatedly and admiringly of the same thing, an ancient tradition
of fairness and equity between rich and poor, in a country where the resource
was scarce and unpredictable, a source of constant concern.[3] The notion of fairness, I would suggest, is essentially one of uniformity and proportionality, principles whose full significance students of irrigation have been slow to recognize,
even though we have known about the concepts for decades. They now appear
to be characteristic of well-run irrigation systems in many parts of the world, at
least of small-scale, community-based systems.[4] The principles are central to
both Garcilaso's and Guaman Poma's accounts, which are not likely to be simply fables or hoaxes.

Although water was used in this manner only when and where it was scarce,
that condition seems to have prevailed throughout much of the sierra during
Inca times. Recent studies have shown that the empire emerged toward the end
of a long dry period of several hundred years (Thompson et al. 1985), and that
the Incas tried to alleviate the arid conditions by expanding and probably intensifying irrigation in the provinces (Denevan 1986; Treacy 1990: 125–35, 1994a,
b). As John Treacy surmised in his work on a community much like Huaynacotas, the Incas probably did have a standard system for water conservation, and
it was this one. Recently, Guillet (1994: 181), in a comparative analysis of communities in the Colca, has moved very close to agreement, after having spoken
originally of an "acephalous" tradition he thought to have been native to that
valley.

If one assumes, therefore, that population density and cultivated acreage
were about the same in Inca times as they are today, so that water would usually
have been scarce, then the small-scale canal systems of the sierra can indeed be
said to have encouraged the emergence of a certain type of village society. Under these conditions, assuming also that conflict over the supply had to be minimized, and that remote communities had to be able to govern themselves effectively, at least in this one vital domain, some options were better than others
and one was best of all: the kind of transparent and equitable system that the
Incas favored and, in some areas, may even have imposed.

I think that, allowing for a few compatible modifications, this is the only system that could establish equity and promote conservation in many parts of the highlands today, and that these practices and principles should be instituted in communities like Cotahuasi, where the legacy of the landlords and the state has created a desperate need for both. Ultimately, this is the most compelling argument I can offer that communities irrigated in this manner during Inca times: it was the best and most efficient way, under the prevailing environmental and demographic conditions, parameters that have re-emerged in modern times. Huaynacotas and its people are living proof of this, a community that has apparently held onto and continually affirmed a real triumph of human achievement—a successful way of sharing scarce water and equitably governing the commons, to the benefit of everyone.

As for why the tradition was not lost during the long era of population collapse and water abundance, which happened in most other places, I cannot begin to say. Perhaps people merely reinvented the tradition when water became scarce, discovering again all the principles that had been worked out long before, which are simple enough and serve very well. But I am more inclined to think that they held onto it, perhaps because they preferred the simplicity, even elegance, of an "egalitarian" tradition.

Tragedy: A Drama of Unintended Consequences

In what ways was this tradition modified during the next four centuries, by the Conquest and all the changes that the Spanish brought with them? It is clear that hacienda owners did not have to be living in a community, using its land and water, for important changes to take place. The population collapse alone was so devastating that few aspects of village life could have escaped its effects. Land and water became abundant for the first time in centuries, eliminating the need for conservation, and labor became extremely scarce. All too often, the result was that communities took the logical step of adopting the hierarchical mode of distribution as a permanent arrangement. And unfortunately, during the long period of water abundance, many of them appear to have forgotten that they had once had a more conservative and effective way of doing things. The other tradition was simply lost in many places.

Other changes that took place during the long colonial era set the stage for conflict later on. Vast expanses of terrain were abandoned and only put back under cultivation very slowly as populations began to recover some two centuries later. Because "Indian" people had many new demands on their time, these eroded lands were oftentimes not restored to their original condition. The result can be seen in many villages, where slopes are cultivated in some areas, and the inundation technique is used on them. This method, clearly incompatible with the management tradition of Huaynacotas, requires more water but uses less labor than the pooling method. Both techniques are practiced today in many villages, and one even sees the inundation technique used widely on terraces, a mixed pattern that strongly suggests that the one method has gradually displaced the other over time. Evidence for this can be seen not only in the Cotahuasi valley, but in every other valley where irrigation practices have been closely studied.[5]

People first adopted the new landscaping and watering techniques during the era of depopulation, but the impact was probably not strongly felt until populations recovered and abandoned cropland was gradually put back into production. This in itself was a recipe for a certain amount of scarcity and conflict, but once alfalfa was added to the equation—a vital commodity in the emerging new political economy—serious problems became inevitable. The impact of alfalfa is clear today in areas where it has only recently been cultivated, such as the Colca, particularly in Lari, the village studied by Guillet (1992: 173–90). His account of conflict in that community puts the blame squarely on pasture production, but it becomes much more comprehensible when one considers the possibility that the watering method in general use there, the inundation technique, and perhaps other aspects of irrigation too are not really so traditional as they seem to be.[6]

Scarcity and conflict over water are almost universal in the highlands today, even in indigenous communities, and the trends set out above seem to me to be some of the reasons why. People do not have an inherent tendency to behave "tragically," to waste water and yet steal it and fight over it, but that is the impression one gets if one assumes that they have always done things the way they do now. But for all their importance, neither the introduction of alfalfa nor the more frequent occurrence today of drought, or even both together, can fully account for this almost universal conflict. The other changes that helped to bring that about are most clearly seen in Pampamarca today: the wholesale destruction of terraces, the switch to the inundation technique, the emergence of hierarchy and inequity in water shares, and ultimately even the privatization of the resource, whether de jure or de facto. We have seen that these changes, all of which the Spaniards introduced along with pasture production, have recently been embraced by certain comuneros involved in cattle-raising for the market. They are beginning to disrupt the traditional system of distribution, effects that would have been felt long ago if water had not been so abundant. This, I think, is the context in which the tragedy in the Andes began, when some community members first began to depart from tradition and adopt the behaviors and

practices of the Spanish elite. These changes had no immediate negative consequences, but, again, they set the stage for conflict later on.[7]

Obviously, I cannot demonstrate that my interpretation is the true or correct one, but I do not claim to be offering anything more than an approximation. My interest in the history of irrigation stems from my desire to understand how serious problems of waste, theft, corruption, and conflict came to be
so common in the highlands today. This historical process, like the related ones
of mestizaje and urban migration, cannot be taken for granted as somehow
self-evident, a product of some "law" of capitalism or of the state in its ongoing
hegemonic encounter with peasants. Nor do I believe that this "tragedy of the
commons" can be attributed to the inherent greed of the rational self-interested
individual, as some would have it. Indeed, one of my primary aims in this book
has been to explain the tragedy as a historical process by "eventalizing" it, to use
Foucault's term. By his definition (1991: 76), eventalizing means: "To show that
things 'weren't as necessary as all that.' [It] means rediscovering the connections, encounters, supports, blockages, plays of forces, strategies, and so on
which at a given moment establish what subsequently counts as being self-
evident, universal, and necessary. In this sense one is indeed effecting a sort of
multiplication or pluralization of causes."

Continuity and Decline

The negative consequences of hierarchy and inequity are most visible in hacienda-dominated districts like Cotahuasi. There, all of the basic changes discussed so far were pushed to their ultimate extreme, in part because another exogenous agent, the state, played a vital role in promoting this process. The state
encouraged estate expansion in an effort to foster the growth of the market and
endorsed the accompanying privatization of water. It promoted the conversion
of land to producing food for animals, to cultivating alfalfa, a crop that has had
more impact on life in the Andes than any other plant the Spanish brought with
them. The only plants with a comparable impact are sugarcane (used mainly in
this part of the world to make alcohol) and the grama, both of which have had
a pernicious effect and are a part of the same story of tragedy and decline.

Let me just briefly review the effects of all this on the adjacent communities.
Hacienda encroachment deprived them steadily of water, changed their customary system of distribution, and then gradually undermined that tradition,
such as it was, by taking away even more of the resource. The resulting scarcity
unleashed a struggle within each village, undermining the traditional way of life
at its very foundation, a process of impoverishment and growing dependency

that had a great deal to do with the turn toward mestizaje. As water grew increasingly scarce, people became dependent on the landlords for more of it, equity gave way to inequity, cooperation gave way to free-riding and conflict, and the yearly ritual of canal cleaning became a form of forced labor or servitude. Gradually, comuneros became merely campesinos, in this case "mestizo" peasants, a term whose meaning I have deliberately left somewhat unclear because it is ambiguous, as we will see below.

In 1969, the state, now under military control, made an extraordinary effort to resolve these problems by imposing water reform. That effort, though well intentioned, failed, instead making the problems even worse. The General Water Law neglected to change the conditions of water use on estate lands and, though it did increase the amount of water generally available for use, it ultimately only weakened the capacity of the communities to manage their own affairs. In reacting against privatization, the government turned to Hardin's other solution to the commons dilemma: state control. It instituted a highly centralized system run by a resident outsider, in which conservation and cooperation brought few if any benefits, whereas self-seeking behavior brought considerable material rewards. Drought played an important role in this by inducing a chronic scarcity that caused an initially well-organized system to be subverted and come unraveled. But these climatic disturbances are inevitable in the Andes, and they only exacerbated the symptoms of the underlying problems, which are systemic, inherent in the law and the administrative system, even in the arrangement for sharing water itself, all of which were imposed by the state.

A similar story has obviously unfolded in many parts of the sierra. The story for the struggle for water has perhaps not been told in so much detail before, but its outlines can be seen in various communities described in the work of numerous anthropologists.[8] Although the specific versions may vary, it is a story of basic changes in water use, of expansion and impoverishment, of exploitation and decline.

I do not mean to suggest, however, that wherever these changes have taken place all continuity with the past has been broken, or that "indigenous" culture, as most anthropologists have depicted it (e.g., Alberti & Mayer 1974; B. Isbell 1978; Allen 1988; Bolin 1998), is dead. On the contrary, I would argue that the "Andean community" is quite real and alive, even in mestizo districts like Cotahuasi, and that peasants throughout the region are struggling for its preservation. To those who would take the opposite position, I would like, before concluding, to point out several things.

The changes that have had the most drastic effect on highland villages were originally imposed on them by outsiders, first by hacienda owners and later also the state, and some of these have happened only during the last few decades. They have ultimately benefited a minority of people, those heavily involved in the market economy, and they have divided the communities roughly along class, but sometimes also along ethnic, lines. Many people would perhaps discount the ethnic aspect, and turn this narrative into an inevitable tragedy wrought by the relentless expansion of capitalism, arguing that there were no real cultural differences at work here, only winners and losers in a game where everyone was really playing by the same set of rules and the same values.

That would be a serious distortion for several reasons. The growth of the market is under constraint in many parts of the Andes, as Gonzalez de Olarte (1984, 1987) clearly showed years ago in his regional study of peasant household economy. Whole areas such as the Cotahuasi valley, and certainly a great many people, are really only on the margins, at least in respect to their agricultural production and their very limited reliance on purchased food. That marginality is partly due to basic limitations imposed by the geography and topography, but it can also be attributed, I think, to cultural preferences and to active resistance.

The impact of changes in irrigation undermined indigenous life at its very foundation, turning neighbors against one another in a process that ultimately became self-reinforcing and ramified widely throughout each affected community. That is what I have tried most to reveal here: the factors that have steadily increased the pressure on all people, even those only marginally involved in the market, to deviate from what I think had once been traditional and the norm. This is how capitalism expands, how it subverts traditional or alternative ways of life. What unfolds is a drama of unintended consequences arising from changes initiated long ago in the past, a slowly ascending spiral of positive feedback that leads to a place where no one intended originally to go. Nevertheless, significant continuities remain because there has always been resistance, both active and passive, to these changes (Scott 1985, 1990), especially at the cultural level. Nowadays there may be a widespread tendency to see resistance in virtually everything that peasants do (Brown 1997), but the various forms that I saw in the valley were no illusion.

This resistance has in some cases become a kind of critique, a local alternative to the dominant society and its norms and values, virtually from the ground up, as in Huaynacotas. But everywhere it expresses a basic continuity that is central to peasant culture: a communal ethos that is shared by comuneros and campesinos alike, by indigenous people as well as mestizo peasants, as both Smith (1975, 1989) and Mallon (1983) have long argued. It persists today as a set of aspirations and concerns, a kind of hope, even where the conditions of life are highly unequal and harsh. Thus the decline that has been under way in Cotahuasi for so long is primarily a social one, not a cultural one, lying more in the realm of practice—or practical necessity—than of theory.

This is indicated by the fact that the peasants of Cotahuasi and Huaynacotas share some of the same basic values: self-reliance in labor and in food production, an attachment to work, and a bond with place and the soil. More important, it is confirmed by their long common struggle for more equitable terms of labor exchange. Here, however, I want to emphasize the commonalities that have to do with irrigation.

Many mestizos in Cotahuasi district clearly know, just as their indigenous neighbors in Huaynacotas and Pampamarca do, that water shares should be proportional to each other, that the resource should be used in the same basic way by everyone, that it should not be wasted, and that the duties of individuals to the community should correspond to the material benefits that people derive from living there. They know that this is the right way, regardless of whether people produce mainly to feed themselves or for the market. Indeed, from what I have seen and heard, the values of equity and proportionality are basic to peasant ideology, regardless of whether institutions have persisted to make them a concrete living reality. That is, after all, why the idea of fairness is used so often in an effort to mask highly unequal and exploitative labor relations (Orlove 1977a; Mitchell 1991a, b).

Some people might ask what difference proportionality makes in a society that is stratified, as all Andean villages are and long have been. What does it matter, when one person has five hectares while his neighbors have only one, so that he uses five times as much water in any case? I would argue that it is everything. In fact, we now have many examples throughout the world of irrigation systems that are organized and managed by the users themselves, and that operate quite effectively, with minimal waste and conflict, avoiding the famous tragedy.[9] In each and every one, proportionality of rights and duties seems to be the central organizing principle. These economies are both moral and political, being stable systems of "common-property" management that work well, based on commonalities and constraints that minimize—but of course do not eliminate—conflict between rich and poor. Fortunately, we are beginning to know a great deal about this general kind of community and about the factors and processes that can lead to either its persistence or its decline (McCay & Acheson 1987; Ostrom 1990, 1992).

Once such a tradition is lost, however, people can do little to restore it, at least under the conditions that prevail today. Much as the campesinos of Cotahuasi complain about the situation, they still carry on an almost daily and sometimes desperate struggle with their neighbors to survive under the current system. They clearly understand that a society can only be just if everyone, large proprietors and small alike, abides by the same rules; and they are quite willing to manipulate or break the rules when this is the only kind of behavior that is rewarded. They do not like it, but they do what they must in order to subsist and survive.

Few campesinos in Cotahuasi can explain exactly how they came to be in their predicament. But many do clearly believe that the wealthier landowners in Cotahuasi, and their ally, the national government, are mainly responsible for their plight.[10] They know that the General Water Law was a genuine attempt by the state to improve conditions and correct the injustices of the past, but they are quite aware that it was passed by a military government, not an elected one—by the hero Velasco—and that, in any case, the end result has been corrupted and fallen short of the desired objectives.

During my fieldwork, the situation was bad enough that some people seemed willing to embrace any regime that would establish order and put an end to the corruption, even the Shining Path—a small number, however, whose significance I do not want to exaggerate. Fortunately, that authoritarian movement has now been virtually extinguished. But what I have tried to show here is that it is within the grasp of the local people to solve their own problems, if only the new government would provide the necessary guidance and support, by amending in a number of ways the existing legislation or by coming up with an entirely new law. The General Water Law can be made to serve the purpose for which it was intended, simply by basing it on a more appropriate model for irrigation, an Andean one. Or a new law, such as the one that is now being considered by the government, could be designed to the same effect.

Looking into the Future:
The Proposed Return to Privatization

Clearly, in this valley and many others, it is up to the state, and perhaps also international lending institutions such as the World Bank and the Inter-American Development Bank, to show the way somehow toward a better way of doing things. The banks, in any case, were responsible for drafting the new law now being considered and for stressing the need for a second water reform. Unfortunately, the proposed new law—based on legislation adopted in Chile under the dictator Augusto Pinochet—would privatize water rights and allow them to be bought and sold, once again creating local water markets. Among organizations that have the power to make policy, this, Hardin's other solution to the commons dilemma, is now the popular trend in water management. The same proposal has been under consideration for several years in Ecuador, Bolivia, Brazil, and most other Latin American countries, where it has met with vigorous, at times even violent, public protest. The banks are exerting enormous pressure on these governments, in the form of massive but contingent loans, to adopt the policy as part of a program of "structural adjustment," the effort to downsize government and get it out of the business of things like managing water, at least at the local level. This is part of an effort, laudable enough and quite necessary in itself, to work out a way of turning ownership and control of the resource over to the communities and user groups.

The goal is supposedly to construct a system with a built-in incentive for people to use water more efficiently, and these institutions, in promoting the expansion of the market even further into new domains of social life, have acknowledged that the current legislation, and the existing system of state administration, have failed to provide such an incentive. However, in the small-scale canal systems of the Andean highlands, monetary concerns and market forces will not provide the desired incentive, as the history of Cotahuasi district makes clear. Privatization would merely restore a policy that has been thoroughly discredited, not just in Peru but in most other Latin American countries, one that caused a lot of hardship and conflict in the past, and it would not achieve the goal for which it is intended.

The main reason for this is simple. In a region where the average household irrigates less than a hectare of land—one characterized mainly by subsistence or peasant agriculture—the amount of water that could be saved by people through more frugal use, though potentially very significant in the aggregate, will rarely be large enough that it could feasibly be sold to someone else, even if the infrastructure existed to make this possible. In the Andes, the motive for conservation can only be found in the link between the efficiency and orderliness of water use and the duration of the irrigation cycle, between "individual" self-interest and the common good. And that link is most direct and obvious to the farmer when watering is done under the kind of regimen used in Huaynacotas and numerous other places in the Andean highlands.

The solutions to the problem lie not in the market and the profit motive, but in the basic principles of Andean irrigation.[11] This is the proposal that I present now to the scholarly community and to my collaborators in Peru, along with the specific recommendations for change outlined in this book. Although my recommendations are based on what I think was the Inca system for water conservation, they are suggestions for policy, not just in the Andes, but also in other arid and mountainous regions, indeed anywhere in the world that small, community-based canal systems are found.

Thus a large part of my original task, and part of my promise to the people of the Cotahuasi valley—that former hole on the historical map—is now fulfilled. I have told the story of irrigation in the province, or my version of it, and arrived at conclusions that I know will be helpful and will give something back to the people who gave so much to me. And, in the final analysis, I have found that my original impression on arriving there was correct. The valley may be a very remote and unusual place, but in many ways its history is that of all highland Peru.

Glossary of Quechua Terms

This list is confined to irrigation terms and a few other words that are used frequently in the text.

Allapay. The second irrigation of the year, for the germination of seeds of maize and other food crops of the *qheshwa* zone; also called *yapay*

Allway. The third irrigation of maize, to promote plant development

Atu. An earthen water-containment feature used in terrace irrigation; its function is to pool water and maximize water absorption

Atura. The first irrigation of the year, to moisten and soften the soil for plowing and planting

Ayllu. A residential and social unit within or composing an indigenous community. Analogous to the barrio, or neighborhood, it is made up of families related by kinship and is often a corporate or territorial landholding unit.

Ayni. A form of cooperative work in which a service is given on the condition that it will be returned in equivalent kind or amount; also refers to loans of a tool, money, or anything else made under the same condition

Chakra. A generic term for a field, parcel, or plot

Chakra miray or *mirachiy.* To enlarge a parcel by terracing adjacent uncultivated slopes

Chawpi tarpuy. The middle phase of the planting cycle, carried out from mid-September through mid-October

Chuchuña. Lands that are dry and hard from lack of water; used to refer to nonirrigated fallowing lands (*laymis*)

Hatun yaku. "Big water" or main water, from a main spring rather than a secondary spring

Huch'uy phayna. A small cooperative work project for cleaning a secondary canal

Kutipay. A quick second irrigation done after the water has had time to drain somewhat. It is often considered an infraction of the rules of water use.

Laymi. Sectorally fallowed lands used for growing tubers and cereal crops; often irrigated for planting and periodically as needed thereafter (sometimes called *t'ikras*)

Mink'a. A traditional form of asymmetrical exchange in which a day of agricultural work is given in return for special foods, chicha, and liquor, plus a share of the eventual harvest

Ñawpa tarpuy. An early or first planting, carried out in late August and early September

Pata. An agricultural terrace

Pata pata. A series of contiguous terraces, or *andenería*

Phaqcha. A small stone ledge, or "fall," extending out from a terrace wall that allows water to drop cleanly to the next terrace without wetting and damaging the wall

Phaspa. A light or superficial irrigation that moistens the soil to a depth of a few inches

Pukyu. A spring used as a source of irrigation water

Pukyu chakra. A field or sector watered by a secondary spring rather than by water from the main supply

Purun. Uncultivated slopes, fallowed or virgin land

Qarpay. To irrigate, the act of irrigating

Qhata. A slope or slopes, sloping unterraced terrain

Qhata pata. A terrace with a pronounced slope

Qhaway. To watch over or guard irrigation water against canal blockage or water theft

Qhepa tarpuy. A late planting, the last phase in the planting cycle, carried out in late October or thereafter

Qhosqay. To irrigate a field or series of terraces by releasing water at the top and allowing gravity to draw it over the whole parcel at once

Qocha. A tank or reservoir; also refers to bodies of water in general

Raki. An "irrigation" or water allotment; a portion of the main canal flow that is sufficient to water one parcel in the normal amount of time

Ranra hallp'a. Gravelly or rocky soil that retains water poorly and must be irrigated slightly longer than other types of soil

Sara chakra. Intensively irrigated lands, used mainly for growing maize but also planted in beans and other crops of the temperate or *qheshwa* zone

T'ikra. Sectorally fallowed lands in the *suni* zone used for growing potatoes and other tubers, wheat, and barley. They are irrigated wherever possible.

Wayka. A form of emergency assistance in which a group of people join together to help in the rapid completion of some task; also refers to the private crop fields of a hacienda owner and the obligatory work done on them by sharecroppers

Yaku. Water

Yana hallp'a. Black or dark soil that absorbs and holds water well

Yut'a. A small dam of rocks and sod that is used to close off a canal and divert its water

Notes

Introduction

1. After a long absence made necessary by the political turmoil of the early 1990's, I was able to make brief trips back to the valley for follow-up research during the summers of 1997, 1998, and 1999.

2. There are numerous excellent studies of irrigation in highland communities, notably Mitchell 1973, 1977, 1981; Meyer & Fonseca 1979; Fonseca 1983; Guillet 1987, 1992, 1994; Gelles, 1984, 1986, 1991, 1994, 1995, 2000; Treacy 1990, 1994a, b; Bunker & Seligmann 1986; Seligmann & Bunker 1994; Paerregaard 1994; Valderamma & Escalante 1986, 1988; and Bolin 1990, 1994. Several of the later works, from the 1990's, are summarized in Mitchell & Guillet, eds., 1994.

3. Sendero Luminoso is also known as the Communist Party of Peru.

4. I also used 1: 90,000-scale stereo pairs, which were essential in enabling informants to identify key topographic features and major landholding units.

5. Any ethnographer working in the highlands at the time would have encountered these suspicions. I am sure that few people seriously thought I was a spy for either the CIA or Shining Path.

6. In all, I was able to make just five visits to Pampamarca, covering a period of slightly more than two months, and only three to Huaynacotas, covering five weeks all together—periods too brief to allow a suitable ethnography of all three communities.

Chapter 1: The Setting

1. This is my hypothesis regarding the name Ocoña's meaning and derivation. Quechua has no vowel "o," only a "u" that is slightly rounded when pronounced in the environment of a velar or glottal consonant (see Note on Orthography). The Spanish colonists tended, however, to substitute "o" for "u" in all kinds of settings, as they did in referring to the Kunti people of this part of the Inca empire as the Condes. Since there appears to be no word *oqo* in the language, *ukhu*, "inside" or "deep," seems to be the most likely root of the original name.

2. The neighboring Colca canyon, with a depth of roughly 2,300 m is commonly touted as the world's deepest, but according to the maps of the Instituto Geografico, it is about 700 m shallower than the Ukhuña. The Grand Canyon of the Colorado is only about half as deep.

3. River water is used for irrigation in the highlands, but usually on a relatively small

scale in most valleys and usually in just a few locations. The major exceptions are the Vil-canota-Urubamba valley near Cusco, parts of the Mantaro and Yanamarca valleys in the department of Junin, parts of a few valleys in the Cajamarca basin, and the area sur-rounding the city of Arequipa, which is irrigated massively by the Chile River.

4. Again, Quechua has no vowel "o," only a "u" whose pronunciation is rounded when it precedes or follows a velar or glottal consonant like "q"; thus it is often spelled as an "o" in that setting. To my knowledge there is no word or prefix *coro* or even *kuru* in any dialect of Quechua. *Qori,* however (hispanicized spelling), means "gold" in the lan-guage. Since we know that the valley and canyon were a primary source of gold for the Inca empire (as discussed in Chap. 2), it seems likely that Qoripuna was the original name. It may well have been deliberately changed to obscure the valley's long association with the mineral, during a time when the Spanish were plundering the empire and searching for its gold sources.

5. According to the local office of the Ministry of Agriculture, roughly 650 mm of rain are needed to grow maize without irrigation.

6. I am generalizing here for the sake of simplicity. In the higher-altitude communi-ties, where less alfalfa is planted, maize production can continue for 10 years or even more if dung fertilizer is heavily used, as is generally the case. Fields may be planted pe-riodically in wheat or barley to enrich the soil, so that maize can be produced almost in-definitely, without planting alfalfa.

7. There is a fifth zone, which is uninhabited and not exploited in any way: the *janka,* or *nevado* (5,000+ m), the zone of high peaks and perpetual snow.

8. Pasture is more scarce and localized here than in other parts of the altiplano, ow-ing to the extremely porous nature of the puna soil, which is volcanic and coarse (Luís Montoya, personal communication).

9. Though the figure for the total cultivated land is only an estimate of the local of-fice of the Ministry of Agriculture, it is useful as a rough approximation.

10. Although this pattern of grazing and agriculture still prevails, some alfalfa is now cultivated in all the indigenous communities, and production is expanding in many of them. From an ecological point of view, this is the primary locus of change.

11. Cotahuasi is also the capital of the district. I refer to it as a town, not because it is especially large, but because of its political and economic importance and because local people speak of it that way.

12. The only exceptions are Puica, capital of the district covering the eastern edge of the province, and Toro, capital of a district of the same name. Both are high-altitude vil-lages, predominantly peasant, but dominated by landlords who are closely related to the wealthy "Spanish" families of the valley bottom.

13. The exact way in which peasants of the lower zone identify themselves depends on the context. When in the city they may sometimes describe themselves, or one an-other as *cholos,* a term referring to a partly "acculturated" Indian. In any case, nearly all of them have Spanish last names, and they all have at least a primary education.

14. Achambi, an annex in the district of Tomepampa, is the only exception. Its pop-ulation was almost completely wiped out after the Conquest, and its lands were later largely expropriated by families who lived in the lower valley. The current residents, who are mestizo, are descendants of peasants, most of whom came from elsewhere to work the estate land. The villages in the canyon are inhabited mainly by Spanish families who

have been there, producing large amounts of wine that is sold heavily in the upper valley, ever since early colonial times.

Chapter 2: Early History

1. I collected several samples directly from the source for one of my advisers, Richard Burger, who was carrying out a massive study of the prehispanic obsidian trade (see Burger et al. 1996).

2. The sites are Cochacallan, Allway, Challkima, and Pitahuasi in Cotahuasi; and Wit'u, Patacapilla, Cunapampa, and Mawka Llaqta in Pampamarca. I surveyed these areas by collecting diagnostic pottery sherds from the surface, taking architectural notes and photographs, and estimating roughly the number of habitations found in each site. The collections were given to Dr. Max Neira and Sr. Pablo de la Vera Cruz, both experts on the archaeology of the Arequipa region. I also surveyed the areas around Huaynacotas and Alca, though not as thoroughly.

3. The ballpark population figure in the text was derived by multiplying the estimated number of habitations in each site by an average family size of five. There are at least 200 dwellings in Cochacallán, at least 200 in Challkima, and 50 in Allway and Pitahuasi together, yielding a conservative total of about 450. The destroyed site at Cotahuasi would have pushed the figure a bit higher.

4. Other sherds were found of a Late Intermediate Period style known as Chiqhra, from the altiplano of the Cusco region, but, at least in my small sample, these were very few.

5. Chavez missed the ancient site high above Cohuana, the contemporary pueblo, that I found during one of my visits to the village.

6. The major exceptions with stone-paved canals are Tiqnay and Ayahuasi, sites adjacent to and closely related to Cahuana, the Inca center.

7. Ayllu is Quechua for "group." These corporate kinship groups generally held their land and water supply in common.

8. Because of the political violence that occurred in Cotahuasi in 1988, I was not able to be there during the project. The coordinator, a good friend, collected a large sample of sherds and fill directly from the canal wall for me. Interestingly, he told me that the surface of the aqueduct had been made with a mixture of lime and sand, apparently baked to form a hard impermeable pavement. At several points along the canal, he had found the remains of large earthen ovens surrounded by lime residue, which seemed to have been used to bake the material during canal construction. This method of lining canals, which has not been reported before, was apparently an alternative to the stone paving, and it could perhaps provide a feasible alternative to cement today, which is so costly that communities need outside sponsorship to purchase it.

9. "Pampas," or flatlands, derives from the Quechua *panpa*, which refers to the same thing (Lira 1970: 266).

10. Although much of the Kuntisuyu highway is in bad shape for lack of maintenance, it is still used by herders and traders traveling to and from Parinocochas, the adjacent province to the northwest (see Bingham 1922). It remained a major route of trade and transport until the 1950's, when roads began to penetrate Parinocochas from the north. This was the route over which cargo passed during the height of the wool trade.

11. The villages of Challkima and Cochacallán appear to have been demolished in a

single episode. Here it is intriguing to note that Cotahuasi was a site of the Spanish Inquisition, which was rarely carried out in the highlands. A cross behind the ancient church marks the event to this day. People claim that the local Indians were the targets, suggesting that the area may have been a center of native religious resistance during the 17th century (see Salomon 1987 on similar events in the Majes valley).

12. The 1689 figures are obviously estimates, probably not very precise ones. They were made by local priests, who may have had reason to exaggerate the decline.

13. Only a handful of documents provide evidence of the valley's importance in the gold trade, and most histories of mining overlook the region altogether (but see Boggio 1983: 13).

14. Both Raimondi (1887) and Babinski (1883) counted numerous veins that extended from the canyon floor all the way up to the puna. Analysis revealed that the gold was 23 carats, or 96% pure, making it among the purest in the world, equal to that of Siberia and Australia. The only obstacles to its exploitation were the canyon's inaccessibility and the scarcity of water, constraints that continue to block large-scale development today.

15. My thanks to Nelson Manrique for giving me a copy of the document on the Ayahuasi, which he found in the Ministry of Agriculture archive in Arequipa.

16. The recovery of the grazing lands in Huaynacotas and Huillac is referred to in the document on Ayahuasi mentioned in the preceding note.

17. Some estate owners claim that their forebears bought these lands, which is at least plausible; there clearly was some buying and selling of puna property. But the counter-claim often made by community members is probably closer to the truth: that the landlords simply moved their herds into these "vacant" areas, that the communities were too weak to resist, and that the hacendados thereby succeeded in gaining legal possession. In any case, to this day people in the communities recall that depopulation led directly to the loss of much of the puna to the landlords.

18. These small puna estates were overseen by native herders in an arrangement analogous to sharecropping (see Inamura 1981, 1986).

19. The landlords frequently had illegitimate children with poor women of native heritage, often many of them, but I know of only one case, among all the casta genealogies I collected, where the man married the Indian mother of his child.

20. I derived the number of Cotahuasi Indians from the total using the method in Gootenberg 1991: 134, by multiplying the number of tribute-payers and Spanish heads-of-household by the presumed average household size for each group. The 710 figure is extremely low, but since the official mita had ended by 1830, there is no reason to think that workers were still being concealed.

21. There were probably just three ayllus originally in Cotahuasi district, although the 1785 figure of four is all we have to go on. It is telling, for one thing, that there are three principal water sources and three major areas of cultivated land. Beyond that, and even more tellingly, one of the four ayllus, Reyparte, alone has a Spanish rather than a Quechua name.

22. The name Reyparte, Spanish for "division" or "allotment," seems to have been routinely given to resettlements of native groups whose land was taken early in the colonial period. This ayllu appears to have been formed when Cachana, one of the original 17th-century estates, was established on Collana ayllu's land. The change split Collana in

two geographically, and a new ayllu was formed on its lower territory. The other ayllu, Quillunsa, also lost a part of its best land: the pampa of Pitahuasi, now a hacienda. But that estate was well separated from the rest of the ayllu's territory, which remained intact until after 1876.

23. My estimate for Cotahuasi in 1831 is 958; the total in the 1876 census was 2,958.

24. Since "criollos" and "mestizos" are lumped into a single category, "mestizos," there is no way to even estimate how many were in each group.

25. An unpublished local census in 1981 showed a total of 3,126 people in Cotahuasi district, only slightly fewer than the 3,353 counted in 1940

26. Mabry & Cleveland 1996: 277 provides a good general definition of indigenous irrigation, valid for the Andes or any other part of the world: "Systems that are locally developed by cultures with unique histories, often over long periods of time, and usually relying on intensive human labor, small-scale water control systems, [and] direct farmer management. . . . Where an adequate degree of local autonomy has been maintained . . . indigenous irrigation systems retain enough of their local adaptations to remain distinctive."

Chapter 3: Huaynacotas

1. This population figure and the others to follow are official numbers from a 1980 census kept by the Office of Statistics in Arequipa, but they are apparently only estimates.

2. Eight other local villages share the official designation *comunidad campesina*.

3. It is likely that moiety organization, known to have been imposed by the Incas (Gelles 1995), once existed here, as it did elsewhere in the valley. Even today, the communities in the district of Puica are grouped into upper and lower moieties (called Wichay and Uray; Inamura 1981: 67), and an early-19th-century document (ADC 1831) refers to Willaq in the district of Alca as Hanansaya, or upper moiety. It may well be that the community of Visve, which is adjacent to Huaynacotas and shares some of its irrigation water, was originally a fourth ayllu that was part of the moiety system there.

4. The topo is the most common unit of land measurement, defined by the Ministry of Agriculture as 3,496 sq. m, or 0.35 ha, but few parcels if any have ever been accurately measured.

5. These land figures are very approximate, based on interviews with ayllu leaders and other landholders, and they are likely to overestimate the number of larger landholders and middle proprietors. It is notoriously difficult to get accurate data on landholdings in remote villages like Huaynacotas, since everyone's property is scattered, and the fields have never been measured. I was unable to acquire the "auto-evaluos," or official landholding estimates of the early 1980's, for Huaynacotas or Cotahuasi in Arequipa, the whereabouts of which were unknown. Nor was the Padrón de Regantes, the official list of irrigated properties, available to me; the water officials had only the list of households, 264 names in all. The property data were sent to the provincial council in Cotahuasi, and on to Arequipa to be registered, but no one seemed to know where they were when I was there.

6. Although the suffix denoting plurals in Quechua is -*kuna*, the Spanish -s is also often used. So that root words can be remembered, I will use the "s" on key terms.

7. Some of the wealthiest families claimed to have as much as 5 irrigated ha when I

did my fieldwork in the mid-1980's, but when I returned to the village 10 years later, in 1998, the village authorities insisted that no one then had more than 3. It is likely that, in the interim, inheritance had fragmented some family landholdings, and that out-migration had made other properties available for purchase by minoristas.

8. Map 6, like the corresponding maps for Pampamarca and Cotahausi, is based on a 1: 50,000–scale aerial photograph taken in 1953. The land sectors were identified by informants at strategic points within the irrigation system, and any recent changes in use were noted. Because of distortions due to large altitudinal differences, the maps are not very accurate, but they are close enough to be useful in studying current patterns of land and water use.

9. Local people seem to agree unanimously that the reservoirs of Huaynacotas have "always" been there and are "very ancient."

10. All of the above are very rough estimates made from the aerial photograph, using sectors of known area as a basis for calculation. The total area of 410 ha for Huaynacotas conforms closely with the figure of 400 provided by the village mayor.

11. "Raki" is derived from the verb *rakiy*, meaning to distribute or divide something into portions (Cusihuamán 1976: 126), the same term used in the province of Lucanas, in the department of Ayacucho to the north (Montoya et al. 1969: 76), and in some villages in the Colca valley (Treacy 1994b).

12. There is an earlier phase of irrigation for plowing and field preparation, called *atura*, which occurs about a month before the planting, in August (the technique is called *phospay*, "light irrigation"). As noted, beans, barley, garden vegetables, alfalfa, and other crops are also grown on *sara chakra* lands. Unless they are intercropped with maize (as is often the case with beans and quinoa), they are planted later in the year.

13. Visve is a small village of about 360 people; Luicho is a dispersed hamlet of roughly 70. Neither is an ayllu, but some landowners are members of the ayllus of Huaynacotas.

14. I was told by several people of another method of reducing demand used during droughts: ordering irrigators to fill their atus only two-thirds full, or even less. I have since learned that this never worked very well, that it may have been tried in the past, but that in any case it is unnecessary once some land has been taken out of production.

15. In this system, users participate in setting, or continually ratifying, collective rules of management, but no user can individually dispose of his or her rights, which are indissolubly tied to the land, nor can any landowner be excluded. These are often called communal rights (Schlager & Ostrom 1992: 253), but they are not recognized as such by law, since the Peruvian state became the legal owner of all the country's water in 1969.

16. The atus usually taper from about 20 cm in diameter at the base to roughly 10 cm at the top.

17. I was not able to do a soil study to determine roughly what percentage of each soil type is found in the territory. The black soil, or sandy loam, clearly prevails throughout most of the valley.

18. I did not observe terraces being built in Huaynacotas, but I did see it done several times in Cotahuasi. The only way I was able to get a thorough explanation of the procedure was to have people build small working models out of earth and rock, a method originally developed by Harold Conklin (1980: 3).

19. Ox-drawn plows are commonly used on terraces, even very narrow ones, but building a larger field makes the work much faster and easier.

20. For thorough analyses of the rituals of communal work elsewhere in the Andes, see, for example, B. Isbell 1978; Ossio 1978; Valderamma & Escalante 1986, 1988; and Gelles 1994, 1995, 2000.

21. But households are required to spend further time on other projects, such as cleaning plazas and major footpaths.

22. It is extremely important to point out that the principle of proportionality is also central to the *cargo* system of ceremonial sponsorship, which I cannot discuss here. In sponsoring fiestas and moving up the status hierarchy, mayoristas are expected to give especially lavish ones, commensurate with their relative wealth. They would be resented and ridiculed as stingy if they did not.

23. Kinship relations are bilaterally structured here, and the terminology employed is precisely the same as that recorded by Sato 1981 for a village in the Cusco region.

24. The other comuneros usually sell their livestock directly to buyers in the lower valley, where they can get a better price.

25. At the time of my visits, there were six shops in the village that sold the usual range of items—cane alcohol, beer, soft drinks, sugar, rice, kerosene, etc. Three of them were owned by the bigger landowners, and one was a co-op run by the community.

26. The amount of land allotted to the special partner (*mink'aq*) is substantial; a typical unit might be a 20 m x 4 m terrace, or two shorter or narrower ones.

27. To repeat, this wage relationship is true only in respect to agriculture. The herding estancias are worked under a sharecropping-like arrangement by pastoral families affiliated with independent communities on the puna.

28. These predictions are speculative and hypothetical responses to my question: "what would happen if . . . ?"

Chapter 4: Pampamarca

1. The other examples of indigenous villages dominated by ethnic minorities are Puica, Achambi, Mungui, Toro, and Charcana.

2. The place-names show the link with mining (Molino means mill, Aqo means sand), and there are remains of gold-extraction equipment (*quimbaletes*) in both locales.

3. The amount of land and water expropriated was clearly small. Labor conscription and depopulation were major impacts, but the collapse may not have been as complete as the figures show because of the absconding of Indian men and the concealment of tributary labor.

4. None of the families living there when I visited had arrived before the early 19th century, by which time the mines had clearly been abandoned. Their genealogies and family histories agree on this point. The one absentee landlord, Sr. Soto, may well have been a descendant of the original mine owners.

5. The family count comes from a 1987 census by COPASA, a development group financed by the Peruvian and West German governments. According to it, the total number of people, 942, had remained unchanged since the 1981 provincial census (as shown in Table 1, above). The number of elites or "criollos" is my own estimate, but it is at best only a rough one because most of their children now live elsewhere most of the time. According to the COPASA survey, 69% of the population were smallholders with 1 ha of land or less, 20% were middle proprietors with 1–4 ha, and 5% were largeholders with more than 4 ha; 6% of families had no land at all. These figures are likely to be inaccurate, since COPASA had no way to confirm the information.

6. The village mayor and ayllu officials said Kupe has 18 families, and Ch'eqa 22; I do not know how accurate those numbers are.

7. The civil *cargos* in Pampamarca—all traditional ayllu positions—are *teniente gobernador*, *varayoq*, *campo*, and *kuraka*, in order of importance. The religious ones are *mayordomo*, *alferado*, and *previste* for the four major fiestas: Santiago (July 25), the Virgen of Asunta (Aug. 15), the Immaculate Conception (Dec. 8), and Christmas.

8. The *medianos propietarios* are also called *chakrasapa* ("people with many fields"), as in Huaynacotas.

9. The abundance of springwater was confirmed by the findings of a hydrological study carried out in the late 1980's (Cabrera 1987b).

10. The Malawata sector is a prime area for maize, a large tract at low altitude, and it already had a canal. But when water was first restored, it became a laymi.

11. Although irrigation is normally men's work, women often irrigate because the men are frequently absent, working on a hacienda in the lower valley or in Majes. And of course there are widows who do the work themselves. Women have been doing this and most other agricultural tasks (except plowing) ever since the beginning of the mita.

12. Seasonal migration to the sugarcane and rice plantations of Majes and Camana, long an integral part of Pampamarquinos's economic strategies (see Tsunekawa 1986), began to decline in the late 1970's because of the mechanization of rice production. The expansion of the cattle trade provided an alternative source of cash.

13. One landlord was generally more cooperative and reduced his irrigation somewhat, and the two smallholders (the schoolteachers) reportedly always did so. My generalizations about the mistis necessarily obscure the fact that some were more sympathetic to the comuneros' situation and less elitist in their attitudes than others.

14. I got conflicting information in Huaynacotas, where only a few people said that the partial filling of atus as a water-saving measure during droughts had been tried. Since I only asked about this after I had learned about it in Pampamarca, my questions may simply have put the idea in people's heads. Nevertheless, it is common practice there for the campo to try to get people to "hurry up," so that they do not use as much water and take so long.

15. The prayer, as I heard it, was, "Tinkarisayki, hatun pukyo, sumaqta purichiwanki, ama yakuyta mich'akuwankichu" (I am offering to you, great spring; make me go [live] well; do not deny me your water).

16. I know of one case where a comunero, falsely accused of stealing a sheep, was hanged upside down from a post and whipped on the bottoms of his feet until he agreed to give up a piece of land.

17. Three of my best informants in Huaynacotas were mayoristas, all of whom agreed that mortgaging land is bad for both the individual and the community. But in any case, since there is no commercial agriculture in the valley, and no milk production for an external market, the mayoristas have little motive to make loans in the hope of acquiring more land, for there is little they could do with it. Certain factors discourage the raising of beef cattle on a larger scale. Thus the ecological and economic conditions in the villages help to sustain the ideology against trafficking in land.

18. In the words of one person, "El nos despertó; nos dió muchos aprendizajes. Nos decía, 'ustedes pueden salir afuera para trabajar; no tienen por qué pisotearse por nadie.'" (He awakened us, taught us many things. He would say, "You can leave here to work on the outside—there is no reason to be trodden upon by anyone.")

19. Again, the Quechua term for middle proprietors is *askha chakrayoq*, "people with many fields," but they are sometimes referred to as *mayoristas campesinas* or, on occasion, even *misti runakuna*, "white Indians."

20. There are no estate properties in Qhayawa territory.

21. Like the landlords, the middle proprietors are prominent padrinos; they too sometimes give loans and often sell alcohol on credit, and most of them have plows and oxen that they rent out to other ayllu members.

22. If one asks about problems in the past, a campo might reveal how he can be pressured into favoritism. Although people usually ask for the favor first, they sometimes just take the water and then confront the campo, trying to buy him off or intimidate him if a problem arises.

Chapter 5: Cotahuasi

1. Lansing's (1991) vivid characterization, in similar terms, of the terraced and irrigated landscape of Bali would apply just as well here.

2. The puna lands above the district are rather barren and have not been used much in historic times. Here the pasture lands are in the suni, a large area lying in a basin formed by a huge collapsed crater, where cattle are grazed today.

3. A document from the Cusco archive (ADC 1785a) shows that this "puna" was still ayllu property in 1785, and the fiscal census of 1830 does not yet include it among the list of estates. It finally appears as a hacienda owned by the Loayza family in the census of 1876 (DNE 1876: 435). The Loayzas originally came from Alca.

4. As noted earlier, the number of mestizo peasants cannot be determined precisely because they were listed along with the landlords, businessmen, etc., in a single category, "mestizos."

5. When the state became involved in local irrigation in 1941, each major settlement and its territory—Cotahuasi, Quillunsa, Cachana, and Chaucavilca—became a sector, or major component of the official distribution system. The hamlet of Reyparte also became a sector, but Chacaylla, a former hacienda area, is considered to be a part of Cotahuasi sector.

6. The total acreage for Cotahuasi district comes from the Padrón de Regantes, or official list of irrigators, in the Ministry of Agriculture office for 1986.

7. This same water-sharing arrangement existed, though on a much smaller scale, in the districts of Tomepampa and Alca. It could be said to have existed, de facto, in Pampamarca too, although the private water there was not based on actual water titles, and the days of the week were not fixed. See Montoya et al. 1979: 78 for a description of this kind of system in southern Ayacucho.

8. But in Pampamarca, the landlords simply came first in order. Their days of water were not fixed but pinned to the same schedule as everyone else.

9. Each community was required to elect an administrator, or water distributor, which was already the tradition, as well as a three-member committee to oversee his activities.

10. My search for elderly people knowledgeable about the water law situation in the early 20th century led me to three principal informants, all of whom now live in Arequipa, and who were in their mid-seventies or older at the time of my fieldwork. I owe a great debt to Segundo Rosas, Maximo Loayza, and Dario Benavides, whose help was

crucial in this aspect of the research, but perhaps most of all to Silvio Rubio, now deceased.

11. Landlords also used the communal water of Chaucavilca, but on different terms. Some of them owned eriazos that had no private rights, and that should have had no rights to communal water either, if, as I was told, they were bought as eriazos after the Water Code was passed. But by renting these fields out to members of the community—sharecropping them—the owners were able to get communal water.

12. Of course, the decrees had also facilitated the establishment of the major estates and their truly private rights. The point is that, even after the Water Code was passed, water continued to be privatized, de facto and by force, as the estate owners acquired more and more community land.

13. I cannot say for certain when the acquisition of land titles by comuneros began. I have seen a few deeds that date to the 1930's. It is possible that some people procured them as early as the late 19th century, but any such titles would have had to be updated to bring the owners' rights under the Water Code.

14. The real muleteers (arrieros) were the hacendados, who had herds of those expensive animals that few peasants could afford, and who ran the wool business. But the men who worked for them were also known as muleteers (*arrieros campesinos*). See Montoya et al. 1979: 80–87 on the importance of this group in long-distance trade in Ayacucho.

15. Because of the subdivision of the major estates, a day of water was often shared by more than one hacendado, together with any smallholders to whom they had sold rights.

16. The administrator appointed in 1941 was Segundo Rosas. He was still alive when I did my fieldwork and, at the age of 93, remarkably lucid. Then living in Arequipa, he was one of my best informants. I also worked closely with Max Loayza, who was one of Segundo Rosas's assistants during the reform process. It is important to note, for purposes of future discussion, that both were members of the same political party, APRA.

17. The Yawarcocha tank was built by the comuneros of Quillunsa and sharecroppers from the major estates. The hacendados helped to finance it, as the Water Code required, but of course did not participate in the work itself.

18. See Montoya 1980: 111; and Montoya et al. 1979: 75–79 for observations on the change in the campo's role in southern Ayacucho, where conditions and events were very similar.

19. My informants never pinpointed the time of the campo's fall, but it clearly happened in the 1940's. They described the change in the course of talking about the decrease in *cargo* participation and the general decline of traditional authority in the villages, and about how it was that the major fiestas in the district came to be held only by landlords and other wealthy members of each community. Their information has interesting implications for the debate on the economic effects of the *cargo* system.

20. The punishments for water theft included incarceration in a tiny cell or sweat box (the *calabazo*), confinement in stocks (the *cepo*), and public floggings. I know of one occasion in Tomepampa when this kind of mistreatment resulted in a campesino's death.

21. For similar findings on two villages on the western slope, see Gelles 1984, 1986, 1994; and for the nearby Colca valley, see Treacy 1994a, b; Guillet 1992, 1994; and Paerre-

gaard 1994. In fact, most studies in the literature have documented such centralized or "unified" systems.

22. According to Ministry of Agriculture data for 1987, 281.7 ha of the district's 563.5 ha were supposedly in pasture at that time.

23. The information was based on "auto-evaluos," self-declarations by each landowner. Although the landholding figures themselves may be quite inaccurate, I cannot think of reasons why the percentages listed in alfalfa would have been distorted.

24. I worked over a period of several months in 1987 with the former sharecroppers who now own the land. The information they gave me on conditions on the estate was quite consistent with what I learned from farmers in other areas, so I am sure that this fundo is representative in most ways. Although it is a small property, it was run in the same manner as the larger estates. Apart from the ownership of the land, surprisingly little had changed on the estate. Shortly before the agrarian reform, the landlord had sold all but 2 of his 6 topos to keep them from being expropriated by the state. Most of that land had been bought by the sharecroppers, and the owner had eventually sold the other 2 topos to another former hacendado. In terms of landscaping, the distribution of terraces (andenes) and sloped fields (canchones) was much the same as when it had been a single property.

25. Most people in the valley know how the grama got its start in the area because Apurimac was one of the regions where local hacendados bought cattle. The grass came directly to Cotahuasi from there and spread very quickly. Ironically enough, the landlord who introduced it to Peru was serving as Minister of Agriculture in Lima at the time.

26. In the case of Wakajara, the only big reservoir in the district, campesinos who lived near the tank stored and released the water. After the reservoir was built in 1942, the hacendados hired for a small wage the family who oversaw the herding hacienda of Huambo, where the tank was located. The comuneros of Quillunsa also benefited from the arrangement, since the tank was operated every day, but apparently they did not have to pay anything for it.

27. The landlords spoke Quechua quite well and typically used it when talking to their workers.

28. The Quechua terms for a daughter-in-law and a son-in-law (*nuera* and *yerno*, respectively, in Spanish) are *q'achun* and *qata*. Kinship terms are the same here as in Huaynacotas and Pampamarca, again identical to those recorded by Sato 1981 in the Cusco area.

29. Since the grama seeds are transported in animal dung, keeping animals out of the fields is the only means of avoiding the spread of the grass altogether. Both means of combating it are quite labor-intensive and expensive.

30. Lira 1970: 42 defines both wayka and waykilla as "a fight in which many intervene against one; an unequal attack"; he defines the verb *waykay* as encompassing this same concept, as well as another, seemingly unrelated usage: "to work at a single thing with the aim of mastering [finishing] it." Cusihuamán's (1976: 163) definitions are closer to the mark, with the nouns defined as a "joint final action," and the verb defined as "to intervene in someone's defense; reinforce; collaborate; to carry out a task among various [people]."

31. Hacienda workers in colonial Cotahuasi were clearly no more than serfs. Local

people refer back to the tradition of *servidumbre* or *pongaje* (also know as *colonaje*) that existed in "ancient" times.

32. Of course, local peasants went through an earlier, centuries-long period when they had to acquire cash to make their tribute payments by selling some of their produce and animals every year. In this sense, there was nothing new about handling money. But that era had ended long before, probably by the middle of the 19th century, when monetary tribute, now known as the "indigenous contribution," was finally abolished successfully by the national government.

33. Montoya 1980 provides a detailed account of how landlords in Puquio, to the north and west of Cotahuasi in Ayacucho, gave loans and manipulated interest rates in such a way as to keep campesinos in perpetual debt, a state that he elsewhere calls "restricted servitude" (Montoya et al. 1979: 93–94).

34. Presumably, mink'a had originally been a form of service to the kuracas (Mayer 1974a, b; Fonseca Martel 1974). Ayllu members had worked the kuracas' fields upon request in exchange for food and drink, but also in return for the services that the chiefs provided for the community. Those services were clearly more numerous and significant than anything the comuneros ever got from the hacendados, who made them poor and kept them in that condition. Furthermore, the differences in status were of a different nature, since the kuracas were of the same ethnicity, were ayllu members, and even participated, at least ritually or symbolically, in the work itself. Thus, even though there was certainly a similarity of form, the two were very different arrangements in terms of content.

Chapter 6: A Failure of Good Intentions

1. On the 1969 reform, see, among others, Lowenthal 1975; Matos Mar & Mejia 1980; Caballero 1981; McClintock & Lowenthal 1983; Mayer 1988; Montoya 1989; and Seligmann 1995.

2. The total of 36 principal hacendados in the province as a whole is based on lists compiled with various people. Everyone seemed to agree that these were the dominant families, and that their property was of roughly this size, including the eight former landlords with whom I worked closely.

3. The census of 1961 (published in 1968) includes no information on how the data were compiled, so that the figures are hard to interpret. The landowners, who furnished the information on their own, may have had reason to understate the extent of their holdings.

4. The proportion of former hacienda land is a rough estimate, based on the data I collected on the estates of Piro, Colcan, Comunidad, Capaya, Aquerana, Salcán Grande and Salcán Chico, Saucay, San Martín, Cascahuilca, and Waminsa, all of Chacaylla; several properties in Quillunsa, Acobamba, Pitahuasi, Cachana, Pumacocha, Cancha, Pampacancha; and a large part of Chaucavilca. The total area is the Ministry of Agriculture's figure.

5. Furthermore, rice production had by now expanded from Camaná all the way up the Majes valley, largely replacing sugarcane and providing local campesinos with a new source of seasonal employment (see Tsunekawa 1986).

6. Here, of course, as elsewhere in the Andes, where most households have at least one member living elsewhere, some of the subsistence crop is usually sent to the city, to

lower that person's cost of living, and money is periodically sent back. But these city dwellers are still counted as village residents in the censuses.

7. In the early 1960's, the National Liberation Army (ENL), a guerrilla organization financed by Cuba, established a "cell" in the valley. Its four leaders, one of whom ultimately became a compadre and good informant of mine, were active in fomenting resistance, though not rebellion, among the campesinos until they were imprisoned and tortured in 1964.

8. The APRA party, populists who opposed the oligarchy and the rural aristocracy, had steadily gained strength during the 1940's and 1950's, even winning a local election, only to be cheated out of the victory. The local Apristas were mostly aspiring middle proprietors, sons who were not from the richest hacendado families and whose inheritance had been meager.

9. Consider, for example, the owner of the hacienda of Acobamba, a former governor of the province—and a good friend and informant. One of the few who continued on in the wool trade, he increased the amount of land planted in alfalfa from 36% in the late 1950's to roughly 50% percent in the early 1960's and to over 75% just before the reform.

10. The reform law declared it a crime to attempt to subvert the reform through bribery, threats, or the dissemination of false information, and the penalties were harsh.

11. According to the law (art. 186), a mayordomo could acquire his usufruct plot but not any of the alfalfa fields. Most of the ones I met ultimately did acquire their plots but several continued to seek the advantages of working for a landlord. There seems to have been a lot of continuity, in part because it had been common for the patrón to give a *chacra* to his mayordomo as a reward for years of service.

12. On the big estates, partidarios typically worked one watered field and one or more eriazos. This was not true on the smaller properties, which did not usually include any adjacent dry-farmed land.

13. This was not so much the case for the larger landowners, simply because I knew most of them and their wives and was able to take their wives' property into account in compiling Tables 4 and 5.

14. I am indebted to three research assistants, Elena Honderman Motta, Rey Chirinos Monga, and Lolo Mamani Dada, for help in carrying out a survey of the percentage of land planted in alfalfa vs. food crops, the number and kinds of livestock, the sources of monetary income, and the forms of labor recruitment. My sample of 7.4% of the district's 667 landowners was not statistically significant. Neither was it random since I could only include people who were willing to talk with me at length. I limited my sampled universe, in a manner fairly representative of the district as a whole, by confining myself to Cotahuasi and the two former indigenous communities of Reyparte and Quillunsa. Nor was I able, with such a small sample, to compose the strata exactly in proportion to their presence in the overall population, since that would have left me with too few large landowners, people in whom I was particularly interested.

15. The observation that the elite equate manual labor with a loss of status is of course a generalization, and as with all such sweeping statements, there are significant exceptions to the "rule." I know two large landowners and members of the elite society who now, after the reform, work their own land, very hard, alongside their peons. Here I am referring to the tradition that is said to have predominated from the colonial era

down to the reform, when labor became scarce enough to force some hacendados to change their attitude.

16. This man, one of the leaders of the National Liberation Army during the 1960's, has served many times as a water distributor, but that is not an elected office.

17. The text definition of the term peasant corresponds well with that given by Trouillot (1988), which focuses on the distinctive characteristics of "the peasant labor process," in which a household or family is the production unit. Michael Kearney (1996) takes the extreme political economist position when he asserts that the term has outlived its usefulness, arguing, based on the Mexican case, that hardly any so-called peasants are significantly self-reliant anymore. But the country that he is generalizing from has had at least 50 years of the "bracero" program of heavy labor migration into the neighboring U.S.

18. Not all of the "rich" campesinos in Sánchez's study engage in reciprocity. Several hardly practice it at all, engaging only in what he calls "ayni" with their parents or children, an arrangement that, in my view, is not ayni at all but rather family labor. The majority of their extra-household work is clearly done by peons (see Sánchez 1982: 171, 179–83).

19. The local peasant association, the Federación Campesina, which was established in the reform years, was not much of a political force when I was there. The members evidently favored the APRA candidates in 1985, who won the provincial and national elections; they did not put forward any candidates of their own. This changed in 1990, after the political violence of 1988, when the president of the federation, Mario Ramirez, running as an Independent, was elected mayor of the province. The first campesino ever to hold provincial office, he was captured and executed by Sendero Luminoso in 1991.

20. Nearly all of the "peons" working for the bigger landowners in Cotahuasi were comuneros from villages like Huaynacotas and Pampamarca who were bent on earning only enough cash to finance a trip elsewhere. This clearly is the predominant pattern.

Chapter 7: Failure Again

1. Montoya et al. 1979 briefly assesses some of the 1969 water law's impact in a district in Ayacucho, where its effects were obviously substantial. Barbara Lynch and her co-authors (1986) discuss what they call the "bureaucratic transition" in a district in Cajamarca, but without looking closely at the law itself. Other authors—Treacy (1994a, b), Gelles (1994, 1999), and Guillet (1992, 1994)—discuss the Ministry of Agriculture's largely unsuccessful efforts to implement the law in the Colca valley (also see Mitchell & Guillet 1994). But, in general, research has tended to focus on communities that never had a tradition of private water ownership and were minimally affected by the reform.

2. As things worked out, the provincial user group, the *junta de usuarios*, played little part in local operations. It now has very few important functions.

3. Since the inundation method was often used on terraces too, as it still is today, a 20 percent drop in the watering time is probably a conservative estimate

4. Cotahuasi is a political district, but not an irrigation district. It is simply a community belonging to the Irrigation District of Ocona.

5. Apristas had also led the first attempt at reform, in 1941.

6. I do not mean to say that these particular landlords—three of my best friends and informants—were necessarily guilty of seeking favoritism and the other kinds of privilege to be described below. Not all former hacendados did this.

7. Even though the drought has eased and perhaps even ended since the period of my fieldwork, that has not eliminated the problem of water scarcity and the resulting conflict. In 1999, after a year of adequate rains, the main cycle in Cotahuasi district was 45 days, and emergency measures were still in effect.

8. Two students from a local technical school, one of whom was my research assistant, gathered much of the 1988 data and did their own report on the hydraulic system as a thesis project (Bellido and Chirinos ms). I had measured most of the water flows during the previous dry year, 1987, or assisted in such measurement, and they did this, maybe more accurately than I had been able to do, during a more normal year. In both cases, a current-meter was used for the main canal just below the tanks.

9. Again, these are Ministry of Agriculture estimates for the alfalfa production in each sector.

10. A new administrator took over when the drought began in 1978 and served for the next eight years, up until the first year of my fieldwork. He tried, unsuccessfully, to continue the policies of his predecessor.

11. Nearly all of the ethnographic studies published to date show that the ministry is wrong in its assumption that crops can thrive if they are given only the amounts of water they are thought to "need." Frequencies of one to three months are common (see, e.g., Treacy 1994a, b; Gelles 1994, 1995; Guillet 1992; and Seligmann & Bunker 1994).

12. The various user groups have consistently voted for the Choccocco Project.

13. There are roughly 100 people in the neighborhood of Santa Ana, where most of the town's peasants and former tenants reside. It is extremely poor.

14. Interestingly, when, after a long absence, I was finally able to go back to the valley in 1997, I found that the stalemate was over: the Tomepampa-Piro project had been resurrected, and the canal was halfway completed. This had happened despite the fact that the Quillunseños had won out in their refusal to contribute. The water-users of lower Cotahuasi sector had appealed to a "benevolent patron" (i.e., the state) for financial help and been given a large grant that was contingent on their first coming up with a rather large contribution themselves, which they did. The canal was being built with wage labor, part of a local program of temporary employment sponsored by CORDEA. It is now nearly finished.

15. Strengthening the faena tradition was the basic approach toward rural development of Belaúnde's Popular Action party. It was adopted by Cooperación Popular, the government's development agency, which continued to work in the valley during the subsequent period of APRA rule. It was also adopted by CORDEA, the regional organization that designed and helped to finance the construction projects.

16. Art. 20 does require all users to "contribute proportionally to the conservation and maintenance of . . . hydraulic structures [and] other communal installations, likewise to the construction of necessary ones" (CEPES 1984: 19), but nowhere does the law stipulate what "proportionally" means.

17. As one Cotahuasino put it to me, referring to the barbecue as a bribe, "Se compró con la grasa, con la picantada" (He was bought with fat, with a barbecue).

18. The Armanca tank's outflow is already shared by three sectors and cannot be made to stretch any further, and there is no need to divide the water of Qochacallán, which serves only one sector and a small part of another.

19. Far from solving the existing problems, the 1989 regulations seemed to me to have made things worse and may have even created new problems.

Chapter 8: Water into Blood

1. The province of La Unión has the highest infant mortality and illiteracy rates, and the lowest per capita income, in the department of Arequipa, according to reports done by CORDEA. It also has the least area connected by roads and the highest per capita consumption of alcohol.

2. The Shining Path's activities in the surrounding area were recounted to me by people from Huaynacotas, migrants who lived in Arequipa.

3. The wording of the threatening letters was different from that used in the previous ones, according to a friend, the secretary of the local *fiscal*, who participated in the ensuing investigation.

4. "Sinchi" is a Quechua term meaning, among other things, terrible, extreme, or ferocious—an appropriate name for members of a death squad. I had dealt with soldiers before, but I had never encountered anything like these professional torturers and killers, trained at the U.S. Army's School of the Americas.

5. For thorough descriptions of the Senderistas, see, among others, Degregori 1989; Starn 1991, 1992; Palmer 1992; Poole & Renique 1992; and Gorriti 1999.

6. I will refrain from using "his or her" everywhere in this discussion; apart from being clumsy, the subject at hand has to do almost entirely with males.

7. My impression of the lack of support for Sendero among campesinos is based not only on the few conversations that I did have with them, but also on later events. Long after the attack on Cotahuasi, the guerrillas briefly took over Alca and Tomepampa, where the most abusive landlords are said to have lived before the reform. They put the more prominent people in each community on trial, asking the campesinos if they were abusive. No one was executed because the answer was no in each case, which was definitely not true of some of the accused.

8. My own sympathies were mostly with García and the Apristas on this issue. García had made his stand very publicly on the foreign debt, half of which had been spent by previous Peruvian military dictators and other strong-arm governments on armaments (part of the U.S.-inspired politics of the Cold War), but he was left standing alone by the other leaders of South American countries. Things clearly could have turned out differently, given the will to make together what I am sure will turn out to have been a very necessary stand.

9. I must admit that at one time I expressed my belief that significant changes had indeed occurred (see Trawick 1994a: 39), though I also made a point of saying that I was not altogether sure that this was the case.

Conclusion

1. As I have shown elsewhere (Trawick 1994b: 206–8), based on what I observed in Pampamarca, one can easily see how the moiety system became distorted in the distant past by a widespread breakdown of endogamy within these social units (i.e., by intermarriage between them, a change that was probably made necessary by the population collapse). Gelles 1995 documents the effects in the Colca valley. The resulting change in inheritance patterns ultimately created a situation where the moieties were no longer distinct territorial and hydraulic units, as apparently they once were. The resulting intermixed pattern of moiety, and therefore of ayllu, landholdings, as in Pampamarca, has

helped to create a dispersed distribution pattern that has consequences for water conservation and vigilance within the system.

2. The main problem with my hypothesis is that it seems to be contradicted by other chroniclers (see Mitchell 1980). In discussing the Inca agricultural cycle, Bernabé Cobo (1964 [1653]: 120–21), for example, stated that all the land in the empire was divided up among the Sun (the state religion), the Inca (the state itself), and the peasantry, and that the peasantry always cultivated the land in that order. Since the planting order determines the watering order, this would seem to indicate that the contiguous sequence described by Garcilaso could not have been followed—assuming, of course, that the various lands relied on the same water sources. Climatic and ecological constraints strictly determine the planting order, and these would have precluded the hierarchical sequence of agricultural work, so that Cobo and the others must be wrong (Mitchell 1980). My research in Cotahuasi valley on the location of the imperial lands, however, confirmed the early observations of John Murra (1960) and the more recent findings of William Denevan for the Colca valley (in Denevan, ed., 1986), and lends support to the assertions of many other ethnohistorians and archaeologists (e.g., D'Altroy 1987; LeVine 1987). Wherever possible, the Incas opened up new lands along the valley bottoms for cultivation and the extraction of labor tribute, as in Collota. They did this by tapping new and previously unused water sources—the rivers. These lands had their own abundant water source and, being warm and virtually invulnerable to frost, they could have been sown at any time, perhaps first in the sequence, as Cobo and others said, so that they did not interfere with local planting and watering cycles in any way.

3. See Guaman Pomas de Ayala's (1978 [1615]) observations at pp. 246, 356, 845, 1040, and 1237.

4. On small irrigation systems in various parts of the world, see Glick 1970; Hunt & Hunt 1976; Coward 1979; Hunt 1992; Ostrom 1990; and Ostrom & Gardner 1993.

5. On irrigation in the Colca valley, see Valderrama & Escalante 1986, 1988; Treacy 1990, 1994a, b; Gelles 1994; Guillet 1992; Paerregaard 1994; and for the Cañete, see Mayer & Fonseca 1979; Fonseca 1983.

6. I strongly suspect that "irrigation by crop"—that is, watering crops one at a time, so that each in effect has its own separate cycle—is a fairly recent adoption. It is very wasteful and is not compatible with the kind of system described by Garcilaso. It may have been introduced by the Ministry of Agriculture; there are several indications, both in Guillet 1992 and in Gelles 1994, 2000, that the bureaucracy began to interfere locally as early as the 1940's.

7. The landlords were never able to establish estates in some communities in the Andes, as we have seen. However, this did not necessarily lead to a continuity of tradition and a "comic" rather than a tragic result. It was sometimes the native elites who adopted the new practices and set a similar sequence of events in motion. An example is provided by Andagua in the neighboring province of Castilla, near the Arcata mine, the one attacked and looted by Sendero Luminoso in 1988. During the 17th and 18th centuries, a small group of landlords was living in that community, but the dominant figures were a group of kuracas, of an ethnic group different from the local Indians, who were heavily involved in long-distance trade as muleteers. Salomon's (1987) account of the extirpation of idolatry among them provides a glimpse, I think, of a situation where hierarchy and

inequity were probably emerging in irrigation, in a context of depopulation, but among indigenous people.

8. See Montoya et al. 1979; Fuenzalida et al. 1982; Skar 1981; Bunker & Seligmann 1986, 1994; Mitchell 1976, 1991a, b, 1994; and Lynch et al. 1986 for discussions of the struggle for water in different kinds of communities.

9. For studies of autonomously organized and managed irrigation systems elsewhere, see, among others, Maass & Anderson 1978; Coward 1979, 1980; Ostrom 1990, 1992; Hunt 1992; and Ostrom & Gardner 1993.

10. I hope I have made it clear that not all of the larger landowners try to manipulate the law in their favor. I know several who seem very conscientious and who apparently observe the rules, just as I know some campesinos who probably were not and do not. With regard to water, most people in the district are involved, and implicated to some extent, in a conflict whose aspects and dimensions they do not fully understand.

11. During work I did as a consultant for both banks on water reform in several South American countries, I made the results of my research available to policy makers, together with the proposals I have presented in this book (see Trawick 1995). In large part, my purpose in writing this book was to bring those proposals to a wider audience, particularly in Peru, where the matter of privatization has not, to this writing at least, come up for public debate.

Bibliography

The following abbreviations are used in this Bibliography and the citations. Publications issued by ministries or other official sources are listed under Peru.

ADC   Archivo Historico Departamental del Cusco
CEPES   Centro Peruano de Estudios Sociales, Lima
DESCO   Centre de Estudios y Promoción del Desarollo, Lima
DL   Decreto Ley
DNE   Dirección Nacional de Estadistica
ONERN   Oficina Nacional de Evaluación de Recursos Naturales

Acuña, Francisco de. 1965. "Relación Hecha por el Corregidor de los Chumbivilcas, Don Francisco de Acuña (1586)." In *Relaciones Geograficas de Indias—Perú*, Tomo 183. Ed. Marcos Jimenez de la Espada, pp. 310–25. Madrid: Biblioteca de Autores Españoles.

Adams, Richard N. 1975. *Energy and Structure*. Austin: University of Texas Press.

Alberti, Giorgio, and Enrique Mayer, eds. 1974. *Reciprocidad e Intercambio en los Andes Peruanos*. Lima: Instituto de Estudios Peruanos.

Allen, Catherine. 1988. *The Hold Life Has: Culture and Identity in an Andean Community*. Washington, D.C.: Smithsonian Institution Press.

Appleby, Gordon. 1976. "Export Monoculture and Regional Social Structure in Puno, Peru." In *Regional Analysis*, Vol. II: *Social Systems*. Ed. Carol A. Smith, pp. 291–308. New York: Academic Press.

Archivo Historico Departamental del Cusco (ADC). 1785a. "Expediente contra la Cacica Juana Vilcapi de Cotahuasi por Usurpación de Tributos," Intendencia, Real Hacienda, No. 165.

———. 1785b. "Expediente Relativo a la Queja del Subdelegado de Chumbivilcas del Cura de Toro por Haber Retenido Cantidad de Tributos," Intendencia, Real Hacienda, No. 517.

———. 1794. "Expediente Relativo a una Mita de Indios por la Hacienda de Francisco Xavier de Boza y su Mina de Orccopampa, en Santo Tomas," Intendencia, Real Hacienda, No. 195.

———. 1830. "Libro Extracto de la Provincia de Chumbivilcas y Condesuyos del Cusco. Indígenas."

———. 1831. "Libro Extracto de la Contribución General de Castas, Provincia de Chumbivilcas y Condesuyos del Cusco."

Arguedas, Jose María. 1969. *Yawar Fiesta, con la Novela y el Problema de las Expresión Literaria en el Perú.* Santiago, Chile: Editorial Universitaria.

Arriaga, Pablo José. 1968 [1621]. *La Extirpación de la Idolatría del Peru.* Tomo CCIX. Biblioteca de Autores Espanoles, Madrid.

Babinski, H. 1883. "Informe sobre las Diferentes Minas de Cobre, Plata y Oro que se Encuentran en la Provincia de La Unión, Departamento de Arequipa." Paper presented at the Sociedad Anónima de las Minas de Oro de Montesclaros y Palmadera, Lima.

Bellido, Beto y Rey Chirinos. n.d. "Estudio Hidrológico de la Sub-cuenca del Distrito de Cotahuasi." Unpublished manuscript, Ministry of Agriculture office, Cotahuasi.

Benavides, María. 1988. "Grupos de Poder en el Valle del Colca (Arequipa), Siglos XVI–XX." In *Sociedad Andina, Pasado y Presente.* Ed. R. Matos Mendieta, pp. 151–77. Lima: Fomciencias.

Bertram, Geoffrey. 1974. "New Thinking on the Peruvian Highland Peasantry," *Pacific Viewpoint,* 15.2: 89–111.

Beyersdorff, Margot. 1984. *Lexico Agropecuario Quechua.* Cusco: Centro de Estudios Rurales Andinos Bartolomé de las Casas.

Bingham, Hiram. 1922. *Inca Land: Explorations in the Highlands of Peru.* New York: Houghton Mifflin.

Boggio, Mario Samamé. 1983. *Minería Peruana,* Tomos IX and X, Vol II. Lima.

Bolin, Inge. 1990. "Upsetting the Power Balance: Cooperation, Competition and Conflict Along an Andean Irrigation System," *Human Organization,* 49.2: 140–48.

———. 1994. "Levels of Autonomy in the Organization of Irrigation in the Highlands of Peru." In Mitchell and Guillet, eds., *Irrigation at High Altitudes,* pp. 233–74.

———. 1998. *Rituals of Respect: The Secret of Survival in the High Peruvian Andes.* Austin: University of Texas Press.

Bolton, Ralph, and Enrique Mayer, eds. 1977. *Andean Kinship and Marriage.* Special Publication No. 7. Washington, D.C.: American Anthropological Association.

Bonavía, Ducio. 1967. "Investigaciones Arqueológicas en el Mantaro Medio," *Revista del Museo Nacional* (Lima), 35: 211–94.

Bonilla, Heraclio. 1987a. "Comunidades Indigenas y Estado Nacion en el Peru." In H. Bonilla, ed., *Comunidades Campesinas,* pp. 13–28.

———, ed. 1987b. *Comunidades Campesinas: Cambios y Permanencias.* Lima: Consejo Nacional de Ciencia y Tecnologia.

Bowlin, John R., and Peter G. Stromberg. 1977. "Representation and Reality in the Study of Culture," *American Anthropologist,* 99.1: 123–34.

Bowman, Isaiah. 1916. *The Andes of Southern Peru.* New York: Greenwood Press.

Brown, Michael F. 1996. "On Resisting Resistance," *American Anthropologist,* 98.4: 729–49.

Brush, Stephen. 1977a. *Mountain, Field and Family: The Human Ecology of an Andean Valley.* College Park: University of Pennsylvania Press.

———. 1977b. "Kinship and Land Use in a Northern Sierra Community." In Bolton and Mayer, eds., *Andean Kinship and Marriage,* pp. 136–52.

Bunker, Stephen, and Linda Seligmann. 1986. "Organización Social y Visión Ecológica de un Sistema de Riego Andino," *Allpanchis,* 27: 149–78.

Burger, Richard, and Frank Asaro. 1977. *Trace Element Analysis of Obsidian Artifacts from the Andes: New Perspectives on Pre-Hispanic Economic Interaction in Peru and Bolivia.*

Berkeley, Calif.: Energy and Environment Division Publication, Berkeley Laboratory.

Burger, Richard, and Lucy Salazar. n.d. "The Second Phase of Investigations at the Initial Period Center of Cardal." Unpublished manuscript.

Burger, Richard, Frank Asaro, Fred Stross, and Paul Trawick. 1998. "The Alca Obsidian Source: The Origin of Raw Material for Cuzco Type Obsidian Artifacts," *Andean Past*, 5: 185–202.

Bustamante, Alberto. 1974. *Legislación sobre Reforma Agraria y Cooperativas*. Lima: Centro de Estudios y Promoción del Desarollo.

Caballero, José María. 1981. *Economía Agraria de la Sierra Peruana antes de la Reforma Agraria de 1969*. Lima: Instituto de Estudios Peruanos.

Cabrera, Luis A. 1987a. "Estudio Hidrológico de las Sub-Cuencas del Rio Cotahuasi, Sector Cotahuasi." Unpublished report to the Corporacion del Desarollo de Arequipa. Arequipa, Peru.

———. 1987b. "Estudio Hidrológico de las Sub-Cuencas del Rio Cotahuasi: Sector Pampamarca-Charcana." Unpublished report to the Corporacion del Desarollo de Arequipa. Arequipa, Peru.

Centro Peruano de Estudios Sociales (CEPES). 1984. "Ley de Aguas," *Informativo Legal Agrario*, No. 18/19.

Chavez, José Antonio. 1982. "Evidencias Archeológicas en la Cuenca del Rio Cotahuasi-Ocona." Tesis Bachiller. Universidad Nacional de San Agustín, Arequipa, Peru.

Cieza de León, Pedro. 1959 [1553]. *The Incas*. Tr. Harriet de Onis. Norman: University of Oklahoma Press.

Clifford, James. 1988. *The Predicament of Culture: Twentieth-Century Ethnography, Literature and Art*. Cambridge, Mass.: Harvard University Press.

Clifford, James, and George E. Marcus. 1986. *Writing Culture: The Poetics and Politics of Ethnography*. Berkeley: University of California Press.

Cobo, Bernabé. 1964 [1653]. *Historia del Nuevo Mundo*. Tomo 92. Madrid: Biblioteca de Autores Españoles.

Concha Contreras, Juan de. 1975. "Relación entre Pastores y Agricultores," *Allpanchis*, 8: 67–102.

Conklin, Harold C. 1957. *Hanunoo Agriculture: A Report on an Integral System of Shifting Cultivation in the Philippines*. Rome: U.N. Food and Agriculture Organization.

———. 1980. *Ethnographic Atlas of Ifugao: A Study of Environment, Culture, and Society in Northern Luzon*. New Haven, Conn.: Yale University Press.

Cook, Noble David. 1975. *Tasa de la Visita General de Francisco de Toledo (1572)*. Lima: Universidad Nacional Mayor de San Marcos.

———. 1981. *Demographic Collapse: Indian Peru, 1520–1620*. New York: Cambridge University Press.

———. 1982. *The People of the Colca Valley: A Population Study*. Boulder, Colo.: Westview Press.

Costa y Cavera, Ramón. 1934. *Legislación de Aguas*. Lima: Biblioteca de Obras Administrativas.

Cotler, Julio. 1968. "La Mecanica de la Dominación Interna y el Cambio Social en el Perú," In *Peru Problema: 5 Ensayos*. Ed. J. Matos Mar and F. Fuenzalida, pp. 145–88. Lima: Instituto de Estudios Peruanos.

Coward, E. Walter. 1979."Principles of Social Organization in an Indigenous Irrigation System," *Human Organization*, 38.1: 28–36.

———. 1980. *Irrigation and Agricultural Development in Asia: Perspectives from the Social Sciences*. Ithaca, N.Y.: Cornell University Press.

Cusihuamán G., Antonio. 1976. *Diccionario Quechua Cuzco-Collao*. Lima: Instituto de Estudios Peruanos.

D'Altroy, Terence. 1987. "Introduction," *Ethnohistory*, 34.1: 1–13.

Davies, Thomas M. 1970. *Indian Integration in Peru: A Half Century of Experience, 1900–1948*. Lincoln: University of Nebraska Press.

Degregori, Carlos Ivan. 1989. "Que Difícil es ser Díos: Ideología y Violencia Política en Sendero Luminoso," *Allpanchis*, 34: 117–40.

Delran, C. Guido. 1981. *Historia Rural del Perú*. Cusco: Centro de Estudios Rurales Andinos Bartolomé de las Casas.

Denevan, William M., ed. 1986. "The Cultural Ecology, Archaeology and History of Terracing and Terrace Abandonment in the Colca Valley of Southern Peru." Technical report to the National Science Foundation and the National Geographic Society. Department of Geography, University of Wisconsin, Madison.

Denevan, William M., Kent Mathewson, and Gregory Knapp. 1987. *Pre-hispanic Agricultural Fields in the Andean Region*. Oxford, Eng.: BAR International Series 359(i).

Dollfus, Oliver. 1981. *El Reto del Espacio Andino*. Instituto de Estudios Peruanos. Publication Series Perú Problema 20.

Donkin, R. A. 1979. *Agricultural Terracing in the Aboriginal New World*. Viking Fund Publication in Anthropology, No. 56. Wenner-Gren Foundation for Anthropological Research.

Earls, John, and Irene Silverblatt. 1978. "Investigaciones Interdisciplinarias en Moray, Cusco." In *Etnohistoria y Antropolgía Andina*. Ed. M. Koth and A. Castelli, pp. 117–22. Lima: Museo Nacional de Historia.

Erasmus, Charles. 1965. "The Occurrence and Disappearance of Reciprocal Farm Labor in Latin America." In *Contemporary Cultures and Societies of Latin America*. Ed. D. Heath and R. N. Adams. New York: Random House.

———. 1977. *In Search of the Common Good*. New York: Free Press.

Escobar, Arturo. 1995. *Encountering Development: The Making and Unmaking of the Third World*. Princeton, N.J.: Princeton University Press.

Figueroa, Adolfo. 1982. "Production and Market Exchange in Peasant Economies: The Case of the Southern Highlands in Peru." In D. Lehman, ed., *Ecology and Exchange*, pp. 122-56.

———. 1984. *Capitalist Development and Peasant Economy in Peru*. Cambridge, Eng.: Cambridge University Press.

Fisher, John R. 1975. *Matrícula de los Mineros del Peru: 1790*. Lima: Universidad Nacional Mayor de San Marcos.

Flores-Galindo, Alberto. 1977. *Arequipa y el Sur Andino: Siglo XVIII*. Lima: Editorial Horizonte.

Flores-Ochoa, Jorge. 1968. *Pastoralists of the Andes: The Alpaca Herders of Paratía*. Philadelphia: Institute for the Study of Human Issues.

Fonseca Martel, Cesar. 1974. "Modalidades de la Minka." In Alberti and Mayer, eds., *Reciprocidad*, pp. 86–109.

————. 1983. "El Control Comunal del Agua en la Cuenca del Río Cañete," *Allpanchis*, 22: 61–74.

Foucault, Michel. 1991. "Questions of Method." In *The Foucault Effect: Studies in Governmentality.* Ed. Graham Burchell, Colin Gordon, and Peter Miller, pp. 73–86. Chicago: University of Chicago Press.

Fuenzalida, Fernando, T. Valiente, J. L. Villarán, J. Golte, C. I. Degrogori, and J. Casaverde. 1982. *El Desafío de Huayopampa: Comuneros y Empresarios.* Lima: Instituto de Estudios Peruanos.

Fuji Tatsuhiko and Hiroyasu Tomoeda. 1981. "Chacra, Laime y Auguénidos: Explotación Ambiental de una Comunidad Andina." In Masuda, ed., *Estudios Etnográficos*, pp. 33–64.

Galdos, Guillermo. 1985. *Kuntisuyu.* Arequipa, Perú: Edición Universitaria.

————. 1988. "Naciones Oriundas en Expansión y Mitmaqs en el Valle de Arequipa," Archivo Departamental de Arequipa, Peru.

Garcilaso de la Vega, Inca. 1961 [1616]. *The Incas: The Royal Commentaries of the Inca.* New York: Orion Press.

————. 1966 [1609, 1617]. *Comentarios Reales de los Incas.* Vols. 1 and 2. Ed. H. V. Livermore. Austin: University of Texas Press.

Geertz, Clifford. 1973. *The Interpretation of Cultures.* New York: Basic Books.

————. 1995. *After the Fact: Two Countries, Four Decades, One Anthropologist.* Cambridge, Mass.: Harvard University Press.

Gelles, Paul. 1984. "Agua, Faenas y Organización Comunal: San Pedro de Casta," *Revista Antropológica del Departamento de Ciencias Sociales, Pontífica Universidad Catolica del Perú,* 2: 305–34.

————. 1986. "Sociedades Hidraúlicas en los Andes: Algunas Perspectivas desde Huarochirí," *Allpanchis*, 27: 99–148.

————. 1994. "Channels of Power, Fields of Contention: The Politics of Irrigation and Land Recovery in an Andean Peasant Community." In Mitchell and Guillet, eds., *Irrigation at High Altitudes*, pp. 233–74.

————. 1995. "Equilibrium and Extraction: Dual Organization in the Andes," *American Ethnologist*, 22.4: 710–42.

————. 2000. *Water and Power in Highland Peru: The Cultural Politics of Irrigation and Development.* Brunswick, N.J.: Rutgers University Press, 1991.

Gitlitz, John S. 1977. "Impressions of the Peruvian Agrarian Reform," *Journal of Inter-American Studies,* 13.3–4: 456–74.

Glave, Luís M. 1987. "Comunidades Campesinas en el Sur Andino, Siglo XVII." In H. Bonilla, ed., *Comunidades Campesinas,* pp. 61–94.

Glick, Thomas, F. 1970. *Irrigation and Society in Medieval Valencia.* Cambridge, Mass.: Harvard University Press.

Golte, Jurgen. 1980. *La Racionalidad de la Organización Andina.* Lima: Instituto de Estudios Peruanos.

Gonzales de Olarte, Efraín. 1984. *Economía de la Comunidad Campesina: Aproximación Regional.* Lima: Instituto de Estudios Peruanos.

————. 1987. *Inflacion y Campesinado: Comunidades y Microregiones Frente a la Crisis.* Lima: Instituto de Estudios Peruanos.

Gootenberg, Paul. 1991. "Population and Ethnicity in Early Republican Peru: Some Revisions," *Latin American Research Review,* 26.3: 109–57.

Gorritti, Gustavo. 1999. *The Shining Path: A History of Millenarian War in Peru*. Chapel Hill: University of North Carolina Press.

Gose, Peter. 1994. *Deathly Waters and Hungry Mountains: Agrarian Ritual and Class Formation in an Andean Town*. Buffalo, N.Y.: University of Toronto Press.

Grieshaber, Erwin. 1979. "Hacienda-Indian Community Relations and Indian Acculturation: An Historiographic Essay," *Latin American Research Review*, 14.3: 107–28.

Guaman Poma de Ayala, Felipe. 1978 [1613]. *Letter to a King: A Peruvian Chief's Account of Life Under the Incas and Under Spanish Rule*. New York: Dutton.

Guillet, David. 1981. "Land Tenure, Ecological Zone and Agricultural Regime in the Central Andes," *American Ethnologist*, 8.1: 139–56.

———. 1987. "Terracing and Irrigation in the Peruvian Highlands," *Current Anthropology*, 28.4: 1–35.

———. 1992. *Covering Ground: Communal Water Management and the State in the Peruvian Highlands*. Ann Arbor: University of Michigan Press.

———. 1994. "Canal Irrigation and the State: The 1969 Water Law and Irrigation Systems of the Colca Valley of Southern Peru." In Mitchell and Guillet, eds., *Irrigation at High Altitudes*, pp. 167–88.

Harvey, David. 1990. *The Condition of Postmodernity: An Enquiry into the Origins of Cultural Change*. Cambridge, Eng.: Blackwell.

Hendriks, Jan. 1986. "Distribución de Aguas en Sistemas de Riego," *Allpanchis*, 28: 185–210.

Hunt, Robert C. 1988. "Size and Structure of Authority in Canal Irrigation Systems," *Journal of Anthropological Research*, 44.4: 335–55.

———. 1989. "Appropriate Social Organization?—Water User Associations in Bureaucratic Canal Irrigation Systems," *Human Organization*, 48.1: 79–89.

———. 1992. "Inequality and Equity in Irrigation Communities." Paper presented at the Third Common Property Conference of the International Association for the Study of Common Property, Washington, D.C., Sept. 17–20.

Hunt, Robert, and Eva Hunt. 1976. "Canal Irrigation and Local Social Organization," *Current Anthropology*, 17: 129–57.

Hyslop, John. 1984. *The Inka Road System*. New York: Academic Press.

Inamura Tetsuya. 1981. "Adaptación Ambiental de los Pastores Altoandinos en el Sur del del Perú: Simbiosis Económico-social con los Agricultores." In Masuda, ed., *Estudios Etnográficos*, pp. 65–84.

———. 1986. "Relaciones Estructurales entre Pastores y Agricultores de un Distrito Altoandino en el Sur del Peru." In Masuda, ed., *Efnografía e Historia*, pp. 141–90.

Isbell, Billie Jean. 1977. "Kuyag: Those Who Love Me—An Analysis of Andean Kinship and Reciprocity in a Ritual Context." In Bolton and Mayer, *Andean Kinship*, pp. 81–105.

———. 1978. *To Defend Ourselves: Ecology and Ritual in an Andean Village*. Austin: University of Texas Press.

Isbell, William. 1988. "City and State in Middle Horizon Huari." In *Peruvian Prehistory: An Overview of Inca and Pre-Inca Society*. Ed. R. W. Keatinge, pp. 164–89. New York: Cambridge University Press.

———. 1991. "Huari Administration and the Orthogonal Cellular Architecture Horizon." In *Huari Administrative Structure: Prehistoric Monumental Architecture and*

State Government. Ed. W. Isbell and G. McEwan, pp. 293–316. Washington, D.C.: Dumbarton Oaks Research Library and Collection.

Isbell, William, and Gordon McEwan. 1991 "A History of Huari Studies and Introduction to Current Interpretations." In *Huari Administrative Structure: Prehistoric Monumental Architecture and State Government*. Ed. W. Isbell and G. McEwan, pp. 1–17. Washington, D.C.: Dumbarton Oaks Research Library and Collection.

Jennings, Justin, and Willy Yepez Alvarez. n.d. "Architecture, Local Elites, and Imperial Entanglements: The Impact of the Wari Empire on the Cotahuasi Valley of Peru." Unpublished manuscript. Department of Anthropology, University of California, Santa Barbara.

Jurado, Joel. 1989. "Tendencias Estructurales del Campesinado en el Perú," *Allpanchis*, 34: 63–116.

Kearney, Michael. 1996. *Reconceptualizing the Peasantry: Anthropology in Global Perspective*. Boulder, Colo.: Westview Press.

Keith, R. G. 1976. *Conquest and Agrarian Change: The Emergence of the Hacienda System on the Peruvian Coast*. Cambridge, Mass.: Harvard University Press.

Kelly, William. 1982. *Water Control in Tokugawa Japan: Irrigation Organization in a Japanese River Basin, 1600–1870*. Cornell University East Asia Papers, 31. Ithaca, N.Y.: Cornell University China-Japan Program.

———. 1983. "Concepts in the Anthropological Study of Irrigation," *American Anthropologist*, No. 85: 880–86.

Kubler, George. 1952. *The Indian Caste of Peru, 1795–1940*. Washington, D.C.: Smithsonian Institution.

Lambert, Bernd. 1977. "Bilaterality in the Andes." In Bolton and Mayer, eds., *Andean Kinship*, pp. 1–27.

Lansing, J. Stephen. 1991. *Priests and Programmers: Technologies of Power in the Engineered Landscape of Bali*. Princeton, N.J.: Princeton University Press.

Leach, Edmund. 1961. *Pul Eliya*. Oxford: Oxford University Press.

Lehman, David, ed. 1982. "Ecology and Exchange in the Andes." In *Andean Societies and the Theory of Peasant Economy*, pp. 1–26. New York: Cambridge University Press.

Levillier, Robert, ed. 1925. *Gobernantes del Perú: Cartas y Papeles Siglo XVI*. Tomo IX. Madrid.

Levine, Terry Y. 1987. "Inka Labor Service at the Regional Levels: The Functional Reality," *Ethnohistory*, 34.1: 14–46.

Lewis, Herbert S. 1998. "The Misrepresentation of Anthropology and Its Consequences," *American Anthropologist*, 100.3: 716–31.

Lira, Jorge A. 1970. *Diccionario Kkechua Espanol*. Cusco: Edición Popular.

Llano Zapata, José. 1904 [1761]. *Memorias Historico-Físico-Apologéticas de la America Meridional*. Lima: Imprenta de San Pedro.

Long, Norman, and Bryan R. Roberts, eds. 1978. *Peasant Cooperation and Capitalist Expansion in Central Peru*. Austin: University of Texas Press.

Lowenthal, Abraham F. 1975. *The Peruvian Experiment*. Princeton, N.J.: Princeton University Press.

Lynch, Barbara, Rudolfo Flores, and José Villarán. 1986. "Irrigación en San Marcos," *Allpanchis*, 28: 9–46.

Maass, Arthur, and Raymond Anderson. 1978. *And the Desert Shall Rejoice: Conflict,*

Growth and Justice in Arid Environments. Cambridge: Massachusetts Institute of Technology Press.

Mabry, Jonathan B., and David A. Cleveland. 1996. "The Relevance of Indigenous Irrigation." In *Canals and Communities: Small-scale Irrigation Systems.* Ed. J. B. Mabry, pp. 227–60. Tucson: University of Arizona Press.

Mallon, Florence. 1983. *The Defense of Community in Peru's Central Highlands: Peasant Struggle and Capitalist Transition, 1860–1940.* Princeton, N.J.: Princeton University Press.

Mannheim, Bruce. 1985. "Southern Peruvian Quechua." In *South American Indian Languages.* Ed. H. Manelis-Klein and L. Stark, pp. 481–688. Austin: University of Texas Press.

Manrique, Nelson. 1983. "Los Arrieros de la Sierra Central," *Allpanchis,* 21: 27–46.

———. 1985. *Colonialismo y Pobreza Campesina: Caylloma y el Valle del Colca, Siglos XVI–XX.* Lima: Centro de Estudios y Promoción del Desarollo.

Masuda Shozo. 1981a. "Cochayuyo, Macha, Camarón y Higos Charqueados." In Masuda, ed., *Estudios Etnográficos,* pp. 173–92.

———, ed. 1981b. *Estudios Etnográficos del Perú Meridional.* Tokyo: University of Tokyo Press.

———. 1986a. "Las Algas en la Etnografía Andina de Ayer y de Hoy." In Masuda, ed., *Etnografía e Historia,* pp. 173–92.

———, ed. 1986b. *Etnografía e Historia del Mundo Andino.* Tokyo: University of Tokyo Press.

Matos Mar, José, and José Manuel Mejía. 1980. *La Reforma Agraria en el Perú.* Instituto de Estudios Peruanos. Publication Series Peru Problema 19.

Mayer, Enrique. 1974a. "Las Reglas del Juego en la Reciprocidad Andina." In Alberti and Mayer, eds., *Reciprocidad,* pp. 37–65.

———. 1974b. *Reciprocity, Self Sufficiency and Market Relations in a Contemporary Community in the Central Andes of Peru.* Cornell University Latin American Studies Program. Dissertation Series 72.

———. 1977. "Beyond the Nuclear Family." In Bolton and Mayer, eds., *Andean Kinship,* pp. 60–80.

———. 1985. "Production Zones." In *Andean Ecology and Civilization.* Ed. S. Masuda, I. Shimada, and C. Morris, pp. 45–84. Tokyo: University of Tokyo Press.

———. 1988. "De la Hacienda a la Comunidad: El Impacto de la Reforma Agraria en la Provincia de Paucartambo, Cusco." In *Sociedad Andina: Pasado y Presente.* Ed. Ramiro Matos, pp. 59–100. Lima: Fomciencias.

———. 2002. *The Articulated Peasant: Household Economies in the Andes.* Boulder, Colo.: Westview Press.

Mayer, Enrique, and Cesar Fonseca. 1979. *Sistemas Agrarios en la Cuenca del Río Cañete.* Lima: Oficina Nacional de Evaluación de Recursos Naturales.

Mayer, Enrique, and Miguel Glave. 1999. "Alguito para Ganar (A Little Something to Earn): Profits and Losses in Peasant Economies," *American Ethnologist,* 26.2: 344–69.

Mayer, Enrique, and Cesar Zamalloa. 1974. "Reciprocidad en las relaciones de producción." In Alberti and Mayer, eds., *Reciprocidad,* pp. 66–86.

McCay, Bonnie, and James Acheson. 1987a. "Human Ecology of the Commons." In McCay and Acheson, eds., *Culture and Ecology,* pp. 1–36.

————, eds. 1987b. *The Culture and Ecology of Communal Resources*. Tucson: University of Arizona Press.

McClintock, Cynthia, and Abraham Lowenthal. 1983. *The Peruvian Experiment Reconsidered*. Princeton, N.J.: Princeton University Press.

Mintz, Sidney. 1953. "The Folk-Urban Continuum and the Rural Proletarian Community," *American Journal of Sociology*, 59: 136–45.

————. 1973. "A Note on the Definition of Peasantries," *Journal of Peasant Studies*, 1.1: 91–106.

————. 1985. *Sweetness and Power: The Place of Sugar in Modern History*. New York: Penguin Books.

Mitchell, William P. 1973. "The Hydraulic Hypothesis: A Reappraisal," *Current Anthropology*, 14: 532–34.

————. 1976. "Irrigation and Community in the Central Peruvian Highlands," *American Anthropologist*, 78.1: 25–44.

————. 1977. "Irrigation Farming in the Andes: Evolutionary Implications." In *Peasant Livelihood*. Ed. R. Halperin and J. Dow, pp. 36–59. New York: St. Martin's Press.

————. 1980. "Local Ecology and the State: Implications of Contemporary Land Use for the Inca Sequence of Agricultural Work." In *Beyond the Myths of Culture: Essays in Cultural Materialism*, pp. 139–54. New York: Academic Press.

————. 1981. "La Agricultura Hidraúlica en los Andes: Implicaciones Evolucionarias." In *Tecnología del Mundo Andino*. Ed. H. Lechtman and A. Soldi, pp. 145–67. Mexico: Universidad Nacional America de Mexico.

————. 1991a. *Peasants on the Edge: Crop, Cult and Crisis in the Andes*. Austin: University of Texas Press.

————. 1991b. "Some Are More Equal Than Others: Labor Supply, Reciprocity and Redistribution in the Andes," *Research in Economic Anthropology*, 13: 191–219.

————. 1994. "Dam the Water: The Ecology and Political Economy of Irrigation in the Ayacucho Valley of Peru." In Mitchell and Guillet, eds., *Irrigation at High Altitudes*, pp. 276–302.

Mitchell, William P., and David Guillet, eds. 1994. *Irrigation at High Altitudes: The Social Organization of Water Control Systems in the Andes*. Society for Latin American Anthropology Series 12. Washington, D.C.: American Anthropological Association.

Montoya, Rodrigo. 1989. *Lucha por la Tierra, Reformas Agrarias y Capitalismo en el Peru del Siglo XX*. Lima: Mosca Azul Editores.

————. 1980. *Capitalismo y No-Capitalismo en el Perú: Un Estudio de su Articulación en un Eje Regional*. Lima: Mosca Azul Editores.

Montoya, Rodrigo, María Silveira, and Felipe Lindoso. 1979. *Producción Parcelaria y Universo Ideológico: El Caso de Puquio*. Lima: Mosca Azul Editores.

Murra, John V. 1960. "Rite and Crop in the Inca State." In *Culture in History*. Ed. S. Diamond. New York: Columbia University Press.

————. 1970. "Current Research and Prospects in Andean Ethnohistory," *Latin American Research Review*, 5.1: 3–36.

————. 1972. "El 'Control Vertical' de un Máximo de Pisos Ecológicos en le Economía de las Sociedades Andinas." In *Visita de la Provincia de León de Huánuco*, Vol. 2. Ed. Iñiga Ortiz de Zuñiga, pp. 429–68. Huánuco, Peru: University Nacional Hermilio Valdizán.

————. 1975. *Formaciones Económicas y Políticas del Mundo Andino*. Lima: Instituto de Estudios Peruanos.

————. 1980. *The Economic Organization of the Inka State*. Greenwich, Conn.: JAI Press.

————. 1985. "The Limits and Limitations of the 'Vertical Archipelago' in the Andes." In *Andean Ecology and Civilization*. Ed. S. Masuda, I. Shimada, and C. Morris, pp. 15–21. Tokyo: University of Tokyo Press.

Murra, John, and Nathan Wachtel. 1986. "Introduction." In *Anthropological History of Andean Polities*. Ed. J. Murra, N. Wachtel, and J. Revel, pp. 1–8. New York: Cambridge University Press.

Netting, Robert McC. 1986. *Cultural Ecology*. 2d ed. Prospect Heights, Ill.: Waveland Press.

Oehm, Victor P. 1984. *Investigaciones sobre Minería y Metalurgía en el Perú Prehispánico: Una Visión Crítica Actualizada*. Bonn: Estudios Americanistas de Bonn.

Onuki Yoshio. 1981. "Aprovechamiento del Medio Ambiente en la Vertiente Occidental de los Andes en la Región Meridional del Perú." In Masuda, ed., *Estudios Etnograficos*, pp. 1–32.

O'Phellan, Scarlett. 1983. "Tierras Comunales y Revuelta Social: Perú y Bolivia en el Siglo XVIII," *Allpanchis*, 22: 75–92.

————. 1978. "El Sur Andino a Fines del Siglo XVIII: Cacique o Corregidor?," *Allpanchis*, 11–12: 11–28.

Orlove, Benjamin S. 1977a. "Inequality Among Peasants: The Forms and Uses of Reciprocal Exchange in Andean Peru." In *Peasant Livelihood: Studies in Economic Anthropology and Cultural Ecology*. Ed. R. Halperin and J. Dow, pp. 22–35. New York: St. Martin's Press.

————. 1977b. *Alpacas, Sheep and Men: The Wool Export Economy and Regional Society in Southern Peru*. New York: Academic Press.

Orlove, Benjamin S., and Ricardo Godoy. 1986. "Sectoral Fallowing Systems in the Central Andes," *Journal of Ethnobiology*, 6.1: 269–304.

Ossio, Juan M. 1978. "El Symbolismo del Agua y la Presentación del Tiempo y el Espacio en la Fiesta de la Aséquia de la Comunidad de Andamarca." In *Actes du Congress XLII Internacional des Americanistes*, 4: 377–96. Paris.

Ostrom, Elinor. 1990. *Governing the Commons: The Evolution of Institutions for Collective Action*. New York: Cambridge University Press.

————. 1992. *Crafting Institutions for Self-Governing Irrigation Systems*. San Francisco: Institute for Contemporary Studies.

Ostrom, Elinor, and Roy Gardner. 1993. "Coping with Asymmetries in the Commons: Self-Governing Irrigation Systems Can Work," *Journal of Economic Perspectives*, 7.4: 93–112.

Paerregaard, Karsten. 1994. "Why Fight Over Water? Power, Conflict and Irrigation in an Andean Village." In Mitchell and Guillet, eds., *Irrigation at High Altitudes*, pp. 189–202.

Painter, Michael. 1992. "Re-Creating Peasant Economy in Southern Peru." In *Golden Ages, Dark Ages: Imagining the Past in Anthropology and History*. Ed. Jay O'Brien and William Roseberry. Berkeley: University of California Press.

Palma, Ricardo. 1951. *Tradiciones Peruanas*. Tomo II, pp. 275–76. Lima: Editorial Cultura Antarctica.

Palmer, David Scott. 1992. *The Shining Path of Peru*. 2d ed. New York: St. Martin's Press.

Pasapera, Manuel S. 1902. *La Ley de Aguas con sus Antecedents*. Lima: Imprenta y Libreria de San Pedro.

Patterson, Thomas C. 1991. *The Inca Empire: The Formation and Disintegration of a Pre-Capitalist State*. New York: St. Martin's Press.

Pease, Franklin. 1986. "La Noción de Propiedad entre los Incas: Una Aproximación." In Masuda, ed., *Etnografía e Historia*, pp. 3–34.

Peru, Ministerio de Fomento. 1970. *Ley General de Aguas: Decreto Ley 17752*.

———, Direccion de Minas y Petroleo. 1924. "Sintesis de la minería Peruana." In *El Centenario de Ayacucho*, Tomo I.

———, Ministerio de Hacienda y Comercio, Dirección Nacional de Estadística. 1876. *Resumen del Censo General de Habitantes del Perú hecho en 1876*.

——— , ———. 1940. Censo Nacional de Población de 1940.

———, Oficina del Consejo Provincial de la Unión, Cotahuasi. 1981. "Censo Poblacional de la Provincia de La Unión." Unpublished document.

———, Oficina Nacional de Estadística y Censos. 1968. *Censos Nacionales de Población, Vivienda y Agropecuario, 1961*. Vol. IV: *Arequipa*.

———, Oficina Nacional de Evaluación de Recursos Naturales (ONERN). 1975. *Inventario, Evaluación y Uso de los Recursos de la Costa: La Cuenca del Río Ocoña*.

Petersen, George G. 1970. *Minería y Metalurgía en el Antiguo Perú*. Lima: Museo Nacional de Antropología y Arqueología.

Polanyi, Karl. 1957. "The Economy as Instituted Process." In *Trade and Market in the Early Empires*. Ed. K. Polanyi, C. M. Arensberg, and H. W. Pearson, pp. 240–73. Glencoe, Ill.: Free Press.

Poole, Deborah. 1987. "Korilazos, Abigeos y Comunidades Campesinas en la Provincia de Chumbivilcas (Cusco)." In H. Bonilla, ed., *Comunidades Campesinas*, pp. 257–96.

Poole, Deborah, and Gerardo Renique. 1992. *Peru: Time of Fear*. Washington, D.C.: Latin American Bureau.

Pulgar Vidal, Javier. 1946. *Las Ocho Regiones Naturales del Perú*, Tomo I: *Historia y Geografía del Perú*. Lima: Universidad Nacional Mayor de San Marcos.

Purser, W. F. C. 1971. *Metal Mining in Peru, Past and Present*. New York: Praeger.

Rabinow, Paul, and William M. Sullivan, eds. 1987. *Interpretive Social Science: A Second Look*. Berkeley: University of California Press.

Raimondi, Antonio. 1944 [1887]. "Observaciones sobre la Explotación de Oro en el Perú. Boletín de Minas, Industria y Construcción, *La Minería Peruana* (Lima), 3.26 (July).

Rappaport, Roy A. 1968. *Pigs for the Ancestors: Ritual in the Ecology of a New Guinea People*. New Haven, Conn.: Yale University Press.

———. 1979. *Ecology, Meaning and Religion*. Berkeley, Calif.: North Atlantic Books.

———. 1993. "Distinguished Lecture in Anthropology: The Anthropology of Trouble," *American Anthropologist*, 95.2: 295–303.

Rengifo Vasquez, Grimaldo. 1984. La Agricultura Tradicional en los Andes: Manejo de Suelos, Sistemas de Labranza y Herramientas Agricolas. Lima: Editorial Horizonte.

Rich, Bruce. 1994. *Mortgaging the Earth: The World Bank, Environmental Impoverishment and the Crisis of Development*. Boston: Beacon Press.

Ricouer, Paul. 1976. *Interpretation Theory: Discourse and the Surplus of Meaning*. Fort Worth: Texas Christian University Press.

Roscoe, Paul B. 1995. "The Perils of 'Positivism' in Cultural Anthropology," *American Anthropologist*, 97.3: 492–504.

Sahlins, Marshall. 1965. "On the Sociology of Primitive Exchange." In *The Relevance of Models for Social Anthropology*. Ed. Michael Banton. ASA Monograph 1. London: Tavistock.

———. 1972. *Stone Age Economics*. Chicago: Aldine.

Salomon, Frank. 1987. "Ancestor Cults and Resistance to the State in Arequipa, ca. 1748–1754." In *Resistance, Rebellion, and Consciousness in the Andean Peasant World, 18th to 20th Centuries*. Ed. Steve Stern, pp. 148–65. Madison: University of Wisconsin Press.

Sánchez, Rodrigo. 1977. "Economy, Ideology and Political Struggle in the Andean Highlands." Ph.D. thesis, University of Sussex.

———. 1982. "The Andean Economic System and Capitalism." In D. Lehman, ed., *Ecology and Exchange*, pp. 157–90. New York: Cambridge University Press.

Sánchez-Albornóz, Nicolas. 1978. *Indios y Tributos en el Alto Perú*. Lima: Instituto de Estudios Peruanos.

Sato Nobuyuki. 1981. "El Concepto de Ayllu, y Qata/Q'achun: Un Estudio de la Familia, el Parentesco y el Ayllu." In Masuda, ed., *Estudios Etnograficos*, pp. 139–72.

Schaedel, Richard P. 1971. "Commonality in Processual Trends in the Urbanization Process: Urbanization and the Redistributive Function in the Central Andes." Discussion Paper, Center for Latin America, University of Wisconsin, Milwaukee.

Schlager, Edella, and Elinor Ostrom. 1992. "Property Rights Regimes and Natural Resources: A Conceptual Analysis," *Land Economics*, 68.3: 249–62.

Scott, James C. 1976. *The Moral Economy of the Peasant: Rebellion and Subsistence in Southeast Asia*. New Haven, Conn.: Yale University Press.

———. 1985. *Weapons of the Weak: Everyday Forms of Peasant Resistance*. New Haven, Conn.: Yale University Press.

———. 1990. *Domination and the Arts of Resistance: Hidden Transcripts*. New Haven, Conn.: Yale University Press.

Seligmann, Linda. 1995. *Between Reform and Revolution: Political Struggles in the Peruvian Andes, 1969–1991*. Stanford, Calif.: Stanford University Press.

Seligmann, Linda, and Stephen G. Bunker. 1994. "An Andean Irrigation System: Ecological Visions and Social Organization." In Mitchell and Guillet, eds., *Irrigation at High Altitudes*, pp. 203–32.

Sherbondy, Jeannette E. 1982. "The Canal Systems of Hanan Cusco." Ph.D. dissertation, University of Illinois, Champaign-Urbana.

———. 1986. "Los Ceques: Código de Canales en el Cusco Incaíco," *Allpanchis*, 27: 39–74.

Silverman, Sydel. 1979. "The Peasant Concept in Anthropology," *Journal of Peasant Studies*, 7.1: 49–69.

Skar, Harold O. 1981. *The Warm Valley People: Duality and Land Reform Among the Quechua Indians of Highland Peru*. Oslo: Universitetsforlaget.

Smith, Gavin. 1975. "The Social Bases of Peasant Political Activity: The Case of the Huasicanchinos of Central Peru." Ph.D. thesis, University of Sussex.

———. 1989. *Livelihood and Resistance: Peasants and the Politics of Land in Peru*. Berkeley: University of California Press.

Spalding, Karen. 1974. *De Indio a Campesino*. Cusco: Tipografía Americana.

Starn, Orin. 1991. "Missing the Revolution: Anthropologists and the War in Peru," *Cultural Anthropology*, 6: 63–91.

———. 1992. "New Literature on Peru's Sendero Luminoso," *Latin American Research Review*, 27.2: 212–26.

———. 1999. *Nightwatch: The Politics of Protest in the Andes*. Durham, N.C.: Duke University Press.

Steward, Julian H. 1949. "Cultural Causality and Law: A Trial Formulation of the Development of Early Civilizations," *American Anthropologist*, 51: 1–27.

———. 1955a. "The Concept and Method of Cultural Ecology." In *Theory of Culture Change*. Ed. J. Steward, pp. 30–42. Urbana: University of Illinois Press.

———, ed. 1955b. *Irrigation Systems: A Comparative Study*. Washington, D.C.: Pan American Union Social Science Monographs 1.

Thomas, Brooke. 1972. "Human Adaptation to a High Andean Energy Flow System." Ph.D. dissertation, Pennsylvania State University.

Thompson, I. G., M. E. Mosely, J. F. Bolzan, and B. R. Koci. 1985. "A 1,500-Year Record of Tropical Precipitation from the Quelccaya Ice Cap," *Science*, 229: 971–73.

Toribio Polo, José. 1911. *Reseña Historica de la Minería en el Peru*. Lima.

Tosi, J. A. 1960. "Zonas de Vida Natural en el Perú," *Boletín Técnico*, 5. Lima: Organización de Estados Americanos.

Trawick, Paul B. 1994a. "Historia de la Irrigación y Conflictos de Classes en la Sierra," *Debate Agrario*, 18: 21–44.

———. 1994b. "The Struggle for Water in the Andes: A Study of Technological Change and Social Decline in the Cotahuasi Valley of Peru." Ph.D. dissertation, Yale University.

———. 1995. "Water Reform and Poverty in the Highlands." In *Peru: A User-Based Approach to Water Management and Irrigation Development*. Ed. Mateen Thobani, Annex B, pp. 1–18. World Bank Report13642-PE. Washington, D.C.

———. 1998a. "La Privatización del Agua: Alternativa Andina para Una Nueva Ley de Aguas, *Quehacer* (DESCO), 115: 36–41.

———. 1998b. "La Nueva Ley de Aguas: Una Alternativa Andina a las Reformas Propuestas," *Debate Agrario* (CEPES), 28: 85–102.

Treacy, John. 1994a. "Teaching Water: Hydraulic Management and Terracing in Corporaque, the Colca Valley, Peru." In Mitchell and Guillet, eds., *Irrigation at High Altitudes*, pp. 99–114.

———. 1994b. *Las Chacras de Corporaque: Andenería y Riego en el Valle del Colca*. Lima: Instituto de Estudios Peruanos.

Trouillot, Michel-Rolph. 1988. *Peasants and Capital: Dominica and the World Economy*. Baltimore, Md.: Johns Hopkins University Press.

Tsunekawa Keiichi. 1986. "Interacción entre los Serranos y los Costeños en la Vida Económica y Política del Valle de Camaná." In Masuda, ed., *Etnografía e Historia*, pp. 191–222.

Urrutia, Jaime. 1983. "De Las Rutas, Ferias y Circuitos en Huamanga," *Allpanchis*, 21: 47–64.

Valderamma, Ricardo, and Carmen Escalante. 1980. "Apu Coropuna: Visión de los Muertos en la Comunidad de Awkimarca," *Debates en Antropología*, 5: 233–64.

———. 1983. "Arrieros, Traperos y Llameros en Huancavelica," *Allpanchis*, 21:65–88.

————. 1986. "Sistema de Riego y Organización Social en el Valle del Colca: Caso Yanque," *Allpanchis*, 27: 179–202.

————. 1988. *Del Tata Mallku a al Mama Pacha: Riego, Sociedad y Ritos en los Andes Peruanos*. Lima: Centro de Estudios y Promocion del Desarollo.

Vasquez de Espinoza, Antonio. 1943 [1621]. *Compendio y Descripción de las Indias Occidentales*. Washington, D.C.: Smithsonian Institution.

Villanueva, Horacio. 1982. *Cusco 1689: Economía y Sociedad en el Sur Andino*. Cusco. Centro de Estudios Rurales Andinos Bartolomé de las Casas.

Villanueva, Horacio, and Jeanette Sherbondy. 1979. *Cusco: Aguas y Poder*. Cusco: Centro de Estudios Rurales Andinos Bartolomé de las Casas.

Weberbauer, Augusto. 1945. *El Mundo Vegetal de los Andes Peruanos*. Lima: Ministerio de Agricultura.

Webster, Steven. 1971. "An Indigenous Quechua Community in the Exploitation of Multiple Ecological Zones." In *Actas y Memorias del XXXIX Congreso Internacional de Americanistas*, 3: 174–83.

————. 1973. "Native Pastoralism in the South Andes," *Ethnology*, 12: 115–34.

Wittfogel, Karl A. 1955. "Developmental Aspects of Hydraulic Civilization." In Steward, ed., *Irrigation Systems*.

Wolf, Eric, and Sidney W. Mintz. 1957. "Hacienda and Plantation in Middle America and the Antilles," *Social and Economic Studies*, 6: 386–412.

Zuidema, R. Tom. 1964. The Ceque System of Cusco: The Social Organization of the Capital of the Inca. Leyden.

————. 1986. "Inka Dynasty and Irrigation: Another Look at Andean Concepts of History." In *Anthropological History of Andean Polities*. Ed. J. Murra, N. Wachtel, and J. Revel, pp. 177–200. New York: Cambridge University Press.

Index

In this index an "f" after a number indicates a separate reference on the next page, and an "ff" indicates separate references on the next two pages. A continuous discussion over two or more pages is indicated by a span of page numbers, e.g., "57–59." *Passim* is used for a cluster of references in close but not consecutive sequence.

Acción Popular, 265

Achambi, 49, 53, 212, 310–11n14, 315n1

Administrators, 269, 323n10; water conflicts and, 258–65, 266–67. *See also* Campos

Agrarian League, 284

Agrarian reform, 11, 66, 106, 197, 199, 237, 321nn10, 11, 326n10; impacts of, 206–9, 210–13, 237; circumvention of, 209–10; large properties and, 246–47

Alca, 21, 43, 47, 54, 59, 215, 287, 313n3, 317n7, 324n7; in Spanish colonial period, 49–55 *passim*; population in, 63f, 66; indigenous communities in, 68–69

Alcohol, 111, 225

Alfalfa, 28, 201, 205; production of, 29–30, 35, 66, 76, 134, 145, 147, 164, 177f, 181, 298, 310n10, 321n9; Spanish production of, 54–55, 111; irrigating, 88, 123–24, 171, 186, 231, 242–47 *passim*; landownership and, 208, 319n23

Alpacas, 67, 74

American Popular Revolutionary Alliance (APRA), 12, 233, 253, 321n8, 322n18, 324n8; water projects and, 252, 323n15; and Cotahuasi, 273–78 *passim*, 286; economic reform and, 283–84

Anchakani, 119

Andamarca, 64

Andean Quadrangle, 274

Antamarca, 156

APRA, *see* American Popular Revolutionary Alliance

Apu, 22

Apurimac, 66, 319n25

Aqo, 110, 124, 315n2

Aquerana, 54

Arcata, 277

Archaeology, 14–15, 39, 311nn2, 3, 4, 5; Huari, 40–41

Arequipa (city), 12, 20f, 274; migration to, 102, 113, 286; contact with, 178, 204

Arequipa (department), 4(map), 5, 18(map), 36, 75

Arequipa (intendencia), 59

Arequipa plateau, 19

Armanca, 54, 156, 158, 255; water flow in, 159f, 313n18; reallotment of, 230, 233, 261

Army: and Sendero Luminoso, 273–74

Arrieraje, arrieros, *see* Muleteering

Aspilcueta family, 62, 111

Auxilio, 244–45, 247–48

Ayacucho (city), 20

Ayacucho (department), 20, 66, 75, 183, 274, 286, 314n11

Ayacucho (intendencia), 59, 273

Ayahuasi, 55, 58–59, 75, 110, 311n6
Ayapata, 110
Ayllus, 49, 55, 62ff, 68, 188, 311n7,
    312–13nn21, 22; and tribute system,
    56–57; and haciendas, 60, 144, 153;
    Huaynacotino's, 72–74; Pampamarca's,
    113ff, 117, 122, 144–45; and canal main-
    tenance, 135–36; Cotahuasi, 151, 155f,
    312n21
Ayni, 98–100, 137, 224, 322n17; Cotahuasi,
    185–86, 197

Belaúnde, Fernando, 207, 253, 323n15
Benavides family, 62
Bolívar, Simón, 64, 68, 162
Bingham, Hiram, 19
Bordas family, 111
Bowman, Isaiah, 19
Businessmen, 217f, 227, 246, 256. *See also*
    Middle proprietors

Cabanaconde, 48
Cachana, 54, 64f, 69, 155, 157, 174, 184, 237,
    255, 268, 312n22, 317n5; water control in,
    156, 241; water rights in, 161, 230; water
    distribution in, 162, 267; canal main-
    tenance in, 192f
Caciques, 56–57, 58
Cahuana, 43–44, 55, 58, 110, 296
Camaná valley, 113, 141, 165, 247
Campesino Federation, 287
Campesinos, *see* Peasants
Campos, 79, 318n19; and water distribu-
    tion, 80–91 *passim*, 317n22; and canal
    maintenance, 97–98; in Pampamarca,
    120–27 *passim*, 135, 136–37, 144–47 *pas-
    sim*; in Cotahuasi, 169–70
Canal systems, 24, 26, 34, 237; pre-
    hispanic, 3, 5, 41, 43–46, 311nn6, 8;
    Huaynacotas', 76–79, 84; maintenance
    of, 96–98, 119, 135–37, 143–44, 191–94,
    195–96, 268; and terraces, 88–92; Pam-
    pamarca's, 114(map), 123; Cotahuasi's,
    150, 155–59, 169; government adminis-
    tration of, 230–34; government projects
    and, 251–53, 255–56, 276

Cancha, 54, 174
Cañete valley, 176
Capac Yupanqui, 43
Capitalism, 219, 279, 301
Carbajal, Sr., 211
Cargo systems, 294, 315n22, 318n19; in
    Pampamarca, 113, 121, 126, 141, 316n7; in
    Cotahuasi, 161–62
Cash, 190, 212, 320n32
Cash crops, 221f
Castas, 62–63
Castilla, 62, 277
Castilla Alta, 142
Catatoria, 110
Cattle raising, 62, 74, 111, 118, 134, 145, 171,
    201, 205, 208, 217, 226, 316n17; cash
    income and, 222, 316n12
Caylloma, 53
Cerro Rico, 142, 165
Cervantes family, 111
Chacaylla, 230, 233, 317n5
Chakrasapa, *see* Mayoristas; Middle pro-
    prietors
Chala, 20, 47, 178
Chaucalla, 52
Chaucavilca, 54, 64f, 69, 155ff, 161, 237,
    268, 317n5; water control in, 159, 318n11;
    water distribution in, 162, 267; canal
    maintenance in, 191ff
Ch'eqa, 72, 113, 117–23 *passim*, 131, 135,
    316n6
Ch'ewqa, 115
Chika chakrayuq, *see* Comuneros;
    Minoristas
Chile, 303
Chinkayllapa, 277
Choccocco Project, 251f, 323n12
Choccocco River, 251, 275
Chumbivilcas, 48
Chuquibamba, 47, 141, 178, 274, 281, 285
Ch'uychu canal, 117, 119
CICDA-PRODAPU, 252
Cigarettes, 225
Class: in Cotahuasi valley, 5, 63, 217–19
Coca, 225
Cochacallán, 255, 311nn2, 3, 311–12n11

Colcán, 209
Colca valley, 35, 42, 48, 176f, 309n2; irrigation system in, 296–97
Collana, 64, 156, 312–13n22
Collota, 40, 45–46, 276, 325n2
Colonial period, 34; population reduction during, 48–49, 312n12; in Cotahuasi valley, 51–59, 311–12nn11, 20; social changes in, 297–98
Communities, 9, 14f, 27, 34, 111; indigenous, 68–76; work relationships within, 100–101; in colonial era, 297–98; social changes in, 300–301
Compadrazgo, 100, 140, 202, 223
Comuneros, 166, 178, 212, 316n16, 318n13; of Pampamarca, 113, 115, 124f, 129–30, 134–35, 139–40; labor relations and, 137–41, 256–57, 318n17, 322n19; and outside world, 141–42; canal maintenance by, 143–44, 191–94; and irrigated land, 162–64; water distribution and, 167–70 *passim*
Condes, 47–48
Condesuyos of Cusco, *see* Cotahuasi valley
Confederations, 42
Conflict: in Huaynacotas, 87–88; over water, 151, 168, 250; over irrigated land, 163–64; Cotahuasi-Quillunsa, 258–68, 269–70, 287, 323n14
COPASA, *see* Peruvian-German Pact for Food Security
CORDEA, *see* Development Corporation of Arequipa
Cornejo family, 111
Coropuna, Nevado, 22
Corruption, 12, 56, 279, 284, 303; land titles and, 163–64; water distribution and, 169–70, 234, 245, 249; of elites, 280, 281–82
Cotahuasi, 10–11, 12f, 29, 34ff, 50(map), 54, 59, 62, 150–51, 152(photo), 154(map), 209, 237, 247, 273, 310n11, 311n2, 319n25, 322nn19, 4; rainfall at, 22, 24f; archaeological evidence in, 39, 40–42; Spanish colonial period and, 49, 53, 55,

311–12n11; haciendas and, 60–61, 156, 157–58, 317n3, 319–20n31; population in, 64, 153, 155, 197–98, 313nn23, 25; indigenous communities and, 68–69; water distribution in, 91–92, 166–70, 244, 245–46, 270–71, 323n7; terraces in, 96, 174–75, 314n18; canal system in, 155–58; land use in, 158–59, 317n2, 319nn22, 23, 24; water control in, 159–60, 171–73, 241, 269; *cargo* structure in, 161–62; irrigated land in, 162–64; water theft in, 165–66; sloping fields in, 174–76; top-down watering system in, 177–78, 242; irrigation units on, 179–90; canal maintenance in, 191–94; government administration in, 194–96, 228, 232, 250f, 317n5; mestizaje in, 196–98; road construction and, 204–5; and Tomepampa-Piro Project, 252, 254, 323n14; water use conflicts, 258–70 *passim*, 287; APRA and, 274–76, 277–78, 286; national identity in, 279–80; as corrupt, 281–82; Sendero Luminoso and, 282–83, 285–87; unrest in, 284–85
Cotahuasi River, 17, 21–22, 117
Cotahuasi valley, 17, 19, 35, 296; as study area, 5–7; and Sendero Luminoso, 12–13; cultural zones of, 36–38; prehistory of, 39–47, 50(map); Spanish colonial period and, 47–49, 51–59; after independence, 59–63; population growth in, 63–64, 66; economy of, 200–201; agrarian reform in, 207–9
Coups d'etat: impacts of, 199, 208
Credit, 200–205 *passim*
Crop rotation, 30, 78, 119
Cruz family, 62
Cultivation and Irrigation Plan, 245
Cultures: of Cotahuasi valley, 36–38
Cusco, 20, 43, 47, 130
Cusco (intendencia), 59
Cutirpo, 54, 155–60 *passim*, 192, 255

Debts, 140, 320n33
Democracy, 282
Demography, 14. *See also* Population

Dependency, 256
Development Corporation of Arequipa
(CORDEA), 251–56 *passim*, 276, 323n15
Dictatorship, 282–83, 289
Dirty war, 273–74
Diseases, 49, 53
Double-cropping, 122
Droughts, 245; and water sources, 25–26;
and irrigation, 27–28; and water distri-
bution, 84f, 117–18, 165–68, 300, 314n15,
316n14; and spring flow, 115, 239–40;
Pampamarca, 119–20, 134–35; and water
supply, 229, 238–39; impacts of, 234–36;
and government administration,
240–41
Dry farming, 118, 237, 310n5

Economy, 6, 115; cultural groups and,
36–37; hacendados and, 59–60,
200–201, 216; Huaynacostas, 100, 101–2;
landownership and, 199f; road construction and, 204–5; peasants and,
220–22; household, 224–25, 320–21n6;
national, 283–84
Elites, 5, 9, 40, 321–22nn8, 14, 325–26n7; in
Cotahuasi, 11, 19, 62, 161–62; land control, 59, 208; status control by, 62–63; in
Pampamarca, 110–11, 113; and water
ownership, 165–66; property owner-
ship, 201–2, 203; landownership, 215,
216–17; political struggle among,
232–33; as corrupt, 279–80, 281–82
Emergency Development Microregions,
12, 274, 276, 286
Empresarios, 217f, 227, 246, 256. *See also*
Middle proprietors
Encomiendas, 62
Epidemics, 49, 53
Eriazos, 163, 237
Escarbo de Asequia (Canal Cleaning),
169, 193
Españoles, 36
Ethnic groups, 40, 47–48, 279
Ethnicity, 5, 9, 72, 110, 301; economy and,
201–3
Ethnography, 3, 5
Exploitation, 223; labor, 187–90

Faena, 192f, 197, 203–4, 256f, 323n15
Fallow lands, 78, 119f, 158–59, 236f
Families, 100; elite, 56, 62, 138–39, 320n2;
landholding, 73–74, 313–14n7; in Huaynacotas, 75, 98–99, 100; reciprocal
work, 98–99, 224; water rights and,
108–9; in Pampamarca, 110f, 112–13, 115,
315nn4, 5, 316n6; middle proprietor,
144–46; mayordomo, 186–87; "rich"
campesino, 222–23
Fatalism, 279–80, 282
Favoritism, 323n17; in water distribution,
258–59, 268f, 317n22, 322n6; government projects and, 259–64
Fields, 119, 314n12, 318n11; agricultural,
29–30; sloping, 174–75, 181–82; hacienda, 179–81; abandonment of,
236–37, 238
Fieldwork: description of, 11–12
Fiestas, 140f, 261–62, 315n22, 316n7
Food production, 28, 225, 245,
320–21n6
Forasteros, 54, 66
Fraud, 276–77
Fujimori, Alberto, 289
Fundos, 179–90

Ganadería, ganaderos, 62, 205, 218, 246
García, Alan, 253, 273f, 324n8
Gastelú family, 56
Genealogies, 14
General Water Law (1969), 37, 242, 256,
270–71, 289, 300, 303, 323nn16, 19;
administration of, 228–34, 249, 258
Gentlemen farmers, 217
Goats, 118
Gold, 46–47, 48, 310n4, 312nn13, 14
Government, 39; and Cotahuasi system,
166–70 *passim*, 194–96; and mestizaje,
196–97; military, 199, 206–9; irrigation
management, 228–29, 230–34, 242–43,
250–52, 317n5, 326n6; drought response
of, 240–41; and water rights, 248–49;
canal and tank projects, 255–56; labor
sharing and, 256–57; water conflicts
and, 258–65; and Cotahuasi district,
273, 274–76; fraud and, 276–77

Grama (*Pennisetum clandestinum*), 182,
187, 319nn25, 29
Grazing, 118
Groundwater, 25–26
Guardia Civil, 278
Guzmán, Abimael, 282

Habitats, 30–31
Haciendas, hacendados, 3, 6, 11, 54, 215,
232, 318n14, 320n2, 321n9, 322n6; and
water management, 8f, 145–46, 318n12;
expansion of, 59–63, 64–66, 153; locations of, 63, 312nn17, 18; labor on,
66–67, 183–86, 319–20n31; irrigation
systems and, 91–92, 179–90; at Pampamarca, 110, 115, 119; water distribution
and, 123–25, 132–33, 159–62, 263,
299–300, 318n15; canal maintenance
and, 136–37, 191–92, 195–96; work relations and, 137–44; in Cotahuasi, 151, 155,
157–59, 317n3, 318n17; water ownership
and, 164, 165–66, 170–72, 228; water
supply and, 167–68; Iskaywayqo,
179–90; breakup of, 199f; property
ownership of, 201–2, 320n4; road construction and, 203–5; agrarian reform
and, 206–13, 246–47. *See also* Landlords
Hanansaya, 294, 323n3
Herding, herders, 31, 33, 61–67 *passim*,
315n27
Herding grounds, 59, 119f, 151, 201, 211,
312n17
Hinajosa family, 111
Households, 126, 142; reciprocal work
and, 98–100, 315n21; in Pampamarca,
112–13; sharecropping and, 185–86;
landholding by, 202, 214(table), 215;
economy of, 224–25, 320–21n6
Huacctapa, 277
Huambo, 151, 156, 160–61, 167, 192, 251, 255
Huancavelica, 53
Huansacocha, Lake, 117
Huarhua, 47, 49, 148, 286
Huari, 39, 40–41, 47
Huayllura, 55
Huaynacotas, 10f, 24, 34, 49, 55, 58, 68, 109,
228, 275, 295, 301, 309n6, 313n3, 315n25,

316n17; land in, 59, 313–14nn7, 10, 16;
population in, 64, 66; maintaining
indigenous identity in, 71–74, 110; irrigation system in, 76–79, 88–92, 291–93,
314n9; water distribution in, 79–88, 127,
231f, 241, 314nn14, 15, 316n14; terraces
in, 88–94, 95–96, 131, 237; canal system
maintenance in, 96–98, 191–94; work
relationships in, 98–101, 219; economies, 101–2; labor relations in, 102–6;
livestock damage in, 140–41; land reform in, 211f; labor from, 246–47;
Sendero Luminoso and, 277, 283
Huillac, 44f, 55, 58f, 75, 110
Hurinsaya, 294
Hyperinflation, 284

Identity, 310n13; national, 279–82
Incahuasi, 67
Incas, 3, 22, 325n2; as conquerors, 42–43;
and Cotahuasi valley, 43–47; water dis-
tribution system of, 127, 304; irrigation
systems of, 292–96
Income: family, 101f, 222; cash, 106–7, 108,
145, 190, 212
Independence, 59
Indigenous communities, 310n10; social
change in, 68–70; structure of, 71–76
Indios, population growth, 63–64. *See also*
Comuneros; Mestizos; Peasants
Insurgencies: armed, 206
Intendencias, 59
Intermarriage, 113
International development, 252–53, 255
Irrigation, 1, 15, 31, 309–10n3, 316n11; state
administration of, 3, 242–44; prehispanic, 9–10; Cotahuasi valley, 23–24;
role of, 27–28; temperature and, 28–29;
and water supply, 118–19, 238–39; planting and, 247, 314n12; of slope fields,
297–98
Irrigation systems, 7–8, 11, 154(map), 238,
298–99, 302–3, 322n3, 325n6; variation
in, 26–27, 178–79; prehispanic, 41,
43–45, 129, 293–94; indigenous, 70,
313n26; in Huaynacotas, 76–84, 88–92,
291–93; egalitarian, 85–88; in Pampa-

marca, 113, 115–20; top-down, 128–34, 174–76, 177–78, 242–43; demography and, 176–77; Iskawayqo, 179–90; government administration of, 228–29, 230–34, 251–52; bottom-up, 247–48; Inca, 294–96; acephalous, 296–97. *See also* Canal systems

Irrigator Commission, 228–33 *passim*, 287; drought response, 240–41; water distribution and, 243, 248, 261, 268; politics, 263–64, 266

Ispanqa, 115, 120

Iskawayqo: irrigation system on, 179–90

Jefe de Aguas y Riego, 194

Jornal, 219f, 224

Kalpa, 142, 165

Kamayuq, *see* Mayordomos

Kinship, 14, 203, 311n7, 313n3, 315n23, 324–25n1; and work parties, 99–100, 188f; reciprocity and, 137, 185

K'uchuqocha, 76, 81f, 85f, 122

Kuntis, 42f, 48

Kuntisuyu, 20, 22, 42, 46–47, 311n10

Kupe, 72, 113, 117ff, 122, 237, 316n6; water distribution in, 123, 135; qhosqay system in, 130, 131–32

Kuracas, 56–62 *passim*, 75

Labor, 131, 217; Inca taxation as, 43, 45–46; Spanish colonial, 49, 53–54, 315n3; in mines, 55, 57–58; haciendas, 60–61, 66, 246–47, 319–20n31; forced, 64f, 67; reciprocity and, 98–100, 107–8, 184–85, 219–20, 315n21; relationships of, 103–6, 137–44, 219, 224, 321–22nn14, 18; wage, 106–7, 145, 190, 212, 218–19, 226; mink'a, 107–8, 138–40, 223, 320n34; and watering techniques, 133–34; exploitation and, 187–90; cooperative, 193–94; and crop planting, 246–47; on government-sponsored projects, 253, 255–57

Labor exchange, 224

Lampa, 67

Lancaroya, 209, 285–86

Land, 230, 238, 256, 324–25n1; arable, 31, 33; under irrigation, 34–35; and Spanish colonial period, 55–59 *passim*; haciendas and, 61–62, 64–65, 201, 320n4, 321nn11, 12, 13; and indigenous communities, 68–75 *passim*; cultivated, 76, 78, 310n9, 313–14nn7, 10, 315n26; in Pampamarca, 111, 113; protection of, 139–40, 162–63; Cotahuasi comuneros and, 162–64, 318n14; registration of, 166–67; ownership of, 199–203, 213–17, 313–14nn5, 7, 316n17, 321nn11, 13; agrarian reform and, 206–12; peasant acquisition of, 225–26, 319n24; and Tomepampa-Piro Project, 253–54; control of, 315n3, 316n16

Landlords, 5, 10, 19, 241, 310n12, 312n19; Spanish, 36, 58; wool trade and, 59–60, 61–62; land acquisition and, 64–65; in Pampamarca, 111, 127, 134, 138–39, 316n13, 317n8; and canal maintenance, 136–37; labor relations and, 137–44, 184–85; in Cotahuasi, 161–62, 195; water distribution and, 183–84, 318n11; and canal systems, 195–96; and land reform, 207–10, 216, 326n10; government projects and, 256–57; water conflicts and, 269–70. *See also* Haciendas, hacendados; Mayoristas; Mistis

Land reform: Bolívar's, 64, 68. *See also* Agrarian reform

Landscape modification, 24, 181. *See also* Terraces, terracing

Land titles, 163–64

Land-use systems, 11, 119, 158–59

Land-use zones, 31–33, 34

Largeholders, *see* Mayoristas

La Unión, 36, 59, 274, 324n1

Laymis, 118f, 122, 131f, 316n10. *See also* T'ikras

Lima, 21, 113

Livestock, 139–40, 171, 315n24

Llamas, 61, 74

Loans: peasants and, 140f, 202, 205, 316n17, 320n33

Loayza family, 62, 151, 160–61, 171, 317n3

Luicho, 82

Maize, 30, 76, 80, 118, 121–22, 310nn5, 6
Majes, 204, 247
Majes valley, 42, 48, 111, 113, 141f, 165, 320n5
Malaria, 141
Malawata, 119, 131, 316n10
Managers, *see* Administrators; Campos; Mayordomos
Market economy, 221
Markets, 205, 223, 226
Marxism, 278–79
Mawka Llaqta, 43, 311n2
Mayordomos, 138, 186–87, 208, 321n11
Mayoristas, 315n22; of Huaynacotas, 73f, 100–104; canal maintenance, 97, 268; wage labor and, 106–7; water rights and, 108–9, 145–46; loans and, 140–41, 316n17. *See also* Haciendas, hacendados; Landlords
Mayta Capac, 43
Medianos proprietarios, *see* Middle proprietors
Meetings: water distribution, 127–28
Mestizaje, 68–69, 300; in Cotahuasi, 153, 155; state management and, 196–97; village life and, 197–98
Mestizos, 5, 36f, 63, 205, 281, 302, 310–11n14, 313n24, 317n4
Middle Horizon, 39, 40–41
Middle proprietors, 115, 134, 142–43, 205, 226, 316n8, 317n19; water distribution and, 144–48 *passim*; land control, 199–200, 202, 208; status as, 218–19, 317n21; labor reciprocity and, 219–20; political issues and, 232f
Migration, 75, 165, 286; from Pampamarca, 113, 141–42, 316n12; and land control, 207–8, 212, 216; labor, 223, 247, 320–21n6
Military government, 199, 206–9, 234
Military service, 142
Mining, mines, 40, 48, 72, 165, 312n14, 315n2; Ocoña, 46–47; Spanish colonial, 52–57 *passim*, 110; Pampamarca, 142, 315n4
Ministry of Agriculture, 37, 228, 230, 248, 326n6

Mink'a, 22ff, 188, 197, 219f, 320n34; Huaynacotas, 103–8 *passim*, 315n26; Pampamarca, 138–39, 143
Minoristas, 98, 162; of Huaynacotas, 73–74, 101; work relationships of, 106–7; water rights and, 108–9; landowner-ship, 113, 115, 213; top-down irrigation, 129–30; drought adaptations of, 134–35; labor relations, 138–44. *See also* Comuneros
Miska, 122
Mistis, 36, 113, 142, 201, 202–3, 279, 316n13; water ownership by, 124–25; resource control, 137–41 *passim*; canal maintenance, 143–44; landownership by, 216–17
Mita, Inca, 43, 45–46; Spanish colonial, 49, 53–58 *passim*, 141
Moieties, 294–95, 313n3, 324–25n1
Molino, 110, 124, 315n2
Money, 205, 320n32; access to, 106–7, 108, 145, 190, 220
Montesclaros, 55
Moral economy, 221, 292–93
Morales-Bermudez, Francisco, 208, 211, 234
Moriberón family, 56
Mules, 201
Muleteering, 55, 61f, 164, 171, 178, 190, 204, 318n14
Multas, 232, 244
Mungui, 21, 49, 315n1
Mutual aid, 98–100. *See also* Reciprocity

Nana Alta, 67
National System for the Support of Social Mobilization (SINAMOS), 206–11 *passim*, 230, 261; canal and tank projects, 255–56
Netahaha, 40

Obsidian: trade in, 39–40, 47
Ocoña, 17, 46–47, 309n1, 322n4
Oracles: Inca, 22
Orcopampa, 57
Orqon, 76, 80

Ownership, 9; of water, 3, 33, 124–25, 134, 159–66 *passim*, 170–72, 241; land, 201–3
Oxen, 139

Pachapaki, 137–38
Padrón de Regantes, 167. *See also* Administrators
Pampacolca, 47
Pampamarca, 10f, 24, 34, 50(map), 55, 59, 114(map), 165, 228, 237, 283, 309n6, 316nn7, 9, 10, 11, 12; prehispanic population in, 42, 311n2; Spanish colonial period and, 49, 57f; population in, 64, 66, 315n5; ayllus in, 68, 324n1; Spanish in, 110–11; residents of, 112–13; irrigation system, 115–20, 294–95, 298; water distribution in, 120–23, 125–28, 144–48, 160, 241, 316n13, 317n8; haciendas in, 123–25; qhosqay system in, 128–34; drought in, 134–35; canal maintenance in, 135–37; labor relations in, 137–44, 219; outside world and, 141–42; agrarian reform in, 209, 212; planting labor, 246–47; roads and, 275f
Pampas, 45–46, 311n9
Pampa Yarqa, 124, 135–36, 143–44
Pararapa, 55, 57f, 72
Parinacochas, 62, 142
Partidarios, 183, 184–85, 191, 321n12. *See also* Sharecropping
Pasture, 31, 59, 33, 111, 310n8; access to, 74–75, 118; watering, 124, 147, 174–76, 178–79, 231, 242; Cotahuasi, 151, 160–61, 177–78, 317n2, 319n22; management of, 186–87
Peasant communities, 3, 55
Peasants, 5, 10, 165, 178, 287–88, 310n13, 322n16; in Cotahuasi, 19, 36–37, 151; land control and, 62, 199–200, 206, 208, 212–16 *passim*, 325n2; population growth, 63–64; water and, 151, 171; activism of, 189–90; economy and, 200–201, 205, 220–22, 320n32; socioeconomy of, 217–19; reciprocity and, 219–20, 322n17; definitions of, 223–24; land acquisition by, 225–26; politics and, 226–27, 283, 322n18; in Quillunsa,

267–68; water conflicts and, 269–70; and Sendero Luminoso, 273–74, 285–86, 324n7; and social change, 301–2; and irrigation system, 302–3. *See also* Comuneros; Mestizos; Runakuna
Pérez family, 56, 62, 171
Peruvian-German Pact for Food Security (COPASA), 255ff, 276, 286
Phaspa, 119
Phaspay, 129
Phayna, 96–97. *See also* Faena
Pinochet, Augusto, 303
Piro, 54, 156f, 174; water supply in, 238–39, 247f; government favoritism in, 259–60
Pitahuasi, 54, 156, 174, 237, 254f, 311nn2, 3; water distribution, 160, 230, 244, 260f, 267; water use, 167, 171; agrarian reform in, 209f; water supply, 238–40, 269
Plan de Cultivos y Riego, 229
Planting system, 77(map), 231, 246; Pampamarca, 116(map), 121–22; labor for, 246–47
Plows, 139, 314n19
Polanco incident, 281–82
Politics: peasants and, 226–27, 283, 322n18; elites and, 232–33; of water distribution, 259–66; government programs and, 274–76
Pomatambo, 49, 53
Pooling technique (bottom-up), 247–48; in Huayancotas, 88–92
Popular Cooperation, 276
Population, 75, 202; prehispanic, 41–42, 311n3; at Spanish conquest, 48–49; Spanish colonial period, 49–56 *passim*, 297, 312nn12, 20; Pampamarca, 112–13, 115, 131, 315n5, 316n6; Cotahuasi, 153, 155, 197–98, 313nn23, 25; and irrigation techniques, 176–77
Precipitation, *see* Rainfall
Prehistory: of Cotahuasi valley, 39–47
Principales, 113
Private estates, *see* Haciendas
Privatization: of water rights, 303–4
Production cycle, 29–30
Production zones: Qheshwa, 31, 78, 237; in Huaynacotas, 76–79

Property, 113; water as, 33, 124–25, 134, 151, 161–66 *passim*, 170–72, 201, 318n12; land as, 58–59, 69–70; in Huaynacotas, 73–74; acquisition of, 140–41; estate, 159–60

Puica, 29, 58f, 66, 148, 277, 310n12, 313n3, 315n1; rainfall at, 23ff; mines near, 55, 57; land reform in, 211f

Puka Puka, 45

Puna (altiplano, meseta), 31, 33, 74, 312nn17, 18, 317n2; land reform on, 210–12

Puñenos, 205

Puquio, 20, 227, 256, 320n33

Qhaqha, 43

Qhayawa, 113–23 *passim*, 130–31, 144, 317n20

Qhosqay system: in Pampamarca, 128–34

Qochapampa, 144

Qocheqa, 113–22 *passim*; water distribution in, 123–25; terraces in, 130–31

Qotanayu, 119

Quechua, 5, 10, 13; use of, 36, 68, 74, 319n27

Quillunsa, 63–69 *passim*, 155–59 *passim*, 171, 238, 312–13n22, 319n26; canal system in, 156–60 *passim*, 318n17; water rights in, 161f; water distribution in, 167–68, 241, 244, 270–71; canal maintenance in, 191ff; government administration in, 232, 250, 317n5; and Tomepampa-Piro Project, 252–54, 323n14; water conflicts in, 258–70 *passim*, 287

Quillunsa Irrigator Committee, 253

Rainfall, 22–23, 24; variation in, 25–26; and irrigation, 28, 81–82; patterns of, 235–36

Reciprocity, 197, 322n17; in agricultural work, 98–100, 183–86, 218; labor, 107–8, 137–44, 187–90, 219–20

Reducciones, 49

Red Zones, 273–74

Reginas, 127–28

Rent, 200, 318n11

Repartimientos, 49

Reservoirs, 76, 158, 167, 230, 255, 314n9, 319n26

Resource allocation, 109

Reyparte, 64f, 69, 153, 155, 161, 184, 237, 241, 312–13nn21, 22; water distribution, 230, 267

Rituals, 26, 68, 316n15; canal cleaning and maintenance, 135–37

Roads, 178, 274, 281; impact of, 203–5

Rock salt, 47

Rompeo, 30

Rondador, 169

Runakuna, 36–37, 74

Salamanca, 49

Salcán Grande, 159, 209f, 237, 263

Santa Ana, 263, 323n13

Santo Tomas, 48

Sara chakra, 76, 78, 118f

School system, 63, 72, 113, 141–42, 143

Self-reliance, 221–22

Sendero Luminoso (Shining Path), 11, 12–13, 199, 212, 272, 303, 309nn3, 5; war against, 273–74; in Cotahuasi, 277, 285–87; goals of, 278–79; support for, 282–83, 324n7

Sharecropping, 66f, 164, 315n27; on Iskawayqo, 183–86; and land reform, 209f, 319n24. *See also* Comuneros; Partidarios

Sheep, 67, 118

Shops, 204–5, 315n25

SINAMOS, *see* National System for the Support of Social Mobilization

Sinchis, 278, 324n4

Sloped fields, 8, 181–82, 297–98

Smallholders, *see* Comuneros; Minoristas

Solimana, 20

Soto family, 111

Spanish, 58, 141, 202, 281; settlement by, 54, 56, 310–11n14; in Pampamarca, 110–11; in Cotahuasi, 150f; and national identity, 279–80

Spanish language, 10, 13, 36f, 74

Spanish Water Law, *see* Water Code (1902)

Springs, 54, 160, 316n15; water volume from, 26–27, 239–41; Huayancotas irrigation system and, 76, 78–79, 86; Pampamarcas irrigation system and, 115–20 *passim*, 316n9; Cotahuasi irrigation system and, 155–56, 159, 181; water distribution and, 231–32

State, 9, 153; administration by, 3, 194–96; water administration by, 37, 228–34; and water distribution, 166–70 *passim*; and mestizaje, 196–97; and drought response, 240–41; and irrigation systems, 242–43

Stores, 204–5

Suni zone, 31, 237

Tacna, 274

Takapo, 119

Taurisma, 21, 44–45, 53, 194, 215

Tawa Rimaq, 44–45

Taxation, 167; Inca, 43, 45f; Spanish colonial, 53–54, 56–58

Technical Administrator, 228, 230

Technology, 3, 7, 24, 27

Temperature, 28–29

Terraces, terracing, 5, 8, 26; prehispanic, 41, 94–95; preparation of, 88–92; construction of, 92–94, 314n18; in Pampamarca, 128–31; flattening of, 174–75, 298; collapse of, 181–82; sharecropping on, 184–85; abandoned, 237f

T'ikras, 78–84 *passim*, 131, 237

Tinterillos, 163

T'iwqa tank, 117

Toledo, Francisco, 49

Tomepampa, 21, 49, 54f, 62ff, 287, 317n7, 318n20, 324n7

Tomepampa-Piro Project, 252–55, 323n14

Toro, 148, 212, 310n12, 315n11

Trade, 17, 111, 142; networks of, 20–21, 56, 311n10; obsidian, 39–40; haciendas and, 59–60; expansion of regional, 68–69

Tranca, 119, 124

Transportation networks, 20–21, 61–62, 178; roads and, 204–5

Trapecio Andino, 274

Tribute, 320n32; Inca, 43, 45–46; Spanish colonial, 49, 51–52, 56–58, 141; cooperative labor as, 193–94

Trucking, 204

Tulla, 45

Tupac Amaru rebellion, 58

Uchupalla, 124, 137–38

Ukhuña, 17, 19–20

United Left, 275

United Nations, 276

Uprisings, 19, 43, 58, 206. *See also* Sendero Luminoso

User groups, 228, 272, 322n2, 323n12

Valdivia, Sr., 141–42, 143, 316n18

Velasco Alvarado, Juan, 199, 205, 210f, 303

Vera-Portocarrero family, 56, 62

Verticality, 33–34

Villages, 49, 313n2; in study, 10–11; water control by, 37–38; prehistoric, 40–42; mestizaje and, 197–98; social change in, 300–301

Viraco, 48

Visve, 34, 82, 276, 313n3

Vivo, vivesa, 280–81, 282

Wages, 106–7, 108, 145, 190, 212, 226, 315n27

Wakajara, 54, 156–60 *passim*, 192, 230, 254f, 319n26

Wakcha, 74

Waqalla, 137–38

Warmunta, 76, 81

War of the Pacific, 68

Warwa, 47

Waskaqocha, 76, 80–86 *passim*

Water: as property, 33, 134, 151, 160–61, 164, 171–72, 228, 318n12; Spanish expropriation of, 54–55; Spanish colonial period, 55–56; privatization of, 70, 303–4; conservation of, 93, 268–69; sharecropping and, 184–85; control of, 201, 210; overuse of, 242–45; legislative reform and, 303–4; conservation of, 304–5

Water Code (1902), 37, 70, 159f, 166, 171,
318nn11, 12, 17; comunero rights,
162–63
Water control: village, 37–38; in Cotahuasi, 171–73
Water distribution, 7f, 323n11; in Huaynacotas, 79–84, 314nn14, 15; egalitarian,
85–88; conflict in, 87–88; in Pampamarca, 116(map), 117–28 *passim*,
144–48, 317n8; hierarchical, 126–27; in
Cotahuasi, 159–62, 166–70, 194–96,
245–46, 317n7, 318n11, 322n7; and
haciendas, 170–72, 299–300, 318n15; in
Iskawayqo, 183–84; sharecropping and,
184–85; government administration of,
194–96, 242–44, 317n9; under General
Water Law, 230–32, 323n16; auxilio,
244–45, 247–48; government concepts
of, 250–51; conflicts in, 258–68, 269;
reforming, 270–72
Water Festival, *see* Yarqa Aspiy
Water management, 8; prehispanic, 9–10;
state, 230–31; village, 37–38
Water rights, 140, 184, 229, 248–49,
314n15, 318n12; equity of, 108–9, 197; in
Pampamarca, 119, 145–46; in Cotahuasi, 151, 156, 159–63, 184; authority
and, 166–67; government administration and, 241, 263–65; privatization
of, 303–4

Water systems, 77(map), 116(map),
183–84. *See also* Irrigation systems
Water supply, 120, 271, 309–10n3; and irri-
gation, 29, 118–19, 238–39, 242–44; for
Pampamarca, 125–26, 148; drought and,
229, 239–41
Water theft, 88, 108–9, 232, 318n20; in
Pampamarca, 144, 145–46; in Cota-
huasi, 170, 172, 194–95
Water use, 26
Wayka, waykilla, 197, 319n30; and hacien-
das, 187–90
Wayki, 72
Wit'u, 120, 311n2
Wool industry, 59–60–67 *passim*, 111, 151,
202, 205
Work parties, 188; reciprocity and,
98–100; poor and, 103–4; organization
of, 104–5; canal maintenance by, 192,
193–94
Work projects: community, 96–97

Yanapakuy, 137
Yanaquihua, 286
Yarqa Aspiy, 96–97, 135–37, 169,193
Yawarcocha, 167, 318n17
Yunka (canyón), 31

Zanabrias family, 111
Zones of Emergency, 273–74, 277–78